The Fragile Leaves of the Sibyl

dante's master plan

The Fragile Leaves
of the Sibyl

by T. K. Swing

THE NEWMAN PRESS
WESTMINSTER, MARYLAND
1962

Nihil Obstat: Edward A. Cerny, S.S., S.T.D.
 Censor Librorum

Imprimatur: Lawrence J. Shehan, D.D.
 Archbishop of Baltimore
April 19, 1962

The *nihil obstat* and *imprimatur* are official declara-
tions that a book or pamphlet is free of doctrinal and
moral error. No implication is contained therein that
those who have granted the *nihil obstat* and *imprimatur*
agree with the opinions expressed.

Dedication

The Fragile Leaves of the Sibyl is an invitation to intuitive reflection on the *Divina Commedia*. This invitation proposes an intuitive insight into the elusive unity of the greatest epic and justifies that insight through a reflective disclosure of Dante's master plan. It promises to unravel the baffling complexity of the most titanic creation in the poetic tradition by revealing the hidden simplicity which governs the formation and progression of the dramatic plot. It does not stop at hoisting a proposal and brandishing a promise, but performs the joyous task of elucidating the profundity of Dante's angelic vision and thereupon illuminating its sublimity.

This joyous invitation to the immortal feast of Dante's divine love is dedicated to my venerable teachers in human love:

DEAN HARTLEY SIMPSON

and

PROFESSOR THOMAS G. BERGIN

Preface

I⊤ is, I suspect, literally true that books on Dante are countless. From the time of Dante's own composition of the famous letter to Can Grande (if indeed it be his) to the present, readers and admirers of the great work have felt an irresistible urge towards exegesis, criticism, or commentary. Indeed, it has reached the point where history and criticism *of* Dante criticism is a legitimate field of endeavor; English speaking readers may find in such a work as W. P. Friederich's *Dante's Fame Abroad* evidence of the interest of successive generations in the *Divine Comedy*. One may think of the work as a cut jewel which scholars, year after year, have turned over in their hands, allowing new facets to catch the light and reveal their own splendor to the eye of the observer. And in truth, the *Comedy* has many facets; it has been examined philologically, philosophically, historically, and frequently esoterically with an eye to proving what the critic himself would have it prove. This bibliographical accumulation, aside from being a tribute to Dante, is almost a history of critical attitudes over the past six hundred years, and it certainly puts a burden on anyone who in the year of Our Lord 1962 feels the need of publishing yet one more work on the *Comedy*. If we are to plant yet one more tree in the *selva spessa* of Dante bibliography it will have to be a sturdy one.

I believe Swing's tree is not only sturdy but *sui generis*—

or, to drop the metaphor, I think his book is both important and original. For one thing, from beginning to end it looks at the *Comedy* as a whole. The fragmentation of the great work is nowadays normally attributed to Croce with his distinction between *poesia* and *non poesia*, but actually, in the area of criticism—as distinct from commentary which is by definition concerned with details—a book, pre- or post-Croce, which keeps steadily in mind the whole of the *Comedy* is rather rare. Some studies are warped by partisan or doctrinal bias; others, while seeking a philosophical unity, ignore the aesthetic and *vice versa*. Even today, when the quest for the *sovrasenso*, which would seem to imply an establishment of unity and consistency, is the primary occupation of scholars, there is a tendency to linger on certain particular episodes, the meeting with Beatrice, the ultimate vision, or the like, with consequent neglect or dwarfing of other parts of the great poem. Swing's search for the unity of the work is twofold: he explores the aesthetic principles which unify the three realms of Dante's other world and at the same time he sees that this unity needs a corresponding philosophical integrity to support it. He does not ignore detail; his book is full of illuminating remarks on the familiar figures and traditional allegories of the *Comedy*, but I think he is unique in preserving his view of the work as a whole from the beginning to the end of his enterprise. I say this, subject to correction of course; I do not claim to have read every work on Dante. But as far as my reading goes, I can think of no other book which has so consistently and successfully kept the impact of the whole *Comedy* ever before the reader. Whether Swing's central theory is valid is almost irrelevant; my friends in the field of philosophy tell me it is ingenious and certainly not unsound, and I confess that I find it very persuasive. But whether the finding is right or wrong, the search is exciting and in itself rewarding. For Swing is searching not for something marginal or tangential but for a vital and determinant principle in Dante's art.

He has the qualifications for it. He is a student of philosophy, well prepared by training and temperament for the Aristotelian-Thomistic aspect of his research. He has at the same time an aesthetic sense which lends to his appreciation of beauty an element of all but passionate participation. This is a truly Dantesque combination. He has, furthermore, through pure circumstances, an advantage denied to many of us. His background, his formation in a foreign culture enables him to see with a peculiar freshness not only the *Comedy* itself but its implications and its significance. I think he has made good use of his endowments and his privileges to give us a very valuable study of the greatest poem of the Western world.

THOMAS G. BERGIN
Yale University

Acknowledgements

LA DIVINA COMMEDIA is an unusual work. It is unusual in assimilating so many diverse fields of human experience as philosophy and theology, psychology and physiognomy, cosmology and astronomy, topography and meteorology, mythology and history, politics and economics, *et cetera*. In any one of these diverse fields and disciplines, I am neither a learned scholar nor an experienced expert. Having no scholarly knowledge and no expert experience of my own in these fields, I have had to draw profusely from the works and efforts of many other people. *The Fragile Leaves of the Sibyl* is *inter alia* a patient product of scissors and paste. It is impossible to enumerate all the persons whose labors have been borrowed because there are too many. But let me try to recall a few of those whose contributions have been generous and indispensible.

Professor Thomas G. Bergin has affectionately nursed my work from its initial inception to its final delivery and left the trace of his graceful hand almost on every line. In the summer of 1960 during which I was writing this volume, he not only gave me recourse to his discriminate judgment and his authoritative command of the subject matter but left at my disposal the charming Chubb Suite of his Timothy Dwight College of Yale University and his handsome Dante library. His secretary, Mrs. Katherine Denison, also went out of her way to aid my work. Professor Bergin finally gave my work the lovely name under which it is to be known and kindly wrote the Preface which it is proud to bear.

xi

Acknowledgements

I planned and prepared for *the Fragile Leaves of the Sibyl* during the first year of my graduate studies at Yale (1959–1960). Since I had to carry the full load of a regular student, I would have had little time left for this extra-curricular activity but for the indulgence of Professor Rulon Wells to accept the first three chapters of this book as the term paper for his course. It was also Professor Wells who drew my attention to the significance of Saint Bernard in *La Divina Commedia*. While I was writing the outline of this volume as a term paper for Professor Wells, I knew little of the Abbot of Clairvaux and had little time to delve into his works. Only later I came to realize the crucial fact that the saint's three works, *De Gradibus humilitatis*, *De diligendo Deo*, and *Sermones in Cantica Canticorum*, jointly constitute the chief model for the architectonic construction of Dante's *Cantica* of divine love.

I also owe my understanding of Aristotle to Professor Wells and to Professor William Earle. I know my Plato as Professor Robert Brumbaugh has taught me. I remember Saint Augustine and Saint Thomas as I read them with Professor George Lindbeck and Professor Irwin Lieb. I drew heavily from the memorable lessons of Professor John E. Smith and Professor George A. Schrader in presenting Dante's doctrines in contrast with modern theology and philosophy. I relied on the valuable courses with Dr. Daniel Freedman, Dr. Thomas Detre and Dr. Jay Katz of the Yale Medical School Psychiatry Department in showing the permanent significance of Dante's incisive insight into the abyss of the human psyche in the light of the current knowledge of psychiatry and psychoanalysis. I derive my critical outlook from Professor Kenneth Connelly and Professor Cleanth Brooks who opened my eyes to the magnificent beauty of the poetic tradition in the West. I have come to appreciate the elegant liturgy of the Catholic Church at St. Thomas More Chapel under Father Edwin O'Brien.

The Fragile Leaves of the Sibyl could not have been written without Dean Hartley Simpson of the Yale Graduate School. It was his fatherly concern and his tender care that enabled me to write this book. Dean Simpson and his Assistant, Dean Alan Douglas Ferguson, sustained my work with gracious aid and kindness.

I am grateful to Mr. T. S. Yoon for having liberally provided me with expensive medieval books; to Mr. John Galm for reading through my manuscript and proofs; and to Mrs. M. W. Kim, my typist, for her patient reading of my difficult handwriting.

Let me finally acknowledge my gratitude for permission to use the many quotations in this volume of the following publishers, authors, editors, and translators:

Benziger Brothers, N. Y.;
The Holy Bible (New American Catholic Edition), 1950
Rev. F. X. Lasance and Rev. F. A. Walsh, the *New Roman Missal*, 1954
Saint Thomas Aquinas, *Summa Theologica*, 1947–1948
The Roman Breviary, an English Version, 1937
Sheed and Ward, N.Y.;
The Holy Bible, trans. by Ronald Knox, 1950
Holt, Rinehart, and Winston, Inc., N.Y.;
The Divine Comedy, trans. by H. R. Huse, Rinehart Editions, 1959, by permission of the translator and Holt, Rinehart and Winston, Inc., Publisher.
E. P. Dutton and Co., Inc, N.Y.;

Acknowledgements

The *Inferno*, the *Purgatorio*, and the *Paradiso* of Dante Alighieri, Temple Classics, 1958

The Book of Saint Bernard on the Love of God, ed. and trans. by Edmund G. Gardner, 1916

Appleton-Century-Crofts, N.Y.;

The *Divine Comedy*, ed. and trans. by Thomas G. Bergin, 1955, by permission of the publisher.

The Viking Press, Inc., N.Y.;

The Portable *Dante*, trans. by D. G. Rossetti, ed. by Paolo Milano, the Viking Portable Library, 1955

A. R. Mowbray and Co., London;

Saint Bernard, *The Steps of Humility*, trans. by Geoffrey Webb and Adrian Walker, 1957

Saint Bernard, *On the Song of Songs*, ed. and trans. by a Religious of C.S.W.V., 1952

Random House, N.Y.;

The Basic Works of Aristotle, ed. by Richard McKeon, 1941

The Basic Writings of Saint Augustine, ed. by Whitney J. Oates, 1948

Harvard University Press, Cambridge, Mass.;

Charles S. Singleton, *Dante Studies* 1, 1954

Henry Holt and Co., N.Y.;

Benedetto Croce, the *Poetry of Dante*, trans. by Douglas Ainslie, 1922

Image Books, Garden City, N.Y.;

Saint Thomas Aquinas, *On the Truth of the Catholic Faith*, 1955–1958

New Haven   T. K. SWING
July 4, 1961

xiv

Contents

Contents

EPIGRAPH

Così la neve al sol si disigilla,
così al vento nelle foglie lievi
si perdea la sentenza di Sibilla.

Par. xxxiii. 64-66

PART I

The Presentation of the Problem

chapter 1

The Quest for the Unity of the
Divina Commedia

THE stage of Dante's *Divina Commedia* presents the most wondrous splendor and the most puzzling enigma of all poetic creations. Neither in its scope nor in its depth has Dante's stage ever been paralleled by any other dramatic setting. For the sake of a brief comparison, let us set Dante's titanic stage side by side with the long course of the perilous voyage on which Virgil launches his epic hero Aeneas, and with the immense Mediterranean world into which Shakespeare tosses his tragic hero Marcus Antonius. In the course of his journey from the burning city of Ilium to his motherland of Latium, Aeneas travels down to Hades, meets his father Anchises on the Field of Elysium, and sees the destiny of the Roman Empire. The beautiful meadow of fresh verdure within the Noble Castle of the virtuous pagans, which reminds us of the grandeur of the Elysian Field, marks the beginning of Dante's descent to the Emperor reigning over the world of darkness and death. At the end of his long journey from exile on the earth, Dante meets his Father face to face in the Empyrean and sees the destiny of the entire human race in his Beatific Vision. Exhausted and defeated by the evil forces of cruel power politics clashing in the immense Mediterranean world, Antonius achieves heroic stature by dying on the bosom of Cleopatra, the Queen of Egypt, who gives herself up to the bite of an asp. Overcoming the bestial wrath of the Centaurs and the fraudulent tricks of the devils, Dante dies, away from the world of sin, and is born and "magnified" in the bosom of Mary, the Queen of Heaven, who has crushed the serpent's head under her heel.

Many may consider Virgil's stage as the greatest stage to come out of the entire epic tradition and Shakepeare's as the greatest stage to emerge from the entire tragic tradition. But even these two great stages shrink down to the size of tiny threshing floors, when they are compared with the titanic stage on which Dante unfolds not only the action of mortal creatures but also that of the Creator, from which he gives us not only the human perspective but the angelic, and through which he does not spin out simply Virgil's theme of *pietas* or Shakespeare's theme of *amor* but weaves both of them together into the single theme of *caritas*. The complexity of action, the immensity of perspective, and the gravity of theme of the *Divina Commedia* is fully reflected in the structure of the stage. Dante's is not a single stage but a triple one. The three realms of spirits stretch from extremity to extremity, from the darkest to the brightest, from the most hideous to the most sublime, from the most despicable to the most splendid, from the greatest woe to the greatest bliss, and from the emptiest to the fullest of Being.

Dante's stage is not only the most wondrous splendor of all poetic creations, but the most baffling enigma. The enigma which has puzzled Dante's readers a little over half a millennium lies in the relation between the form and the content of the *Divina Commedia*. What is the relation between the stage and the action of the poetic drama? This relation of form and matter is one of the oldest problems in philosophy, older than Plato and Aristotle. As a philosophical problem, the relation of form and matter offers only a harmless occasion for theoretical disputations involving no practical consequence. But this harmless philosophical problem has a decisive practical relevance for Dante's epic. For, if there is no relation between its stage and action, its form and content, then Dante's titanic edifice has no unity and should be condemned as the greatest chaos ever created. If there is a definite relation between the stage and the action, Dante's epic can be rightly admired as the greatest single poem ever written since the dawn of human civilization.

Though the problem of unity sounds very exotic in its philosophical formulation as the relation of form and content, it is in our context quite simple. In plain words, the question is: what is the principle governing the structure of the three worlds of the *Inferno*, the *Purgatorio* and the *Paradiso?* Is there such a principle or principles? If so, how are the principles governing the structures of the three worlds related to the themes and actions which develop in the three worlds? Each of the three worlds is divided into ten regions. The progressive grouping of the ten regions takes on a different form in all the three worlds. The structure of the *Inferno* can be expressed in the form of $10 = 1 + 1 + 8$ (the Vestibule, the Limbo, and the eight Circles of Sins); the structure of the *Purgatorio* in the form of $10 = 2 + 7 + 1$ (two Antepurgatorial Terraces, the seven Purgatorial Terraces, and the Terrestrial Paradise); and the structure of the *Paradiso* in the form of $10 = 7 + 1 + 1 + 1$ (the seven Planets, the Fixed Stars, the *Primum Mobile*, and the Empyrean).

$$10 = 1 + 1 + 8 \ (Inferno)$$
$$10 = 2 + 7 + 1 \ (Purgatorio)$$
$$10 = 7 + 1 + 1 + 1 \ (Paradiso)$$

This simple table seems to show at least one thing: there is no common principle governing the structures of the three worlds, and each of the three worlds is built on its own unique plan. This is the opinion that has been established and sanctified by a long tradition. It has been believed that the Circles of sins in the *Inferno* and the Terraces of sins on the *Purgatorio* are not related at all except that sinners are punished in the one and purged in the other. It has also been assumed that the seven Terraces and the seven Planets do not correspond except in number. Snugly resting on the aged assumption that there is no common principle governing the structure of the three worlds, the host of Dante critics have turned their attention to the question of whether the lack of correspondence and contrast between the three worlds is a poetic success or failure, virtue or sin. On this question, there have in general been three schools of opinion: (i) the school of damnation, (ii) the school of adulation, and (iii) the school of silence.

The school of damnation, which can see no order in Dante's three worlds, accuses the poet of being confused and confusing his readers, and condemns him to the intricate complexity of his own creation. For example, Coleridge, fascinated and obsessed with the vivid contrast of imagination as the fundamental principle of poetic presentation, was quite disappointed in Dante's three worlds of fantastic imagination and labels the *Divina Commedia* as nothing more than "a system of moral, political, and theological truths with arbitrary personal exemplification."[1] He even ventures to attribute the chaos of Dante's epic to the chaotic emotional atmosphere of the politically lacerated Italy in which Dante had to live and write.

The school of adulation maintains that Dante's three

worlds are ordered and constructed on the basis of the Aristotelian-Thomistic classification of virtues and sins. They further claim that the poet fully reveals his genius in avoiding a mechanical application of the common principle of virtues and sins as a ground plan for the construction of the three worlds. If the poet were to use a ground plan with no variation, he would have to produce three uniform worlds in a monotonous repetition. It is through the marvelous combination of the common ground plan and its subtle variation that the three worlds are not only saved from boring monotony but are linked together in a daring fusion of uniformity and diversity, familiarity and novelty, repetition and variety. For example, Professor Charles Singleton who has devoted many faithful years to the explication of many difficult features of the *Comedy* echoes a typical note of this school:

[Every scene] will ever display a variety which defies simple formulation. The poet's work was not done by preconceived formula mechanically applied. Each scene arises from its own real center of inspiration, nor in a single instance do we feel that the poet is near the risk of repetition. . . . The variety of beings and states of being which arise before the eye of his reader acknowledges only such limits as the design of one hundred cantos can itself impose. It is to the greater glory of the poem that our own willful purposes of abstractive analysis are quite defeated in this regard. [2]

Thus Professor Singleton exhorts us not to tire our feeble eyes any more by looking for the principle governing the unity of the three worlds, and to be grateful for the splendid variety of beings and states of being which Dante spins out with his inexhaustible imagination throughout his one hundred cantos. We are urged to take the lack of

7

unity in Dante's three worlds not as an inexcusable disgrace to the poet but as an inexplicable glory to him.

Caught between this harsh exchange of adulation and denunciation, the third school cautiously holds its peace. For example, Croce, who has propounded "expression" as the fundamental form of poetic intuition, cautions us against expressing our judgment on the *Divina Commedia*.[3]

Before joining any of these three well-established schools, let us first examine the merit of their arguments. We will begin with the contention of the second school, since it alone offers a positive view. According to the school of adulation, the Aristotelian-Thomistic classification of virtues and sins is the ground plan for the construction of Dante's three worlds. The poet has told us that the state of the soul after death is the central theme of his epic. The state of a soul is nothing other than its virtues and sins, its bliss and woe which are the consequences of virtues and sins. It is quite probable or even necessary that the nature of the virtues and sins should be the fundamental principle governing the structure of Dante's three worlds.

St. Thomas makes up his well-known table of ten virtues by adopting from Aristotle the three cardinal virtues of temperance, fortitude, and justice and the four intellectual virtues of understanding, knowledge, wisdom, and prudence, and adding to them the three theological virtues of faith, hope, and charity. The cardinal and intellectual virtues are the natural powers of the soul for the fulfillment of its natural end. The theological virtues are the supernatural powers for the realization of the supernatural end. The natural virtues are connatural to man as much as his natural end is. The natural end and the natural virtues are in conformity with the nature of man. Unlike the bliss on earth, the bliss in heaven surpasses the nature of man. It is man's supernatural end. Man comes to know and achieve his supernatural end not through his own power but through divine grace. The supernatural end and virtues are not in conformity with the nature of man, whereas the connatural end and virtues are.

The number of the ten virtues coincides with the number of the ten regions in each of Dante's three worlds, but the order of the ten virtues does not agree with the order of the ten regions in any of the three worlds. This can be readily seen in the formal grouping of the ten virtues and of the ten regions in each of the three worlds.

$$10 = 3 + 4 + 3 \text{ (order of virtues)}$$
$$10 = 1 + 1 + 8 \text{ (order of } Inferno)$$
$$10 = 2 + 7 + 1 \text{ (order of } Purgatorio)$$
$$10 = 7 + 1 + 1 + 1 \text{ (order of } Paradiso)$$

It is at this point that the school of adulation brings in its argument of variation. That is, the order of virtues and sins as the ground plan is modified and varied in the construction of each of the three worlds. Let us now see what sort of modifications the Aristotelian-Thomistic table of virtues and sins has to undergo in accounting for the structure of the three worlds.

The structure of the *Inferno* is supposed to follow Aristotle's classification of all evil acts into three groups. This theory is based on Virgil's discourse in the eleventh canto of the *Inferno*. Aristotle divides evil acts into three classes: incontinence, bestiality, and malice. Incontinence is the inordinate appetite which escapes the control of the will. It is the vice of soft, weak people.[4] Bestiality differs from incontinence. While the latter is the evil of inordinate appetite, the former is the evil of bestial temper. While the acts of incontinence seek the immediate object of appetite, the acts of bestiality aim at ferocious revenge and destruction.[5] Malice differs from both incontinence and

9

bestiality. Acts of malice involve neither overpowering appetite as do acts of incontinence, nor overwhelming bestial anger as do acts of bestiality.[6] A malicious man plots and works evil through his cold, calculating reason. Acts of malice stem directly from the highest "originative source" of man's action, his reason. While reason is overpowered by appetite in acts of incontinence and by temper in acts of bestiality, it takes a cruel command in acts of malice.

Of the three classes of evil acts, malice is the gravest because it stems from man's highest faculty and is the uniquely human evil. Incontinence is the least grave of the three groups. In the order of gravity, bestiality stands between incontinence and malice. Bestiality is graver than incontinence, because the faculty of temper and anger is more closely related to reason than sheer appetite. Anger and temper listen to and obey the argument of reason to some extent, but sheer appetite never does.[7] The order of gravity of the three evils conversely reflects the order of their dignity. Incontinence is more disgraceful than bestiality, and bestiality more than malice. A man who cannot control his appetite is a greater disgrace to human dignity than a man who cannot control his temper. The gravest evil is the least disgraceful one, and the least grave evil is the most disgraceful one.

It is a prevalent belief that the Aristotelian order of the three classes of evil acts is the fundamental order of Dante's underground world. The lowest two Circles represent the sins of malice. The Seventh Circle represents the sins of bestiality. The Second, the Third, the Fourth, and the Fifth Circles represent the sins of lust, gluttony, avarice, and wrath, that is, the sins of incontinence. These three groups constitute seven Circles. Dante is then supposed to add three more regions for the uniquely Christian sins:

the Vestibule for the sin of indifference, the Limbo for the sin of unbelief, and the Sixth Circle for the sin of heresy. With the exception of the Vestibule and the Limbo, the entire *Inferno* is thus divided and ordered into three sections of incontinence, bestiality and malice. The sins become more and more grievous and intellectual as we move down from the fringe to the center of the *Inferno*. The sins of the higher Circles are more disgraceful and less intellectual than the sins of the lower Circles.

This is a rough outline of the Aristotelian explanation of the structure of the *Inferno*. Let us subject it to a few tests. Why is the sin of wrath in the Fifth Circle and included in the region of incontinence? Aristotle specifically distinguishes it from incontinence and brings it under the heading of bestiality. Does the inclusion of the sin of wrath in the region of incontinence show our poet's oversight and ignorance or his deliberate variation and modification of Aristotle's doctrine for poetic purpose? The Circle which seems to violate most conspicuously the Aristotelian maxim of intellect as the measure of vices is the Sixth Circle for heretics. The sin of heresy seems to be more intellectual than any other sin in the *Inferno*, but is placed between incontinence and bestiality. Are we to understand that heresy is graver than incontinence and less intellectual than bestiality? Is the Sixth Circle only a heretical violation of Aristotle's doctrine of virtues and sins? Even by the most faithful students in the school of adulation, the location of the Sixth Circle has been conceded as an abominable anomaly and a blemish disfiguring the Aristotelian order of the *Inferno*. In his masterly and adulatory commentary on the *Divina Commedia*, C. H. Grandgent has nothing to say about Dante's heretical violation of Aristotle's doctrine but this lament: "Here Aristotle, who furnishes the general plan of Dante's Hell, offers no help."[8]

The sin of heresy resembles the sin of violence against God in the Third Ring of the Seventh Circle and the sin of the schismatics in the ninth *bolgia* of the Eighth Circle. Why are these three sins and other similar sins separated from one another and placed differently? Do they involve intellect in different degrees? If so, how?

Let us now shift our inquiry from the inter-relation of the three main sections of incontinence, bestiality, and malice to their internal order. There are four Circles in the section of incontinence: lust, gluttony, avarice, and wrath. Are these four sins placed in the order of gravity? The Circle of gluttony is placed below the Circle of lust. Are we to understand that the sin of gluttony is more grievous and requires a greater use of intellect than the sin of lust? Is it a more serious sin to bloat one's stomach than to feast in the joy of the flesh? Our concern is to know whether or not there is an internal order in each of the three main sections as well as the order in the external relation of the three sections.

There are many other features in the structure of the *Inferno*, which can never be adequately accounted for by the Aristotelian doctrine of virtues and vices, whatever elaborate modifications and revisions are imposed on that doctrine. Let us now shift our inquiry from the gravity of sins and the order of the Circles to the scenery of Hell. The *Inferno* is divided into the Upper Hell and the Lower Hell, and the latter is protected by gigantic fortifications. Our poet runs into difficulty in getting through the gate of the Lower Hell. This unique feature of the *Inferno* cannot be traced back to any of Aristotle's teachings or to any other previous tradition. Are we to see any special significance in this conspicuous feature of Dante's Hell or just see it as a delightful occasion for diversion and relief to refresh us in the middle of the tiresome descent to the center of the *Inferno?* There are four rivers in the *Inferno*, and they are different from one another. Are we to see any particular significance in these four rivers or just feast our eyes on the fantastic scenery of the four rivers and be grateful for Dante's fertile imagination?

Let us now move on to the *Purgatorio* and see how well its structure can be explained by the Aristotelian-Thomistic table of virtues and sins. The seven Terraces are piled one upon another in the order of the seven deadly sins. Our question then is simply: How are the seven deadly sins related to the Aristotelian-Thomistic scheme of virtues and sins? We can turn directly to the Angelic Doctor for the answer to this question. In the examination of virtues and sins, St. Thomas confronts the question: Why do the seven capital vices correspond neither in number nor in kind to the ten virtues.[9] He evades the issue by giving a clearly un-Aristotelian answer that "there is no need for the principal vices to be contrary to the principal virtues." And yet he wants to defend the adequacy of the enumeration of the seven deadly sins. In this defense, he does not appeal to the Aristotelian metaphysical and psychological system, but wishes to stand on "the authority of Gregory who enumerates them in this way." Since the Angelic Doctor accepts the enumeration of the seven deadly sins on the authority of St. Gregory, the structure of the *Purgatorio* should be called Gregorian-Thomistic rather than Aristotelian-Thomistic.

Near the end of Canto XVII of the *Purgatorio*, Virgil explains the order of the seven Terraces. He says that human love can be perverted in three general ways: it can be misdirected, deficient, or excessive. The sins of pride, envy, and wrath are the expressions of misdirected love and are placed on the first three Terraces. The sin of sloth is deficient love and is placed on the middle Terrace. The

13

sins of avarice, gluttony, and lust are the consequences of excessive love and are placed on the top three Terraces. Notice the difference between the division of the *Inferno* and that of the *Purgatorio*. Both *Inferno* and *Purgatorio* are divided into three main sections, but they are divided by different criteria. The division of the *Inferno* into three main sections is made in accordance with the three sinful powers of the soul. The ancient Greeks thought the soul to be composed of three parts: reason, temper, and appetite. The three Infernal sections of malice, bestiality, and incontinence correspond to the three parts of the soul. Incontinence is the vice of appetite, bestiality the vice of temper, and malice the vice of intellect. While the *Inferno* is divided and ordered in accordance with the three sinful powers of the soul, the *Purgatorio* is divided and structured in the light of the three states of sinful love. We cannot but ask: What is the relation between the three perverted parts of the soul and the three states of perverted love?

This question is one of the many possible technical formulations of the fundamental problem: How is regeneration related to degeneration? The *Inferno* reveals the state of degenerate souls, and the *Purgatorio* shows the process of regenerating the degenerate souls. To be sure, not all the sins of the *Inferno* can be purged in the *Purgatorio*. The sins of the *Inferno* can be divided into two groups: the positive and negative sins. The sins in the Vestibule and the Limbo are negative sins, and the sins in the eight Circles of the *Inferno* proper are the positive sins. All the seven sins which are purged on the *Purgatorio* are positive sins. This is one of the reasons why Virgil explains the order of the seven Terraces in the light of perverted love. Each of the seven deadly sins embodies a positive love for certain objects. There is no perversion of positive love in the sin of the indifferent in the Vestibule and in the sin of the virtuous pagans in the Limbo. The positive sins in the eight Circles of the *Inferno* proper must involve perversion of love in one state or another and should be able to find a place on one of the seven Terraces for regeneration. It is obvious that the sins of the Second, the Third, and the Fourth Circles can be purged on the top three Terraces. We are not quite certain on which Terraces the sins of the rest of the *Inferno* proper can be purged. It is even doubtful whether the sin of heresy can find a place for its cure on any of the seven Terraces. Are we to understand that some positive sins can never be purged and pardoned even by climbing the mountain that cures?

So much for the order of sins and their purgation. Let us now turn our inquiry to the scenery of *Purgatorio*. What is the function of the *Ante-Purgatorio?* Is there any resemblance between the function of *Ante-Purgatorio* and *Ante-Inferno* (the Vestibule and the Limbo)? Why is the *Purgatorio* proper bare and devoid of natural beauty, while the *Ante-Purgatorio* and the Terrestrial Paradise are adorned with beautiful, fresh natural scenes? What should we make of the peculiar rule that the penitents cannot take a single step upward after the sunset? Should we invoke the ghosts of Aristotle and St. Thomas for the answers to these questions?

Our problem becomes far more acute, once we fly up to the *Paradiso*. Unlike Virgil who strains his natural reason to explain the order of the *Inferno* and the *Purgatorio*, Beatrice does not bother to explicate the structure of the heavenly world. Has Dante grown up enough to see the order of the kingdom of heaven without his guide's explanation? Though our poet labels each Circle and each Terrace with the names of sins, he neither labels nor names any of the ten Heavens in any way to show their relation to virtues and sins. Does he expect us to see the nature of the ten Heavens and their order through the effulgent divine light and without the cumbersome method of naming and labeling? If so, his expectation has not been defeated. His readers have been able to see too much and too well in his labelless *Paradiso*. Almost every commentator seems to see a different order and significance in Dante's ten Heavens. Let me cite a few examples at random from my Dante library:

1. Moon	The Inconstant	Inconstancy	Weakness in Faith
2. Mercury	The Ambitious	Ambition	Weakness in Hope
3. Venus	The Sensual	Earthly Love	Weakness in Love
4. Sun	Teachers	Prudence	Strength in Prudence
5. Mars	Warriors	Fortitude	Strength in Fortitude
6. Jupiter	Rulers	Justice	Strength in Justice
7. Saturn	The Contemplative	Temperance	Strength in Temperance
8. Stellar Heaven	Apostles	Souls	Faith, Hope, Love
9. *Primum Mobile*	Angels	Angels	Angels
10. Empyrean	The True Heaven (T. G. Bergin)	God (P. H. Wicksteed)	Beatific Vision (H. R. Huse)

Everyone seems to see his own vision and speak his own language in Dante's *Paradiso*. This is surely a sign of madness. Having had a memorable lesson with Plato, we should not forget that there is madness and madness. There is the human insanity that makes a man lose himself and become less than a man. There is the divine insanity that transforms a mortal creature into an immortal. I am not quite sure what sort of insanity it is that makes the host of Dantists lose themselves and enables them to see every possible vision they long to see. I am only grateful for retaining my sane self, in spite of the unbearable torment of not even knowing what I miss, since I have not been initiated into the sacred college of Dante mysteries. This is the price I have to pay for my feeble sight and my timid soul.

Timid as I may be, I seem to see something wrong with all the visions of the sacred college of Dante mysteries. The members of the college seem to see everything but the one thing they should all see. What is it that they should all see, but no one of them can see? Virtues contrary to the seven deadly sins. The purpose of purgation is not to purge away the sins, but to regenerate the sinful powers into virtuous powers. On each Terrace of Purgatory, purgation begins with the examples of virtue contrary to the sin that is to be purged. The penitents not only cleanse themselves of the seven deadly sins, but cultivate seven principal virtues during their ascent through the seven Terraces. These virtues should be preserved and revealed in the *Paradiso*, but none of the Dante visionaries seem to see all of the seven virtues in the *Paradiso*. Are we to understand that the seven virtues are not essential to heavenly bliss? Are we to understand that the penitents get rid of the hard-earned virtues as well as their memory of sins, when they drink from Lethe? When one sees everything but does not see one thing that one should see, one has surely lost oneself as well as the object of one's quest.

Knowing better than anyone else that his *Paradiso* is a far more difficult and perilous ocean to sail through than his *Inferno* or *Purgatorio*, our poet, at the beginning of his heavenly voyage, gently bids the timid souls to leave and go back to their safe homes:

> O you, who in your little skiff
>   longing to hear, have followed on my keel
>   that sings on its way,

The Fragile Leaves of the Sibyl

Turn around and go back to your own shores:
commit you not to the open sea, lest it may hap
that, losing me, you may be left astray.

Par. ii. 1–6

In the oceanic frenzy and in the diabolical insanity, we
have lost our poet, lost our epic, and finally lost ourselves.
Whatever trickery we may employ in conjuring up the
authority of Aristotle and whatever jugglery we may
exercise in modifying the Angelic Doctor's table of virtues
and sins, the ghosts of the philosopher and the theologian
cannot save Dante's epic from chaos nor rescue us from
our demonic frenzy. No wonder, then, that many honest
readers give up their quest for the unity of Dante's epic
and dare condemn the poet to the chaotic abyss of his own
creation. The unity of the *Divina Commedia* cannot be
defended on the ground of variety for variety's sake. Every
defense based on the ground of variety entails a threefold
task. In the first place, we have to specify what is varied.
In the second place, we have to articulate how the variation
is executed. In the third place, we have to evaluate the
merit of variation. We cannot know what a variation is
without knowing what is the original plan that is varied and
then what is the method of variation. Since not every
variation is desirable and successful, we have to determine
further the merit of variations. I have not yet encountered
anyone who can specify and elucidate these three important
features in his admiration of the inexplicable variations in
the *Divina Commedia*. I have not yet seen anyone who can
even show what is the common plan that is varied in the
construction of Dante's three worlds and what is the common theme that is expressed differently in his three canticles.

Those who venture to defend the unity of Dante's

epic on the ground of variety and variation without even being able to specify the ground and the manner of variation seldom realize that their devout defense is not only a poorly disguised denial of the unity of Dante's stage but an outright insult to his poetic genius. They only reveal their low estimation of Dante's power in assuming that our poet could not but have turned out three dreadfully monotonous and uniform worlds, if he were to have followed one common principle in creating his three realms of spirits and if he were not allowed to inject profuse elements of variation and diversion. On what ground are they so sure that Dante's power was not equal to the task of lending poetic beauty and dramatic movement to the sequential development of his three worlds if he were to construct them under one common principle? On what ground are they so sure that it would be dreadfully boring rather than delightfully edifying to go through the three worlds if we could see the common structural principle through which all the three worlds can come into a beautiful mutual reflection and an elegant contrast?

We should not forget that to defend the structure of a poem on the ground of variety for variety's sake is to admit in the most derogatory manner the gravest disparagement of poetry in general. That would imply that poetry is a medium of decoration and diversion at its best and a medium of concealment and confusion at its worst. What a comical adventure it is to defend the unity of the *Divina Commedia* by showering on the poet of all poets the crudest insult to poetry in its entirety. If only to avoid the danger of making comical figures out of ourselves and our poet, should we reject this pseudo-defense of Dante's epic, join the honest rebels, and even curse the day when we were invited to the angelic feast of Dante's divine love?

We could not but pause for a serious second thought

which arises even at a cursory view of the awesome structure of Dante's stage. Behind the colossal edifice of delicate lines and crystalline circles, our poet may be veiling his central theme as Moses veiled his face lest our mortal eyes should be blinded. Since we lose our courage of revolt at this dreadful suspicion, should we not seal our foul lips in devout silence, shut our feeble eyes in rapturous ecstasy, drive out of our mind once and for all the thorny question of its unity and order, and relish its splendor and sublimity in carefree joy? This is the only advice Benedetto Croce can give us after many years of faithful striving to penetrate the hidden mystery of the *Divina Commedia:*

We should read Dante just as all ingenious readers do and are right in doing, paying little heed to the other world, very little to the moral divisions, none at all to the allegories, and greatly enjoying the poetic representations, in which all the poet's multiform passion is condensed, purified, and expressed.[10]

Croce may be showing us the right way to enjoy Dante's epic, but he certainly shows us the sure way to lose it. A significant poem is like life itself, because it is a reflection of life. Once you begin merely to enjoy it, you begin to lose it or you have already lost it. You have already lost its significance in frivolity and triviality and the only thing you can do is to sport with it. Our poet never meant his epic to be an occasion of sport and diversion if for anything else. When the Centaurs try to interfere with Dante's journey in the *Inferno*, his guide Virgil solemnly pronounces the gravity of Dante's mission: "Necessity brings him here, and not sport" (*Inf.* xii. 87). At the outset of his journey, our poet compares his adventure with the descent of Aeneas to Hades for the vision of the destiny of the Roman Empire whose foundation he was to lay and with the rapturous ascent of St. Paul into the third heaven for the vision of the foundation of Faith. Our poet ventures to fathom the lowest pit of perdition and scale the highest heaven of salvation; he attempts to reveal the nature and destiny of the human race and dares to see the mystery of the Holy Trinity. His epic is a little too cumbersome to be recommended for diversion and entertainment.

It is thus through clever frivolity and foolish sincerity that the greatest epic has been lost in the turmoil of adulation and condemnation. We know that there are three canticles in the *Divina Commedia,* but do not know how the three canticles constitute one poem. We see three worlds in Dante's creation, but do not see how the three worlds are unified in one cosmos. We hear of many themes and disputations in the course of Dante's pilgrimage, but do not understand how the many topics of discourse and the many scenes of action are woven into the central plot of the epic. In the course of praising the many fragmentary scenes and sporadic actions, we have carved out a host of poems and lost one great poem in its totality and unity. There have been too many books written explicating each canticle of the *Divina Commedia* in isolation from the other canticles and too many essays composed to unravel the hidden mystery of almost every corner of the stage of Dante, but not a single fruitful venture to unveil Dante's entire *Comedy* in its totality and illumine its unity.

Thus, in the past six hundred years, Dante's titanic epic has been torn apart canto by canto and scattered tercet by tercet and his angelic vision has been lost:

> As, in sunlight, the snow melts away;
>> as the oracles of the Sibyl, written
>>> upon the fragile leaves, were scattered in the wind.
>>>> *Par.* xxxiii. 64–66

The Fragile Leaves of the Sibyl

It is not very hard to know what a great loss it has been to lose the unity of Dante's epic. It is a matter of common knowledge that the *Divina Commedia* is the crystallization of the entire medieval experience and civilization which were nurtured and cultivated under the tutelage of the Holy Church during the first twelve centuries of the Christianization of Europe. This common understanding is an understatement of Dante's epic. In the *Divina Commedia*, the long Israelite history of slavery and tribulation dating back to many centuries before Christianity is re-lived and re-experienced; the flowering Greek civilization of intellect and wisdom bears a new fruit; the slow development of the Roman Empire takes on a new significance. Dante is a rare bird; he is a phoenix. The phoenix is said to spend five hundred years in the Arabian wilderness for the preparation of one sweet song it is to sing before burning itself on its funeral pyre of spices. It took five times five hundred years to prepare Dante's one great song. The fire and flame in which our phoenix burns himself and sings out his immortal song are set and fanned on one of the greatest pyres of human experience: it is built of the legacies from sinful Jews and virtuous Gentiles and of the heritage of the profane and the holy Roman Empires. If such a rare phoenix as Dante is allowed to be born even once in a millennium and to bless our earth with his immortal song, the human race can find rich recompense for its toiling and wailing in the vale of tears. Just as Jeremiah's immortal *Lamentations* were the distillation of Israel's tears and moans in the Babylonian captivity, so Dante's epic was the crystallization of the tears which the human race had long shed in the torment of the bitter exile on the earth and the sighs which it had long heaved in its agony and struggle to return to the mansions of the Father. The *Divina Commedia* is a great treasure and legacy which has been earned through the tears not of one man, but of the whole race.

No true treasure can be possessed except through intuitive knowledge and appreciation. An estate can be inherited through a piece of paper and be possessed in a title deed or even in mortgage, but the possession of a woman cannot be attained through a title deed. This is enough to show that a woman is a far greater treasure than a plot of land. A true treasure can be possessed and appreciated only through intuitive knowledge. Adam had his son only when he had knowledge of Eve. *And Adam knew Eve his wife: who conceived and brought forth Cain* (Gen. 4:1).

Intuitive knowledge cannot be sold or inherited any more than the power of sight can. It thus becomes impossible to inherit any true treasure in the ordinary sense of inheritance. Everyone has to develop his own intuitive knowledge of the true treasure he wants to inherit. Goethe was more keenly aware of this point than anyone else in our modern age. In the *Faust*, which he wrote in imitation of Dante's epic, Goethe thus sings:

> Whatever legacy your fathers left you,
> To own it, you must earn it dear.

We have to earn back Dante's epic and secure its possession in sound knowledge. We have not been able to unveil Dante's colossal work and reveal its unity simply because we have not known the true meaning of unity. Unity is often mistaken for uniformity or confused with diversity. Those who mistake unity for uniformity demand that Dante's three worlds be uniform if the three realms are to come into unity. But if the three worlds were completely uniform, they would become indistinguishable one from another and cease to be three worlds. Those who confuse unity with diversity praise Dante for sustaining his power to inject variety and novelty into every scene with no danger of repetition throughout one hundred cantos. They try to depict Dante's three worlds in such disparate colors that we have no knowledge of how the *Paradiso* disposes of the seven virtues cultivated in the *Purgatorio* or how the *Purgatorio* can accommodate all the positive sins displayed in the *Inferno*. In short, the three worlds become so disparate that they cannot be linked into one cosmos.

Unity is neither uniformity nor diversity, but their union. Uniformity and diversity are the two essential features of unity. As the essence of substances lies in the union of *genera* and *differentiae*, so the unity of Dante's three worlds must reside in the union of their uniformity and diversity. We learn from Aristotle that every entity requires two principles for the constitution of its essence: the formal and the material principles. For example, the nature of a gold ring can be understood through its form of a circle and its matter of gold. The form of a circle can take on silver instead of gold for its matter, and become a silver ring. The same form can be realized in the matter of bronze. The three rings are uniform to the extent that they are the realization of the same form. The three rings are different from one another to the extent that they are made of diverse matters. We can see the unity of the three rings through their uniformity and diversity.

Dante's three worlds are the three realms in which the human soul comes to be realized and perfected. The soul is a substantial form, a potential form that seeks actualization. The same soul attains different modes of actualization in the three worlds, because the three worlds present different matters and ends to the soul. The souls become differentiated in the three worlds, because they participate in the different media of realization. The three worlds should be uniform to the extent that the potential powers of the soul are the same in all. The three worlds should be diverse to the extent that the soul participates in diverse media of actualization. In seeking the unity of Dante's titanic stage, we should specify the formal principle of uniformity and articulate the material principles of diversity for the three worlds. In the following two chapters, we will try to disclose these two constitutive principles and reveal the unity of Dante's epic. It will be a somewhat difficult task, but a worthy toil to recover the immortal melody of our phoenix which has been stifled by the trumpets of idolatrous adulation and blasphemous denunciation. In this worthy toil, we will gather up one by one all the scattered leaves of Dante's great epic and reveal the wondrous splendor of his immortal vision.

PART II

The Formulation of a Solution

chapter 2

The Principle of Uniformity

THE soul is the first principle of life; it is the act and form of the body. This is Aristotle's famous definition of the soul which Dante adopts as the ground plan for the construction of the titanic stage for his epic drama of the soul.[1] On the Seventh Terrace, Statius explains the genesis of a human soul (*Purg.* xxv. 37 ff.). In the first stage, the reproductive cells on impregnation form a vegetative soul in "nature's vessel." Whereas the vegetative soul of a plant "is already at the goal," the human soul has just begun its long journey. In the second stage, it develops into a sensitive soul "till it can feel and move." At this stage, the human soul is like the souls of animals. In the last stage, it undergoes a mysterious metamorphosis from an animal soul to a human soul when the Prime Mover breathes into it "a new spirit replete with powers." Thus, activated and reactivated on three successive stages, the human soul becomes "one single soul" with three different powers.

Statius' account of the genesis of the soul explains the relation of the essence and powers in one soul. St. Thomas says that the soul is one essence but has many powers.[2] The powers of a soul can be distinguished into three levels: the vegetative, the sensitive, and the intellectual.[3] The vegetative power of the human soul is capable of all the functions of the soul of a plant, namely, nutrition and reproduction. The sensitive power of the human soul is capable of all the functions of an animal soul, namely, sensation and locomotion. On these two lower levels of power, the human soul shares in the life and activities of animals and plants. The intellectual power is, however, unique to the human soul in the corporeal world. Through this power, the human soul is capable of cognition and shares in the life of the intellectual substances such as angels and God.

Among these three powers, there is a two-fold order: generation and activation.[4] In the order of generation, the vegetative level is prior to the sensitive level, and the sensitive level is prior to the intellectual level. In the order of activation, the intellectual power is superior to the sensitive power, and the sensitive power to the vegetative power. The relation between the higher and the lower levels of the soul is the relation of form and matter, soul and body. The sensitive power is the form and soul that activates the vegetative level as its matter and body. The intellectual power is the form and soul that activates the sensitive level as its matter and body. In the process of genesis, the vegetative level prepares the body to be activated by the sensitive power, and the sensitive level in turn prepares the body to be activated by the intellectual soul. It is through these three stages of activation that the human soul comes to have three different powers. Statius explains that the human soul becomes, on reaching its mature stage, replete with all the three levels of power. The human soul is capable of living like plants, capable of sensation like animals, and capable of self-reflection like spiritual substances (*Purg.* xxv. 75).

The division of the soul's powers into three levels is a triadic division. Besides this triadic division, the Angelic Doctor employs a dyadic division in his examination of the nature of the soul and particularly in his discourse on virtues and vices. St. Thomas first divides the soul into the rational part and the non-rational part. The rational part is the intellect, and the non-rational part is the sensuality. St. Thomas further divides the non-rational part into the irascible and the concupiscible.[5] The concupiscible is composed of those passions immediately related to the objects of attraction and aversion, namely, direct appetite for sex, food, drink, clothes, etc. The irascible passions are not immediately related to the objects of attraction and aversion, but are reactions to the satisfaction and frustration of the concupiscible. The irascible feels hope or despair in reaction to the objects of good, and fear or daring in reaction to the objects of evil.[6] Anger is the fifth passion of the irascible and has no contrary passion.[7] The irascible presupposes the concupiscible and works for its satisfaction. St. Thomas calls the irascible "the champion and defender of the concupiscible."[8] The Angelic Doctor further specifies the concupiscible as the ground of concupiscence.[9] He explains that concupiscence takes its name from the concupiscible and that the former should be distinguished from the latter because concupiscence refers only to appetite and the concupiscible to love and pleasure as well as to appetite.

Let us now compare the results of the dyadic division with the results of the triadic division. Notice first that the dyadic division has distinguished three parts in the soul: the intellect, the irascible and the concupiscible. Notice also that these three parts resemble the three parts into which Plato divides the soul. The tripartite elements of the soul in the Platonic scheme are reason, the spirited element, and appetite. These three Platonic elements of the soul can be correlated with the three Aristotelian parts of the soul: reason with the intellect, the spirited element with the irascible, and appetite with the concupiscible. Of these three pairs of correlation, the first and the third are too obvious to require explanation. The second pair can be explained briefly. Plato regards the spirited element as the symbol of courage and warriorship and compares it to the warrior class of a state. St. Thomas recognizes the same function for the irascible, when he calls it "the champion and defender of the concupiscible."

It is far less difficult to see how the doctrine of the Platonic school agrees with that of the Aristotelian school than to find out how the two doctrines of the Aristotelian school cohere with each other. We will now face this more difficult question: How are the results of the triadic division related to the dyadic division of the soul? How are the intellect, the irascible, and the concupiscible to be related with the intellectual power, the sensitive power, and the vegetative power? The Angelic Doctor never bothers to face this question and keeps an angelic silence on this point. We have to struggle with this problem without his help. The first parts of the two tripartite groups are identical; they are both intellect. Our question narrows down: How are the irascible and the concupiscible related to the sensitive and the vegetative levels of the soul? Though the Angelic Doctor never wrestles with this question, we have enough evidence to conclude that he believes both the irascible and the concupiscible belong to the sensitive level. He says that the irascible and the concupiscible are the two distinct powers of the sensitive appetite.[10] This is in faithful adherence to Aristotle's observation that the vegetative level does not participate in the conscious life of the soul.[11] Aristotle says that we are not conscious of the nutrition and growth of the bodily organs and that the vegetative level functions primarily in sleep. Whereas the vegetative level does not come within the conscious domain of the soul, the irascible and the concupiscible are the powers under conscious control of the soul. For this reason, the Angelic Doctor has every right to call the irascible and the concupiscible the two distinct powers of the sensitive level.

The Formulation of a Solution

The identification of the irascible and the concupiscible as two distinct powers of the sensitive soul leaves us with one grave problem. Though the irascible and the concupiscible are both non-rational elements, they participate in the rational principle in different ways. Whereas the concupiscible is deaf to the arguments of reason, the irascible listens to reason to some extent. St. Thomas was quite conscious of this Aristotelian observation.[12] If both the irascible and the concupiscible belong to the same sensitive level, why do they respond to the command of reason in different ways? For the solution of this problem, let us postulate that the irascible emanates from the sensitive soul proper and the concupiscible from the body of the sensitive soul, that is, the vegetative level. This postulate is somewhat like the one in which St. Thomas divides all the human appetition into the intellectual and the sensitive appetite. He regards the intellectual appetite as emanating directly from the highest soul and the sensitive appetite from its body.

Under our postulation, the concupiscible is the appetite in which both animals and plants have their shares. Whereas plants have no conscious sensation of their appetite, animals consciously feel the appetite arising in their bodies to the extent that the vegetative appetite is sensitized through their animal souls. The example is the appetite for food, drink, and sex which both animals and plants alike have and which only animals can feel through the sensation of their souls. Just as the power of the sensitive soul becomes human and rational only to the extent that it participates in the formal principle of reason, so the vegetative soul becomes sensitive and animalistic only to the extent that it is sensitized and participates in the formal principle of the sensitive soul.

With this postulation, we can explain why the irascible and the concupiscible react to reason in different manners.

Temper and anger of the irascible stem directly from the sensitive level and are one step removed in their origin from reason. The sheer appetite of the concupiscible arises out of the vegetative level and is two steps removed in its origin from reason. Because the irascible is under the immediate control of reason and the concupiscible comes under the control of reason through the mediation of the irascible, the irascible is far more responsive to the argument and command of reason than the concupiscible. We can now see that both the dyadic and the triadic divisions of the soul lead to the same result. That should be so. All roads may not lead to Rome, but all right ways of analysis must lead to the same truth. Let us review our investigation of the Aristotelian-Thomistic notion of the soul. The powers which emanate from one essence of the soul can be divided into the intellectual, the irascible, and the concupiscible. The distinction of these three powers is made in accordance with the three levels of the soul from which they originate: the intellectual, the sensitive, and the vegetative.

These three powers are called the subjects of act in the Thomistic language. It is through these powers that the soul acts. Besides the subjects, the soul requires objects for its act. The subjects and the objects are the two principles of an act. The relation of the subject and the object can be either active or passive.[13] The active act is called action, and the passive act, passion. In action, the subject acts as an agent on the object. In passion, the subject is acted upon as a patient by the object.[14] The Passion of our Lord is a passion because He is acted upon by His crucifiers and suffers as a patient. Now each of the three powers of the soul can be diversified into an active and a passive power.[15] The three principal powers can be diversified into six powers, three sets of active and passive powers. These three levels of active and passive powers constitute the principle of uniformity for the seven Planets of the *Paradiso*, the seven

34

Terraces of the *Purgatorio* proper and the eight Circles of the *Inferno* proper. To be precise, Dante adds one more power to the concupiscible, namely, love. St. Augustine says that love is the root of all other passions.[16] St. Thomas calls love the first of the concupiscible passions.[17] Dante places love above the active and the passive powers of the concupiscible.

Let us now see how these seven powers emanating from the three levels of the soul can explain the structure of the three worlds. We will begin with the concupiscible which emanates from the vegetative level. St. Thomas sees three distinct powers in the vegetative soul: the generative, the nutritive, and the augmentative powers.[18] The generative power aims at the reproduction and preservation of the species and is the source of the sexual impulse. The nutritive power is meant for the preservation of the individual and is the source of the appetite for food and drink. The augmentative power aims at the growth of an individual and is the source of the desire to mature and expand. St. Thomas articulates the functions of these three powers in the light of plant life.

Since Dante is concerned with these powers in human life, he makes some modifications. He assigns the reproductive function of the generative power to the augmentative power. It is the unique human privilege that sexual impulse can be divorced from the procreative function while the former is always conjoined with the latter in animal and plant life. Furthermore, the procreation of offspring can be regarded as the extension and expansion of the parents. Dante places the sexual impulse at the top of the concupiscible powers, the nutritive power in the middle, and the augmentative power at the bottom. When we compare the nutritive and the augmentative powers, we can regard the former as a passive power and the latter as an active power. The nutritive power aims at the preservation

35

of an individual, while the augmentative power aims at his expansion and procreation. The act of the former is negative, and that of the latter is positive.

Dante places the generative power at the top of the concupiscible primarily because it is the ground of love and because his epic is a song of love. Love is neither active nor passive; rather it is both active and passive. In a perfect love, one loves and is loved, is an agent and a patient. The three powers of the concupiscible constitute the principle of uniformity in the construction of the top three Planets, the top three Terraces, and the Second, the Third, and the Fourth Circles. Lust and chaste love are the sin and the virtue of the generative power. The penitents of the Seventh Terrace purge themselves for the transformation of their lust into chaste love. In the Seventh Heaven, Dante meets St. Benedict and St. Peter Damian, a distinguished son of the Benedictine order. St. Benedict and St. Peter Damian represent the chaste love of monks. The Benedictine monastery on Monte Cassino is the symbol of the conversion of Europe from adulterous idolatry to the chaste love of God (*Par.* xxii. 37–45). On Saturn, Dante sees Jacob's Ladder rising beyond the range of his sight. Jacob's Ladder is the symbol of the love of God and reminds us of the flames of the Seventh Terrace which burn up all the residue of lust.

The Second Circle is the domain where the sin of lust reigns with its tearful singing and moaning. The blast of lust perpetually blows about the sinners and invariably brings them back to the eternal ruin, as the blast of the Seventh Terrace fans the flames which give eternal cure to the final wound (*Inf.* v. 34; *Purg.* xxv. 113 and 139). Singing characterizes both the Second Circle and the Seventh Terrace, because singing is the most appropriate expression for the joy of love and lust. The sinners and penitents go singing like cranes. Of all the seven Planets, Saturn is the only place where music is not allowed. Beatrice explains to Dante that she cannot smile and the heavenly chorus cannot sing on the Seventh Heaven because Dante, a mortal soul, could not stand the expression of the heavenly joy of Saturn. The chaste love of the blessed burns like a volcano under a snow-cap. Our pilgrim is given only a glimpse of the dreadful intensity of spiritual love in the thunderous outcry that follows Peter Damian's denunciation of the bestial clergy (*Par.* xxi. 130–142).

Temperance and gluttony are the virtue and the sin of the nutritive power, the passive power of the concupiscible. The penitents of the Sixth Terrace are striving to purge themselves of gluttony and gain temperance. Jupiter is the "temperate star," namely, the symbol of temperance (*Par.* xviii. 68). The Third Circle is the abode of the intemperate sinners. The nourishment which is the object of the nutritive appetite is symbolized by water. The cold, eternal rain which perpetually beats down upon the gluttons and keeps them submerged under mire represents the excessive hunger for earthly food and drink. The clear water which flows down from rock to rock on the Seventh Terrace stands for heavenly food and drink. The penitents are abstaining from earthly food to strengthen their hunger for heavenly food. In the Sixth Heaven, Dante sees how the Eagle drinks the water flowing out of the heavenly fountain (*Par.* xx. 19–30). The Eagle is the symbol of justice; justice is a consequent virtue of temperance. Justice means, among other things, the order of the appetites. Dante learns from the Imperial Eagle that divine will is the fountain of justice and that human justice is to be in conformity with divine will. The Eagle represents the human appetite which is in a perfect harmony with the divine will. That is why it can mean *We* and *Our* by *I* and *Me*, i.e., why it can express communal desires through individual utterances. The penitents are so emaciated that Dante can read the M's of *Homo Dei* on their faces (*Purg.* xxiii. 31–33). To hunger for the food and the drink from God is the sign that man is made in the image of God. Cerberus, the captain of the gluttons, has three gullets and looks like M set upside down. A glutton is a perverted image of God. Notice how the Imperial Eagle emerges with a slight change from the shape of M (*Par.* xviii. 94–114). The just rulers of the Eagle are the perfected forms of the mortal creatures made in the image of God.

Liberality and avarice are the virtue and the sin of the augmentative power, the active power of the concupiscible. The penitents on the Fifth Terrace are purging themselves of avarice and its contrary vice, prodigality, and working for the virtue of liberality. The penitents are lying on the ground and moaning like women in travail (*Purg.* xx. 16–21). Procreation is an extension of the individual. The penitents are giving birth to their new souls as the adopted sons of the heavenly Father. It is through His liberality that the Father in Heaven has opened the way for mortal creatures to become His sons through the Crucifixion and Resurrection of His only Son. Statius rises up from his long travail under the angelic hymn *Gloria in excelsis Deo* which celebrated the birth of Christ (*Purg.* xx. 127–138). Statius appears to Dante and Virgil in the way Christ appeared to two of his disciples on their way to Emmaus after His Resurrection (*Purg.* xxi. 7–9). The Advent and the Resurrection are the two termini of one great lesson Christ gave the sinful souls, namely, how to conquer sin and death and to be born in the eternal glory. *What is sown corruptible, rises incorruptible: what is sown in weakness, is raised in power* (1 Cor. 15:42–44).

On the Fifth Heaven, Dante sees Christ flashing forth from the Cross, the symbol of the power which has conquered death and raised the mortal soul from exile on the sinful earth. The warriors of the Cross sing the martial hymn for the battle against death "Arise and conquer" (*Par.* xiv. 125). Treasure is the chain and the master of soul; one's heart is where one's treasure is. When a rich man asked Christ for advice on the eternal life, Jesus told him to give all his wealth to the poor and follow him. *If anyone wishes to come after me, let him deny himself, and take up his cross, and follow me* (Mark 8:34). One cannot keep treasures both in heaven and on earth any more than one can serve two masters. The crusaders and the martyrs liberally gave not only their wealth but also their bodies and souls in becoming the warriors of the Cross. The avaricious and the prodigal sold and enchained their hearts to the earthly treasure and are engaged in the arduous labor of pushing around the heavy weights with their chest (*Inf.* vii. 27). They have become the sons and slaves of Plutus.

Let us now move on to the second level of the soul, the irascible. The irascible can be divided into an active and a passive power. It is through the passive power of the irascible that the soul suffers under the difficulties which frustrate the satisfaction of the concupiscible. Fortitude and sloth are the virtue and the sin of the passive irascible. Fortitude enables us not to lose courage and hope, and to strengthen the will power in the face of difficult obstacles.[19] Sloth is the sorrow and rancor arising from frustration and despair.[20] The two groups of penitents on the Fourth Terrace keep running to save their sluggish will from the sin of sloth and to transform it into the will of vigor and fortitude. In the Fourth Heaven, Dante sees two circles of theologians whose two representatives sing the eulogy of St. Francis and St. Dominic. These two great saints are the two princes who rescued the Church from her long sluggish decline. St. Francis and St. Dominic exemplify fortitude and courage in overcoming sloth and despair.

Sloth and despair are represented by the Fifth and the Sixth Circles. Technically viewed, the two Circles are not

39

two independent Circles but two Rings of one Circle. Dante sees the Furies from the Fifth Circle, while the Furies appear on the other side of the walls of the City of Dis, that is, in the Sixth Circle. The Furies are "girt with greenest hydras" and have little serpents for hair (*Inf.* ix. 40–41). Green is the color of hope. The Furies represent the hope which has been perverted into poisonous despair. They threaten to turn Dante into stone with the head of the Gorgon Medusa, the symbol of fatal despair (*Inf.* ix. 52). The vision of the Furies establishes the link of the Fifth and the Sixth Circles. We shall shortly come back to this point for a fuller explanation.

The Fifth Circle represents sloth and rancor arising from the despair of the earthly good, and the Sixth Circle sloth and rancor arising from the despair of the heavenly good. The despairers of the earthly good are sinking in the stagnant water of Styx, and the despairers of the heavenly good are burning in the fire of the open tombs. The stagnant water in the mire and marsh of Styx flows down from the Second, the Third, and the Fourth Circles, which represent the direct appetite for the earthly good. The stagnant marsh stands for the despondency and rancor into which the irascible falls at the exasperating frustration of the concupiscible. The eternally burning fire in the open tomb represents the sullen wrath which comes from the despair of the heavenly good. Dante gives only one example of heresy in the Sixth Circle, the Epicureans who denied the immortality of soul (*Inf.* x. 14). The immortality of soul can never be denied or affirmed on rational ground alone. Reason has no sufficient evidence to settle this grave matter. Its denial is only a reflection of the despair of the celestial bliss. Dante distinguishes the despair of the earthly good and that of the heavenly good with the difference of water and fire, because water falls to the ground and fire flares upward. The sinners in both Circles are burning with anger;

Farinata and Argenti are two good examples. Their anger is of a passive nature. They rather suffer from it as patients than act on it as agents. They can at best bite and pinch their neighbors, but cannot wreak their wrath through manly or bestial actions.

Meekness and wrath are the virtue and the sin of the active irascible. The penitents of the Third Terrace begin all their prayers with *Agnus Dei* (*Purg*. xvi. 19). The Lamb of God is the supreme exemplification of the virtuous irascible in perfect subjection to reason. The sin of the Seventh Circle is represented by the Minotaur in whom bestial wrath overpowers human reason (*Inf*. xii. 10–15). The boiling blood of Phlegethon represents the wrathful animal passion. Blood is the symbol of animal life. Aristotle says that the physiological definition of anger is the boiling of blood around the heart.[21] The anger of the Seventh Circle is active; it can vent itself in ferocious action. In the Third Heaven, Dante meets Carlo Martello, the only member of the house of Anjou that Dante could tolerate. The house of Anjou was a bestial family, and Carlo Martello was its only member to overcome bestial passion. Besides Carlo Martello, Dante meets three souls—Cunizza, Folco, and Rahab—who were once victims of bestial passion and who transformed their bestial passion into faithful valor for the service of the Lord.

We now come to the highest level of the soul. St. Thomas says that the intellect of the human soul is similar in its nature to the soul of an angel and that both of them are devoid of the irascible and the concupiscible passions.[22] Their only appetite is the spiritual passion for excellence. The passion for excellence and glory can be expressed in an active or a passive way. One may defy and reject his superiors and masters in order to secure his excellence and glory. This is the active expression of an inordinate passion for glory and is called *pride*. One may suffer at the excellence of other people because others' excellence eclipses one's own excellence. The grief at the prosperity of other people is the passive expression of inordinate passion for excellence and is called envy.[23] Humility is the virtue contrary to the sin of pride, and mercy, to the sin of envy.

Mercy and envy are the virtue and the sin of the passive intellect. Mercy seeks good for others, while envy works evil for others. The penitents of the Second Terrace labor for the transformation of their envious passion into a merciful passion. They sustain each other by leaning against each other in the spirit of mercy (*Purg.* xiii. 61–63).They recite the Litany of the Saints, the prayer which begs for the mercy of God (*Purg.* xiii. 50–51). In the Second Heaven, Dante meets Emperor Justinian. Justinian narrates the brilliant growth of the Roman Empire. The Empire culminates in the *Pax Romana* under which justice prevails up to the coast of the Red Sea (*Par.* vi. 79–81). All these brilliant achievements of the Roman Empire become pale when compared with the great event under Tiberius. The peace and justice of the Roman Empire were established to prepare the ground on which the Son of God was to pay the ransom for the sin of man with His own blood. This is the supreme exemplification of mercy.

Mercury, as the planet which gladly "veils itself with another's ray," is a proper symbol of mercy (*Par.* v. 129). The spirit of mercy does not seek one's own glory but rejoices in others' glory. Christ warned against the danger of becoming hypocrites while doing works of mercy: *When thou givest alms, do not sound a trumpet before thee, as the hypocrites do . . . But when thou givest alms, do not let thy left hand know what thy right hand is doing* (Matt. 6:2–3). The sinners of the Eighth Circle are all thrown into and hidden in the evil pouches. Envy loves secrecy as much as mercy does. Aristotle makes an interesting comparison between anger and malice.[24] He says that an angry man is not given to plotting and that a malicious man loves secrecy and plotting, while anger itself is open. The ten deep pouches of the *Malebolge* are the secret pouches where the envious plot and bring about the misfortune and disaster of other people. In the descent of the *Inferno*, Dante meets the devils, the black angels, for the first time in the *Malebolge*. St. Thomas says that the angels are capable of only the sins of spirits, pride and envy, and that they cannot commit the other human sins because they are devoid of the irascible and the concupiscible.[25] He further says that the devil's envy of man's good is the consequent sin of pride. After losing his own good, the devil becomes envious of the good of man and works for its destruction.

Humility and pride are the virtue and the sin of the active intellect. The sin of pride lies in the obstinacy of trying to be the master of one's own will and the creator of one's own bliss. The penitents on the First Terrace are bending their proud wills by bending down their proud necks under the heavy weight of stones (*Purg.* x. 118–120). They recite the *Pater Noster* in which they recognize the impotence of the created will and the omnipotence of the Uncreated Will (*Purg.* xi. 7–12). In the First Heaven, Dante meets Piccarda who was too humble and too weak even to keep her vow. Humility comes only with the recognition of the impotence and weakness of oneself. The virtue of humility is to accept one's weakness and entrust oneself to the strength of God. This is the central lesson Christ exemplifies through His own death. *Though he was crucified through weakness, yet he lives through the power of God. Yes, we also are weak in him, yet we shall live with him through the power of God* (2 Cor. 13:4). Weakness in God is stronger than firmness in man.

The Ninth Circle is Satan's inner court, while the *Malebolge* constitutes his outer ten dominions. It is in this

43

inner court that the Emperor of all sins and the princes of pride are engaged in the vision of their own glories and excellences. It is so dark that they cannot see even beyond their eyelashes. They need not see anyone else except themselves; they are too intoxicated with their own glories. The dark mist and the tight ice of Cocytus depict the state of prideful intellect. It is cold and immovable; it is devoid of love and knowledge. The proud will is a strong will; it seeks to be the master of itself and slave to none. Bocca will not identify himself even when Dante threatens to pull off his hair (*Inf.* xxxii. 100). Here is the mystery of the will. The firm and strong will freezes itself in its own obstinacy. The sinners of *Tolomea* cannot even freely shed their tears (*Inf.* xxxiii. 94–99). Whereas the weak and humble will of Piccarda gains strength in its humble submission, the firm and proud will becomes impotent in its willful defiance.

We can now see that Dante is a far more faithful Aristotelian than St. Thomas. It has been a well accepted assumption that Dante's epic is nothing more than a poetification of the Angelic Doctor's beautiful system. It has been often said that the *Divina Commedia* corresponds "point by point" to St. Thomas. We could not but wonder at the intuitive insight which can see all the points of correspondence between an intuitive poetic system and a discursive philosophical system without even knowing the frameworks of the two systems. Whereas St. Thomas does not even expect that there should be virtues contrary to the seven principal sins, Dante enumerates the contrary virtues. Our poet further regards the seven pairs of principal virtues and vices as the perfection and perversion of the seven principal powers which emanate from the three levels of the soul. The seven Planets reveal the nature of the seven principal powers in perfection, and the eight Circles disclose their nature in perversion. The seven Terraces describe the process of transforming the seven principal powers from perversion to perfection. The seven Terraces further bring into contrast the seven Planets and the eight Circles. For this special function of contrast, Dante places the examples of the seven pairs of virtues and sins on the seven Terraces. The seven pairs of virtues and sins are: humility and pride, mercy and envy, meekness and wrath, fortitude and sloth, liberality and avarice, temperance and gluttony, and spiritual love and carnal love. The examples of these virtues and vices are generally known as the whips and the bridles of purgation. Besides indicating the initial and final termini of purgation on each Terrace, the whips and bridles establish the correspondence and contrast between the *Inferno* and the *Paradiso*. For example, the examples of pride on the First Terrace point to the Ninth Circle, and the examples of humility to the First Heaven.

Dante's notion of the soul is one of the most consistent resolutions of a long struggle to articulate the nature of man as conceived in the Judeo-Christian tradition through the conceptual framework developed in the Greco-Roman tradition. The nature of man as conceived in the Greco-Roman tradition is quite different from the concept of man as developed in the Judeo-Christian tradition. Man is a spiritual creature, the spirit enchained in flesh, in the Judeo-Christian tradition. Man is a rational animal, reason embodied in animality, in the Greco-Roman tradition. The difference between these two ideas of man may disappear, if reason is equated with spirit, animality with carnality. But the reason in animal and the spirit in flesh do not come into a neat relation of identity, because the former has a radically different nature from the latter.

The radical difference between these two notions of man is clearly reflected in the contrast between the Greco-Roman concept of virtue and the Judeo-Christian concept of sin. In the Greco-Roman view, all the vices of the

45

rational animal arise from the ignorance of reason or the irrationality of the animal passion. A perfect reason cannot err; it errs only through ignorance. This is why Socrates identifies virtue with knowledge. So conceived, the reason of man is quite different from the spirit of man. In the Judeo-Christian tradition, every sin begins with the spirit. The perfect spirits of angels have sinned not through their ignorance but through their will. The spirit is the only ground of sin also in man. The first man sins not from his flesh but with his spirit. The corruption and degeneration of the flesh are only consequences of the sin of the spirit.

Because of this radical difference between the reason of the Greco-Roman man and the spirit of the Judeo-Christian man, the ancient Greeks always put their stress on virtues and the ancient Jews on sins. In the examination of man's actions and passions, the Greeks saw the virtues of intellect in many forms and its vice only in one form, namely, the ignorance of the intellect. The Jews viewed the sins of spirit in many forms and its virtue only in one form, namely, the humble and obedient will of the spirit. Whereas the perfection of the intellect through knowledge and wisdom is for the Greeks the requisite pre-condition for all other virtues, even knowledge and wisdom is for the Jews only a consequence of a humble and obedient will. While Socrates identifies knowledge with virtue, the psalmist declares, *The fear of the Lord is the beginning of wisdom* (Psalm 110 [111]:10). For the Jews, it is not the knowledge of intellect but the obedience of will that is the root of all virtues and the only safeguard against all sins.

The contrast between the Greek intellectualism and the Judaic volitionism is beautifully reflected in St. Bernard's examination of the Socratic command: "Know thyself." St. Bernard preaches that self-knowledge is the first step of the soul's ascent to its Creator.[26] That is, we have to know how miserable and contemptible we are before we can turn to God. At this point, St. Bernard appears to be a faithful disciple of Socrates. But he concludes his long, persuasive sermon on the importance of the Socratic knowledge with an orthodox Judeo-Christian dictum that the self-knowledge which is the first essential step toward conversion can come only through humility and obedience.

The two notions of the soul from Greece and Israel make their formal encounter at the beginning of Christianity under the names of philosophy and religion. On this fateful encounter, the Fathers of the early Church were divided in their attitude and approach. While in Tertullian's eyes pagan philosophy was little more than the foolish gibberish of the sinful world, Clement of Alexandria regarded philosophy as a gift of God, a means of educating and preparing the pagan world for the revealed wisdom of God. In the end, the Clementine conciliatory spirit triumphed over the reactionary Tertullian spirit, and the Greek philosophy was formally adopted as the handmaid in the articulation of the religion inherited from Israel. This was the birth of the revealed theology in which the discipline of philosophy is employed for the exegesis of the revealed wisdom of God.

The entire intellectual movement throughout the medieval era is the consistent attempt to bring together the Greco-Roman philosophy and the Judeo-Christian religion into harmonious union. In this long endeavor, philosophy has provided the form of thought, and religion the content of thought, that is, the contents of the revealed truth are to be elucidated by the highly developed form and system of the Greek philosophy. Religion and philosophy have thus been placed in the relation of content and form, end and means, and master and servant. It is this long established relation of the legacies from Greece and Israel that is reasserted and reaffirmed in St. Thomas' explanation and definition of theology, that is, he accepts the revealed truth

47

in faith and only articulates it through discursive exegesis.

In the long, persistent endeavor to harmonize religion and philosophy, the central theme of disputation and speculation has been the nature of the soul. The soul was the central target of inquiry throughout the medieval era. For medieval people, the internal world of man was the first object of knowledge. In the investigation of this first object of knowledge, one of the thorniest problems was to reconcile the Greco-Roman notion of virtue and the Judeo-Christian notion of sin. In the Judeo-Christian tradition, sins have been in general classified into the spiritual and the carnal sins in accordance with the dual elements of man, his spirit and his flesh. In the Greco-Roman tradition, the virtues have been divided into the intellectual and moral virtues in accordance with the two elements of the soul, the intellect and the sensitive passions. When these two systems of classification come together, they present two technical problems. How are the spiritual and the carnal sins to be related to the intellectual and moral virtues? How can the carnal and the spiritual sins be related to the powers of the soul as known in the Greek faculty psychology? Dante's notion of the soul and its virtues and sins is the most elaborate, systematic solution to these problems.

We can readily see how drastic and systematic Dante's solution is when we compare his notion of the soul with that of St. Thomas. The Angelic Doctor is fully aware of the grave disparity between the Greco-Roman idea of the rational animal and the Judeo-Christian idea of the spiritual flesh. When he encounters this grave disparity in the form of the ultimate metaphysical questions, such as the relation of the good and the true and that of the will and the intellect, he takes extra caution and care by piling qualification upon qualification to avoid both the error of logic and the sin of heresy.[27] When the Angelic Doctor comes down from the lofty metaphysical plane to the mundane level of our daily life and examines the human virtues and sins, he relaxes his angelic intellectual strain and leaves quite a few loose ends.

The Angelic Doctor examines virtues and sins under the categories both of spirit in flesh and of reason in animal but never achieves a satisfactory union of these two perspectives. His table of ten virtues is perhaps the simplest fusion of the two perspectives. It is not really a fusion of the Judaic and the Greek thought. He adopts Aristotle's seven intellectual and moral virtues for the natural end and places above them St. Paul's three theological virtues for the supernatural end. It is a grafting of Paul's spiritual man on Aristotle's natural man. The grafting is of a very poor workmanship, because the natural virtues and the supernatural virtues have nothing to do with each other.[28] The grafting is so poorly done that not even a drop of blood circulates between the two men grafted together, the natural man and the spiritual man. When St. Thomas relates the ten virtues to the three traditional categories of sins: (i) against God, (ii) against oneself, and (iii) against one's neighbor, he can find no place for the four intellectual virtues among these Christian categories.[29] This is because the highest part of the soul has neither been considered as primarily intellectual nor its virtues as the intellectual virtues in the Judeo-Christian tradition.

When the Angelic Doctor examines virtues and sins under the category of spirit in flesh, he seldom bothers to sustain the Aristotelian spirit of systematization and classification. He never composes a table of spiritual and carnal sins. Once he even refuses to seek their contraries on the most un-Aristotelian pretext that sins need not be contrary to virtues. Here and there, he makes a few sporadic efforts to relate spiritual and carnal sins to the powers of the soul. These sporadic efforts indicate that he regards all spiritual and carnal sins as what Aristotle calls the vices of the

49

sensitive appetite. St. Thomas claims that all spiritual and carnal sins can be reduced to the passions of the irascible and the concupiscible.[30] He regards even the sin of pride, "the inordinate appetite for excellence," as stemming from the irascible passion of the sensitive soul.[31] His definition of pride and its origin faithfully repeats that of Aristotle. But the Angelic Doctor follows the teaching of his Church and condemns pride as the root of all sins, whereas his philosopher, Aristotle, praises it as the crown of all virtues.

Though the Angelic Doctor reduces all spiritual and carnal sins to animal passions and cannot conceive of the human intellect as the ground of sheer spiritual sins in its own right and in independence of sensitive passions, he changes his view when he confronts the fall of the angels. The angels are pure spirits and have no sensitive passion. St. Thomas accepts the traditional description of the status of the angelic mind before the fall: "There was no habit preceding his sinful act or any passion fettering his mind."[32] The sin of such an angelic mind cannot be accounted for within the teachings of Aristotle. But the angels did fall. Only when confronted with this dilemma, does the Angelic Doctor admit the possibility of a pure spiritual sin of a pure spiritual power which defies and revolts against its Creator and the order of His creation. It is indeed a puzzle why St. Thomas does not see the possibility of the same diabolical sin for the spirit of man that he admits for the angelic spirit.

Dante's drastic attempt lies in this: he carries over the nature of pure spiritual power, which the Angelic Doctor accepts for the angels on the authority of St. Augustine, to the human spirit and designates humility and pride as the roots of all virtues and sins. On this point, Dante is a faithful follower of the Platonic-Augustine school rather than of the Aristotelian-Thomistic school. If the Angelic Doctor may be said to have Christianized only the lower two levels of the soul, leaving its highest level in the pagan form, because he attributes all the Christian sins of spirit and flesh to the irascible and the concupiscible, Dante can be said to have completed the Christianization of the human soul right up to its highest peak. Dante's thorough spiritualization of the soul is clearly shown in his poetic description of the generative process of the soul, which we have seen in Statius' discourse. Dante stresses the spiritual power of the soul rather than its intellectual power by characterizing the highest power of the soul as a pure spirit (*spirito nuovo*, *Purg.* xxv. 72). Our poet has often been called a philosophical poet, but he should have been known as a poetical philosopher if there is any difference between these two titles.

Let us now look back over the poetic characterization of the seven principal virtues and sins in the three worlds and notice Dante's technique in representing the difference between the active and the passive powers. In the *Inferno*, the distinction between the active and the passive powers is represented by the position of the sinner's body in relation to the principal medium of punishment. Let us take the Eighth and the Ninth Circles for our first example. The Ninth Circle presents the sin of the active intellect and the Eighth Circle the sin of the passive intellect. The bodies of the sinners in the Eighth Circle are completely submerged below the surface of the livid stone of the *Malebolge*, while the bodies of the sinners in the Ninth Circle are only partially sunk below the surface of the ice of Cocytus. The hard cold ice of Cocytus and the livid stone of *Malebolge* represent the active and the passive powers of the intellect hardened in sin. The sinners of envy are sunk below the surface of the livid stone and in the deep pouches of the *Malebolge* because they are patients of a sinful power. The sinners of pride stick out their heads above the surface of the ice because they are agents of a sinful power. The former suffer from envy, and the latter act from pride.

A similar contrast of action and passion is shown in the active and the passive sin of the irascible. The sinners of the Fifth and the Sixth Circles are those who sinned as patients of the passive irascible. They are submerged in the marsh of Styx or buried in the open tombs of fire. The sinners of the Seventh Circle are those who sinned as agents of the active irascible. All of them project some parts of their bodies above the surface. Even those who are thrown into the boiling blood of Phlegethon do stand on their own feet, while the sinners of the Fifth and the Sixth Circle are floating around in marsh or lying in the tombs. Even the tyrants who are submerged in Phlegethon deeper than any other group do stick out their skulls above the boiling blood (*Inf.* xii. 103). While the sinners of the Fifth and the Sixth Circle are complete slaves of the irascible passion, the sinners of the Seventh Circle retain some measure of mastery over it. The former only suffer as patients from their anger, but the latter act as agents of their anger.

The contrast of action and passion is also indicated in the Third and the Fourth Circles. The Third Circle stands for the passive sin of the concupiscible and the Fourth Circle its active sin. The gluttons of the Third Circle are lying on the ground and submerged in the rain (*Inf.* vi. 34–37). The avaricious and the prodigal sinners of the Fourth Circle stand on their own feet and push around the heavy weight. The sinners of the Third Circle merely suffer as patients from the concupiscible passion, but the sinners of the Fourth Circle act as agents on the concupiscible passion. Lust is the concupiscible passion which is both active and passive, and this duality is reflected in the motion and posture of the sinners of the Second Circle. The lustful are neither allowed to stand on their own feet nor submerged below the surface. They are blown about like cranes by the blast of lust. They can be said to be moving on their feet and above the ground and also to be floating and submerged in the blast. This ambiguity reflects the duality of lust, namely, its dual nature of being active and passive at once.

The roles of the active and the passive are reversed in the transition of the seven powers of the soul from sins to virtues. The active sins in the *Inferno* become the passive virtues in the *Paradiso,* and the passive sins in the *Inferno* become the active virtues in the *Paradiso.* The First Heaven reflects the virtue of the active intellect and corresponds to the Ninth Circle. The Second Heaven reflects the virtue of the passive intellect and corresponds to the Eighth Circle. Piccarda on the Moon suffered violence and could not keep her vow. Justinian of Mercury sings of the mercy of Christ who suffered violence but kept His vow, the promise to save the human race from Adam's sin. In the virtue of humility, which is represented by the Moon, violence is the obstacle to the fulfillment of mission. In the virtue of mercy, which is represented by Mercury, violence is overcome and employed as an instrument to the fulfillment of a mission. Humility is a virtue concerned only with the individual's will, but mercy is a virtue concerned with his neighbors' will. Humility is passive because it is essentially the subjection of the will to the superior and the community, while mercy is active because it aims beyond the mere subjection of the will to the improvement of the welfare of the community. Mercy is a higher virtue than humility, while pride is a graver sin than envy.

In the transition from the world of sin to the world of virtue, the active becomes the passive and the lower becomes the higher. This reversal reflects the diametrically opposite principles of order in the world of bliss and in the world of sin:

The Fragile Leaves of the Sibyl

You know that those who are regarded as rulers among the Gentiles lord it over them, and their great men exercise authority over them. But it is not so among you. On the contrary, whoever wishes to become great shall be your servant; and whoever wishes to be first among you shall be the slave of all (Mark 10:42–44).

The reversal of the active and the passive is also reflected in the contrast of the Third and the Fourth Heaven. Venus reflects the virtue of the active irascible and corresponds to the Seventh Circle, while the Sun reflects the virtue of the passive irascible and corresponds to the Fifth and the Sixth Circles. Carlo Martello of the Third Heaven stands for the failure and decline of the secular government, and St. Thomas and St. Bonaventure of the Fourth Heaven sing of St. Francis and St. Dominic for their success in rescuing the Holy Church from decline and misery. Carlo Martello suffers as a patient from the bestial passion which has shattered the Empire to pieces, and St. Francis and St. Dominic are the agents who have overcome the sloth of the Church. The virtue of meekness is a passive subjection, and the virtue of fortitude is an active conquest. While the sin of the active irascible is graver than the sin of the passive irascible, fortitude is a higher virtue than meekness.

The Fifth Heaven reflects the virtue of the active concupiscible and corresponds to the Fourth Circle. The Sixth Heaven reflects the virtue of the passive concupiscible and corresponds to the Third Circle. The warriors of the Cross on Mars have suffered death in their battle for God, while the just rulers on Jupiter ruled over their subjects in implementing divine justice on the earth. The former were patients in the execution of their missions, and the latter were agents in the execution of their tasks. The liberality of the former was the power to give up all the earthly treasures and take on the cross, and the temperance of the latter was the capacity to be entrusted with the government of

54

the earthly good for the children of God on the earth. Temperance is an active virtue, while liberality is a passive one. The former is a higher virtue than the latter, while avarice and prodigality are graver sins than gluttony and intemperance.

The duality of the active and the passive nature of love is reflected in the chaste love of the monks of the Seventh Heaven. On Saturn, Dante presents the tradition of the Benedictine order as the supreme exemplifier of the chaste love of God. The monk's chaste love appears to be passive because it secludes itself from the worldly affairs. In spite of this apparent passivity, the Benedictine monastery on Monte Cassino stands as the symbol for the conversion of the Western world from the pagan idolatry to the chaste love of God. The virtue of chaste love is at once active and passive like the sin of lust. This duality is reflected in the combination of the tranquility which pervades the atmosphere of Saturn and the thunderous cry which follows Peter Damian's denunciation of the clergy. The duality is further reflected in the combination of the two blessed souls with whom Dante talks in the Seventh Heaven. While Dante talks with one person each in the Fifth and the Sixth Heaven, Cacciaguida on Mars and the Eagle on Jupiter, he talks with two persons on Saturn, Peter Damian and St. Benedict. This is because the Fifth and the Sixth Heavens represent respectively the virtues of the active and the passive concupiscible, while the Seventh Heaven stands for the virtue of the concupiscible which is both active and passive. While St. Peter Damian is vehement and truculent, St. Benedict is gentle and calm.

The transformation of an active sin into a passive virtue and of a passive sin into an active virtue, that is, the reversal of the order of Hell into the order of Heaven, is indicated by the methods of purgation on the seven Terraces. While the sinners of the Ninth Circle stick out their heads above the ice of Cocytus, the penitents of the First Terrace bend down their heads under heavy stone. The sinners of the Eighth Circle are thrown down beneath the surface of the livid stone of the *Malebolge,* but the penitents of the Second Terrace are placed on the surface of livid stones. While the sinners of the Seventh Circle are not completely submerged below the surface of the boiling blood and the burning ground, the penitents of the Third Terrace are completely submerged in the choking smoke. The sinners of the Fifth and the Sixth Circle are floating in water and lying in fire and do not stand on their feet, but the penitents of the Fourth Terrace keep running on their feet. The sinners of the Fourth Circle are pushing around the heavy weights; the penitents of the Fifth Terrace are lying on the ground. The sinners of the Third Circle are lying in mud and rain; the penitents of the Sixth Terrace hop and gallop. Both the Second Circle and the Seventh Terrace are characterized by the blast of wind. The blast of the Second Circle blows the sinners around, but the blast of the Seventh Terrace fans the purgatorial fire and does not carry the penitents around. The fire represents the transformation of the blast of lust into chaste love.

The difference between the active and the passive powers is further represented by the individual and communal modes of act. The acts can be divided into the acts which are primarily individual acts and the acts which are primarily communal acts, though both classes of acts require the individual and the community as instrument and medium. For example, acts of humility and pride are individual acts, while the acts of mercy and envy are communal acts. The stress falls on the individual in pride and humility, while the stress falls on the community in mercy and envy. A proud man is chiefly concerned with his individual excellence, and an envious man with the excellence of his neighbors in his community. A humble man is primarily conscious of his own misery, and a merciful man of the misery of the neighbors in his community. St. Bernard tells his monks that one can become humble only by knowing how miserable and contemptible one is in his own eyes.[33] One can come to be merciful only through the knowledge of the misery of others. Humility is the virtue and knowledge of the individual affairs, and mercy is the virtue and knowledge of the communal problems. The former precedes the latter. St. Bernard says that one can come to know the misery of others only through the knowledge of one's own misery.

We can call the virtues and sins of the active power the private virtues and sins or the individual virtues and sins, because the chief domain and concern of these virtues and sins are the individuals in privacy. We can call the virtues and sins of the passive power the public or the communal virtues and sins, because the chief domain and concern of these virtues and sins are the communities in public. Each of the penitents on the First Terrace carries his own rock over his head and shoulders, while the penitents of the Second Terrace are leaning against one another. The purgation of the First Terrace is individual, and that of the Second Terrace is communal. Humility and pride are of the active intellect and individual in their nature. For the same reason, the sinners of the Ninth Circle are all frozen, each in his own hole, and live in deadly solitude, while the sinners of the Eighth Circle are engaged in busy communal activities. Only two blessed souls appear in tranquility on the First Heaven, while the souls on the Second Heaven rush to Dante like a school of fish (*Par.* v. 101). The humility of the Moon is an individual virtue, and the mercy of Mercury is a communal one.

The penitents on the Third Terrace individually walk through the smoke, and the penitents on the Fourth Terrace run around in groups. The sinners of the Seventh

57

Circle are individually placed, while the sinners of the
Fifth and the Sixth Circle are dumped in groups. Compare
the punishment in Styx with the punishment in Phlegethon.
While the sullen sinners are floating and roaming about in
the marsh of Styx, the bestial criminals are individually
submerged in the boiling blood of Phlegethon in accordance with the gravity of their individual sins. Compare the
tombs of the Sixth Circle and the suicide wood of the
Seventh Circle. While many heretics are dumped together
in each of the tombs, each of the suiciders has his own tree
or shrub. The Heaven of Venus has only one ring of celestial dance, while the Heaven of the Sun has two rings of
celestial dance (*Par.* viii. 26). One ring is a symbol of the
singleness of the individual, while two rings are a symbol
of the togetherness of the community. Meekness and
wrath are of the active irascible power and individual virtue
and sin, whereas fortitude and sloth are of the passive
irascible power and communal virtue and sin.

The penitents on the Fifth Terrace moan and weep individually, and the penitents of the Sixth Terrace move
around in groups (*Purg.* xx. 118–120; xxiii. 20). The sinners of the Fourth Circle are divided into two groups, but
the sinners of the Third Circle are all indiscriminately submerged under rain and mud. The warriors on Mars individually move around within the Cross, while the rulers
on Jupiter constitute members of one bird and speak
through a communal voice. Liberality and avarice are of
the active concupiscible and the individual virtue and sin,
whereas temperance and intemperance are of the passive
concupiscible and the communal virtue and vice.

The penitents of the Seventh Terrace are divided into
two trains. These two trains of penitents are different in
constitution from the two groups of slothful penitents of
the Fourth Terrace. Dante sees one group of the slothful
reciting the examples of fortitude and the other group re-

citing the examples of sloth. These two groups are purging the same sin and are not divided by the difference of their sins, but the lustful penitents are divided into two groups of different sins. The division of the lustful penitents into two different groups reflects the individual feature of lust and love as does the division of the sinners of the active concupiscible into two different groups in the Fourth Circle. Whereas the avaricious and the prodigal clash with each other, the two files of penitents on the Seventh Terrace greet each other with the kiss of communal love. This is because the virtue and sin of the active concupiscible are only active and individual whereas love and lust are at once active and passive, individual and communal. The dual feature of lust is reflected in the ambiguity of the nature of the punishment in the Second Circle. It is hard to tell whether the sinners of lust are floating around individually or communally. Some of them move around in a communal bond like Paolo and Francesca, and others do not. The same thing is also true of the host of blessed souls moving along Jacob's Ladder on Saturn. Each of them seems to move individually up and down the Ladder, but all of them show their communal bond when they all together fly upward and disappear from Dante's sight. Individuality and communality come into a perfect balance in love and lust.

Let us now examine the inter-relation and inter-action of the three levels of the soul. Statius distinguishes the will (*voler*) and the desire (*talento*) (*Purg.* xxi. 63–65). The concupiscible is the appetite immediately related to the objects of attraction and aversion and constitutes the ground for desires. The will can be divided into two levels. When Beatrice talks of the will power on the Moon, she distinguishes two features in the will: the absolute will which can never be coerced by an external force and "the other" will which can be crushed by violence (*Par.* iv. 109–114).

The former can be called the will of choice and decision and the latter the will of execution and prudence. It is one thing to decide on the alternative goals and choose one of them, and another thing to execute the decision and achieve the goal. The former function belongs to the will of the intellect, and the latter to the will of the irascible. The will which the penitents of the First Terrace strive to sacrifice to God, the will which the sinners of Ninth Circle insist on retaining even in the ice-bound lake, and the will which the humble nuns of the Moon could preserve in their inner hearts in spite of adverse circumstances are of the intellect.

The intellect is a universal faculty; it deals only with the concepts of generality and universality. Its choice and decision are general, that is, its choice and decision are in general between good and evil, virtue and sin, salvation and perdition. Because its decision and choice are only general and abstract, the will of the intellect can be preserved even against adverse circumstances. Because the circumstances and situations are particular and concrete, they cannot encroach on the domain of the abstract, general will. You can never intervene directly in the realm of abstract thought with particular things. That is why the weak vow breakers could preserve the sanctity of their absolute will in adverse circumstances.

How can the abstract decision and choice of the intellect be translated into the concrete circumstances? This is one of the oldest questions in human psychology. The desires of the concupiscible are particular, and the will of the intellect is general. Every ethical action can be considered as the mediation and reconciliation of the particular desires and the general will. This meditation is provided by the executive will in the Aristotelian-Thomistic language. It is this mediation which St. Thomas has in his mind when he says that moral virtues dealing with sensitive appetite cannot be without prudence of the intellect and prudence cannot be without the rectitude of the sensitive appetite.[34] Prudence is the virtue of the executive will and its function is to coordinate the particular desires of the concupiscible with the general counsel and choice of the intellect. St. Thomas regards the executive will and its prudence as a joint operation of the intellect and the sensitive appetite, the two elements of the soul, the rational and the non-rational; but Dante assigns the executive will to the irascible. While St. Thomas explains the nature of the executive will in the light of the dyadic division of the soul, Dante articulates it in the light of the triadic division of the soul. In the triadic scheme, the irascible stands between the intellect and the concupiscible; it occupies a logical position for their mediation and reconciliation. Virgil's discourse on the Fourth Terrace explains the mysterious role which the irascible plays in mediating the intellect and the concupiscible (*Purg.* xviii. 19–33). The soul is awakened to activity by the pleasant object of appetite, forms its own ideal image of love from the object of pleasure, and invests the real object with its own ideal. Dante sees the demonstration of this lesson in his dream of the Siren (*Purg.* xix. 7–36). A hideous stuttering woman appears and draws Dante's attention. Dante becomes captivated in his own ideal image of love, with which he invests the Siren in his long gaze. Her pallid face begins to take on love's hue, and her stuttering tongue begins to sing a love song.

The dream of the Siren shows the function of imagination in transforming the abstract ideal of the intellect into a particular image for the love of the concupiscible. Imagination is a faculty of the irascible, that is, an animal faculty. For a fuller understanding of the function that Dante assigns to the irascible in its mediation of the intellect and the concupiscible in the triadic scheme of the soul, we can get valuable help from Kant. Kant was an articulate Aristotelian, well-schooled in the tradition of the

Schoolman, and was puzzled by the relation of the universal and the particular, the intellect and the sense, the will and the desire. All these problems are different facets of one problem, the central problem in the Aristotelian tradition. Kant offers us valuable help, because he confronts these problems within the framework of the triadic scheme of the soul as Dante does, while St. Thomas faces the same problem mostly in the dyadic scheme of the soul. Kant presents the nature of the problem most articulately in his doctrine of schematization and judgment.

In the process of judgment, Kant says particulars are subsumed under general concepts. In this, the process of judgment is viewed from the standpoint of the particular objects. When the same process is viewed from the standpoint of the general concepts, the abstract, non-sensuous concepts of the understanding are given concrete content from the particulars. Kant was very puzzled by this process, namely, how the concepts and percepts which are totally different in nature can come together in the process of judgment. Kant did not regard this puzzle as an exotic problem in the theoretical scholarly world, but as a pervasive mystery in the daily life of common people. Those who have fine theoretical knowledge often make poor judgments in the application of their fine theories. On the other hand, those who have little theoretical knowledge often make marvelous judgments. It is possible to bestow conceptual knowledge, but impossible to impart the power of judgment.

Of this mysterious process of judgment, Kant could see at least one obvious feature, that is, the universal concepts and the particular objects come together. It is to the faculty of imagination that Kant assigns the important function of mediating the concepts and the percepts in judgment. The image has a peculiar dual nature; it can stand for both the particular and the universal. With Kant, thus, imagination becomes the faculty of faculties. Dante's notion of imagination is quite similar to Kant's notion. It is the imagination of the irascible which translates the abstract ideal of the intellect into a particular image of love. It is also imagination which constitutes the link between the general counsel of the intellect and the particular desires of the concupiscible. This mediational function of the irascible is the virtue of prudence. Dante places Solomon, the paragon of this virtue, in the Sun, the Heaven which corresponds to the Fourth Terrace where Virgil extolls his doctrine of imagination and where Dante sees its demonstration in a dream (*Par.* xiii. 91–105).

Love and lust, the highest desire of the concupiscible, constitute one end of the spectrum of the seven powers of the soul, and the active intellect constitutes its other end. Placed at equal distance from the two ends, the passive irascible constitutes the point of mediation and transition. The transition from the Upper Hell to the Lower Hell is made in the boundary of the Fifth and Sixth Circles. On the Fourth Terrace, Dante spends the night between the two days which he spends on the seven Terraces. The Sun stands between the three Planets below and the three Planets above.

The top three Planets can be called the Upper Planetary Heaven, and the bottom three Planets the Lower Planetary Heaven. The blessed souls of the Upper Planetary Heaven appear in the formation of distinct symbols, the Cross, the Eagle and Jacob's Ladder, and the blessed souls of the Lower Planetary Heaven do not. The blessed souls of the Third Heaven appear in a circle of cosmic dance on Dante's ascent but break up the circle immediately. The theologians appear in two circles and maintain that formation, but the two circles are not any distinct symbol like the symbolic formations of the Upper Planetary Heaven. The two circles constitute the transition from the formless presentation of the blessed on the Lower Planetary Heaven to the formational presentation of the blessed on the Upper Planetary Heaven. The *Purgatorio* proper can also be divided into the upper and the lower region. The top three Terraces can be called the Upper *Purgatorio* proper, and the lower three Terraces the Lower *Purgatorio* proper. This is one of the reasons for Virgil's comprehensive definition of the sins of the lower three Terraces as misdirected love and that of the sins of the top three Terraces as excessive love. The sin of the Fourth Terrace as deficient love constitutes the transition between the upper and the lower regions of the *Purgatorio* proper. Virgil explains the structure of the *Inferno* and the *Purgatorio* on the Terrace and in the Circle of the passive irascible, because the transitional point is the ideal place for the prospect and retrospect of the journey and because the explanation of the structure of the two worlds is given to help Dante on his journey.

The difference between the upper and the lower regions of the three worlds reflects the difference between the levels of participation, i.e., the direct and the indirect participation in the chain of being. The three concupiscible powers are immediate appetites and directly participate in the objects of good, whereas the intellect and the irascible sustain the appetite and participate in the objects of good only indirectly through the concupiscible. Dante represents this difference in participation through his spatial position in relation to the blessed and the damned. In the Circles of the Upper Hell, Dante, in general, stands on the same level and ground with the damned. In the Circles of the Lower Hell, Dante usually stands above the damned. The sullen are submerged in the marsh over which Dante is carried in a boat, and the heretics are imprisoned in the tombs. Even in the Third Ring of the Seventh Circle where the sinners may appear to be running about on the same level as

Dante's, our poet makes it clear that he maintains a different level even with his dear teacher Brunetto Latini: "I durst not descend from the bank/ to go level with him" (*Inf.* xv. 43–44). Dante walks over the surface of the *Malebolge*, whose pouches hold the fraudulent sinners, and over the ice of Cocytus, kicking the heads of the proud sinners. When he goes down to the bottom of the evil pouches, he gets off the bridges over the *Malebolge*, the regular passageway in the Eighth Circle. When he goes through the Wall of the Giants, he passes over the head and shoulders of one of the Giants (*Inf.* xxxi. 124–145).

In the ascent of the *Paradiso*, Dante stands on the same level with the blessed up to the Sun where the circles of theologians revolve around Dante and Beatrice as their center (*Par.* x. 65). From Mars on, where Caccicaguida rushes down to the lower end of the Cross to meet Dante, our pilgrim places himself below the symbolic figures in which the blessed appear. As in the case of the Cross of Mars, Dante sees the Eagle of Jupiter and the Ladder of Saturn above his head.

Dante maintains uniform spatial relation with the penitents; he always walks or stands on the same level with them on all the seven Terraces. This can be justified because the powers of the soul on the *Purgatorio* are withdrawn from actual participation in the chain of being and remain in the state of potentiality. The difference of the levels of participation comes about only in the world of actuality. The powers of the soul on the *Purgatorio* have only potential difference in their levels of participation, and this potential difference is indicated by the emergence of Statius. Dante is guided on the Lower *Purgatorio* proper by Virgil, who will go down the Mount back to the Limbo, and on the Upper *Purgatorio* proper by Statius, who will go up to Heaven for his eternal sojourn.

Dante employs the technique of repetition to mark the

transition between the upper and the lower regions in the three worlds. On reaching the Sun, Beatrice tells Dante to express his gratitude for his ascent (*Par.* x. 52). On reaching the First Heaven, she told him to do the same (*Par.* ii. 29). Dante is aided by a heavenly lady in his ascent to the First Terrace during his sleep. He receives a similar aid on the Fourth Terrace when another heavenly lady comes to rescue him from the Siren's bewitchment. When he ascends from the Fourth Terrace, he climbs through "two walls of hard stone," which recalls the entrance to the First Terrace (*Purg.* xix. 48).

Dante's technique of repetition is very dramatic in his transition from the Upper Hell to the Lower Hell. Phlegyas comes with his boat to the shore of Styx, as Charon comes with his boat to the shore of Acheron. Both Phlegyas and Charon refuse to transport Dante on the ground that he is still alive. After crossing Acheron, Dante comes within the view of the Noble Castle. After crossing Styx, he sees the tower of the City of Dis. The glowing summit of the City of Dis reminds us of the fire over the Noble Castle which conquers a hemisphere of darkness (*Inf.* iv. 68; ix. 36). Dante carefully balances his technique of repetition with that of variation. He places the gate of the Upper Hell outside Acheron, and the gate of the Lower Hell inside Styx. The gate of the Upper Hell is unguarded, but that of the Lower Hell is guarded. Virgil explains that the devils who are guarding the gate of the Lower Hell used to guard the gate of the Upper Hell, too (*Inf.* viii. 124–126). Dante crosses over Acheron in unconsciousness but over Styx in full consciousness. These elements of variation do not merely avoid the monotony of excessive repetition, but mark Dante's growth during his travel over the Upper Hell. While he is scared and loses consciousness at Acheron, he has become bold enough to fight with the damned souls in Styx. He has grown enough to be exposed to the devil's harassment in entering the Lower Hell.

The technique of repetition in marking the transition from the Upper to the Lower Hell clearly shows that the Fifth and the Sixth Circles are technically two rings of one Circle. Styx and the walls are the demarcation between the Upper and the Lower Hell. The sinners of sullen anger are dumped into the marsh of Styx, and Dante notices them while crossing over Styx. Only after experiencing enormous difficulty in entering the Lower Hell and seeing its grave citizens and its great company, one begins to realize that the Lower Hell does not allow the sinners of sullen anger within its domain for the same reason the trimmers of the Vestibule are not allowed to cross Acheron (*Inf.* iii. 37–42; viii. 69). The indifferent of the Vestibule failed to take any positive stand, and the sinners of the Fifth Circle failed to vent their anger through any positive act.

It would mar the glory of Hell to allow the indifferent to cross Acheron and disgrace the grandeur of the Lower Hell to admit the sullen sinners into the Lower Hell. The indifferent have to long for a real death, and the sullen have to gurgle out their anger in the marsh. Those who lived in sullen anger and despair of the heavenly good are separated and placed inside the Lower Hell, even though they could not vent their anger through positive act. The despair of the heavenly good is a direct sin against God and deserves a special treatment.

In spite of the separation of the sinners in despair of the earthly good and the sinners in despair of heavenly good, Dante clearly establishes the link of the Fifth and the Sixth Circles by the even ground which connects the outside and the inside of the gate of the Lower Hell (*Inf.* ix. 106–108). In contrast to the even ground which marks the transition from the Fifth to the Sixth Circle, every descent from one Circle to another is marked by a spatial descent from a higher to a lower level of ground. Furthermore, the entrance to every Circle is guarded by a monster who personifies the sin of that Circle. But when Dante enters the gate of the Lower Hell, he sees no monster standing there. The black angels who tried to block Dante's entry into the Lower Hell are not the guards of the Sixth Circle but of the Lower Hell. Once inside the gate of the Lower Hell, that is, in the Sixth Circle, Dante sees none of the black angels. The samples of anger Dante finds in the Fifth and the Sixth Circle are of the same type as that of Phlegyas, that is, a sullen rancor. In short, the Fifth and the Sixth Circles are two Rings of one Circle under the dominion of Phlegyas.

Let us now turn to the remainder of the three worlds whose structure has yet to be accounted for. We can expect Dante to add three theological virtues to his table of seven virtues and seven sins. The theological virtues are faith, hope, and charity. They are supernatural virtues which surpass the connatural powers of the soul, while the seven pairs of virtues and sins are connatural and consonant with man's nature. Faith is established by the mission of the Son, namely through the Incarnation. Hope is sustained by the mission of the Holy Spirit, namely, through His preservation and providence. The Father sends His Son and His Spirit on a mission, but does not send Himself.[35] The Son is visibly sent, and the Holy Spirit invisibly.[36] The Trinity comes to man through the visible and the invisible missions to establish faith and sustain hope. Charity can never be fulfilled until man's soul goes up to the mansion of the Father. The Father waits to embrace the soul as His own bride in His chamber.[37] The wisdom of the Son establishes faith in the truth of the invisible good through His Revelation; the Love of the Spirit sustains hope for the heavenly bliss through His Sanctification; and the Power of the Father consummates love of God through His Illumination.

68

In the Eighth Heaven, Dante sees the Ascension of Christ and the Assumption of the Queen of Heaven in glory. The Ascension of Christ marks the conclusion of His visible mission. Christ conquers and triumphs over death through His Passion and Resurrection. He shows the mortal souls the way to die in the sinful world and rise in glory: *What is sown corruptible, rises incorruptible . . . what is sown a natural body, rises a spiritual body* (1 Cor. 15:42–44). All the faithful will rise in the incorruptible, spiritual bodies on the Day of Judgment as Christ and His Mother have been raised from the world of sin and death. This is the central tenet of faith, and the purpose of the visible mission was to demonstrate this article of faith. The Apostles, who are left behind on the Eighth Heaven after the Ascension of Christ, stand for the Apostolic Church entrusted with the continuation of the visible mission of the Son. The three apostles' examination of Dante stands for the mission of the Church to instruct and guide the faithful.

On the Terrestrial Paradise, Beatrice comes with a majestic procession which unfolds the long chain of historical events preparing for and leading up to the visible coming of the Messiah. The Griffin with his two natures stands for the dual nature of Christ, divine and human. Dante sees the dual nature of the Griffin reflected in Beatrice's eyes (*Purg.* xxxi. 120–123). Beatrice is the visible medium through which Christ came visibly to Dante. The mission of the Son is the visible manifestation of the invisible truth. Christ comes communally and individually, publicly and privately. He is born not only for the race in Bethlehem, but in the heart of each of the faithful.

Before Dante is allowed to see the dual nature of the Griffin through Beatrice's eyes, Dante goes through an ordeal of humiliation and repentance. St. Bernard says that we have to know the truth in ourselves before receiving the revealed truth.[38] To know the truth in ourselves is to reveal our sinful nature. The revelation of ourselves is the requisite preparation for the revelation of God. To reveal ourselves is to repent. Only after the revelation and repentance of our sinful souls, are we allowed to cross Lethe and see the manifestation of divine truth. John the Baptist prepared the way for the Coming of the Son by preaching repentance at the Jordan.

The Griffin draws the Chariot of the Church to the tree of the forbidden fruit. When the Chariot is tied to it, the tree which has been stricken and shrivelled through Adam's sin is revived and renewed. The tree of the forbidden fruit embodies God's first decree and stands for justice. The return of the Chariot to the tree stands for the restoration of justice which Christ achieved through the ransom of His own blood. The Griffin ascends to Heaven, leaving the Chariot under the tree. The Griffin's ascension is the Ascension of Christ. At this point, the Beatricean Procession comes to an end, and Beatrice sits down on the root of the tree. The visible mission of Christ is concluded, and the foundation of faith is laid down.

In the Limbo, Dante meets the virtuous pagans. The Noble Castle represents the perfection of natural virtues. In spite of the natural perfection, the pagans are far from perfect bliss. They live in sadness without torment. Dante learns that natural perfection can never achieve perfect bliss. Virgil explains that faith and baptism are indispensable to man's salvation (*Inf.* iv. 34–42). The human intellect even in its perfection can never know divine truth without the Revelation, and faith comes only through the Revelation. The fire of the human intellect which "conquers a hemisphere of darkness" is not capable of illuminating the mystery of the Trinity (*Inf.* iv. 69).

The *Ante-Purgatorio* can be divided into three sections: the Upper *Ante-Purgatorio* where Dante meets the unshriven and the negligent princes, the Middle *Ante-Purga-torio* where Dante meets the excommunicate and the in-dolent, and the Lower *Ante-Purgatorio* where the penitents land. Notice the contrast between the Limbo and the Upper *Ante-Purgatorio*. In the Limbo, Dante first meets a crowd of ordinary virtuous pagans and then sees their nobility in the Noble Castle. In the Upper *Ante-Purgatorio*, he first runs into a throng of ordinary sinful Christians and then the Christian nobilities and principalities in the Flowery Valley. While the pagans lived in virtue, the Christians lived in sin. The pagan nobility is protected by the seven walls of the Castle, and the Christian nobility by the angels from Mary's bosom (*Purg.* viii. 37). The former perfected the seven natural powers of the soul, but the latter perverted them. This radical difference of perfection and perversion in natural life is overshadowed by the difference in their orientations toward the supernatural bliss. Though the pagans lived in virtues and achieved perfect natural bliss, they cannot expect supernatural bliss. Though the Chris-tians lived in sin and never achieved perfect earthly bliss, they do look forward to the heavenly bliss. The pagans lived in virtue but without faith, and the Christians lived in sin but with faith.

On the Ninth Heaven, Dante sees the nine angelic orders revolving in nine concentric circles around one point. This point with nine angelic orders stands for the invisible mission of the Holy Spirit from the Father, while Christ with his Apostles on the Eighth Heaven represents the visible mission of the Son from the Father. Beatrice refers to Christ with His Apostles on the Starry Heaven with the attributes of the Son and the Father ("Wisdom and Power") and to the Holy Spirit with nine angelic orders on the *Primum Mobile* with the attributes of the Father and the Spirit, "Light and Love" (*Par.* xxiii. 37; xxvii. 112). This is because the Starry Heaven presents the Son in His mission from the Father and the *Primum Mobile* presents the Spirit in His mission from the Father. Angels and human beings are two orders of the intellectual substances in God's creation. The former resembles His Spirit, and the latter His Son. The former is pure spirit and invisible, and the latter is of spirit and flesh and visible. The *Primum Mobile*, in which the Holy Spirit appears with the confirmed angels, has no stars and is an appropriate medium for the presentation of the pure, invisible substances. The Starry Heaven, in which the Son appears with the redeemed human souls, has many stars and is an appropriate medium for the presentation of the visible substances.

The angelic orders stand for the supernatural virtue of hope for two reasons. The angels exemplify the virtue of hope through their own salvation and sustain the hope of the faithful through their ministration. The angelic intellect is far greater than the human intellect. Whereas the human intellect has no intuitive knowledge of divine nature and needs the visible mission of the Son, the angelic intellect has some knowledge of the Trinity even before divine illumination and does not have to wait for the Incarnation for salvation. Whereas the salvation of man begins with faith established by the Incarnation of the Son, the angelic beatification begins with hope infused by the Gift of the Holy Spirit. St. Augustine says that the chief problem of the angels was the uncertainty about the eternal future.[39] The angels knew that they would be rewarded if they persevered, but were not certain whether or not they would be able to persevere. The bliss in God surpasses not only human nature but also angelic nature. Hence the hope for the supernatural bliss is not within the power of creatures. *But hope that is seen is not hope. For how can a man hope for what he sees? But if we hope for what we do not see, we wait for it with patience* (Rom. 8:24–25). The wills of the angels that have been saved were sanctified by the grace of the Holy Spirit.[40] The angels exemplify, through their confirmation, the hope that is sustained by the sanctification of the Holy Spirit.

The angels are the ministers of providence.[41] Every gift comes through the invisible mission of the Spirit from the Father; Gift is the proper name of the Spirit.[42] The nine angelic orders are the ministering spirits for the dispensation of the gifts of the Holy Spirit. The highest gift is the grace that preserves and sanctifies the adopted sons of the Father in hope of the final glory. At the end of the Beatricean Procession, the Griffin leaves the Chariot in charge of Beatrice and ascends to Heaven. When Beatrice sits down at the foot of the tree and beside the Chariot, she stands for the Holy Spirit. The seven lights of the Holy Spirit form a ring around her. Christ sends down the Holy Spirit to guide His Church after His Ascension. The Chariot stands not only for the visible Church, but for the invisible tabernacle of the Spirit in the heart of the faithful. Dante perseveres to the end throughout the seven catastrophes visited on the tabernacle. Through this trial of hope, Dante is prepared for the bliss in Heaven. Whereas the angels have to survive only the test of hope, human souls have to live through the repentance for faith and the perseverance in hope. The angels have only to be confirmed, but the human souls have to receive the two sacraments of baptism and confirmation.

The trimmers in the Vestibule had neither concern nor hope for the supernatural bliss. The caitiff choir of angels were neither for nor against God (*Inf.* iii. 37–39). These angels neither despaired of nor hoped for the bliss in God. The Vestibule is negatively related to hope, while the Limbo is negatively related to faith. On the Middle *Ante-Purgatorio*, Dante meets two groups: the excommunicate and the indolent. Though the former were expelled from the fold of the Church, they sustained hope for salvation.

73

Manfred concludes his episode with his conviction in the power of hope (*Purg.* iii. 131, 135). The indolent are the victims of sloth which stems from despair. Though they lived in sloth and despair, they retained a spark of hope for salvation through their late repentance.

Acheron is the real entrance to Hell, while the gate of Hell is the nominal entrance. The souls who have no love of God have to cross Acheron with the exception of the trimmers of the Vestibule. Dante's loss of consciousness at Acheron stands for the blindness and stupor into which the damned fall in their estrangement from God. *The chosen have obtained it, and the rest have been blinded, as it is written, "God has given them a spirit of stupor . . ."* (Rom. 11:7–8). Those who have the love of God assemble on the shore of Tiber and are transported to the foot of *Purgatorio*. It is the love of God that liberates the soul from the chain of sin and elevates it to the mansion of the Father. Casella sings a love song on meeting Dante at the foot of *Purgatorio* (*Purg.* ii. 112). At the fountain head of Eunoë and Lethe, Dante's love is fully reconciled and purified. Dante completely forgets his past estrangement and defilement of his love (*Purg.* xxxiii. 91–93). He can now walk and discourse in a perfect familiarity and intimacy with Beatrice.

In the River of Light in the Empyrean, Dante's human nature is superhumanized. The human power is too weak to see the Divine Essence and has to be illuminated by divine light. It is through the divine illumination that the love of God is fulfilled in the rapture of the beatific vision. The two orders of creation and salvation, the redeemed souls and the confirmed angels, which appeared in their works of the visible and the invisible missions on the Eighth and the Ninth Heavens, are presented in their feast of love in the Empyrean. Dante joins this celestial feast and sees the One Essence and the Three Persons of the Holy Trinity. This is the final consummation of Dante's love.

Dante for the first time sees the Father in the highest Heaven. He has seen the Son in His visible mission from the Father in the Eighth Heaven and the Spirit in His invisible mission from the Father in the Ninth Heaven; he now sees the Father in his union with His Son and His Spirit in celebration of the conclusion of the missions of His Son and His Spirit. Dante presents the Tenth Heaven as it would appear on the Day of Judgment, that is, at the conclusion of salvation. While the Son in His mission was praised with the attributes of the Father and the Son ("Wisdom and Power") on the Eighth Heaven and the Spirit in His mission by the attributes of the Father and the Spirit ("Light and Love") on the Ninth Heaven, the Father in His union with His Son and His Spirit is praised by the union of the three attributes on the Tenth Heaven:

> O Light eternal who only in thyself abidest,
> Only thyself dost understand, and self-understood
> and self-understanding, dost love and smile on
> thyself.
>
> *Par.* xxxiii. 124–126

Thus, the three theological virtues from God and the seven powers in the soul constitute the formal principle which explains the uniformity of Dante's three words. The structure of the *Inferno* can be expressed in the formula: $3+7$; that of the *Purgatorio* in the formula: $3+7+3$; and that of the *Paradiso* in the formula: $7+3$. The three sections of the *Ante-Inferno* are the Vestibule, Acheron and the Limbo, and stand for the privation of the theological virtues in the damned. Every sinner has to pass through these three regions except the trimmers who never really lived and can never die. The three sections of the *Ante-Inferno* lead to the seven Circles of vices or positive sins. The

75

Inferno proper is composed of seven Circles and not eight.

While the three sections of the *Ante-Inferno* show the privation of the theological virtues, the three sections of the *Ante-Purgatorio* show the possession of those virtues. It is the theological virtues that divide sheep from goats. The *Ante-Purgatorio* leads to the seven Terraces of the *Purgatorio* proper which purge the sins of the seven Circles of the *Inferno* proper. The three events of faith, hope, and love on the top of the *Purgatorio* can be spatially related to the three landmarks of the Terrestrial Paradise; the event of faith to Lethe, the event of hope to the tree of the forbidden fruit, and the event of love to Eunoë.

The *Paradiso* has no *Ante-Paradiso*. The preparation for the entrance into the *Paradiso* is perfected on the top of the *Purgatorio* where Beatrice takes over Dante from Virgil. The seven virtues gained on the seven Terraces are shown in glory on the seven Planets. On the highest three Heavens, the theological virtues are consummated. The seven glorified powers of the soul are contrasted with the seven perverted powers in the *Inferno*. While the damned begin their descent into the kingdom of darkness with the privation of the theological virtues, the blessed end their ascent into the kingdom of light with the consummation of the theological virtues. The three worlds come into a multiple parallel contrast through their common formal principle of the seven powers of the soul and the three virtues from God. Their parallel contrast cannot be fully understood until we know the material principles which diversify them. We will now turn to this feature of our problem.

chapter 3

The Principle of Diversity

Every nature desires its own being and its own perfection. Every soul strives for the realization of its potential powers. Happiness lies in the activity of self-realization. This is the central theme of self-realization in teleological ethics.[1] The powers of the soul are neither virtuous not sinful until they are actualized. The powers of the soul are the subjects of virtues and sins and require objects for their actualization. By acting on different objects, the soul attains different kinds of bliss. The objects, on which the soul acts, constitute the worlds in which it participates. No creature is the cause of its own being, and its actuality and existence are possible only through participation in the chain of being emanating from the Creator.[2]

The two orders of being in which the soul can participate are the material and the immaterial, the corporeal and the incorporeal, the carnal and the spiritual, the natural and the supernatural. Damnation is the actualization of the soul in the material and natural order, and salvation is its actualization in the spiritual and supernatural order. The soul achieves its natural end in the former, and its supernatural end in the latter. Purgation is the transition between these two orders and two ends. Thus the soul can participate in three different worlds, two terminal worlds and one transitional world.

The *Inferno* is the world and the final end for the damned soul. It is composed of the material, corporeal elements, placed under the dust of the earth ,and occupies the lowest region of the cosmos. This is the world out of which man came; it is the connatural world of man. *For dust thou art, and into dust thou shalt return* (Gen. 3:19). The damned soul returns to the world of dust and lives in the labor and toil of the cursed earth (Gen. 3:17). The *Paradiso* is the world and the final end of the redeemed soul. It is composed of the incorporeal, spiritual substance, that is, light. Light is the symbol of spiritual things.[3] The *Paradiso* is placed above the sub-lunary world. In the Aristotelian cosmology, the Moon is the dividing line between the incorruptible world of permanence and the corruptible world of impermanence. Furthermore, the blessed are all placed in the highest region of the cosmos, the timeless and spaceless Heaven of Light. Pure spirits transcend the limit of time and space.

While the damned are positively related to the natural end and privatively to the supernatural end, the redeemed are positively related to the supernatural end and privatively to the natural end. The corporeal world is devoid of light; it is the kingdom of eternal darkness. The ethereal world is devoid of material elements; it is the kingdom of eternal light. The penitents are engaged in the labour of turning away from the kingdom of eternal darkness and moving toward the kingdom of eternal light. The *Purgatorio* is placed between the lower atmosphere of the earth and the ethereal atmosphere of heaven and sees the alternation of day and night. In this transitional stage, the penitents are deprived of both the natural and the supernatural end. The *Purgatorio* is a privative world, while the *Paradiso* and the *Inferno* are the positive worlds. The former is a temporal world, while the latter are eternal worlds.

Dante's sensible and spatial representation of these three worlds should not make us forget that the three realms of spirits are not external but internal. *The kingdom of God is within you* (Luke 17:21). So is the kingdom of Satan. The world is in the self, and the self is in the world. This statement sounds quite modern and seems to echo Hegel's dictum: the self is the world and the world is the self. Dante is not modern; Hegel is medieval. Hegel owes his philosophy of the spirit more to the medieval Christian spirit than to the modern Teutonic spirit. The conception of the self and the world in their intimate internal relation is one of the dominant themes which governed the medieval spiritual life. It is in this intimate internal relation of the soul and his world that St. Augustine propounds his idea of two cities, Jerusalem and Babylon, the City of God and the City of Satan. Because of this intimate relation of the self and the world, the realization of the self and the participation in the world constitute one and the same activity. In the labour and toil to achieve bliss, the self is realized and the world is participated in. Souls are of a uniform nature, insofar as their potential powers are concerned. The orders of being in which souls can participate for their actualization are of diverse natures. It is this diversity which differentiates the three worlds from one another, while the common potential nature of souls constitutes their uniformity. We will now focus our attention on the principle of diversity.

The sinful souls traverse the three regions of the *Ante-Inferno* before they are assigned to proper Circles. They assemble in the Vestibule on the shore of Acheron, cross Acheron, pass the Limbo, and reach the Circle of lust where Minos flings down the sinners with his tail to appropriate Circles. Passage through the *Ante-Inferno* represents the alienation of the soul from its Creator. The three regions

79

of the *Ante-Inferno* stand for the privation of the supernatural virtues, which direct the soul to its Creator. The
alienation from the Creator constitutes the essence of mortal
sin. The Creator is the principle of spiritual life, and to turn
away from Him is the spiritual death of the soul.[4] Mortal
sin is the sickness of the soul which leads to death. It is
this spiritual death that Charon pronounces to the damned:
"Woe to you, depraved spirits!" (*Inf.* iii. 84).

Because the mortal sinners are spiritually dead, they
deserve to be buried underground. The *Inferno* is the
sepulchre for the damned. On the Day of Judgment, the
gate of the *Inferno* will be sealed and the damned will be
enclosed in it with their bodies (*Inf.* x. 10). The estrangement of the soul from its Creator is the injustice the sinful
soul brings about through its mortal sin. Justice is right
relation and order. Original sin has disrupted the right
relation and order between the soul and the Holy Trinity.
The soul is lost from its Creator through sin to the world
of sorrow and pain. The eternal loss of the soul from the
Trinity and the injustice involved in this loss are pronounced by the obscure inscription over the gate of the
Inferno.

> "Through me is the way into the city of sorrow;
>   through me the way into the eternal pain;
>   through me the way among the lost people
>
> Justice moved my High Maker;
>   Divine Power made me,
>   Wisdom Supreme and Primal Love.
>
> Before me were no things created,
>   but eternal; and eternal I endure;
>   leave all hope, ye that enter here."
>
>   *Inf.* iii. 1–9

The Formulation of a Solution

There is no struggle to enter the gate of Hell. Every off-spring of Adam is born in the stain of original sin which is his birthright to the kingdom of Satan.

The sinful soul has no love of God, but lives in love of the natural order. Dante's stupor in the crossing of Acheron not only signifies the eternal loss and estrangement of the sinful soul from the Creator, but also the rapture of carnal love for the natural order of creation. The trimmers of the Vestibule cannot experience this rapture, because they lived only for themselves (*Inf.* iii. 39). Those who live only for themselves and for no one else never come to know love. Love is possible only with the care for and the attachment to others. Those who know of no love never develop the will. As Virgil explains, the will is awakened into activity with the kindling of love (*Purg.* xviii. 19–66). The trimmers had no experience of love and never exercised the will. They were neither rebellious nor faithful to God; they never made a decisive choice of the will (*Inf.* iii. 38–39). Love and will are the unique features which distinguish the rational animal from brute animals. Having failed to achieve human dignity, the trimmers exist and move around like herds of animals. They have neither virtue nor vice; virtue and vice are not possible with brute animals.

The Limbo is the virtuous realization of natural love. The light of natural intellect conquers a hemisphere of darkness. The virtuous realization of natural love falls into two categories, which are represented by the two groups of people Dante meets inside and outside the Noble Castle. The virtue of the pagans outside the Castle was only to be trapped in no vice, while that of those inside the Castle was to attain eminence and distinction. The former group is nameless and blameless, and the latter is famous and praise-worthy. In spite of the dignity and solemnity of the eminent, Dante can see no trace of joy in the Noble Castle.

81

The joy of the perfect bliss does not lie within the power of the human soul.

While the *Ante-Inferno* is the viceless realization of natural love, the *Inferno* proper is its vicious realization. Every Circle of the *Inferno* proper presents the sinners as engaged in their acts of sin. The lustful are eternally captivated by the blast; the gluttons languish in the rain and mud; and the avaricious and the prodigal are rolling heavy weights. The blast is the symbol of lust; the rain is the symbol of nourishment; and the rolling stone is the symbol of wealth. It requires just a little imagination to see that each Circle of the *Inferno* represents the sinners as engaged in the activity of their sinful powers. The sensible representation of the sinful act aims at the disclosure of the nature of sin as it is in itself. The real nature of sin is often hidden behind pleasant façades. For example, the sin of lust often presents itself as something beautiful and lovely, though it is shameful and beastly in its essence. Dante aims at stripping all sins of their misleading appearances and at revealing the internal states of the sinners as well as their external acts.

Each Circle is the perfection of a sinful power. For example, Paolo and Francesca are allowed to enact and re-enact the act of lust for eternity. The sullen in the marsh of Styx are allowed to gurgle out their rancor for eternity. The Second Circle is the perfection of lust, and the Fifth Circle is the perfection of the passive irascible. The damned are allowed to devote their entire energy to the realization of their sinful powers in the most consistent manner. The perfection of a sinful power is its tyranny over other powers. All the powers and passions of the lustful are under the complete tyranny of lust. Every sinful soul can find an ideal kingdom in the *Inferno* for the perfect tyranny of its sinful power.

This is the irony of perfection in Hell. The entire being

of a sinner is sacrificed and distorted for the perfection of his sin. This is the nature of vice. While virtue is order and harmony of the soul, vice is its disorder and distortion. The disorder and distortion of soul are the inevitable consequences of having to achieve and maintain the unity of the soul in vice. The vicious soul has to achieve its unity for its existence. Even the kingdom of the devil cannot stand, if divided against itself. For this reason, Dante repeatedly stresses the unity of the soul (*Purg.* iv. 1 ff.). In his stress on the unity of the soul, St. Thomas says, "Since all the powers of the soul are rooted in one essence of the soul, when the intention of the soul is strongly drawn toward the action of one power, it is withdrawn from the action of another power: because the soul, being one, can only have one intention."[5] In the *Inferno*, every soul has only one tyrannical intention, one eternal intention, for the realization of one sinful power at the expense of all other powers.

The diabolical distortion and perfection of sinful souls are represented by the tight barriers which disconnect all the Circles and Rings from one another and which the damned neither are allowed nor desire to cross (*Inf.* xxiii. 55). The damned soul has no desire to get out of its own Circle and to go over to some other Circles, because it has reduced all its powers and passions to the tyranny of its sinful power and has no more interest in the activities of the powers represented by other Circles. For example, the lustful are completely absorbed in the activity of lust and have no more interest in the act of gluttony or wrath. That tight disconnection of all the Circles and Rings is the austere discommunion of the sinners.

Every Circle of the *Inferno* proper is a sinful expression of love and pride. The *Inferno* proper begins with the Circle of love and ends with the Circle of pride. Pride is the root of all sins, and love the end of all sins. In the perfection of a sinful power, the sinner seeks the excellence with which he can and wishes to identify himself. It is through the sinful perfection and excellence that pride is expressed and love is fulfilled. An avaricious man fulfills his love and pride in the accumulation of a great fortune. Through the expression of love and pride, the sinner realizes himself. Aristotle says, "Just as a city or any other systematic whole is most properly identified with the most authoritative element in it, so is a man."[6] The identity of a sinful soul is established and realized in the authoritative tyranny of its sinful power.

Because each sin is the expression of pride and love, no sinner can repent. As long as a soul strives to achieve its self-realization in a sin and as long as it identifies its excellence with the sin, it cannot be expected to repent of the sin. Repentance is possible only with disillusion and disappointment. With disappointment and disillusion, the source of pride turns into the source of humiliation and the target of love into the target of hate. Dante repeatedly stresses that no penitent soul is thrown into the *Inferno* or stays in it against its desire (*Inf.* iii. 126). Every soul is assigned to the Circle it not only deserves but also desires. Every Circle is a kingdom of perfect freedom.

The excellence and eminence of the sinners differ in accordance with the levels of the sinful powers. For example, the sin of the irascible achieves a greater eminence than the sin of the concupiscible; the irascible is a higher power than the concupiscible. The increasing eminence of the sinful powers in the descent of the *Inferno* is represented not only by the increasing grandeur and depth of the Circles, but by their increasing subdivision. The two regions of the *Ante-Inferno* and the three Circles of the concupiscible do not undergo any further subdivision into Rings. The Circle of the passive irascible is divided into two Rings which are generally known as the Fifth and the Sixth Circles, and the Circle of the active irascible into three Rings. The five Rings of the irascible match in number with the five regions of the Upper Hell, that is, the two sections of the *Ante-Inferno* and the three Circles of the concupiscible. This means that the sin of the irascible is as grave as all the sins of the Upper Hell put together. These ten sections match in number with the ten *bolge* of the passive intellect. This means that the sin of the *Malebolge* is as grave as all the sins of the first seven Circles and the Vestibule put together. This progressive trend of subdivision seems to be reversed in the lowest Circle, because it has only three Rings and one center. In truth, every sinner of the Ninth Circle constitutes its own isolated Ring, because he is tightly frozen into the ice of Cocytus.

Notice also the contrapuntal progression of two and three in subdivision of the *Inferno*. The two sections of the *Ante-Inferno* and the three Circles of the concupiscible constitute the first pair of two and three. The two Rings of the passive irascible and the three Rings of the active irascible constitute the second pair of two and three. The *Malebolge* is divided into two sections by the broken bridge over the sixth *bolgia*. The two sections of the *Malebolge* and the three Rings of the Ninth Circle constitute the final pair of two and three. The contrapuntal progression of two and three reflects the relation of the active and the passive, the positive and the negative. The first pair of two and three is not strictly related as the active and the passive, similar to the second and the third pairs, but as the positive and the negative. Of the five regions of the Upper Hell, the two sections of the *Ante-Inferno* represent no positive vice, while the three Circles of the concupiscible represent positive vices.

Why should the relation of the active and the passive be represented by the contrast of two and three? In the Aristotelian psychology, a passive act is a two term relation and an active act is a three term relation. In the passive act, the object acts upon the soul's passive power. In the active act, the soul acts on the object. The motive power of the soul is always a moved mover. Before the soul acts on an object, it is always moved by an object. When the soul is moved by an object and the motion is terminated in the soul, the motion is a passive act and is a two term relation. When the soul is moved by an object and the soul in turn acts on the object, the motion is an active act and is a three term relation.[7] Because of this technical difference between action and passion in the number of terms of relation, the contrapuntal progression of two and three is appropriate for the progressive subdivision of the *Inferno*.

The increasing degree of damnation is the progressive carnalization. The *Inferno* proper begins with carnal love and ends with the carnal feast of Satan. The spiritual element in the sinful man and in the black angel has been converted into the carnal element. The Creator is the only source of spiritual life. By turning away from this principle of spiritual life, the sinful spirit hardens into the flesh. As we descend in Hell, the bodies of the damned become harder and harder, and heavier and heavier. In the Circle of lust, the bodies are as light as the bodies of birds. In the lowest Circle, the bodies become as hard as the tight ice of Cocytus. That the carnalization of spirit is the effect of sin is shown in the sin of the first man. Adam rebels against God by succumbing to the instigation of Eve. Eve came out of the flesh and bone of Adam, and represents the carnal feature of man. On the other hand, the spirit of Adam came from the breath of the Lord, and God is the fountain of man's spiritual life. Original sin was to turn against the source of spiritual life for the love of the carnal world. Thus, Adam becomes first conscious of the nakedness of his body. His expulsion from Eden is his exile into the carnal world. The world of sin is the world of flesh. That

86

is why all sinners appear in stark nudity and why their highest feast is the feast of flesh.

While the degeneration of the soul is its carnalization, its regeneration is the spiritualization of its carnal powers. The degeneration of the soul is shown in the *Inferno;* its regeneration in the *Purgatorio.* The spiritualization of a sinful soul is possible only with divine help. The divine help for the inclination of the will toward the supernatural end is grace.[8] No soul can reach and climb the *Purgatorio* without the ministration of angels, for the angels are the ministers of grace. The power of grace is further indicated by the power of light. It is the light of the Sun that leads and guides the penitents in their ascent (*Purg.* i. 107; xiii. 16–20). It is impossible to climb the *Purgatorio* even a single step in darkness (*Purg.* vii. 52–57). Light is the symbol of grace, and no one who is in a state of grace walks in darkness.[9]

While all sinners first pass through the *Ante-Inferno* which represents the privation of the three supernatural virtues, all penitents first traverse the *Ante-Purgatorio* which represents the possession of the three supernatural virtues. The penitents arrive at the foot of the *Ante-Purgatorio* in the love of God and climb its Terraces of hope and faith. The climbing of the *Ante-Purgatorio* is the regeneration of the supernatural virtues. The order of generation of the three virtues is faith, hope, and love and the order of their regeneration is its reversal. The regeneration of the supernatural virtues re-directs and re-orients the soul to its Creator. This is the beginning of the cure of the diseased soul. While the sinners complete the death of their diseased soul by passing through the *Ante-Inferno,* the penitents escape the trap of death by climbing through the *Ante-Purgatorio.* The *Purgatorio* is the mountain that cures the soul of its mortal disease (*Purg.* xiii. 2–3).

Because the sinful soul begins its repentance by loving

God as its final end, repentance is essentially a matter of love and joy. This initial joy and delight of the penitents are beautifully conveyed by their gaiety and cheerfulness on arrival at the foot of the *Purgatorio*. While the perverted souls cross Acheron in cursing and weeping, the repentant souls sing of their liberation in their passage from the Tiber to the *Purgatorio: "In exitu Israel de Aegypto"* (*Purg.* ii. 46). The theological virtues of the penitents on the *Ante-Purgatorio* are in the innocent and insubstantial state. This is first shown by their innocent dawdling and dallying which evoke Cato's stern rebuke. Cato has his function; he knows how to put an end to their innocent dawdling.

Cato's appearance and his solemn rebuke throw into a sharp contrast repentance in the moral sense and repentance in the theological sense. The moral repentance is a matter of bitter remorse and firm resolve. There is no room for joy and love. Compared with the moralistic repentance, the joy of returning to God as the ground of bliss appears like a childish affair to the pagan moralists. The end of the moralistic repentance is to climb out of the traps of vice and return to the Limbo, whereas the end of the theological repentance is the kingdom of heaven. Theologically understood, the child-like penitents stand on a higher level than the mature, virtuous pagan Cato. Cato knows nothing of the nature of purgation and shows his ignorance in his incapacity to show the way up to the *Purgatorio*. Childish as they are, penitents find their own ways up to purgation.

Besides this negative function of being an outsider to the kingdom of purgation, Cato has a positive function. The moral wisdom and the upright will symbolized in Cato are requisite conditions for returning to God as the source of the spiritual life. An apostate soul would not even think of returning to God, unless it had the wisdom of knowing the pernicious nature of its estrangement and the will to turn away from the chain of perdition. Cato of Utica sacrificed his earthly life for the liberty of his will. This is the pagan version of Exodus and the pagan pre-figure of the Crucifixion. The Crucifixion teaches the sinful soul to die to the world of sin for the life in the kingdom of heaven. As life in the natural order demands the alienation from God, life in the spiritual order requires the weaning away of the soul from the milk of the earth.

The penitents on the *Ante-Purgatorio* are too sick to begin the positive cures for their diseased souls. The princes of the Flowery Valley are being nursed in the bosom of the Virgin Mother (*Purg.* vii. 68; viii. 37). Those who are stationed even lower than the negligent rulers are too sick even to be lifted up to their mother's bosom. The supernatural virtues of the penitents on the *Ante-Purgatorio* are as insubstantial as those of children. Like children, they spend their time in harmless ease and without work, which comes in a sharp contrast to the rigor and tension of the souls in the *Purgatorio* proper. Belaqua neither appreciates nor cares for Dante's eagerness and excitement.

Only after regenerating and restoring the supernatural virtues, can the penitents begin their works of purgation. Purgation begins with the regeneration of the active intellect, because every sinful act requires the consent of the highest power of the soul. The penitent has to gain the virtue of humility as his initial step of purgation. Humility is the foundation of all virtues, while pride is the root of all sins. What is the purpose of purging the non-intellectual powers? St. Thomas can see no use of sensitive powers in the celestial life. He says, "In the other life, men are happy through beatitude, not through moral life."[10] He firmly believes that only intellect can participate in beatific vision of the Primal Intellect and that non-rational powers have nothing to do with the heavenly bliss. The blessed in Heaven retain only the formal elements of moral virtues.[11] This is true of the damned. It is only the intellectual power of the soul that fully survives the bodily death. While the intellect is independent of the body, all the non-rational powers are dependent on the union of soul and body for their actual operation. The non-rational powers can be retained only in the formal elements, that is, in a potential state, after the death of the body.

On the relation of the powers of the soul to the body, Dante differs with St. Thomas. In Dante's three worlds, all the powers of the soul, rational and non-rational, remain in full actuality after the death of the body and are keener than ever. If Dante were to follow St. Thomas, he would not be able to write two-thirds of the three canticles of his Comedy. Dante's doctrine of purgation is as simple as his doctrine of damnation. While damnation is the carnalization of the entire soul, purgation is its spiritualization. He repeatedly stresses the solidity and heaviness of the damned shades in the *Inferno*, and keeps calling our attention to the lightness and airiness of the shades on the *Purgatorio*. While the shades of the *Inferno* can be kicked and pulled, the shades of the *Purgatorio* cannot even be embraced.

Dante identifies the weight of the shades with the weight of their sins. In the *Inferno*, the souls sink in proportion to the weight of their sins. In the *Purgatorio*, the shades become lighter and lighter as they erase more and more P's from their foreheads (*Purg.* ix. 112–114; xii. 118–136; xxii. 7–9). The climbing becomes easier and easier as purgation progresses and the weight of sin decreases. Because light is the constitutive medium of the heavenly world, the penitent shades have to make themselves completely ethereal in the course of purgation. The angels radiate with increasing light, as Dante ascends Terrace after Terrace (*Purg.* xv. 10–15). The light of angels is very hard to bear at the initial stage of purgation, but becomes joy to behold at its late stage (*Purg.* xv. 31–33). The power to receive light is in inverse proportion to the weight of sins. The former stands for the powers of the soul that have been purged and spiritualized, and the latter for the powers that have been carnalized through sin and are yet to be purged.

That purgation is a process of spiritualization is also shown by the emergence of the sinful powers in darkness. The serpent which appears in the Flowery Valley right after sunset stands for the powers which are still carnal. The serpent is the supreme example of a carnalized spirit; it crawls in a body on the dust. When Dante falls into sleep at night, he attributes the exhaustion of his powers to the carnality inherited from Adam (*Purg.* ix. 10). There are no exhaustion and fatigue in the perfect spiritual life of heaven. Fatigue is an effect of carnal powers in the spiritual exercises. The more spiritualized Dante becomes, the less fatigue he feels in the works of purgation.

On the Fourth Terrace, Dante has to sit down as soon as the night falls. In his dream of the Siren, Dante sees again the emergence of the carnalized powers. In the absence of the rays of grace, the sinful powers come back to life in memory and dream. The dream of the Siren and the appearance of the serpent show different degrees and forces of the sinful carnality. The latter is the emergence of the carnal powers during the waking hours, and the former during sleeping hours. The latter is far stronger than the former. The latter indicates the state of the soul which has not been initiated into the toil of spiritualization, and the former shows the state of a soul which has already been initiated into the toil of purgation. The two different states of carnality are reflected in the two different kinds of climate of the *Purgatorio* (Purg. xxi. 40–57). While the *Ante-Purgatorio* is within the range of the lower atmosphere, the *Purgatorio* proper is beyond the range of all the evil vapors and effects of the terrestrial climate such as rain, hail, snow, dew, clouds or lightning. The evil vapors and effects of the terrestrial climate indicate the defilement of the earth through sin. Sin has come into the world through the sin of man. The lower atmosphere is not only the prison for the punishment of the devils, but also the dominion over which the black angels reign.[12] The *Ante-Purgatorio* is still within the range of the dominion of the devil. It is only through the protection of the angels and grace that the serpent can make no assault on the penitents.

Because the carnal powers of the penitents on the *Ante-Purgatorio* are within the dominion of the carnal atmosphere of the devil, the snake can appear during the waking hours on the withdrawal of the rays of grace. Because the carnal powers on the *Purgatorio* proper are beyond the proper atmosphere of carnal forces, they can appear only in dreams. While the snake moves with vigor and ease, the Siren appears in languor and awkwardness. The former is at home, and the latter is like fish out of water. This difference again shows the contrast between the carnal power within its proper sphere and the carnal power outside its proper sphere.

On the Fifth Terrace, Dante learns that the penitents recite the examples of virtue during the day and the examples of vice during the night. This may be the special rule for the Fifth Terrace, but shows the general principle of purgation. It is possible only with the rays of grace to convert the carnal powers into the spiritual powers. With the withdrawal of the rays of grace, the only thing the penitents can do is to retain control of the carnal powers and wait for the dawn. The carnal powers are the only burdens and chains which hold the penitents down to the ground. As soon as the carnal powers which cleave to the carnal things are completely spiritualized, the soul feels its freedom and attests the completion of its purgation (*Purg.* xxi. 61).

Purgation as spiritualization is what is meant by spiritual birth: *Unless a man be born again of water and of the*

Spirit, he cannot enter into the Kingdom of God. That which is born of the flesh is flesh, and that which is born of the spirit is spirit (John 3:5–6). The completion of purgation is the completion of spiritual birth. Dante presents the completion of Statius' purgation in the analogy of the Advent of Christ and His Resurrection. When Statius finishes his purgation and arises from the ground, the entire *Purgatorio* resounds with the angelic hymn that celebrated the birth of Christ (*Purg.* xx. 136). When he approaches Dante and Virgil, he appears in the manner Christ appeared after His Resurrection to two of His disciples on their way to Emmaus (*Purg.* xxi. 7). The Advent and the Resurrection are the two terminal ends of one lesson: how to be born again from flesh to spirit.

By the time the penitents go through the fire of the top Terrace, they have nothing to burn because all their powers have been thoroughly spiritualized and contain nothing carnal. It is then no wonder that the purgatorial fire does not singe a single hair though the fires of Hell "burn and char bodies" (*Purg.* xxvii. 18, 27). It has been one of the long debated problems whether the purgatorial fire is only for the Seventh Terrace or for the entire *Purgatorio*. St. Augustine says that all virtues are for the perfection of the love of God.[13] All the spiritual powers are for the perfection of spiritual love. It makes little difference whether the purgatorial fire is to be understood as the test of the purgation of the Seventh Terrace or of the entire purgation. Notice the continuity of all the Terraces in contrast to the discontinuity of all the Circles. The angel who approves the completion of work on one Terrace with his benediction initiates the penitent to the next Terrace, while the guards of one Circle have nothing to do with the affairs of other Circles. Because all the powers are for the perfection of spiritual love, all of them come under the final test in the purgatorial fire even if the fire is considered as the test of only the Seventh Terrace.

Dante is too precise to leave this problem to our conjecture. He goes through the fire after receiving the benediction from the angel on the Seventh Terrace, whereas the work of purgation precedes the benediction on other Terraces. The test of fire performs the same function as the judgment of Minos' tail does. Minos' tail determines the weight and gravity of carnal love of the damned, and the purgatorial fire tests the purity and sanctity of spiritual love of the penitents. The important difference between these two tests is that the purgatorial fire gathers together all the penitents into one place, while Minos' tail disperses all the sinners to different Circles. While the penitents work for the spiritualization of all the powers for the love of one God, the damned strive for the carnalization of their love in different levels of the carnal order. It is this difference between spiritualization and carnalization which justifies the different criteria employed in Virgil's accounts of the plans of the *Inferno* and the *Purgatorio*. Virgil uses the state of love in explaining the structure of the *Purgatorio* and the three levels of the soul in explaining that of the *Inferno*. This is because the test of purgation is the test of all powers spiritualized for love, and the test of damnation is the test of the powers carnalized for the tyranny of one single power for each soul.

On arrival at the top of the *Purgatorio*, Virgil proclaims Dante as the king and bishop over his soul (*Purg.* xxvii. 139–142). The purgation of the natural powers appears to be the end of the whole matter to the pagan. For the Christian, the works of purgation on the seven Terraces are only preparations for the substantiation of the supernatural virtues. The warning against mistaking the end of purgation as the final end first comes in Dante's last dream on the

94

Purgatorio. This is the dream of Leah and Rachel. Jacob slaved for seven years for the hand of Rachel. At the end of his labour, he was given not Rachel but Leah. When he thought he was coming to the end of his toil, he had to begin the real labour for Rachel, the ultimate object of his toil. After the toil of climbing through the seven Terraces, Dante has to begin his labour for the hand of Beatrice. His dream is confirmed by the relation of Matelda and Beatrice. Matelda represents the works on the seven Terraces; she is the personification of the purged soul. Dante's ultimate end is not to meet Matelda but Beatrice. Matelda turns out to be only a handmaid to Beatrice.

Dante undergoes the most strenuous and arduous discipline in regaining Beatrice. All the active works on the *Purgatorio* proper are nothing compared with the agony and torture in the contemplative, visual works in the Terrestrial Paradise. Dante experiences the bitterest humiliation in the test of his faith and the most torturing tension in the test of his hope. Through the substantiation of faith and hope, Dante overcomes the estrangement from Beatrice. Dante's final union with Beatrice in harmony and intimacy marks the consolidation of his charity. With his love of God restored and refreshed and with all powers of his soul purged and spirtualized, Dante becomes "pure and ready to mount to the stars" (*Purg.* xxxiii. 145).

What is the relation of the supernatural virtues and the seven virtues which are gained through purgation? The seven virtues are the infused virtues.[14] The Angelic Doctor sees the need of the infused virtues for the realization of the supernatural end. The moral and the intellectual virtues are for the natural end and have nothing to do with the realization of the supernatural end. The theological virtues are not sufficient for the realization of the supernatural end in the way the natural virtues are for that of the natural end. The natural virtues are not only the means of orientation to the natural end, but the actual habits and instruments for its realization. The theological virtues only orient and direct man to his supernatural end and are not concrete habits and means governing the spiritual life to its end.

For the actual implementation of the dictates of theological virtues, St. Thomas sees the need of the infused virtues: "Therefore we need to receive from God other habits annexed proportionately to the theological virtues, which are to the theological virtues what the moral and intellectual virtues are to the natural principle of the virtues."[15] What are the infused virtues? The Angelic Doctor cannot specify their nature and offers an inchoate account. Like the natural virtues, the infused virtues must be the concrete habits and means to govern the daily conduct. The infused virtues and the natural virtues differ in two important aspects. First, they guide the daily life towards different ends, the one toward the natural end and the other toward the supernatural end. Second, they differ in their specified rules of conduct. For example, the temperance of natural virtue aims at the mean fixed by reason, but the temperance of infused virtue rejects the rule of the golden mean and adopts excess as the ideal. The infused virtue of temperance will "chastise his body and bring it into subjection, by abstinence from food, drink and the like."[16]

The Angelic Doctor is quite baffled at the disparity between the human rule of natural virtue and the divine rule of infused virtue, and cannot account for the reason for this grave disparity. He would be equally baffled at the severe rules of purgation Dante imposes on the penitents. For example, the penitents on the Sixth Terrace neither drink nor eat. Their rule is not the moderation of desires but their alienation from the natural order. By alienating the power of the soul from the natural order, the penitents can orient them to the supernatural order. This is "the subjection of the body by abstinence." This is the spiritualization of the carnal powers. There can be no excess in the desires for the supernatural good because the worth and good of the Creator are infinite. The order of Heaven "excludes temperance by essence . . . renders all chastity wanton, and all abstinence gluttonous."[17] For this reason, the rules of infused virtue aim at excess as the ideal, and the rule of purgation dictates excessive abstinence and complete alienation from the natural good.

It is the dictate of the infused virtues that the *Purgatorio* proper be starkly bare and rocky. If the purpose of purgation were only to restore the natural powers from a disorderly condition to an orderly state in the domain of natural good, purgation should be conducted in the natural world with all its beauty and good and should avoid all excess. Aristotle says that deficiency of appetite is as bad as its excess and that insensible man is as unwholesome as an indulgent man. Purgation is not for the restoration of the soul to the natural order but for its initation into the supernatural order. Before the actual purgation begins, the soul is still attached to the natural good. For this reason, the *Ante-Purgatorio* is adorned with the fresh beauty of nature. During purgation, the soul has to be deprived of natural good. The *Purgatorio* proper has to be rocky and barren. After purgation, the soul can be exposed to the charm and beauty of nature without coming under the temptation and attraction of natural good. The top of the *Purgatorio* is adorned with the charm and good of nature for this different reason.

The beauty of nature on the *Ante-Purgatorio* is marred by the snake, and the charm of nature on the Terrestrial Paradise is marred by the bruise and wound the snake has left on the tree of the forbidden fruit. The snake is chased away only temporarily and is certain to come back, but the bruise and wound of the tree are permanently cured and the tree regains its health. The powers of the soul on the

97

Ante-Purgatorio are still under the shackle of Satan's carnal power and cannot become the concrete means for the realization of the supernatural end to which the soul is directed by the theological virtues. The powers of the soul on the top of the *Purgatorio* are perfect instruments for the substantiation of the theological virtues. St. Thomas distinguishes two states of virtues: the perfect and the imperfect or the complete and the inchoate.[18] The theological virtues become complete and perfect on the top of the *Purgatorio*, while they are inchoate and imperfect on the *Ante-Purgatorio*. It is with the perfection of the theological virtues and with the spiritualization of the soul that the soul can fly up to Heaven. The perfect etherealness of the soul enables it to leave the earth, and the longing for the Creator enables it to guide its flight to the source of heavenly bliss.

While the *Inferno* is the order of nature and the *Purgatorio* the order of grace, the *Paradiso* is the order of glory. The powers of the soul that have been alienated from the order of nature and perfected in the order of grace are glorified in the *Paradiso*. The glorification of the blessed lies in the single act of the beatific vision which saturates all the powers of the soul. To Piccarda on the Moon it sounds quite foolish to be asked whether she desires any greater mode of beatitude or any more exalted station in Heaven (*Par.* ii. 60 ff.). The blessed cannot desire any greater bliss than the bliss their souls can receive, just as the damned cannot desire to hop around from one Circle to another. Whereas the sinful soul achieves the realization of itself by exalting one of its natural powers to the place of God, the saintly soul realizes its bliss by subjecting all its powers to the love of one God.

While there is only one God in the *Paradiso*, there are many gods in the *Inferno*. The guard of each Circle is the god for the sinners in that Circle. Cerberus is the personification and deification of the passive concupiscible power, and Plutus is the personification and deification of the active concupiscible power. The gluttons have deified their gluttonous appetite and live in a complete subjection and adoration of Cerberus. Phlegyas and the Minotaur are the passive and the active irascible powers which have become the idols for the sinners of these two powers. Geryon and Satan are the apotheoses of the two intellectual powers.

While the discommunity of the damned is the reflection of the disunity of their gods, the communion of the blessed reflects the unity of the Holy Trinity. Whereas the sinful souls scatter themselves into different Circles and Rings in pursuit of their gods, the saintly souls all gather together in the Mystical Rose for their feast of love in one God. The former is the discommunion of the sinners, and the latter the communion of the saints. All the redeemed see each other's thoughts and feelings through the single act of gazing into the Prime Mover. The harmony and unity of the City of God is also reflected in the heavenly music in which motion chimes with motion and song with song, and the disunity and disorder of the City of Dis is found in the hellish clamor in which wailing clashes with wailing and cursing with cursing.

Do the unity and order of the celestial world demolish the individuality of the blessed? How do the blessed, engaged in the same act of gazing into the same Essence of one God, attain their individuality? The Angelic Doctor's solution of this problem is at once very clear and vague, simple and perplexing. He firmly believes on the authority of St. Paul that the modes of beatitude cannot be uniform and equal for all the blessed.[19] One blessed soul will see God more perfectly than another. *For star differs from star in glory* (1 Cor. 15:41). The created intellect cannot see the Divine Essence without the illumination of the light of glory. Every soul will be given the light of glory in proportion to the intensity of its charity. The measure of beatitude will be determined by the intensity of charity.

Up to this point, the Angelic Doctor is quite clear and simple in his reasoning. His simple reasoning becomes quite vague and confusing if we ask him to relate his simple doctrine of diversity in beatitude to two more elements relevant to the celestial life. One of these two relevant features is the relation of charity to other virtues; the other the relation of the beatific vision to the intellect. Is the intensity of charity to be determined in itself alone or in relation to the other virtues? If the intensity of charity is to be determined in itself alone and in isolation from other virtues, the other virtues would have nothing to do with the ultimate beatitude of the soul. All the labours and toils in developing the infused virtues and other theological virtues would turn out to be great waste. The infused virtues and other theological virtues may be regarded as mere instrumental process for the generation and nurture of charity. Even if that is the case, we are left with the question of whether or not these virtues determine the quality and quantity of charity in any manner. On this point, St. Thomas is silent.

The second of the two relevant points about beatitude is the function of the intellect. St. Thomas says that beatitude is the perfect good of an intellectual nature.[20] This is quite understandable because God is the Supreme Intellect and because the vision of the Supreme Intellect is an act of the intellect. St. Thomas firmly believes that the intellect is the only power of the soul to participate in the heavenly bliss. He is also certain that the natural quality of the intellect is irrelevant to the measure of beatitude.[21] The difference between the keenest and the dullest intellect is infinitesimal in comparison with the infinite charm between the created intellect and the Primal Intellect. Every intellect, keen or dull, can be illumined and elevated to the divine level of beatitude.

St. Thomas can convince us of this point. Let us bring together the two assertions he makes: that the intellect is the only power of the soul for the act of beatific vision and that the quality of beatitude is determined by the intensity of charity. Virtue means the perfection of a power of the soul. We may conclude that charity is the virtue of the intellect. We need not draw this conclusion, because St. Thomas defines charity as an intellectual appetite.[22] This simple definition of charity presents one problem in connection with the infused virtues. St. Thomas has defined the infused virtues as the concrete habits and means governing spiritual life. The end of spiritual life is to nurture charity, and charity is the intellectual appetition for God. Not all the infused virtues are necessarily virtues of the intellect. What have the non-intellectual infused virtues to do with the intellectual appetition of God? This is the same question we encountered earlier: What is the relation of the infused virtues to charity?

Though the Angelic Doctor is silent on this issue, he seems to believe that charity is the only principle for differentiating the modes of beatitude. In some cases, he refers under the general name of "virtue" to the principle which is to determine the modes of beatitude.[23] Even then, he talks of the virtue in the singular and probably means charity. He often talks of the different levels of beatitude not in qualitative terms but in a quantitative term. He seems to believe that all the beatific visions are of one quality and of different quantitative measures.

Whereas St. Thomas sees only one principle for determining the nature and quality of all beatific visions, Dante presents seven principles. The seven powers that have been spiritualized through the works in grace are these seven principles. The seven Planets present the seven virtues in glory and splendor. Splendor is a highly technical word with Dante, meaning the glory which comes in the reflection of the rays of divine light. The Moon and Mercury show the splendors of the two intellectual powers, Venus and the Sun those of the two irascible powers, and the top three Planets those of the three concupiscible powers. These seven different splendors show the seven different types of glory which the seven virtues can have in the reflection of one light. The *Paradiso* is an ocean of one light. Every soul can receive and reflect the rays of divine light in proportion to its capacity which is determined by its seven virtues. In the kingdom of heaven as conceived by St. Thomas, it is God who measures out the amount of light to each soul in proportion to its charity. In Dante's *Paradiso*, all the souls are immersed in the ocean of infinite light and reflect divine rays as much as they can.

One of the prevalent errors in interpreting Dante's *Paradiso* is to assume the splendor of each Planet to characterize the entire bliss of the blessed on that Planet. To be sure, the splendor of every Planet does characterize the dominant feature of the blessed appearing on that Planet because their dominant virtue is the one represented by that Planet. But all the blessed participate in all the seven splendors of the seven Planets, insofar as they all have not one but seven virtues. It is a grave error to regard any one of the seven types of splendor as the only principle for determining the entire bliss of a blessed soul, as grave as to assume that each blessed soul can retain only one of the seven virtues at the expense of the others. For example, the splendor reflected on the Moon does not constitute the entire bliss for those appearing on the Moon, but simply the dominant feature of their beatitude. They share in the other six splendors to the extent that they have six more virtues.

The bliss of each soul is determined by the quality of its seven virtues. Many readers, who do not understand this general principle of individuation in the *Paradiso*, shed many tears for the blessed appearing on the lower Planets because their beatitude seems to be too feeble and too lowly. When these readers see Piccarda in her dim and feeble splendor, they feel the same sort of pity for her as they do for Paolo and Francesca. It is for the benefit of these readers that Dante voices a compassionate protest in asking her whether or not she would like to get on a higher station. Our pity for Francesca is confirmed by her pitiful account of her sin and fate, but our pity for Piccarda is rebutted by her proud account of her bliss. Francesca reinforces our pity with her self-pity, and Piccarda takes pity on our feeble understanding of the kingdom of heaven.

Dante does not give a direct exposition of the seven principles for the determination of beatitude, but an analogical explanation of this matter in the First Heaven. This analogical explanation is Beatrice's account of the moon spots (*Par.* ii. 62 ff.). This long discourse purports to be very scientific in its approach to the problem and yet turns out to be a very un-scientific doctrine in its content. For this reason, this discourse has been at once hailed as astonishingly scientific in spirit and ridiculed as unbelievably unscientific in its conclusion. On Dante's inquiry about moon spots, Beatrice tells him to express his own view of the matter. Dante's view is that the moon spots are caused by different densities of matter. Beatrice says this is wrong and explains why. Dante's view rests on the assumption that there is only one principle for differentiating the splendor of the heavenly bodies.

All the virtues flow out of the Creator in the Empyrean. The vital principle first flows out to the *Primum Mobile*. This sphere which has no stars and is uniform in all its parts does not perform the function of dividing and distributing the vital principle but transmits it to the Eighth Heaven. The Fixed Stars of that sphere differentiate and diffuse the vital principle to the lower spheres. The stars of the Eighth Heaven are "diverse in kind and in size"; they are different in quality as well as in quantity (*Par.* ii. 66). The splendors of these stars could not differ in quality and quantity, if the Heaven of the Fixed Stars were to distribute "one only virtue, more or less or equally" (*Par.* ii. 68–69). Therefore the differentiation of the stars requires the different formal principles:

> Diverse virtues [of stars] must be the fruits
> of formal principles, and all of these except one
> would be excluded by your reasoning.
> *Par.* ii. 70–72

This analogical discourse on the heavenly science is Dante's expansion of St. Paul's analogy of stars on which St. Thomas relies in formulating the doctrine of diversity in beatitude.[24] *There is one glory of the sun, and another glory of the moon, and another of the stars; for star differs from star in glory. So also with the resurrection of the dead* (1 Cor. 15:41–42). The stars differ not only materially but formally. So it is with the seven Planets which represent the seven virtues in glory and splendor. The seven virtues differ formally and qualitatively and as such constitute the seven formal principles for the qualitative determination of beatitude. Though all the blessed have all the seven virtues, their virtues can differ materially and quantitatively. These differences constitute the material principles for the quantitative determination of beatitude.

Dante's ascent of the *Paradiso* further elucidates the way in which the seven virtues participate in beatific vision. His ascent is the reverse process of the diffusion of the vital principle. While the Eighth Heaven distributes the vi-

tal principle down to the Planets, Dante accumulates the
virtues as he mounts from one Planet to another. Beatrice
grows more beautiful at every Planet, and her increasing
beauty is the objectification of Dante's growing virtues:

> And I saw her eyes so clear,
>   so joyous that her semblance
>   surpassed all her former usage and her latest too.
>
> And, as by feeling more delight
>   in doing well, one notices from day to day
>   the steady progress of one's virtue,
>
> So I, seeing that miracle more lovely,
>   became aware that with along the heavens
>   my circling had increased its arc.
>   *Par.* xviii. 55–63

All the seven virtues Dante accumulates in his ascent of
the seven Planets come into a single unity. This unity of
virtues is indicated by his instantaneous passage from one
Planet to another. The first interval of passage he notices in
his voyage of heaven is the interval between the Seventh
and the Eighth Heavens. The contiguity of the seven
Planets has the same significance as the contiguity of the
seven Terraces. As Dante sees the purgation of seven
powers of his soul by climbing up the seven Terraces, so
he sees the glorification of the seven virtues by flying up
the seven Planets. As the seven spiritualized powers of the
soul come together for the final test of love, so the seven
glorified powers of the soul come together to sustain the
final glorification of love, Jacob's Ladder on Saturn.
Jacob's Ladder soars to the highest Heaven, the bower of
love. Dante passes through the purgatorial fire after receiving the angel's benediction and climbs up Jacob's Ladder
after the discourses on the Seventh Heaven. Just as all the

blessed souls fly up along the Ladder to the highest Heaven, so all the seven powers of the soul are lifted and exalted along the Ladder to the highest Heaven.

The relation of the seven Planets and the highest three Heavens is that of action and contemplation. In the Aristotelian ethics, contemplation is the ultimate end of life and action is the preparation for this ultimate end. The active works on the seven Terraces prepare for the contemplative vision and toil on the top of the *Purgatorio*. We have seen this relation in the dream of Leah and Rachel. Leah takes delight in field works, and Rachel in the rapture of vision. Jacob's Ladder marks the same transition from action to contemplation as is marked by the dream of Jacob's wives. In the seven Planets, Dante sees the result of the active spiritual life, namely, the seven infused virtues. From the Eighth Heaven on, he sees the nature of the Trinity. In the Eighth Heaven, he begins to have the fore-taste of the feast of love (*Par.* xxiv. 1–9).

The heavenly feast of divine love begins in the Heaven of faith, because faith is already the beginning and germ of charity. The order of generation of the theological virtues is faith, hope, and charity, and the order of their perfection is charity, hope, and faith.[25] When St. Thomas talks of these two orders, he means to see the three theological virtues in one organic, teleological unity. If we compare charity to the fruit of a tree, faith is the seed out of which the tree grows, and hope is the tree which bears the fruit. Faith and hope are the initial and the intermediate stages in the growth of charity and can be called the initial and the intermediate forms of charity. In the Eighth Heaven, Dante sees the Son in His visible mission for the revelation of the truth of faith. This is the initial vision of the Trinity. In the Ninth Heaven, he sees the Spirit in His invisible mission for the sanctification of the faithful in hope. This is the intermediate vision of the Trinity. The final vision of the Trinity comes with the vision of the Father in union with His Son and His Spirit in the bower of love, the spaceless and timeless heaven of pure light. And charity comes to its fullest perfection.

In the perfection of charity, all the powers of the entire soul are fully actualized. Whereas the perfection of carnal love necessitates the distortion of the entire soul, the perfection of spiritual love glorifies the entire soul through the single act of charity. St. Thomas says that the divine perfection embraces all other perfection as the divine beatitude embraces all other beatitude.[26] This could not be the case if the sensitive powers of the soul were to remain in potentiality in heaven. A power in potentiality cannot be called perfect; nothing is perfect unless it is in act.

The powers of the human soul are not only perfected in heavenly bliss, but superhumanized. The human soul becomes like God; the blessed are made *deiform*.[27] Dante calls it the experience of transhumanization (*Par.* i. 70). The blessed see not only all the substances and accidents of the cosmos but the mystery of the Holy Trinity in a single timeless vision. This is the divine joy consonant only to the nature of divinity and far surpassing the nature of humanity. The heavenly bliss is to participate in the Godhead, and the soul becomes a partaker of divine nature.[28]

The deification of the human soul is the reward Christ promised to his faithful: *Rejoice and exult, because your reward is great in heaven* (Matt. 5:12). This promise sums up all the blessings in the seven beatitudes:

Blessed are the poor in spirit, for theirs is the kingdom of heaven. Blessed are the meek, for they shall possess the earth. Blessed are they who mourn, for they shall be comforted. Blessed are they who hunger and thirst for justice, for they shall be satisfied. Blessed are the merciful, for they shall obtain

*mercy. Blessed are the clean of heart, for they shall see God.
Blessed are the peacemakers, for they shall be called children
of God . . . Rejoice and exult, because your reward is great
in heaven* (Matt. 5:3–12).

Each of the seven beatitudes is composed of two parts: the
act of virtue and its reward. On each of the seven Terraces,
the angel pronounces one of the seven beatitudes in benediction on the penitents for the completion of purgation on
that Terrace. The order of the seven beatitudes on the *Purgatorio* differs from their original order. In the re-arrange-
ment of the seven beatitudes, Dante joins together the
second and the seventh beatitudes into one, and divides the
fourth one into two beatitudes. He then places one beatitude
on each of the seven Terraces as benediction: (1) *Beati
pauperes spiritu* to those who have transformed their pride
into humility; (2) *Beati misericordes* to those who have
transformed envy into mercy; (3) *Beati pacifici* to those
who have transformed wrath into meekness; (4) *Benedicti
qui lugent* to those who have transformed sloth and sorrow
into fortitude and vigor; (5) *Beati qui esuriunt* to those
who have transformed avarice into liberality; (6) *Beati qui
sitiunt* to those who have transformed intemperance to
temperance; (7) *Beati mundo corde* to those who have
transformed carnal love into spiritual love.

St. Thomas confronts the thorny question of whether the
rewards assigned to the beatitudes refer to this life or to
the life after death.[29] He says that the rewards promised in
the beatitudes can be fully received only in the kingdom of
heaven. This conclusion coheres with his conviction that
perfect bliss is impossible in this life and can be realized
only in the kingdom of heaven.[30] The glorification of the
seven spiritualized powers as seen on the seven Planets are
the rewards for the spiritual works done in grace on the

earth. The rewards are the rays of divine light in which the spiritualized powers display glory and splendor.

Notice now the triangular arrangement of the bridle, the whip, and the beatitude on each Terrace. Each of the seven whips is correlated with one of the seven beatitudes which indicate the mode of reward, but none of the seven bridles is correlated with anything that shows the mode of punishment for the corresponding sin. Is it merely because no penitent is destined to be flung down into Hell and interested in the nature of punishment? The answer is: the sinners have already received their rewards. The act of sin is its own punishment and reward. We have seen that every Circle is nothing other than the representation of an act of sin in perfection. St. Thomas says that sin can be the punishment to itself.[31] This idea of autonomous retribution is a little older than St. Thomas: . . . *such foolish reasonings led them astray, that they worshipped brute reptiles and despicable vermin. And swarms of brute beasts thou didst send to execute thy vengeance, for the more proof that a man's own sins are the instrument of his punishment* (Wisdom 11:16–17).

Dante's *Inferno* perfectly realizes the principle of autonomous and simultaneous retribution. There is no special device for punishing the sinners. The only device is to leave the sinners in perfect freedom for the eternal, perfect realization of their sinful powers. The guards of Hell may appear to be special instruments of torment, but they are the personification and deification of the sinful powers of the soul. The principle of autonomous retribution is eloquently stated in Capaneus' defiant identification of himself: "That which in life I was, in death I am" (*Inf.* xiv. 51). Some of the scenes in Hell may not appear to be the acts of sin but only the instruments for punishment. For example, the shrubs of the suicide wood in the Seventh Circle may appear to represent not the brutal act of suicide, but the punishment of immobility appropriate for those who destroy their own lives and bodies. But a closer examination will show that the life of the shrubs is a sensible representation of the anger that leads to suicide. Those who take their own lives vent their anger through the violence on themselves, because they cannot wreak their anger on the people who provoke their anger. They feel as though they were living in a wood full of black bitches freed from the leash (*Inf.* xiii. 124–126). Without being able to fight back the bitches and the Harpies, like the shrubs of the suicide wood, they can find outlet for their anger only through the damage and destruction of their own bodies (*Inf.* xiii. 101–102).

It requires some imagination to see how each scene of Hell is a sensible representation of sin in its actuality and that every sin is its own punishment. Every sin is also its own reward. What is the reward of an act but its end? To regard sin as its own punishment is a negative view, and to regard it as its own reward is a positive view. The positive view focuses its attention on the good realized, and the negative view on the evil produced. Evil is the absence or loss of good.[32] Every act aims at some good for its end, and every evil is a by-product of an act seeking some good. There is no possible source of evil except good.[33] The good that is realized as the end of an evil act is its reward. Thus every sin in the *Inferno* is its own reward as well as its own punishment.

Why should we not apply the same principle of autonomous retribution to virtues as well? The same principle is applicable to the natural virtues, but not to the infused virtues. The natural virtues are for the realization of the natural end, and virtuous acts are their own rewards. The infused virtues are spiritual powers and can find no proper end and medium for their act in this world, while the natural powers, virtuous or vicious, have the proper end and medium in this world. The former has to wait for the kingdom of heaven for its end and act, and the latter has already attained its end and realization. This is why Christ cheers up his faithful with the promise of the heavenly reward: *"Rejoice and exult, because your reward is great in heaven";* and repeatedly points out the earthly reward which the pharisees and hypocrites have already gained: *"They have already received their reward."*

Because the purged powers of the soul have to remain in potency, the seven Terraces do not undergo any subdivision. The relation of potency to acts is the relation of one to many. One potential power can be actualized in different kinds of act. Because all the powers in Hell are in full actuality, the Circles are subdivided into Rings. The relation of one to many holds for the relation of the *Paradiso* to the *Purgatorio*. The *Paradiso* is a world of actuality, but its divine actuality differs from the human actuality of the *Inferno*. All the blessed are gathered in one place on the Empyrean, because all the powers are actualized through a single act, whereas the penitents are divided by Terraces because the works of purgation cannot be accomplished by a single instantaneous act.

The different principles of reward in the *Paradiso* and in the *Inferno* appear in the contrast between the nakedness of the damned and the radiant garments of the blessed. Because the damned have already their reward in their sin and need no additional reward, they are presented in stark nudity. The reward the purged soul seeks is the ocean of divine light, the proper medium in which its powers can be actualized. The blessed appear like silkworms enclosed in their silk, the silk woven of divine light (*Par.* viii. 54). The participation in the natural order is the reward for the natural powers, and the participation in the spiritual order is the reward for the spiritual powers. The garment of light shows the latter, and the body of flesh the former.

Though the glory of heaven is given in proportion to the virtues as their reward, we should not forget that the heavenly glory is a gratuitous reward. The virtues which are rewarded in heaven cannot be developed in the order of nature but only in the order of grace. No one deserves grace; grace is a gift. The fruit of labour in grace is the virtue which is glorified in heaven. Let us now focus our attention on the relation of these three orders of nature, grace, and glory in the scheme of salvation. In the previous chapter, we focused our main attention on the parallel contrast of these three orders. Let us now view the three orders in a linear progression, because their linear progression is the eternal plan of salvation.

The creation began with two orders: the natural and the spiritual. Adam was the perfection of the natural order (*Par.* xiii. 82–83). He stands on the border line between the two orders; He is made of spirit and flesh. When Eve entices him with the forbidden fruit, Adam is forced to make the choice between the primal source of spiritual life and the flower of carnal life. Eve is the exemplification of Adam's carnality: *This is bone of my bones, and flesh of my flesh* (Gen. 2:23). For the sake of carnality, Adam alienates himself from the spiritual order. Thus he becomes a slave of the carnal world. This is his fall and his sin. The second Adam comes through the womb of the second Eve. It is one of the problematic points of dogma whether or not Christ would have been born in flesh but for the sin of man. St. Thomas holds that the Son of God would not have become incarnate except for Adam's sin.[34] Christ Himself clarifies the purpose of His visible mission: *"It is not the healthy who need a physician, but the sick. For I have not come to call the just, but sinners"* (Mark 2:17).

The Incarnation opens the way for the regeneration of the degenerate soul, but the regeneration does not merely restore what has been lost. If the regeneration were to aim at mere restoration, the Terrestrial Paradise would be the final destiny of the penitents. The Garden of Eden has been transformed from the permanent habitat of man to the final preparatory ground for the flight of the soul to the spiritual order. While Adam was falling from the Garden of Eden, the Garden of Eden was projected into the upper atmosphere from its original site on the sea level (*Purg.* xxviii. 97–102). Adam in his innocent stage did not know of the spiritual end; his bliss was the bliss in the undefiled natural order. By the time the soul climbs up to the Terrestrial Paradise, it becomes ready to participate in the bliss of the spiritual order. It becomes "equal unto angels of heaven," because its powers are perfectly spiritualized and because the redeemed and the angels do not constitute two societies but one city of God.[35]

What would have happened, if Adam had not consented to Eve's enticement and had retained his innocence? Cato is the answer to this question. Like Cato, Adam would be standing alone in the Garden of Eden. If Adam had not sinned, the Garden of Eden would still remain at the foot of the *Purgatorio*. Eve alone would have been exiled to the world of sin. Because of the chasm between the world of sin and the world of innocence, Cato has no interest and no concern for his dear wife Marcia. If Adam and Eve had been separated like Cato and Marcia, Adam would be standing in his solitary innocence in eternal estrangement from Eve. To be sure, he would not have suffered sin and death, but like Cato would not have known of the bliss in the spiritual order.

Flesh and sin, woman and fall, are the essential foundation for the salvation of man. This is why three ladies of heaven initiate Dante's epic journey. While Cato shows no interest in Marcia, Dante begins his climb with a love song. Casella sings Dante's love song in which the virtues of the lady are praised (*Purg.* ii. 112). Every step on the *Purga-*

torio is guided by ladies. Lucia lifts Dante to the gate of the *Purgatorio* proper. The virtues the penitents cultivate on the seven Terraces are exemplified by the Queen of Heaven. Beatrice takes over the charge of Dante from Virgil whom she sent for his succor. She guides him to the highest Heaven. The final beatific vision comes through the intercession of the Queen of Heaven.

The sin from flesh is an essential and indispensable instrument for the works in grace. Grace comes through sin; it would not have come without sin. The sins purged on the seven Terraces can be said to be the children of the first Eve, and their contrary virtues to be the children of the second Eve. The former and the latter are inseparable, because they are contraries. The latter is not possible without the former. Sin is the indispensable progenetrix for virtue. Grace that opens heaven for man comes only through sin that has expelled man from the Garden of Innocence. It is this indispensability of the fall into sin that Christ means among other things when He says: *"Amen, amen, I say to you, unless the grain of wheat falls into the ground and dies, it remains alone. But if it dies, it brings forth much fruit"* (John 12:24–25). He says this in explanation of His impending Passion and Death.

His Death and Resurrection show the way of life for the sinful soul which has to die because of sin. Death is the consequence of sin, and as such is powerless against the sinless body of Christ. That is, Christ does not need to go through the death and resurrection of a natural body for His own sake. The damnation of the sinners lies in their unwillingness to die in sin; they will to live in sin. In order to die in sin, however, one has first to live in sin. Dante's descent in the *Inferno* is his life in sin, and his ascent of the *Purgatorio* is his death in sin. The latter is impossible without the former. No one can climb the *Purgatorio* without the power of sin any more than without the power of grace. Grace does not come and work in the soul which has not been fermented in sin. Grace works its miracle only where sin has prepared a fertile soul. *Where the offense has abounded, grace has abounded yet more* (Rom. 5:20). Christ could not have shown His Resurrection without dying and being buried.

The linear progression of the three orders of nature, grace, and glory is in imitation of Christ's Passion, Resurrection, and Ascension. In imitation of Christ's burial, Dante falls into the underground world. In imitation of His Resurrection, Dante overcomes the world of death and is born for the fellowship in the spiritual order. In imitation of His Ascension, Dante flies up to the mansion of the Father. Every stage of the linear progression is an essential link on the way from the world of sin to the world of bliss as exemplified by the three events which conclude the Son's visible mission: the Passion, the Resurrection, and the Ascension. Dante could not have found any better model for his epic plan than the Son of Man who says: *I am the way, the truth, and the life* (John 14:6).

The paradox of salvation lies with the crucial functions which woman plays. Woman is the manifestation of the lower of man's two natures. It is through woman that man falls and rises. Adam falls through Eve, and Christ comes through Mary. This paradox of salvation is presented in the transformation of the carnal powers into the spiritual powers. The higher powers in the order of nature become the lower powers in the order of glory, and vice versa. The active powers in the natural order become the passive powers in the spiritual order, and vice versa. While Satan with his three male offspring hanging down from his three mouths reigns in the kingdom of sin, the humble handmaid of God reigns in the kingdom of heaven. The paradox of salvation is beautifully condensed in St. Bernard's salutation to the Queen of Heaven:

The Fragile Leaves of the Sibyl

Virgin mother, daughter of thy son,
  lowly and exalted above all creatures,
  the final terminus of the eternal design.

Par. xxxiii. 1–3

Before concluding this chapter, let us examine one more feature of the soul: its relation to the body which will be restored to it on the Day of Judgment. We have to begin with Plato, the beginning of the soul's self-recollection. Plato's doctrine came quite early into Christendom and established a long venerable tradition from St. Augustine down to St. Bonaventure, while Aristotle's theory came quite late through St. Albertus Magnus and was fully consolidated by his disciple St. Thomas, the bull whose voice his discerning teacher confidently predicted would resound throughout the world. Plato regarded the body as a chain and burden imposed on the soul as a punishment. The body drags down the soul to the corruptible world of copies. The real world is the bodiless world of Ideas. Plato presents, in *Phaedo*, Socrates rather anxiously waiting for his death as the liberation of his soul from the fetters of the body.

Though Aristotle owes a great deal to Plato, Aristotle takes a view exactly opposite to Plato's. For Aristotle the real is the concrete and the living, while the Ideas are empty copies of abstraction from the real. The body is the medium through which the soul attains life and bliss. The relation of the soul and the body is the relation of form and matter, and their union is indispensible for their concretion. The body is not a burden or chain imposed on the soul, but the medium of its actualization and perfection. It is obvious that the soul cannot achieve the happiness of active life without a body. Even in the contemplative life of the intellect, the soul cannot dispense with the aid of the

116

body because no intellectual contemplation is possible without the bodily image.

Their radically different views on the relation of the soul to its body are reflected in their conceptions of the relation of the rational part of the soul to its non-rational elements. Plato and Aristotle agree in holding that the non-rational elements of the soul have their origin in the body. They differ about the relation of the rational element to the non-rational elements in the soul. Aristotle sees an *essential* relation, and Plato an *accidental* relation. We have seen Aristotle's *essential* relation in the examination of Statius' discourse at the beginning of the preceding chapter. The non-rational powers are related to the rational level in the way matter is united with form in a substance. This is the *essential* relation. In Plato's *accidental* relation, the rational soul is joined with its non-rational companions by the mere accident that they are placed in one body. It is for this difference of the *essential* and the *accidental* relation that Aristotle stresses the unicity of the powers in one essence of the soul while Plato argues for the plurality of souls and their separability.

After Plato's doctrine was taken up into Christendom, it was very effective and useful for the articulation of the Christian belief. The soul's longing for the liberation from this world and for the excursion to the other world could be readily translated into its longing for the liberation from the world of sin and for the ascent to the kingdom of God. The *accidental* relation of the soul and body was an effective premise for the proof of the immortality of the soul. Plato's doctrine, however, had its thorn as well as its rose. On the Day of Resurrection, the soul is to regain its body for the perfection of its bliss. If the body is a burden and chain on the soul, the Day of Judgment will be the day of curse and woe that will terminate the freedom of the soul. Plato's doctrine works marvellously well for the death of a Christian and very poorly for his resurrection. Augustine resolves this dilemma by appealing to St. Paul. The body which the blessed will regain is not a natural body but a spiritual body.[36] While the natural body is corruptible and unruly, the spiritual body will be incorruptible and perfectly adapted to the spiritual bliss. How can the natural body be transformed into the spiritual body? St. Augustine explains, "God gives the soul such a powerful nature that from its exceeding fullness of happiness the vigor of incorruption overflows into the lower nature."[37]

When Aristotle's doctrine makes its appearance, it displays the comeliness and ugliness which are exactly opposite to those of Plato's. God did not give the body to punish the soul, and this is in the line of Aristotle's thinking. Aristotle's doctrine explains quite well the union of the soul with its body, but faces a grave difficulty in accounting for its separation. While Plato's *accidental* relation can make a plausible case for the independent life of the soul in separation from its body, Aristotle's *essential* relation is bound to offer reasons counter to the immortality of the soul. This is one of the main reasons why the Angelic Doctor's absorption in Aristotle was looked upon by many devout Christians with uneasiness and suspicion.

To be sure, Aristotle himself argues for the imperishability of the intellect, but the intellect whose immortality Aristotle vouches for is not exactly the same as the individual soul whose immortality the Christians are promised. Aristotle's intellect is the universal, impersonal *nous*.[38] For these reasons, some Aristotelians like Averroes were compelled to deny the immortality of the individual soul (*Purg.* xxv. 63–66). In a faithful adherence to the teaching of his Church, St. Thomas tries to refute Averroes and prove the immortality of the individual soul. To prove the separability of the soul within the Aristotelian psychology is not so simple as to do so within the Platonic system. In the Platonic system, the rational soul can be easily separated from the non-rational soul of the body, because the former is accidentally linked with the latter. Within the framework of the Aristotelian psychology, the individual intellect can not be easily separated from the non-rational powers, because all the elements, rational and irrational, are the powers of one essence. The *unicity* of the soul grounded in its *essential* relation makes it impossible for the intellect to be simply separated from the sensitive powers. Furthermore, the sensitive powers cannot survive the separation of the soul and the body, because they reside in the union of the soul and the body.

St. Thomas overcomes this problem by distinguishing the formal elements and the material elements of the sensitive powers. Every sensitive power is composed of a rational element and an irrational element, a rational mode of operation and an irrational appetite. The former is the formal element and the latter is the material element. The latter requires the union of the soul and the body for its existence, but the former can survive the separation of the soul from its body. When the soul is separated from the body, it retains only the formal elements of moral virtues and the sensitive powers.[39] Thus the soul can retain its *essential* unity of all its powers even after the death of the body.

Though St. Thomas has established a fine case for the immortality of the soul and its separability from the body without impairing its unity, his task is not yet over. He has yet to prepare the soul for the Day of Judgment. The soul that retains the formal elements of the sensitive powers may appear to be fully prepared to exercise all the moral virtues whenever it regains its body, but the case is not so simple as it may appear. St. Thomas believes that all the business of the active, natural life will come to a halt in the world after the Last Judgment.[40] In short, the blessed will not return to the natural order but stay in the spiritual order even after regaining their bodies. The blessed will not have a chance to exercise their moral virtues whose formal elements they retain on leaving the natural order. What is the use of retaining the formal elements which will never be used for eternity?

Neither Plato nor Aristotle is of any great help in explaining the bliss of the spiritual order after the Day of Judgment; both of them were Gentiles to whom the bliss exemplified by the Resurrection of Christ would be mere folly. No wonder, then, St. Thomas does not invoke the authority of Aristotle, but falls back on that of St. Paul as St. Augustine does, whenever he talks of the Day of Resurrection: *What is sown corruptible, rises incorruptible; what is sown unhonored, rises in glory; what is sown in weakness, is raised in power; what is sown a natural body, rises a spiritual body* (1 Cor. 15:42-44). In explaining this passage, St. Thomas says that the bodies of the blessed will be spiritual and the bodies of the damned carnal.[41] The former will be lightsome and ethereal (*claritas*), and the latter darksome and heavy. How does this difference come about between the two kinds of bodies? The Angelic Doctor's answer to this question rests on the premise that the nature of the body should be consonant with the nature of the soul.[42] The spiritual lightsomeness of the blessed will overflow to their bodies, adapting the bodies to the glory of the souls.[43] While the bodies of the blessed will become spiritual by refulgence, the bodies of the damned will be carnal by affection.[44]

In explaining these major tenets of faith, St. Thomas makes little use of Aristotle's fine theoretical system and falls back to the Augustinian tradition. Dante's significant contribution lies in his dextrous use of Aristotle's theoretical framework for a masterly elucidation of these theological problems. Dante consistently sticks to the unicity of the soul and employs the metaphor of fermentation in explaining the unity of its three powers. As the heat of the sun transforms grape juice into wine, the spirit of the human soul transmutes the non-rational powers into its own one essence (*Purg.* xxv. 76–78). St. Thomas also recognizes a similar possibility in the conversion of concupiscence into the appetite for the spiritual good.[45] Because of the unity of the three powers in one essence of the soul in Dante's scheme, all the three powers of the soul stand on the same footing in their separability from the body. All the three powers stay together in one essence of the soul, whether the soul is in union with or in separation from the body. After the separation from the body, the soul's destiny is settled between the spiritual and the carnal order by its own state. If the soul is neither fully carnal nor completely spiritual, it is initiated into the medium of purgation. The purpose of purgation is not to separate the formal elements from the material elements of the sensitive power, but to spiritualize the carnal powers. All the powers are in full actuality both in Heaven and Hell.

What sorts of bodies will the souls have on the Day of Resurrection? Dante offers a clear answer to this question in his explanation of the bodies of the penitents:

> As soon as space encloses it (the soul) there
>   the *formative power* radiates around,
>   in *form* and *quantity* as in shaping the living members,
>
> And as the air when it is moist
>   becomes adorned with diverse colors
>   through rays reflected in it,
>
> So the air here takes on that *form*,
>   which the soul that is enclosed in it,
>   impresses upon it through its *power*. (Italics mine.)
>   *Purg.* xxv. 88–93

121

In the relation of form and matter, matter is totally devoid of form. Form means quality and nature. Matter has no nature of its own and only reflects the nature of the form it embodies. It is this relation of form and matter on which Dante settles the relation of the soul and the body. The soul is "the formative power," that is, the power that gives the form to the body. The body is the matter which has no nature of its own and only reflects the formative power of the soul. Now you can see what sort of bodies the blessed and the damned will regain and why. The bodies of the blessed will be spiritual because they embody and reflect the spiritual powers, and the bodies of the damned will be carnal because they embody and reflect the carnal powers. This is as simple and as clear as to say that the body of a man is human because it embodies a human soul and the body of a plant is vegetative because it embodies a vegetative soul.

When St. Thomas talks of the bodies of the resurrected, he never thinks of this simple principle of form and matter to account for the nature of their bodies. He tries to solve the problem through the principles of "refulgence" and "affection" which are as alien to his philosophical system as St. Paul's theological virtues are to Aristotle's natural virtues. Furthermore, he is not quite sure whether the souls will transform the bodies in such a way as to suit the nature of the souls or the bodies will be of suitable nature before being given to the souls.[46] In St. Thomas' view, the intellect does not gain anything for having lived and suffered in the natural order because it has to divest itself of all the sensitive powers on the death of the body. We may as well ask St. Thomas what the intellect gains on recovering the body. The human soul which becomes pure intellect like the angelic substances in the kingdom of heaven may be more perfect in separation from the body than in union with it. If the human intellect becomes more perfect by regaining the body, the angelic substances must remain less perfect for having no bodies.

If I am not mistaken, Dante is the first to accomplish a consistent elucidation of the teleological destiny of the Christian soul through a metaphysical scheme. In his vision, the soul retains every power it has gained through its toil and labour in the natural order. The soul is fully prepared to regain the body because it retains the irascible and the concupiscible which are the powers governing the body. The angels are not given bodies because they have no bodily powers. The human soul becomes perfect in its re-union with the body because its bodily powers are re-gaining the medium of action. It lies within the formative power of the soul to determine the nature of the body by transfusing its power into the body. The Transfiguration of Christ is precisely meant to show the *claritas* of the body which comes through the transfusion of the spiritual glory into the natural body (*Purg.* xxxii. 72–90).[47]

Whereas St. Paul's spiritual man is poorly grafted on Aristotle's natural man in the Angelic Doctor's workman-ship as is shown by the discommunion of the natural virtues and the spiritual virtues and by the discontinuity in the soul's transition from the natural order to the spiritual order, St. Paul's doctrine of the spiritual life transfuses and radiates through Aristotle's natural system in Dante's masterful craftsmanship as the *claritas* of the spiritual glory transfuses and radiates through the natural body of Christ in the Transfiguration.

We are now in a position to place Dante's magnificent achievement in the proper historical context. The momen-tous goal of medieval thought was to elucidate the Judaic religious ideals through the Greek philosophical systems. The first monumental accomplishment toward this goal was the works of St. Augustine, and the second was the works of St. Thomas. The Bishop of Hippo relied on Plato, and

Thomas of Aquino on Aristotle. The significant difference between Plato and Aristotle, as handmaids of the revealed theology, is twofold. Plato's is a triadic system, and Aristotle's is a dyadic one. The latter's eyes are focused on this world, and the former's eyes on the other world.

To be sure, Aristotle mentions the triadic division of the soul but only with a passing interest.[48] In his exploration of the human psyche and its powers, he consistently employs the dyadic division: the rational and the non-rational.[49] St. Thomas takes note of the triadic division of the soul only once in his *Summa* and never employs it in his examination of virtues and vices.[50] Faithfully following the well-established path of the "Philosopher," the Angelic Doctor attempts to see all human passions and powers through the dyadic scheme.

St. Bonaventura scrupulously follows the Platonic-Augustinian tradition and views the nature of the soul through the triadic scheme. The Seraphic Doctor holds that the soul has three powers: memory, intelligence, and will, because the soul is an *imago Dei*.[51] There is a unity of Nature in the Holy Trinity of the Three Persons; there is a unity of essence with a trinity of the three powers in the soul. Dante reformulates the unity of the soul's essence and the trinity of its powers through the Aristotelian scheme of entelechy (cf. Statius' discourse on the genesis of the soul). This is his conversion of the Platonic *accidental* relation of the soul's three parts into the Aristotelian *essential* relation of the three levels of powers.

Both Plato's idealistic and Aristotle's realistic outlooks offer grave obstacles to the elucidation of the teleological movement of the Christian soul. The Christian soul has to be saved through its works in this world for its bliss in the other world. Whereas the teleological movement of the Christian soul cuts across the boundary between the two worlds, Plato's longing is firmly attached to the other world and Aristotle's bliss is securely anchored in this world. If Plato is right, the soul has only one aim, the liberation from the fetters of this corruptible world. The soul would gain nothing for having lived, toiled, and suffered in the vale of tears. The whole earth would have nothing to contribute toward the fulfillment of the eternal plan of salvation. But it is a major tenet of the Christian faith that natural life is the preparation of spiritual life: *Mankind begins with Adam who became, as Scripture tells us, a living soul; it is fulfilled in the Adam who has become a life-giving spirit. It was not the principle of spiritual life that came first; natural life came first, then spiritual life* (1 Cor. 15:45–46).

In contrast to Plato, Aristotle is fully appreciative of natural life but knows of no spiritual life. In adopting Aristotle's system, Thomas of Aquino has to clarify the relation of Aristotle's natural life to Paul's spiritual life. It is for the clarification of this issue that he makes up the table of ten virtues. The cardinal and the intellectual virtues are for Aristotle's natural life and the theological virtues for Paul's spiritual life. The Christian soul has two ends: the natural and the spiritual. But the two ends are independent of each other; one cannot be reduced or converted to the other.[52] St. Thomas is well aware that no man can serve two masters. The two ends cannot stand on equal level; the natural end should be subject to the supernatural end.

St. Thomas can establish an axiological order but no teleological movement between natural and spiritual life. Spiritual life has a higher end than natural life, but the latter has nothing to contribute toward the fulfillment of the former. In the Angelic Doctor's view, the soul gains nothing for having lived and toiled in the natural order when it moves into the spiritual order. On this point, St. Thomas is scarcely distinguishable from the Platonic-Augustinian tradition. It is then no wonder that he always relies on that venerable tradition when he ponders on the soul's after-life.

Dante's adventurous aim is to bring together the principle of natural life and the principle of spiritual life into one teleological movement. Natural life is the preparation of spiritual life, and spiritual life is the consummation of natural life. The first Adam is the beginning of the second Adam, and the second Adam is the end of the first Adam. The fall of the first Adam is essential to the rise of the second Adam. Dante extols Paul's faith in the emergence of the bliss of the spiritual man out of the sin of the natural man through the Aristotelian entelechy. He not only converts the Platonic *accidental* relation of the triadic scheme into the Aristotelian *essential* relation, but also transforms Aristotle's natural entelechy into Paul's spiritual entelechy. We will defer the fuller discussion of this point to Part III of this book. Let it suffice to say for the moment that Dante's *Divina Commedia* fuses Plato and Aristotle into one elegant system for the elucidation of Paul's vital ideal of the life-giving spirit.

At the opening of this chapter, we noticed that the participation in the world and the realization of the soul are one and the same act. Dante's three worlds embody three well-known metaphors for the soul in act. The three metaphors are Plato's receptacle, Aristotle's arrow, and St. Benedict's angelic ladder. Plato was fond of comparing the soul to a vessel. The *Inferno* is the vessel filled with the good of the natural order, and the Mystical Rose is the vessel brimming with the good of the spiritual order. The *Purgatorio* is being transformed from a natural vessel to a spiritual vessel. The nature of the vessel should be consonant with the nature of the contents. New wine cannot be put into old skin.

The metaphor of a vessel presents only the receptive role of the soul. For the representation of the active role of the soul in search of bliss, Dante employs the metaphor of shooting at a target. Aristotle was fond of this metaphor in his illustration of the golden mean and virtue. He says that the attaining of virtue is like shooting at a target. There is only one way of hitting it and many ways of missing it. Dante extensively uses the metaphor of shooting. The natural end and the supernatural end are the two targets a soul can shoot at. With many Circles and Rings, the *Inferno* represents the target of the natural end. Minos shoots down the arrows of sinful souls to the target of sin. The nine concentric circles of angels revolving around the Creator on the *Primum Mobile* constitute the target of the supernatural end. The *Purgatorio* is the turret where the arrows of the blessed souls are released for the heavenly target. Every arrow that reaches its heavenly destiny opens its tip into a blossom on one of the petals of the *Rosa Mystica*.

Since there is not one but two targets in Dante's cosmos, we have to revise Aristotle's dictum. There is only one way of shooting toward the spiritual target, namely, the way of grace. There are many ways of hitting the mark, because every point on the infinite spiritual order is a point of perfection. There is only one way to shoot for the natural target, namely, the way of sin. There are many ways of hitting the mark, because every point on the natural target is a point of perfection. There is only one way to gain the kingdom of heaven, that is, to lose the earth. There is only one way to gain the earth, that is, to lose the bliss of heaven. No one can serve two masters; no soul can shoot for both of the targets.

St. Benedict gave his famous Rule as the ladder for his monks to ascend to God. The two sides of the ladder are the soul and the body, and the twelve rungs are the twelve virtues. The ascent of the ladder begins with the virtue of humility and ends with the love of God. This is the ladder of humility. The ladder of pride is exactly the opposite path to the ladder of humility, and begins with pride and ends with the habit of sinning. The ladder of humility is the gradual ascent to God, and the ladder of pride is the gradual descent to Satan. The metaphor of the ladder comes from Jacob's vision. Jacob saw a ladder with angels going up and down on it. The soul becomes equal to angels through baptism and can climb the angelic ladder of divine love. The *Inferno* is the ladder of pride, and the *Purgatorio* is the ladder of humility. They are one and the same path leading to the diametrically opposite destinations:

But you know that they are one and the same path, although they are called by different names and are completely unlike: the road of falsehood and evil is the one by which the proud slip to their ruin, while the way of truth and faithfulness is for those who are climbing in humility. A prince mounts his throne by the same steps as he comes down from it; the road leading us to a city also brings us away from it . . . and Jacob saw only one ladder with angels ascending and descending . . . if you want to return to the truth, there is no need to seek for some new and unknown path for you already know the road down which you slipped . . . you will no longer worry about finding a way of humility.⁵³

Dante does not bother to devise a new itinerary for the ascent of the *Purgatorio*, but only reverses the descent of the *Inferno*. There are not two different paths but two phases of the same path. Truth and error are not two entirely different things, but two different reflections of one and the same reality. Knowledge and ignorance are not two entirely different states of the soul, but two different self-reflections of the same soul. This is the paradox of contraries Socrates wants to express in his statement that he knows only that he does not know.

Though St. Bernard sees only two phases of climbing

and descending of the angelic ladder, Dante sees a third phase. While the *Inferno* is the ladder of pride and the *Purgatorio* the ladder of humility, the *Paradiso* is the ladder of joy. Dante may owe his idea of the third phase also to St. Bernard. In his exegesis on the opening line of the Canticle of Canticles (*Let Him kiss me with the kiss of His mouth*), St. Bernard wants to counsel that a sinful soul, defiled in carnal passions, should not presume to lift up its foul lips directly for the joy of kissing the holy lips of the Divine Bridegroom:

You must (first) prostrate yourself upon the ground, kissing His Feet and washing them with tears . . . Between Feet and Mouth, you need the intermediate stage (of repentance)—His Hand, which first must cleanse you and then raise you up. How shall it raise you up? By giving you the grace of self-control, the fruits of penitence . . . Give Him one kiss because He has forgiven you; another, for the virtues that He has bestowed. When in these two kisses you have received twin proofs of the divine condescension, you may perhaps be bold enough to seek yet holier things . . . So this, then, is the way, the order we must follow. First we fall at the Lord's Feet . . . Next, we seek His Hand to lift us up and strengthen our knees . . . And, when we have won two graces . . . we may at last dare to lift up our heads to that all-glorious Mouth, not only to behold it but to kiss. For the Spirit Whom we thus behold is Christ the Lord, Who deigns to make us of one spirit with Himself when we cleave to Him in this holy kiss.[54]

The ladder of pride in the *Inferno* is for the kiss of His Feet. *Heaven is my throne and the earth my footstool* (Isa. 66:1). The ladder of humility is for the kiss of His Hand which cleanses the sickly soul. The ladder of joy is for the final rapture of kissing the holy lips of the Lord. Dante's three worlds constitute the three phases of climbing one angelic ladder of divine love, and its ten rungs are made of the seven powers of the soul and three virtues from its Creator.

Our poet may owe the time table of his journey to St. Bonaventura's *The Mind's Road to God,* another famous exposition on the angelic ladder. St. Bonaventura compares the three stages of journey on the angelic ladder to the three phases of one day: the evening, the morning, and the noon.[55] Dante descends to the *Inferno* in the evening of Good Friday, begins his ascent of the *Purgatorio* on the morning of Easter Sunday, and begins his ascent to the *Paradiso* at noon of the following Wednesday. St. Bonaventura also compares the whole journey of the soul to God to the cycle of one week; Dante completes his entire journey in one week.[56] The cycles of one day and one week were the two fundamental units for the medieval spiritual life; the creation of the whole world was measured through these two cyclical units, namely, one week of seven days.

I hope to have convinced you that Dante's titanic stage is not a monstrous chaos but a careful design of the highest order. The structure of his stage is not meant for the diversion and amusement of his fatigued readers, but is the sensible representation of the theme of the epic and the theatrical objectification of the dramatic action. Thus the beauty of Dante's stage is its splendor in his own technical usage. The common formal principle accounts for the uniformity of the three worlds, and the different material principles for their diversity. These two principles jointly constitute the unity of Dante's titanic stage, lining up its three worlds in the linear progression of damnation, purgation, and salvation and of the three orders of nature, grace, and glory, and bringing them together in the parallel contrast of the natural and the supernatural, the privative and the positive, the carnal and the spiritual.

In Dante's stage, you can find not only one kind of unity but three kinds: linear unity, parallel unity, and the joint unity of the linear and the parallel. This is the trinity of Dante's stage, which reflects the Holy Trinity, the main theme of Dante's epic. It is through the trinity of his epic stage that our poet takes an angelic perspective. He has every right to the title of the Angelic Poet, and his epic to the title of the Angelic Epic. Because of the trinity of the Angelic Epic, the three canticles can be viewed from many different perspectives. If we designate the first canticle as I, the second as II, and the third as III, we can have the following nine major ways of reading the angelic epic.

(1) I	(2) II	(3) III
(4) I–II	(5) II–III	(6) III–I
(7) I–II & III	(8) II–III & I	(9) III–I & II

The first three ways are to read each canticle separately. This is the most conventional procedure for the teachers and commentators. For example, J. S. Carroll handles the three canticles separately in his voluminous commentary. The middle three ways are to go through one canticle in contrast with another canticle. There have been some sporadic, fragmentary attempts at this method, but never a systematic, consistent one. I can give you two notable examples of this method. The first is the long debate about the relation between the arrangement of sins on the *Purgatorio* and that in the *Inferno*. The second is the often mentioned similarity of the garden imagery in the Terrestrial Paradise and the Garden of Apostles on the Eighth Heaven. The last three of the nine major modes are to read one of the three canticles in contrast with the other two canticles. Many of those who have complained of the lack of unity in the Angelic Epic have been groping for one of these three methods.

Because of these many possible ways of reading the Angelic Epic, almost everyone has been able to find some sort of unity, though imperfect, in the *Divina Commedia*.

Because of the intricate trinity of the three worlds, the titanic stage for the Angelic Epic remained without being unveiled for a little over half a millennium, and its splendour buried under the ever piling heap of adulation and denunciation. This is the severe price that Dante has to pay for bestowing his great epic on the pygmies of the dull earth. The oriental sage, Mencius, was keenly aware of the heavy sacrifice a mortal soul has to pay for his greatness. Mencius says, "When Heaven singles out the man to be entrusted with Its Mandate, It humiliates him, torments him and makes him suffer in order to make him great for the great mission." Greatness is no plant to be nurtured on the soil of comfort and ease. Dante well knew this:

> ....sitting on down
> or lying under coverlet, no man comes to fame,
>
> Without which whoever consumes his life
> leaves such vestige of himself on earth
> as smoke in air or foam on water.
>
> Therefore get up, overcome your panting
> with the spirit which wins every battle
> if it does not sink with its heavy body.
> *Inf.* xxiv. 47–54

The Angelic Poet wrote his Angelic Epic with the panting and moaning of his spirit, while dragging his weary body along the dreary ways of his long exile from his home. Mencius can rightly call Dante's harsh lot of exile the worthy medium of preparation for his august angelic stature. But did he know the cruel lot which is consequent upon having attained greatness? This is not to be understood; the greatness is too great to be understood by the puny pygmies. There is even a more cruel lot than not to be understood; it is to be misunderstood. In their pitiful struggle to understand a great man. the pygmies scale down his titanic stature to their own miniature level and rejoice in the feast of butchering their titan. They should not be severely chided but tenderly forgiven because they know not what they are doing.

Getting back to the nine major ways of reading the Angelic Epic, the last way is the best one. It is to mount the ten rungs of the ladder of joy one by one, simultaneously viewing in a parallel contrast the corresponding rungs of the ladder of humility and of the ladder of pride. It is the best way because the *Paradiso* is the ladder of absolute truth and because truth is the measure of itself and its contraries. It offers the best perspective for the immortal splendor of the titanic stage for the Angelic Epic. Without further dawdling, which can only evoke Cato's stern rebuke, let us climb up the ten rungs of the angelic ladder of divine love, and "strip bare the truth and its contraries."

PART III

The Elucidation of a Solution

chapteR 4

Lesson on the Rung of Humility and Pride

The First Heaven, the First Terrace, and the Ninth Circle

WE ARE beginning the long climb up the angelic ladder of divine love and stepping on its first rung. The first rung is grounded on the active spiritual power, which is the subject for the virtue of humility and the sin of pride. The active spiritual power is the "absolute will" which Beatrice talks of on the Moon (*Par.* iv. 113). The object of this will is excellence and glory. Though the humble and the proud will alike seek excellence and glory, their difference comes with the manner of seeking them. Whereas the humble soul knows of its own powerlessness and seeks excellence in the will and power of the Creator, the proud soul dares to be like its Creator and attempts to attain excellence with its own will and power.[1]

The humble soul readily admits the will of others into the domain of its own will, but the proud soul demands to be the master of its own will and never allows the intrusion of others' will into the dominion of its own will. The contrast between the soft humble will and the hard proud will is presented by the difference of the material grounds in the three regions which constitute the first rung of the angelic ladder. The proud will is as hard as the ice of Cocytus, which has "the semblance of glass and not of water" (*Inf.* xxxii. 24). The humble will is as soft as "the eternal pearl of the moon" which receives Dante as water receives a ray of light (*Par.* ii. 34–36). The ray of divine light is the emanation of divine will. The humble will gladly receives the ray of divine light and shines like a diamond (*Par.* ii. 32–33). The proud will cannot accept the divine ray and has to freeze in darkness. On the First Terrace, the proud will is being exposed to divine light for its infusion and its frozen willfulness is being melted into a placid humbleness. The rifted rock through which Dante climbs to the First Terrace is "moving on one side and the other,/ even as a wave that recedes and draws near" (*Purg.* x. 8–9).

Cognitively viewed, the first rung of the angelic ladder is made of the power of the active intellect. The active intellect is the intuitive faculty which reflects the real and the true. For the representation of the reflective feature of the intellect, Dante employs the metaphor of a mirror. The ice of Cocytus has "the semblance of glass" but reflects nothing because it is devoid of light. The Moon is "the eternal pearl" and shines like a diamond in the reflection of divine light. It is a divine mirror for the reflection of the Trinity, the highest reality. On the First Terrace, the examples of virtues and sins are carved on marble. The penitents see their lessons in a pictorial mirror. Another feature of the intellect is its tranquility. Aristotle says that the intellectual passion is never violent like the sensitive passions. The entire lake of Cocytus is quiet and chilly. The First Terrace is more solitary than the roads in a desert (*Purg.* x. 21). The Moon is calm and placid. Humility and pride are the virtue and the sin of solitude and tranquility and alien to a gregarious atmosphere.

For a proper understanding of the Circle of pride, we

should first overcome the conventional error of seeing four Rings in it. There are not four Rings, but three Rings and one center in the Ninth Circle. You may ask what difference it would make to regard *Giudecca* as a Ring or the center. The difference is as important as the difference between a circle and a point. Let us begin with the examination of the three Rings. If you know the circumference of a circle, you can determine its center. *Giudecca* is the triple center of the three concentric Rings. If you know the nature of the three Rings, you can clarify the nature of the center of the Ninth Circle.

The three Rings represent the three grades of betrayal: *Caina* for the betrayal of family, *Antenora* for the betrayal of country, and *Tolomea* for the betrayal of friends. Betrayal is only the negative feature of pride. St. Thomas says that every act aims at good and that every evil is the negative feature of the good sought.[2] What is the positive good that the sinners of pride seek in their evil acts of rejecting their families, their countries, and their friends? We come to understand the positive aims of the sins of pride when the penitents of the First Terrace explain the nature of their sins. This is because the penitent sinners know the nature of their sins and the hardened sinners do not.

On the First Terrace, three sins of pride are distinguished and explained (*Purg.* xi. 58–136). The first sin of pride is the pride of family, the second sin the pride of talent, and the third sin the pride of power. Notice carefully the ascending order of the three sins of pride. The pride of family is dependent on the family, because it is the pride of the inheritance which comes through the family. The pride of talent is not dependent on the family. Talent is an inborn gift. The pride of power is even less dependent than the pride of talent. Power is neither inherited nor inborn, but is created by the individual. The creation of power most resembles the act of the Creator

139

because one can build up and develop one's power with one's own power. Whereas inherited fortune resides in the family and inborn talent in the man, created power rests on the friendship one cultivates. It is therefore no accident that Salvani, proud of his power, knew the importance of friends, put away all shame and became a beggar in the market-place to earn the ransom of his friend (*Purg.* xi. 133–138).

The three Rings of the Ninth Circle represent the three grades of pride. *Caina* represents the pride of the family. Cain killed his brother Abel to secure the inheritance of his family (Gen. 4). The great inheritance which Cain was anxious to secure was the blessing of his family God. Cain would not have bothered to kill Abel but for his pride in his family and his inordinate desire for the glory as the heir to the fortune and blessing of the earth. The sons of Alberti and all other sinners of *Caina* had great pride in their families and sinned in their attempt to appropriate and monopolize their family inheritance.

Antenora represents the pride of individual talent. Antenor was a Trojan who did not approve of the cause of his country in the war of Troy. He advised the return of Helen to the Greeks and finally proved the rightness of his original judgment by concluding the peace treaty with the Greeks. He was so proud of his power of judgment that he had to prove its rightness even at the price of his country's defeat. Bocca was another slave of the pride of talent (*Inf.* xxxii. 76). At the critical moment in the battle of Montaperti, he cut off the hand of the Florentine standard bearer and brought about the defeat of his country. Like Antenor, Bocca proved the excellence of his talent at the severe price of the defeat of his country.

Tolomea represents the pride of power. Ptolemy was very greedy for power (I Machabees 16:11–17). Simon who was his father-in-law and the high priest of his country was the original source of Ptolemy's power. Ptolemy invited Simon to a banquet and murdered him in order to usurp Simon's power and make himself the master of the whole country. Both Alberigo and Branca d'Oria of *Tolomea* invited to a banquet and killed their friends and relatives for the consolidation of their power. The denizens of *Tolomea* turned against the friends and benefactors who were the original source of their power in order to secure and increase their power.

The triple center of these three Rings is *Giudecca*. As the circumference of a circle emanates from its center, the three Rings reflect the triple sin of Satan. Satan is understood to imitate the Holy Trinity. How does he imitate? He imitates in sin. His sin is a triple pride and is reflected by the three Rings. The three creatures whom Satan is chewing represent the three sins of Satan's pride. In the conventional understanding, Judas is the traitor to the Lord of the heavenly empire, and Brutus and Cassius are the traitors to the Lord of the earthly empire. This conventional understanding does not fit in well with Satan's imitation of the Trinity. If Brutus and Cassius embody an identical sin, Satan becomes a symmetrical figure. The relation of the Three Person is not symmetrical, but asymmetrical. That is why Satan's three faces are all differently colored. The sins of Brutus and Cassius must be different to allow Satan's sinful imitation of the Trinity. Negatively viewed, Brutus and Cassius committed the same sin. Their sins differ in their positive nature, namely, different kinds of pride motivated Brutus and Cassius. If you know the nature of their pride, you will see Brutus belongs to *Caina*, Cassius to *Antenora*, and Judas to *Tolomea*.

For the understanding of the nature of pride in Brutus and Cassius, we have to turn to Plutarch. Plutarch tells us that Brutus and Cassius had different motives and played different roles in their conspiracy against Caesar. It was

Cassius who master-minded the entire conspiracy. Brutus did not even think of rising against Caesar until he was entreated by Cassius. Though Cassius was quite confident of his talent of intrigue and plotting, he knew that he could not overthrow Caesar's force without Brutus' prestige on his side. Brutus' motive for joining Cassius' conspiracy was not so much his love of the republican cause as his pride. Brutus came from a family which had enjoyed such a long reputation of having fought against the enemies of the Roman Republic as to be regarded as the standard-bearer of the republican cause. When Caesar assumed the dictatorship, Brutus was tormented and humiliated time and again by the accusation that he was not living up to his family tradition. Brutus often found written on his chair the agonizing message from the unknown people: "You are not a Brutus!" By the time Cassius came around to enlist Brutus' name on his side, Brutus joined the conspiracy with a great sigh of relief. It was the tormenting and humiliated pride of his family that drove Brutus into Cassius' conspiracy and forced him to draw his knife against his great friend and benefactor. Cassius master-minded his conspiracy through his pride of talent.

Judas' pride is the pride of *Tolomea*. Like Ptolemy, Judas betrayed his Lord during a feast. During the Last Supper, Judas slipped out of the gathering and made arrangement for the arrest of Christ (John 13:30). Judas' pride is the pride of power which rests on friendship. In betraying Christ, Judas did what only the close friends of Christ could do. Judas was one of the few who had an intimate knowledge of Christ and could point Him out with his kiss to the persecutors (Matt. 26:48–50). As an Apostle, Judas received from Christ one of the greatest powers a mortal soul can wield and finally turned against the original bestower of his power as Ptolemy did.

The pride of power which turns against one's friends

is far graver than the pride of family and talent. Friendship transcends the boundaries of family and country. In
Aristotle's famous definition, a friend is "another self."
To turn against one's friend is to turn against oneself. Because of this heinous nature of the pride of power, Dante
gives a special punishment to the denizens of *Tolomea*.
Their faces are turned upward and they cannot shed
their own tears:

> The very weeping there forbids them to weep,
> and the grief, finding in the eyes a stop,
> turns inward, to make anguish bite more deep.
> *Inf.* xxxiii. 94–96

Their grief gnaws inwardly into the self, as the poison of
their pride was turning against their other selves. Judas
is also given this special punishment of *Tolomea*. Unlike
Brutus and Cassius, Judas is dangling down with his head
inside one of Satan's mouths (*Inf.* xxxiv. 63–64). We can
assume that Judas cannot bend his neck and turn down
his face to shed his tears as he wishes.

Giudecca is the cumulative representation of the three
Rings. Notice the difference between the way Dante
presents the three Rings and the way he presents *Giudecca*.
In each of the three Rings, Dante talks with their
representatives to find out the nature of their sins. In
Giudecca, he does not talk with any sinners and does not
bother to explore the nature of their sins. He merely points
out the three heads of Satan and his three companions.
Through this visual representation, Dante brings together
all the sins of the three Rings on *Giudecca*. He does not
even explain Satan's carnal feast, because he has already
explained it in the episode of Count Ugolino. To understand
the nature of *Giudecca* is to recall all the things Dante has
disclosed in the three Rings. *Giudecca* condenses all the

sins of three Rings into itself. This is what I mean by the cumulative representation.

As a corollary technique of cumulative representation, Dante uses different methods of naming the three Rings and *Giudecca*. Our poet names the three Rings while he is in each of the three Rings, but does not even give the name of *Giudecca* while he is in it (*Inf.* xxxii. 59, 88; xxxiii. 124; xxxiv. 117). The names of the three Rings are a part of the explanation of the three sins of pride. That is why you do not meet Cain in *Caina*, Antenor in *Antenora* and Ptolemy in *Tolomea*. Cain, Antenor, and Ptolemy embody the sins of the three Rings, and Dante to avoid duplication does not place these three sinners in the three Rings. Dante does not name *Giudecca* while he is in it for two reasons. First, *Giudecca* need not be identified because it is cumulatively identified through cumulative representation. If Dante were to name the center of the three Rings after any one of the three companions of Satan, he would run the risk of misleading his readers to identify the nature of the center as the embodiment of the pride of that sinner and of destroying the effect of the cumulative representation. Dante gives the name of *Giudecca* only after finishing the description of *Giudecca*. He gives it when he is on the other side of the *Inferno*. The names of the three Rings and the name of *Giudecca* differ in their functions. The latter is for orientation and the former for characterization. The former is to characterize the nature of the three Rings, and the latter is to orient Dante in his spatial relation to *Giudecca*. It is because of this functional difference that the names of the three Rings are given inside the Rings and the name of *Giudecca* outside *Giudecca*, and it explains why the owners of the names of the three Rings are not mentioned in the Rings and why Judas is present in *Giudecca*.

Through cumulative representation, the sins of the

three Rings and the sins of Satan are interchangeable. Pride is Satan's sin, and every sinner of pride is an embodiment of Satan. Christ identifies Judas as a devil, *Yet one of you is a devil* (John 6:72). All the sinners of the Ninth Circle are Satan's offspring, and Judas, Cassius, and Brutus are three personifications and embodiments of Satan. St. Bernard calls the devil the king over all the sons of pride.[3] While all the sinners of the three Rings embody Satan, Satan embodies all the sins of the three Rings, the pride of family, talent, and power. In rebelling against God, Satan tried to usurp the inheritance of his family. What is the family inheritance he tried to usurp? It is the source of beatitude. It is God, Satan's Father, who has this source. Satan attempted to be the source of beatitude like his Creator. Further, Satan was proud of his talent; he was created as the greatest angel. With his talent, Satan masterminded the conspiracy against God and turned one-tenth of the angels against Him. Lastly, Satan wanted to consolidate his power by overthrowing his friend and the original bestower of his power.

With these three sins of pride, Satan imitates the Trinity. Power, wisdom, and love are the three attributes of the Three Persons. Pride of family corresponds to love, because the family is the fountain of love and because the love of the Holy Spirit is God's love of His family. We should remember Brutus' defense of his assassination of Caesar, "I loved Caesar, but I loved Rome more!" Pride of individual talent corresponds to the wisdom of the Son. Like talent, wisdom is an inborn gift. Finally, pride of power corresponds to the power of the Father. Both the divine and the human power are the powers of creation. The colors of Satan's three faces further characterize and explain his sinful imitation of the Trinity. The face from whose mouth Brutus hangs is black (*Inf.* xxxiv. 45). Satan has burned and scorched himself in hatred. The face from whose mouth Cassius hangs, is of a feeble color between white and yellow (*Inf.* xxxiv. 43). This feeble color represents Satan's folly and stupidity with which he ruined himself like Cassius. The face whose mouth is chewing up Judas is fiery red (*Inf.* xxxiv. 39). This color stands for the fire of the power which is burning for self-consumption. All these three attributes are working for the final end of self-destruction. Satan is gnawing into the flesh of his own offspring; all three of them took their own lives through the sin of pride. To complete Satan's inverted imitation of the Trinity, Dante places Cassius on the right side of Judas (*Inf.* xxxiv. 43, 67). The Son of God sits on the right hand of the Father; Cassius is hanging on the right side of Judas.

While perdition is the perverted imitation of the Trinity, purgation is the true imitation of the Trinity. This was one of the prevalent ideas of the medieval era. *Giudecca* is the bottom of perdition and consummates the sinful imitation of the Holy Trinity. The beginning of purgation must then be the beginning of the virtuous imitation of the Trinity, the fountain and exemplar of all virtues. This is represented by the three steps at the bottom of the *Purgatorio* proper:

> The first step which we reached
> > was of white marble, so polished and smooth
> > that my true image was mirrored in it.

> The second was darker than purplish black,
> > of a rough and burned stone,
> > cracked through its length and across.

> The third which rises on top
> > seemed of porphyry, as flaming red
> > as blood that spurts from a vein.
> > > *Purg.* ix. 94–102

In the conventional understanding, the three steps are taken for the symbols of the three steps of penance: contrition, confession, and satisfaction. That is, the cracked step stands for the contrite heart, the polished step for confession, and the flaming step for satisfaction. This interpretation has one irredeemable blemish. The blemish is the order of the three steps. The order of the three steps of penance are contrition, confession, and satisfaction. It is mandatory that the sinner be contrite before confession. This mandatory rule is violated if the three steps of the First Terrace are taken for the three steps of penance because the polished step of confession precedes the cracked step of contrition.

The three steps represent the penitent who prostrates himself for the beginning of the true imitation of the Trinity. Try to imagine the three persons of the fiendish trinity prostrating themselves on the ground and to correlate the colors of Satan's three faces to the colors of the three steps: the white face tinged with yellow to the white, polished step; the fiery face to the black, cracked step; the black face to the flaming step. When our pilgrim reaches the bottom of the *Inferno,* his soul reaches the nadir of perdition, and becomes the most perverted image of the Trinity. When he flings himself down at the angel's feet and strikes his breasts three times, he is reciting the *Confiteor* and acknowledges his guilt: *mea culpa, mea culpa, mea maxima culpa* (through my fault, through my fault, through my most grievous fault) (*Purg.* ix. 109–111). The sinner who reaches *Giudecca* knows nothing but his excellence, and the penitent who is about to begin the works of purgation is aware of nothing but his guilt and sin. The three steps of the First Terrace depict the state of the soul which has gone through the conversion from the Satanical defiance of pride to the humble recognition of one's misery.

Ignorance and stupidity in pride turn into knowledge and wisdom in humility; Satan's whitish and yellowish face changes to the white polished step. Hatred in pride turns into love in humility; Satan's black face scorched in hatred changes to the red step flaming in love. The self-consuming power in pride becomes the recognition of one's powerlessness in humility; Satan's fiery face has burned itself and become the cracked black step. The cross which is formed by the crack of the middle step is the trace of the self-crucifixion of Judas. Judas is dangling down with his head in Satan's middle mouth and looks as if he were being crucified.

As the three persons of the fiendish trinity cumulatively represent the last step on the ladder of pride, so the three steps of the *Purgatorio* proper collectively represent the first step on the ladder of humility. That is, the three steps exemplify the three essential features of purgation on the First Terrace. On the first of the three steps, Dante can see his own image because it is well polished. One of the favorite themes of St. Bernard's eloquent sermons was: "Know thyself." He told his monks to know that they were the souls made in the image of God but separated from Him by sin, ignorance, and wretchedness.[4] Not to know the true destiny of one's soul is to mistake oneself for a fellow of cattle or a fellow of demons.[5] By joining the cattle and the demons, St. Bernard preaches, we try to seek our glories in the transitory, worthless, devilish things and cheat ourselves out of the eternal glory. St. Bernard concludes, "It is therefore necessary to know both what thou art and what thou art not of thyself."[6]

The Angelic Poet eloquently elucidates the destiny of the human souls through the metaphor of birds and butterflies:

> O proud Christians, miserable and weary,
>   who, sick in your mental vision,
>   put your trust in backward steps,

Do you not see that you are insects
   born to form the angelic butterfly
   which flies without defense to judgment?

Why does your vain pride soar so high,
   since you are imperfect and incomplete,
   like worms which remain undeveloped?

Purg. x. 121–129

Satan is the biggest worm which has refused to grow into
an angelic butterfly. His hideous sail-like wings have no
plumes (*Inf.* xxxiv. 49). He has mistaken the initial point
of his destiny for its final terminus. He was created the
greatest angel, but has become the biggest animal. The
Ninth Circle is the pen of worms and fiends, frogs and
storks (*Inf.* xxxii. 31–36).

Dante shows in his dream of Lucia what it is like to be
fully developed into an angelic butterfly. Lady Lucia
swoops down in the form of an eagle "with golden feathers
and wings outspread," snatches our poet and soars up into
the fiery zone (*Purg.* ix. 13–42). This dream, among other
things, foretells Dante's flight to the *Paradiso*. At the
beginning of his flight to the First Heaven, Dante compares
Beatrice to an eagle (*Par.* i. 48). The vision of the eagle is
the vision of the heavenly destiny of the human soul. It is
this image of the superhuman destiny of himself that Dante
sees on the first of the three steps. The recognition of this
image surpasses the natural intellect and is possible only
with grace.

On the second step, the step of power, Dante sees his
powerlessness. The more willful the sinner of pride becomes, the more impotent he becomes. St. Bernard says
that to assert one's proud will as the law to oneself in
defiance of God's law and will is to impose an unbearable
burden upon oneself.[7] The proud soul sinks to the bottom

of the *Inferno* and freezes himself into the ice of Cocytus with the weight of his own pride. We crucify not only Christ but ourselves with our own pride. By nailing ourselves down on the cross of pride, we become the impotent victims of our own defiant will. No mortal creature has the power to wrench himself out of the tightly frozen pride. It is only with the power of grace that one can rise from sin and perform the works of purgation.[8] Lady Lucia is the power of grace that lifts up the sinner from his sin and sets him on the way of purgation. Dante soars into the air with her like an eagle: *It is he that giveth strength to the weary, and increaseth force and might to them . . . Youths shall faint . . . But they who hope in the Lord shall renew their strength. They shall take wings as eagles; they shall run and not be weary. . . .*(Isa. 40:29–31).

On the third step, the step of love, Dante sees his love of God flaming red. Pride knows no love but only hate. Satan is having a feast of hatred with the flesh of his offspring. No mortal soul can love God without first receiving love from God.[9] It is always God who can and does take the initiative in establishing the love relation between Him and His creature. Grace is the gift of the Holy Spirit, and the Spirit is the love of God. By receiving the grace of the Spirit, one can begin to love. Lady Lucia appears in the form of the eagle. The Eagle is the symbol of the Holy Spirit which Dante extensively and consistently uses in the *Divina Commedia*. We will soon encounter a few more examples of this symbol. In the grace of the Eagle, Dante's self-consuming hatred turns into the love of God.

It is thus the Eagle of the Holy Spirit that lifts the soul out of its frozen will exemplified by the Satanical trinity and enables it to prostrate itself like the three steps before the angel. The power of Satan's pride is reflected in his three faces and three companions, and the power of grace is manifested in the three steps. The power of grace which is manifested in the three steps is further manifested in the power, wisdom, and love of the penitents. They are bending down their stiff necks by pressing them down with heavy stones. It takes indeed a great will power to assert one's will, but a far greater power to bend it down. At this point, we should avoid one grave error which conventional understanding has imposed on the medium of purgation. It has been a prevalent opinion that the medium of purgation is the sin that is being purged. For example, the stones which the penitents of the First Terrace are carrying over their heads are the symbol of pride and its weight. We cannot allow this interpretation because sin can never be the remedy to itself. In the third chapter of this book, we argued that sin is its own reward and punishment in the *Inferno*. If the stones were to represent the nature of pride, Dante would place them on the heads of the sinners of the Ninth Circle. As we climb the angelic ladder, we will try to show that no medium of purgation has sin as its component. In the meantime, let us remember that sin is not and cannot be its own cure any more than a disease can be its own medicine.

The important feature of the purgational medium is not so much the weight of the stones as the bending of the heads and necks. It is precisely the first step of humility that St. Benedict recommends to his monks in his Rule: "to show humility of heart and behaviour by always having the head bowed and the eyes downcast."[10] The weight of the stone is not the weight of pride; the weight of sin can never bend the will to God, though it can sink the sinner to the bottom of Hell. The power of the penitents is exemplified not only in their capacity to bend their necks, but in their capacity to walk. Whereas the proud will cannot budge a single step from its frozen pride, the humble will can walk toward God.

The wisdom of the penitents is exemplified in their knowledge of the nature of pride. As we have already seen, the Ninth Circle does not explain the positive good which the sin of pride seeks, but the penitents can explain the cause of their pride. To know sin is to know its cause. They further know that the glories which pride of family, talent, or power seeks are empty glories and a breath of wind in the span of eternity (*Purg.* xi. 91–120). The earthly glories are the foul vapors of the world (*Purg.* xi. 30). We can now see the meaning of the dark vapors which wrap up the Ninth Circle (*Inf.* xxi. 34–39). The dark vapors are the empty glories which the proud mistake for the true glories just as Dante mistakes the giants for towers (*Inf.* xxxi. 30). With their knowledge of the transitoriness of the earthly glories, the penitents can now seek and love the true glory. The spiritual food from God is the true glory and the object of the penitents' love.

These three attributes of power, wisdom, and love as symbolized by the three steps and manifested in the penitents are the effects and works of one virtue: humility, the foundation of all virtues. The virtue of humility lays down the mortal's impotent will before the all-powerful will of God. This surrender of the human will is to acknowledge the Lordship of the Lord from Whose power comes every perfect gift and without Whose power no eternal glory is possible. The Lordship of the Lord is sung in the Ambrosian hymn, *Te Deum Laudamus*, which greets the entrance of the penitent into the First Terrace:

We praise Thee, O God; we acknowledge Thee to be the Lord.
Thee, the Father everlasting, all the earth doth worship.
To Thee all the angels, to Thee the heavens, and all the powers,
To Thee the cherubim and seraphim cry out unceasingly:

Holy, holy, holy, Lord God of hosts.

Full are the heavens and the earth of the majesty of Thy glory.

Thee, the glorious choir of the apostles,

Thee, the admirable company of the prophets,

Thee, the white-robed army of the martyrs doth praise.

Thee, the holy Church throughout the world doth confess,

The Father of infinite majesty.

Thine adorable, true, and only Son.

And the Holy Spirit the Paraclete.

Thou, O Christ, art the King of glory.

Thou art the everlasting Son of the Father.

Thou, having taken upon Thee to deliver man, didst not disdain the Virgin's womb.

Thou, having overcome the sting of death, hast opened to believers the kingdom of heaven.

Thou sittest at the right hand of God, in the glory of the Father.

Thou, we believe, art the Judge to come.

We beseech Thee, therefore, to help Thy servants whom Thou hast redeemed with Thy precious blood.

Make them to be numbered with Thy saints in glory everlasting.

O Lord, save Thy people, and bless Thine inheritance.

And govern them, and exalt them for ever.

Day by day, we bless Thee.

And we praise Thy name for ever; yea, for ever and for ever.

Vouchsafe, O Lord, this day, to keep us without sin.

Have mercy on us, Lord; have mercy on us.

Let Thy mercy, O Lord, be upon us; as we have hoped in Thee.

In Thee, O Lord, have I hoped: let me never be confounded.

(*The New Roman Missal*, pp. 1836–1837)

This is the Ambrosian hymn, which praises the majesty and glory of the Father, His Son, and His Spirit. To be proud is to be intoxicated and blinded with the paltry glory of the earth. To come to know the majesty and glory of God before which all earthly glories become pale and dim is the first step on the way to humility. One can be frozen in the glory of dust by becoming the master of one's will in defiance of God's will or become a partaker of His glory by sacrificing one's will to the divine will. By reciting the Lord's Prayer, the penitents are offering their will as their first sacrifice to God:

> May the peace of Thy kingdom come to us,
>   for we can do nothing by ourselves
>   with all our thought, unless it comes.

> Just as the angels sacrifice their will
>   to Thee, singing hosannas,
>   so may men do theirs.

> *Purg.* xi. 7–12

The First Heaven shows how God raises the weak human will in glory and power. The humble will joyfully and gracefully accepts the will of others like the everlasting pearl of the Moon which receives Dante "as water does a ray of light, remaining undisturbed" (*Par.* ii. 34–36). The essence of a humble will is embodied in the episodes of the two nuns who could not keep their vows (*Par.* iii. 97–123). The two episodes are one story, or rather show the two aspects of one humble will. Piccarda tells Dante how the force of evil made her break her vow. She also tells him how the constant will of Constance held fast to the object of her love even after her sacred veil was defiled against her will. Piccarda speaks of her demerit and the merit of Constance. To admit the weakness of oneself and praise the firmness of others is a sign of humility. When Piccarda begins to talk of Constance, she says that her misfortune and demerit can be applied to Constance. We can expect that the merit and virtue she tells of Constance are also her merit and virtue. Piccarda ran away while yet a child for the sacred marriage with the Holy Spouse and succumbed like a child to the cruel force that stripped her of the sacred veil.

After the discourse with Piccarda, Beatrice goes into a long explanation on the nature of the will (*Par.* iv. 71–114). She distinguishes two features in the will. What Beatrice calls "the absolute will" is the will of choice and decision. What she refers to as "the other" will is the executive will. The former is the will of the spirit and the intellect, and the latter is the will of the irascible. The former makes decision and choice, and the latter executes and implements the decision of the former. The shortcomings and failure of Piccarda and Constance lay in their executive will. They could not overcome adverse circumstances and could not implement the decision of their absolute will.

Their virtue was their humble absolute will. The absolute will is the innermost sanctuary of man which no external force can invade or violate and which only God and the self can have access to.[11] Because the absolute will is the inviolable sphere, Constance could maintain her devotion and attachment to God even after she was dragged away from the convent. Because humility and pride are the virtue and the sin of the innermost sanctuary of the absolute will, the atmosphere of tranquility and solitude pervades both the Moon and the Ninth Circle. The solitude of the Ninth Circle reflects fiendish defiance, and the tranquility of the Moon child-like submission. Notice the difference between Bocca's defiant will and Piccarda's lowly will. While Piccarda calmly admits her failure, Bocca will not identify himself even when Dante threatens to pluck his hair (*Inf.* xxxii. 100–102). St. Thomas says that the main feature of the religious vow is to lay down the will before God as an offering.[12] To lay down one's will before God and live in accordance with His almighty will is to become a child. A child has no will of its own. To become a child is the first requisite step for entering the kingdom of God.

On the rung of humility, our pilgrim himself becomes a child. When he is snatched up to the zone of fire by Lucia, he compares himself to the startled baby, Achilles, who was carried in his mother's arms from Chiron to Scyros (*Purg.* ix. 34–42). He behaves like a child and is treated like one in the First Heaven. Caught between two equally attractive questions, our baby-like pilgrim cannot make up his mind about which question he should first put to Beatrice (*Par.* iv. 1–12). Beatrice is amused and smiles at his "child-like thought" (*Par.* iii. 25–27).

Dante is very cruel in the Circle of pride. The cruel Dante coils Bocca's hair on his hand and threatens to pluck it in order to force the willful sinner to identify himself (*Inf.* xxxii. 97–105). In *Tolomea*, where the sinners do not even have the comfort of freely shedding tears, the merciless Dante induces Friar Alberigo to speak by the fraudulent promise to remove the icicles from his eyes (*Inf.* xxiii. 109–117). After hearing Alberigo's pitiful story, the pitiless Dante ruthlessly ignores his plea: "But reach out your hand, open my eyes" (*Inf.* xxxiii. 148). He is not only cruel to Alberigo, but justifies and praises himself for being rude to him: "to be rude to him was courtesy" (*Inf.* xxxiii. 150).

How should we take Dante's malicious delight in his cruelty and his self-righteousness? St. Bernard says that the proud can never have compassion for the misery of their fellow creatures. Why? The proud soul revels in the delusion of his own excellence and knows nothing of his misery. St. Bernard repeats time and again that we can come to know the misery of others and have compassion for them only by knowing our own misery.[13] This is why God took on the flesh and experienced the wretched state of humanity. If we do not know our own misery and remain intoxicated with our own excellence, St. Bernard says, we not only can take no compassion for our neighbors but have contempt on them for their misery, praying like the proud Pharisee: *"O God, I thank Thee that I am not like the rest of them."*

When a proud man takes interest in the misery and fault of other people, he takes others' faults and failings as a medium of illuminating and magnifying his excellence. A proud man lives in the pride of himself and in the contempt of others. Pride and contempt are the only motives with which Dante seeks out the sinners and wants to hear their episodes. One can become even so proud as to show no contempt, that is, to hold the faults and failings of others beneath his contempt. This is the highest peak of pride which Dante reaches at *Giudecca*. He does not bother to talk with the sinners and find out the nature of their sins in *Giudecca*, but merely looks and passes.

Dante's dreadful pride and cold heart at *Giudecca* reflect the bottom of perdition to which Satan has sunk. Compared with Dante's Satan, Milton's Satan is a childish devil. Milton's Satan bewails to his cohorts and reviles against the Creator. One who has reached the apex of pride knows of neither praise nor blame, because he holds the whole world beneath his contempt. To revile against someone is to pay him a great deal of respect; an insignificant, worthless creature is never taken as a target of denunciation. To express one's grief to someone is also to hold him in great respect; you disclose your grief only to those who you believe can understand your agony and share it with you. Dante's Satan weeps but bewails to no one. He does not express his sorrow to mortal creatures lest they may presume to understand the nature of his sorrow. *There is no sorrow like unto mine.* The sorrow and agony which are the consequences of his pride become the source of his pride. Thus Satan has become sufficient to himself in his pride and is the alpha and omega of his fiendish bliss. This is the apex of the disunity of sin; Satan knows and needs nothing but deadly silence and complete isolation from all other sinners. Bewailing and reviling are below the majesty and dignity of the king of all sins. Dante accomplishes with silence what Milton can never expect to achieve with torrents of eloquence.

The proud will sinks to the bottom of the world, but the humble will is raised to the highest Heaven. Satan's will and Piccarda's will constitute the two opposite extreme ends in the spectrum of the will power. This is not only to say that Satan secured the mastery of his will in defiance against God and Piccarda obediently laid down her will in her humble trust of God. Whereas Piccarda had no executive will to keep her sacred vow, Satan had a strong executive will as well in executing his conspiracy against God. Piccarda is the quintessence of the humble absolute will; she embodies a pure absolute will with no adornment.

While the proud will sinks with its own momentum to the center whither "all weights are drawn," the humble will is raised by the almighty will to the eternal feast on the highest Heaven (*Inf.* xxxii. 74; *Par.* iv. 28–36). The Emperor of Hell scatters all the proud with his power of repulsion and freezes them with the wind of hatred; the Emperor of Heaven brings all the humble into one body and quickens them with His eternal breath of love, *Inf.* xxxiv. 49–52; *Par.* ii. 121–148, iv. 28–36). While the *Inferno* is the discord of many wills, the *Paradiso* is the concord in one will:

> Rather it is the essence of the blessed state
> to hold ourselves within the divine will
> so that our wills are themselves made one.

Thus wherever we may be from threshold to
    threshold
      throughout this kingdom pleases all the realm
      as it does the King who bends our wills to His.

And His will is our peace;
      it is that sea to which all moves
      that He and nature create.

Par. iii. 79–87

While the proud will sinks to the carnal repast of Satanical hatred, the humble will is raised to the spiritual feast of divine love. This is the main theme on the first rung of the angelic ladder. Dante presents Piccarda as the symbolic medium for the elucidation of the humility of Christ. The humility of Christ begins with His Incarnation and culminates in His Passion. As Piccarda suffered all the violence with no resistance, so Christ subjected Himself with no resistence to spitting, slashing, and mocking. If He had wanted to resist the persecutors, He could have marshalled more than twelve legions of angels (Matt. 26:53). It is through His suffering that He wished to show us how to sacrifice our will in the infinite trust of the almighty will of the Father. It takes the power of the absolute humble will to bear all the sufferings and violence with no resistance. Only when one knows the impotence of one's own weak will and only when one believes in the omnipotence of the divine will, can one entrust everything to the will of God and bear all iniquities with no resistance. The virtue of humility in which one leaves, in the infinite resignation, everything to God's will is the first lesson Christ wished to show us through His Passion. With absolute trust in the will of the Father, he remained obedient unto death: *If it is possible, let this cup pass away from me; yet not as I will but as thou willest* (Matt. 26:39).

Because Piccarda appears as the symbolic medium for the elucidation of Christ's humility, she disappears singing *Ave Maria* (Par. iii. 122). *Ave Maria* is the angelic salutation which announced the Incarnation of Christ. Christ's humility begins with His birth and culminates in His death. I cannot properly explain His humility without resorting to the Pauline eloquence:

Yours is to be the same mind which Christ showed. His nature is, from the first, divine, and yet he did not see, in the rank of Godhead, a prize to be coveted; He dispossessed himself, took the nature of a slave, fashioned in the likeness of man, and presented himself to us in human form; and then he lowered his own dignity, accepted an obedience which brought him to death, death on a cross (Phil. 2:5–9).

Besides explaining the humility of Christ, this passage gives an eloquent elucidation of Satan's incarnation at the center of Hell. While Christ in humility dispossessed Himself of His divinity, Satan in pride tried to invest himself with the privilege of divinity, namely, to be the source of his own beatitude. Christ in humility came down to earth and took on flesh, and Satan in pride also came down to the bottom of the earth and put on flesh. While Christ gave up the dignity of being the Son of God in His Incarnation, Satan gave up the dignity of being the highest angel in his incarnation. As Christ's humility culminates in His Crucifixion, so does Satan's pride in his crucifixion.

On reaching the center of Hell, Virgil points out Satan to Dante by singing *Vexilla Regis prodeunt inferni*. Except the last word, *inferni*, this is the first line of the hymn the Holy Church sings in memory and praise of the Crucifixion after setting up anew the cross on the stripped altar in the evening of Good Friday. The hymn of Good Friday is as follows:

The Elucidation of a Solution

The royal banners now unfurled,
  The mystic cross illumines the world,
For life the sting of death hath borne,
  And death of all its poison shorn.

Thereupon with steel of cruel spear,
  His side is pierced, whence there appear
Of blood and water hallowed streams,
  To cleanse the souls He now redeems.

Hereon fulfilled is David's word,
  That wandering nations deeply stirred,
When crying in prophetic strain,
  "The Lord our God from tree doth reign."

O comely tree! thou radiant bride!
  By kingly purple sanctified,
Thou chosen from a high-born race,
  God's hallowed members to embrace.

O happy tree! to thee doth cling
  The sinful world's redeeming King,
Thou, balance, where His body lies,
  To snatch from hell its stolen prize.

O cross, our only hope, all hail!
  This passion-tide, thy balm exhale:
In loving hearts, augment thy grace,
  The sinner's stains entire efface.

O Trinity, Thou loving fount,
  To praise Thee every spirit mount!
The cross's victory to those who share,
  O grant reward without compare.

Amen.
(*The New Roman Missal*, pp. 490–491)

With three sinners dangling from his three mouths, Satan imitates the scene on Calvary where Christ was crucified between two thieves. While "the mystic cross illumines the world," Satan's cross darkens the whole kingdom of sin. Christ bears the sting of death for life.* It was on the eve of His Crucifixion that Christ instituted the Holy Eucharist. In this sacrament, Christ feeds His faithful with His flesh and blood: *I am the bread of life . . . I am the living bread that has come down from heaven . . . and the bread that I will give is my flesh for the life of the world . . . unless you eat the flesh of the Son of Man and drink his blood, you shall not have life in you* (John 6:48–54).

St. Thomas calls the Holy Eucharist the sacrament of all sacraments.[14] All other sacraments prepare for and end in the Holy Communion which gives life to the mortal soul. The institution of the Eucharist and the Crucifixion are integral features of one momentous miracle which saves man from death. It is the same body of Christ which was given in the Last Supper and which was delivered up for the Crucifixion. By dying on the cross, the Son of Man becomes the Paschal Lamb who takes away the sins of the world and delivers the sinful man from the poison and sting of death. By instituting the Holy Eucharist, the Son of God becomes the bread and wine that gives life to the mortal soul. Fully knowing the integral relation of the Crucifixion and the Last Supper, Satan imitates not only the scene of the Crucifixion but that of the Last Supper.

What is the nature of the Satanical carnal feast? The answer lies in the episode of Count Ugolino (*Inf.* xxxiii. 1–75). Count Ugolino was locked up with his four sons in a prison and left to starvation. The sons in whose faces he

---

* Satan's inverted imitation of the Crucifixion can be described by the inversion of *Vexilla Regis prodeunt*. This is intended and indicated by the addition of *inferni* to *Vexilla Regis prodeunt*.

could see his own image offered their flesh for the father to eat. Count Ugolino restrained his hunger for a few days. On the fourth day, one of his sons died, saying: "My father! why don't you help me?" The other three sons all died one after another on the following two days. After groping over the bodies of his sons, going blind and calling his sons, he started eating their flesh: "Then fasting had more power than grief" (*Inf.* xxxiii. 75).

Compare this episode with the scene of the Last Supper. Christ offers His flesh and blood to His children, and Ugolino's sons offer themselves to their father for food. Ugolino is too powerless to do anything for his sons locked up in the prison, and Christ releases His children from the prison of death with His death and feeds them with His body and blood. Ugolino and his children are the victims on the cross of pride, and Christ and His children are the lambs on the cross of humility. The penitents in Purgatory are crucifying their will on the cross of humility. They drag their weary feet with heavy stones on their shoulders in imitation of Christ who carried His cross on His shoulders to Calvary.

The prison in which Count Ugolino was locked is the symbol of the proud will. The proud man locks himself in the prison of his defiant will by alienating himself from the bounty of grace. The proud will has to freeze into itself like the sinners in Cocytus and feed on itself. This is the feast of pride, the feast of sorrow and death. This is the feast of self-destruction; all the three companions of Satan took their own lives in the sin of their pride. The penitents are releasing their will from the tightly frozen ice of pride and offering it in humility for the food that gives the life eternal. They sing the sacrifice of their will and pray for the divine food (*Purg.* xi. 10–15). The humble will is the first step on the way to the joy and glory of the heavenly feast. Christ not only gives the Last Supper, but shows how to participate in it through His Passion: *Though he was crucified through weakness, yet he lives through the power of God. Yes, we also are weak in him yet we shall live with him through the power of God* (2 Cor. 13:4). Dante shows in Piccarda how the humble will crucified in weakness lives through the power of the Father, and in Satan how the strong will crucified on the cross of pride is strangled and frozen in its own defiant power.

The virtue of Christ in which Piccarda shines on the Moon and the sin of Satan in which the proud are frozen in Cocytus are elucidated by the whip and the bridle of the First Terrace. The examples of pride are given in thirteen tercets (*Purg.* xii. 25–63). These thirteen tercets consist of three groups of four tercets each and one concluding tercet. Each tercet begins with *Vedea* (I saw) in the first group, with *O* (Oh) in the second group, and with *Mostrava* (It showed) in the third group. *Vedea, O,* and *Mostrava* are brought together in the last concluding tercet:

> I saw (*Vedea*) Troy in ashes and in ruins.
> Oh (*O*) Ilion! thee how base and vile
> it showed (*Mostrava*)—the sculpture which there is
> discerned. *Purg. xii.* 61–63

In arranging the examples of pride, Dante employs the technique of cumulative representation which he uses in the construction of the Circle of pride. As he brings together the three Rings at the center of the Ninth Circle, so he gathers together the three groups of four tercets into the concluding tercet. In this cumulative arrangement of the examples of pride, he uses *Vedea, O,* and *Mostrava* because pride is the sin of the active intellect. The active intellect is the power for intuitive knowledge, while the passive intellect is the faculty for discursive knowledge. While one has to reason from premise to conclusion in discursive knowledge, one intuitively sees the objects of cognition in intuitive knowledge. In intuitive understanding, one sees the object and the object shows itself and nothing intervenes between the subject that sees and the object that shows itself except the wonder of intuitive vision. Thus *Vedea, O* and *Mostrava* are the appropriate words in describing the vision of the sin of the intuitive intellect.

The three examples of humility begin with the scene of the Annunciation (*Purg.* x. 34–93). Dante says that *Ecce ancilla Dei* (*Behold the handmaid of the Lord*) seems to be written in the posture of St. Mary which is sculptured on the bank of the First Terrace. The humility of the Virgin Mary lies in her obedient sacrifice of her virginity for the Miraculous Conception of the Son. *Fiat mihi secundum verbum tuum* (*Be it done unto me according to thy word*). With these simple words, the Eternal Virgin submitted herself to the divine mission. The Virgin Mary is the sacred vessel and mirror which reflects the virtues of the Holy Trinity. Her humility is indeed great, but only reflects a far greater humility, the humility of the king of heaven who did not disdain to be conceived in the human womb. This humility of Christ was first recognized by the mother of God, who said to Elizabeth, *He has gracefully looked upon the lowliness of His handmaid* (Luke 1:48).

The examples of King David and Emperor Trajan are meant to further explain the humility of the king of heaven. King David is mindless of the dignity and authority of being a king in his joyful and humble dance before the tabernacle. King David stands for Christ and the tabernacle for the Virgin Mary. Mary has been honored as the tabernacle of God in her universal Church.[15] She was conceived with no stain of original sin. God preserved His Tabernacle from the stain of sin by the Immaculate Conception. Christ comes on the earth as the heir to the throne of King David. *He shall sit upon the throne of David and upon his kingdom* (Isa. 9:7). At the Annunciation, the Angel Gabriel foretold to Mary the destiny of the child she was to conceive: *He shall be great, and men will know him for the Son of the most High; the Lord God will give him the throne of his father David* (Luke 1:32). The humble joy of King David before the tabernacle represents Christ's humble joy in the womb of the Virgin Mother.

When Emperor Trajan was about to go off on an important expedition, a poor widow begged him to avenge the death of her son before his departure. Trajan tried to persuade her to wait for his return from the expedition. The poor widow would not give in, and the following dialogue takes place between the Emperor and the widow:

> "My lord, suppose you do not come back?" And he,
>   "Whoever takes my place will do it." She, "Of what use
>   is another's virtue, if you forget your own?"
>
> Whereupon he: "Now be comforted;
>   I must do my duty before I leave.
>   Justice demands it, and pity makes me stay."
>
> *Purg.* x. 88–93

The Virgin Mother is the second Eve, and Eve means the mother of all men. *The name which Adam gave his wife was Eve* (Life) *because she was the mother of all living men* (Gen. 3:20). Virgin Mother is not only the mother of Christ, but the mother of all men. Humanity has been killed through the temptation of Satan. *Death came into the world through sin.* The poor widow's entreaty to Trajan stands for the plea of the universal Mother for the vengeance of a spiritually dead son. The Incarnation and the Crucifixion were not the only possible means for the salvation of man. The omnipotent God could have employed any other means for the justification of the sinful

166

man, but chose to become the Paschal Lamb for the remission of man's sin. This personal sacrifice on the part of Christ is echoed in the poor widow's words: "Of what use / is another's virtue . . ." Christ paves the way of salvation with His own virtues. *I am the way, the truth, and the life.*

The two main reasons for the Incarnation are justice and mercy. Christ fulfills the vengeance God promised Eve against Satan. *Now is the judgment of the world; now will the prince of the world be cast out* (John 12:31). By this act of justice Christ restores to God the human race which has been lost to the dominion of Satan. Justice alone does not entitle the sinful man to the grace that has been brought through the suffering of Christ. It is through mercy that Christ offers Himself as the ransom. These two motives of the Incarnation are reflected in Emperor Trajan's words: "Justice demands it, and pity makes me stay." Compared with the cosmic mission which is entrusted to the Son of God, the salvation of mankind is insignificant just as the poor widow's plea is trivial in comparison with the imperial expedition of Trajan. It is only because of His humility that Christ took on the flesh for the salvation of man.

Let me explain the simple rule governing the function of the bridles and the whips of the seven Terraces. The examples of a vice always reflect the design of the Circle to which the vice belongs. On each of the Seven Planets, Dante sings one virtue of one of the Three Persons of the Trinity. It is this divine virtue, which a virtue of the Virgin Mother reflects as the first of the examples of the whip on each of the seven Terraces. The examples of virtue which follow the first example elucidate the divine virtue reflected in the Holy Queen's example. The bridles constitute the traces of sins which the penitents cleanse, and the whips constitute the images of the Holy Trinity which they imitate. The Trinity is the ultimate source of all virtues and the ultimate object for imitation in the way of truth. The purgation is a long course of imitating the virtues of the Trinity which are represented on the seven Planets and reflected on the whips of the seven Terraces. This is why the three steps of the First Terrace represent the initial stage in the imitation of the Trinity and why the penitent is greeted on entering the First Terrace by the hymn *Te Deum Laudamus*, which sings the majesty and glory of the Trinity. It is through the imitation of the virtues of the Trinity that the penitent becomes like God.

It is the humility of the Son toward the Father that our Angelic Poet sings on the first rung of the angelic ladder of divine love. *Learn of me, because I am meek and humble* (Matt. 11:29). It is the humble and the poor in spirit that the Father raises to the heavenly glory and majesty.

chapter 5

Lesson on the Rung of Mercy and Envy

The Second Heaven, the Second Terrace and the Eighth Circle

On the second rung of the angelic ladder, the power of the soul which constitutes this rung is the passive spirit or intellect. While the active spirit is primarily concerned with one's own glory and misery, the passive spirit is more interested in others' glory and misery. Envy takes delight in others' misfortune and grief in their fortune, and mercy rejoices in others' fortune and grieves in their misfortune.[1] On the Second Terrace, Sapia explains the nature of her sin: "I was much happier at others' harm than at my own good fortune" (*Purg.* xiii. 110–111). Guido del Duca says that the flame of envy at the happiness of other people used to suffuse his face with "lividness" (*Purg.* xiv. 82–84).

The "livid" stone which constitutes the Second Terrace represents the heartless heart of envy (*Purg.* xiii. 9). The penitents are dressed in the cloaks whose color is "not different from the hue of stone" (*Purg.* xiii. 48). The *Malebolge* is a monstrous livid stone whose ten pouches hold the envious sinners (*Inf.* xviii. 1–3). Dante descends to the *Malebolge* on the back of Geryon, the image of fraud (*Inf.* xvii. 7). How is envy related to fraud? Envy is the

motive force of fraud. Aristotle says that one may do evil
out of passion or out of guile.[2] The intellect is overpowered
in the act of passion, but takes a cool command in the act
of fraud and guile. Envy is the motive for calculating and
executing the evil for others.

Aristotle says that guileful people are given to secrecy
and plotting while passionate people are always open.[3] The
envious seldom reveal their malicious will. Geryon hides
his poisonous tail behind the face of an honest person (*Inf.*
xvii. 10). One of the sinners in the *Malebolge* says that the
devil is the father of lies (*Inf.* xxiii. 144). Falsification and
dissimulation are the essence of the devil who is the father
of all envy. *When he tells a lie he speaks from his very
nature, for he is a liar and the father of lies* (John 8:44).

Mercy loves secrecy as much as envy. When the intention of doing good is proclaimed and the works of mercy
are displayed on the street, it is hypocrisy and not mercy.
Christ commands us to do all works of mercy in secrecy:
*Therefore when thou givest alms, do not sound a trumpet
before thee, as the hypocrites do in the synagogues and
streets, in order that they may be honored by men . . .
But when thou givest alms do not let thy left hand know
what thy right hand is doing* (Matt. 6:2–3). When Justinian
talks of Romeo's merciful works on Mercury, he says that
the entire world did not notice the virtue deeply hidden in
Romeo's heart (*Par.* vi. 140).

Secrecy and concealment characterize the second rung of
the angelic ladder. The envious are buried in the deep evil
pouches of the Eighth Circle. The penitents are not placed
on an open spot but in a corner of the Second Terrace.
Dante and Virgil encounter them after walking about a
mile. Even when Virgil points them out, Dante notices
them only after a long gaze (*Purg.* xiii. 43). The blessed of
the Second Heaven come out like a throng of fish in a fish-

pool to meet Dante (*Par.* v. 100). Mercury is a fish-pool
veiled and hidden under the rays of the Sun (*Par.* v. 129).

St. Thomas explains the origin of envy: envy is the sin
of the devil which follows his sin of pride.[4] Having lost
their good through pride, the wicked angels become envious
of the good of man. Being sheer spirits, the fallen angels
could not turn to the corporeal good with which man was
blessed.[5] They decided to destroy the corporeal good of
man. The ten evil pouches of the *Malebolge* are the ten
dominions of evil into which the devil seduces human souls.
At this point, we may ask St. Thomas whether the origin
of envy in man can be accounted for in the same way it is
explained in the fallen angels.

The Angelic Doctor's explanation of the cause of envy
cannot work very well for the origin of human envy.
Whereas fallen angel could not turn to the corporeal good
for bliss, fallen man could. Why should fallen man consume
his energy in the envy of others' good instead of in the
pursuit of his own good? Dante's answer to this question is
Virgil's discourse on the difference of the heavenly and the
earthly good in the modes of possession (*Purg.* xv. 45–81).
Virgil explains that the possession of the heavenly good is
communal and that of the earthly good is exclusive. One
man's possession of the material good has to exclude another's possession of the same property. The visual demonstration of the principle of exclusive possession is given in
the seventh *bolgia* where the thieves exchange their shapes
and forms. One has to lose the shape which another steals
from him; no two thieves can share one same form.* In the
possession of the earthly goods, one's gain is always an-

---

* The scene of metamorphosis in *Inf.* xxv. 34–151 may appear to be an
exception to this rule because the Florentine thieves seem to share their
bodily forms in the process of transformation. Viewed technically, however, the thieves do not share their forms in the sense of communal
possession but are exchanging them and stealing their bodily forms
from each other.

other's loss. The more people there are for the possession of the earthly good, the smaller share each will have.

The mode of possessing the heavenly good is exactly opposite to that of the earthly good. The more blessed souls there are to participate in the heavenly bliss, the greater share they receive:

> The infinite and ineffable good above
>   runs toward love for itself
>   as a ray of light to a bright surface.
>
> As much brightness as it finds, so much it gives,
>   so that the more widely love extends
>   the more eternal good grows upon it,
>
> and the greater the number who comprehend
>   and love each other, the more love there is,
>   since one gives to another, like a mirror.
>
> Purg. xv. 67–75

On Mercury, Dante gives a visual demonstration of this mystical mode of communal possession. On reaching the Second Heaven, Dante and Beatrice are greeted and praised by the blessed for the love that will be increased by their arrival: "*Lo! one who shall increase our loves*" (*Par.* v. 105). Compare this joyful reception of love and mercy with the dreadful treatment Dante gets in the *Malebolge* where he is cheated, harrowed, resented, scared, and hated. The mystery of heavenly bliss, which grows in communal possession, is further illustrated by the twin flame in which Justinian glows. At his initial appearance, Emperor Justinian glows in "his own rays" (*Par.* v. 137). After the eulogy of Romeo's hidden virtue, Justinian begins to glow in a twin light. The single light in which Justinian first appears is the splendour representing his own share of heavenly bliss. The twin light indicates the doubling of his bliss through his communion with Romeo and through his praise of Romeo's virtue. Notice the contrast between Justinian's flame and the flame which is burning on the soles of Nicholas III in the third *bolgia*. When Boniface comes, he will be planted upside down on top of Nicholas, and Nicholas will lose the flame on his soles. The holes of the simoniacs are the symbols for the acts of simony; Nicholas calls his hole "the purse" (*Inf.* xix. 72). The flame on his soles represents the gain and fruits of simony, which Nicholas cannot retain when he is succeeded by his heir in simony. While Nicholas will be deprived of his flame by his companion, Justinian has his flame doubled by his companion.

While Justinian is shining in the twin flame, he sings:

> *Osanna, sanctus Deus Sabaoth*
> *superillustrans claritate tua*
> *felices ignes horum malachoth!*
> (Hail! Holy God of hosts!
>   doubly illuminating the brightness from above
>   the blessed fires of these kingdoms!)
>   *Par.* vii. 1–3

Justinian is singing of the mystery of communal participation in which the flames of splendors are doubly illuminated. This hymn is adapted from the *Sanctus:*

> *Sanctus, Sanctus, Sanctus, Dominus Deus Sabaoth.*
> *Pleni sunt caeli et terra gloria tua. Hosanna in excelsis.*
> (Holy, Holy, Holy, Lord God of hosts! Heaven and
> earth are filled with Thy glory. Hosanna in the
> highest.)

The *Sanctus* is the hymn in which the angels praise the glory of God which fills heaven and earth. If the glory of God were like the earthly good which necessitates exclusive

173

possession, God would become poorer by sharing His glory with his creatures. Because the divine good is beneficent, God receives richer and fuller glory by filling heaven and earth with His infinite good.

The *Sanctus* has a further significance through its place and function in the Mass. This angelic hymn concludes the Preface to the Canon, the most solemn part of the Mass. It is in the Canon that the bread and wine are consecrated and the sacrifice of the Pascal Lamb is re-enacted. The sacrifice is offered in the name of the entire Mystical Body of Christ, the saints and the sinners, the dead and the living. It is through the communal bond of the Church that all the faithful participate not only in the offering of the sacrifice but in receiving it when the sacrifice is distributed in the Holy Eucharist. Because the Canon marks the communal participation in the spiritual food, its Preface praises the unity of the Three Persons and the trinity of Their single nature:

. . . Father almighty, eternal God, who with Thine only-be-gotten Son and the Holy Spirit art one God, one Lord; not in the unity of a single person, but in the trinity of a single nature . . .

(*The New Roman Missal*, the Preface)

The Holy Trinity is the exemplar of the heavenly community. Coming at the end of the Preface and at the beginning of the Canon, the *Sanctus* sings the mystery of the infinite glory of the Trinity which is magnified through communal participation.

When the sinful souls become blind to the heavenly good and try to seek the earthly good, they are bound to degenerate into the warfare of envy. Dante takes the feud of the Guelfs and the Ghibellines as the example of the strife of envy. One Guelf and one Ghibelline are leaning against one another on the Second Terrace (*Purg.* xiv. 7). The penitents are reciting the Litany of the Saints (*Purg.* xiii. 50). The Litany of the Saints is a prayer for the mercy of God, addressed severally and jointly to the Three Persons of the Trinity and conveyed through the intercession of all the saints. The penitents' eyes are all stitched up. The two men, with their eyes stitched and leaning against each other, remind us of the two blind men at Jericho:

And behold, two blind men sitting by the wayside heard that Jesus was passing by, and cried out, "Lord, Son of David, have mercy on us!" And the crowd angrily tried to silence them. But they cried out all the louder, "Lord, have mercy on us, Son of David!" Then Jesus stopped, and called them, and said, "What will you have me do for you?" They said to him, "Lord, that our eyes be opened" (Matt. 20:30-34).

By reciting the Litany of the Saints, the penitents are praying for the mercy of the Lord to open their eyes which have been blinded through the envious pursuit of the earthly good.

Blessed are the merciful, for they shall obtain mercy (*Purg.* xv. 38). One has to be merciful in order to obtain mercy. The former Guelf and the former Ghibelline have forgotten their envy and are sustaining each other through the communal bond of mercy. The two blind men bitterly denounce the entire Christendom which has been plagued by envious strife and corruption (*Purg.* xiv. 7 ff.). Dante hears from them two long invectives, one against the valley of the Arno and the other against Romagna.

The Arno's source is a summit of the Tuscan Apennines. The source of the Arno is "so fruitful that in few places is exceeds that mark" (*Purg.* xiv. 33). Throughout the entire valley of the Arno, virtue is avoided and driven out like a snake. The inhabitants have so changed their nature that the entire valley looks like Circe's den. The first part of the Arno valley is filled with filthy hogs, and the second part with snarling dogs. The dogs grow into wolves in the third part of the long valley. The valley finally turns into a valley of foxes. The invective against the Arno valley is followed by the denunciation of Romagna (*Purg.* xiv. 94 ff.) The entire Romagna is choked with poisonous shoots. Every son that is bred in this region is a bastard. The pestilence of degeneration is becoming so universal that to have no son is a great fortune and the only way to keep unsullied the name of a family.

Just after hearing these two invectives and leaving behind the two blind men, Dante hears Cain's voice like a clash of thunder. What does it signify? The two invectives recapture the Biblical account of the degeneration of the human race. Adam's sin of pride turns into Cain's sin of envy. Out of pride, Adam rejects the bliss of innocence for the fruits of toil and sweat in the dust. The possession of the fruits of the sinful earth necessitates exclusive ownership. Cain and Abel have to fight against each other for the fruits of the earth. Cain and Abel are only the beginning of the long course of degeneration. As the seeds of Adam and Eve multiply, their sins also increase and become so abominable that God has to destroy the entire human race except Noah with a deluge (Gen. 6). Romagna where every son is a bastard and to have no son is a great fortune has become so abominable and degenerate as to need and deserve Noah's deluge. As the Arno begins to breed sins from its source and multiplies them as it flows down, so Adam's race begins with sin and multiplies it as the race is multiplied. The history of Adam's race is a history of persistent degeneration.

The invective against Romagna is linked with the history of Rome which Emperor Justinian narrates to Dante. Justinian recounts the history of the Roman Empire in order to place the feud of the Guelfs and the Ghibellines in a right perspective (*Par.* vi. 31–33). Justinian tells Dante that Rome grew into a great Empire by following the spirit of justice which was shown by the Eagle, the bird of God (*Par.* vi. 1–6). The blessings and woes in the history of the Roman Empire were the rewards and punishments for the Romans' faithfulness and faithlessness to the spirit and virtue of the guiding Eagle. For example, the first secure foundation of Rome was established with the virtue of Pallas, Evander's only son, who gave his life for Rome (*Par.* vi. 34–36). The monarchy was swept away as the punishment for the violation of the Sabine women and the outrage to Lucretia (*Par.* vi. 40–42). The Roman republic was born out of the ashes of the Roman monarchy and was later transformed by Caesar into an empire, which was to culminate in the *Pax Romana* under the reign of Augustus. This long, painful growth of the Roman Empire was necessary in order to prepare the domain of justice on which the injustice of the first man and his descendants against the Creator was to be avenged (*Par.* vi. 82–90). All the great events in the history of the Roman Empire look very pale and small in comparison with the greatest event of history, the Crucifixion. The final goal of the long, painful growth of Rome was the justification of the sinful human race through the ransom of the only-begotten Son.

After recounting the history of Rome, Justinian tells Dante that our poet should now be able to see the nature of the feud between the Guelfs and the Ghibellines, which is the cause of all the ills on the earth (*Par.* vi. 97–99). In mediaeval thought, all law and justice on earth are derived from the eternal law of God.[6] The Eagle, the justice of Rome, is the bird of God. Furthermore, the aim of justice and law is not to promote the private interests of individuals, but to subject them to the public welfare and order of the community.[7] This communal spirit of justice is the spirit of the Eagle that guided the destiny of the Roman Empire. This communal spirit of the Eagle can be followed by those who have mercy and concern for the welfare of the fellow members of the community. It is with this spirit of communal justice that even the once envious Sapia can become a citizen of the true city of God and greet Dante as "my brother" (*Purg.* xiii. 94).

Though justice is a heavenly gift, it is easily mistaken for an earthly good in its implementation. When this happens, the thirst for justice easily turns into a greed for honor and fame:

> This little star embellishes itself
> > with good spirits who have been active
> > so that honor and fame could follow them,

> And when desires lean on that,
> > thus deviating, the rays of true love
> > must mount upward less eagerly.
> > > *Par.* vi. 112–117

When the heavenly origin and spirit of the earthly justice are completely forgotten, justice degenerates into the ferocious weapon of envious strife. This is the state to which the Roman Eagle as the symbol of justice has degenerated in the feud of the Guelfs and the Ghibellines. If the two parties were to seek the spirit of the Eagle, they could share it in the communal spirit. They have degraded the Eagle to another item of vainglory. That is why one party tries to monopolize it and the other tries to reject it (*Par.* vi. 100–102). No object of vainglory can be shared by two envious parties. Their claims and counterclaims to the secular power and authority whose sole purpose is to administer justice are as vain as the vainglory of the Sienese who are squandering their fortune in their futile and ludicrous attempt to become a maritime power only for the sake of competing with the neighboring cities (*Purg.* xiii. 151–154).

In the hands of the envious, justice becomes not only the object of vainglory but the instrument of mutual destruction. The Guelfs and the Ghibellines have been butchering each other in the name of justice. This is the justice of the *vendetta*. One of Dante's relatives in the ninth *bolgia* points his finger of accusation at Dante and will not even speak to him because his death has not been avenged by his relatives (*Inf.* xxix. 19–36). The black devil claimed the soul of Guido da Montefeltro in the name of justice (*Inf.* xxvii. 114). The schismatic who carries his amputated head like a lantern hanging from his hand regards his punishment as the right measure of justice (*Inf.* xxviii. 142). The *Malebolge* is the state of justice where the devils have degraded justice into a ferocious instrument of destruction and torture through envy just as the Guelfs and the Ghibellines have turned justice into a weapon of mutual destruction. It is through envy that the original spirit of justice has been forgotten and the justice of Roma has degenerated into the injustice of Romagna.

While the invective against Romagna is linked with Justinian's account of Roma, the denunciation of the Arno compares the Arno to the *Inferno*. The entire Arno valley is compared to Circe's den (*Purg.* xiv. 42). In the third chapter of this book, we explained that damnation is carnalization. The men and angels who are made in the image of God are changed into beasts in the *Inferno;* the *Inferno* is Circe's den. Compare now the four divisions of the valley of the Arno with the major divisions of the *Inferno*. The first part of the Arno valley is the valley of hogs and resembles the Circles of the concupiscible which hold the slaves of appetite who can be properly called hogs. The only sinner with whom Dante talks in the Second Circle presents himself under his nickname Ciacco, *the pig* (*Inf.* vi. 52).

The second division of the Arno valley is the valley of dogs which snarl but cannot bite and resembles the two Circles of the passive irascible which hold the sullen who cannot wreak their anger on other people. Dante calls the sullen sinners dogs (*Inf.* viii. 42). The dogs change into wolves in the third division of the Arno valley, and this transition resembles the transition from the Circles of the passive irascible to the Circles of the active irascible. The last division of the Arno valley corresponds to the *Malebolge*, the valleys of fraud:

> Having descended through many deep gorges
> it finds the foxes, so full of fraud
> that they fear no guile that may trap them.
> *Purg.* xiv. 52–54

As all the gorges of the Arno valley are irrigated by the fertile water which flows down from the Apennines, so all the Circles of the *Inferno* are nourished by the turgid rivers flowing down from the Mount Ida (*Inf.* xiv. 97). All the rivers of Hell flow through many valleys of beasts and pour into the lake of Cocytus. The Arno passes through the many sections of the Circe's den and flows into the lake of Rome, the Mediterranean.

While the justice of the Roman Empire has degenerated into the justice of Romagna, the lake of Roma has become the lake of the Arno valley. While the justice of Romagna resembles the justice of the *Malebolge*, the valleys of the Arno resemble the valleys of the *Inferno*. This is the subtle implication Dante wants to convey through his invectives against the Arno valley and Romagna. To facilitate the understanding of this implication, he correlates Roma with

Romagna through alliteration and the *Inferno* with the Arno through rhythmical association.

The process of degeneration is the inevitable consequence of man's fall; sin breeds only sins. Man has no power to save himself from the devil's snare once he falls into it; he is as powerless as Guido's soul against the black angel's claim. The redemption of the sinful man involves two tasks: the lost man must be restored to God and the debt of punishment must be paid for his sin.[8] Beatrice explains that the sinful man has no power to render satisfaction for his sin (*Par.* vii. 97). Justice in the world of evil knows nothing but the payment of evil for evil. Justice is to render everyone what is due him. What is due to a sinner is only evil. In the *Malebolge*, Dante sees innumerable instances of the justice of retribution: "the infallible justice," "the rigid justice," "the divine justice," etc. (*Inf.* xix. 12, xxiv. 119, xxix, 56; xxx. 70).

The sinful man can gain and retain the *Malebolge* through the justice of retribution but cannot save himself. The lost man must be restored to God, and this is the demand of the justice of restitution. For the restoration of the sinful man, the Son of God becomes a man and offers Himself for the ransom of man. The dual nature of Christ is essential to His function as the Paschal Lamb, and the change of Justinian's belief from one nature of Christ to His dual nature is important (*Par.* vi. 13–18). The justice which restores the fallen man to his Creator is the justice of the New Law.[9] The New Law simplifies and perfects the Old Law: "*Thou shalt love the Lord thy God with thy whole heart, and with thy whole soul, and with thy whole mind." This is the greatest commandment. And the second is like it, "Thou shalt love thy neighbor as thyself." On these two commandments depend the whole Law and the Prophets* (Matt. 22:37–40). The consummation of the Old Law in the New Law is represented by Justinian's codification which simplified and perfected the Roman laws (*Par.* vi. 11–12).

The sinful man does not deserve the justice of the New Law which the Son of God has instituted as the Lamb of God. It is only through His infinite mercy that the only-begotten Son takes on the flesh and offers Himself for the remission of man's sin: *How pitying and gracious the Lord is, how patient, how rich in mercy! He will not always be finding fault, his frown does not last forever; he does not treat us as our sins deserve, does not exact the penalty of our wrong-doing* (Psalm 102[103]:8–11).

The contrast between Christ's mercy and Satan's envy is illustrated by the episodes of Romeo and Ulysses. Satan's envy broke up the family of God, by luring away Adam and Eve from the Garden of Eden. Every sin which is charged against Ulysses is the sin of breaking up a family (*Inf.* 55–142). Ulysses lured away Achilles and led him to death, for which Deidamia still sorrows (*Inf.* xxvi. 62). He destroyed the great family of Troy by stealing the Palladium from Troy and by driving the Wooden Horse into Troy. He refused to return to his home in Ithaca, thus breaking up his own family. He deserted again his aged father, his little son and his lovely wife, instigated his men to follow him, and finally perished in a whirlpool.

The episode of Ulysses embodies Satan's history of sin. As the life of Ulysses was a chain of acts to break up families through his guile, so is the life of Satan. Satan first deserts his Father and drags away a host of angels from the heavenly family and then entices Adam and Eve to leave the Father and join him. The mission of Christ is to reunite the heavenly family that has been broken up by Satan. To restore to the Father the sinful man who has been lured away by the devil's envy, Christ comes to the earth and institutes the marriage between man and God. *The king-*

dom of heaven is like a king who made a marriage feast for his Son (Matt. 22:2).

The episode of Romeo illustrates the merciful mission of Christ to unite the sinful man to the king of heaven through the nuptial sacrament. Romeo, a lowly stranger, married off all the four daughters of Raymond Berenger to kings through his counsel of mercy. After making queens of all the four daughters of a rather prominent but not royal family, Romeo was chased out of his master's home through envious calumny (*Par.* vi. 133–138). Romeo "took his way in poverty and age . . . begging his life crust by crust" (*Par.* vi. 139–140). This is the reward Romeo received for his faithful, merciful works. Christ was rewarded by the death on the cross for the wedding feast He prepared for the marriage of the sinful souls to the king of heaven. As Romeo was always concerned with the welfare of others and took no heed for his own well-being, so Christ gave everything to the sinful men and took nothing for Himself. Like Romeo, who begged his way crust by crust, Christ was a mendicant throughout his life and was nailed down with his naked body on the cross. *The foxes have dens, and the birds of the air have nests, but the Son of Man has nowhere to lay his head* (Luke 9:58).

The self-abasement Christ put on in His Incarnation is represented by Romeo and Mercury. Christ came not in power and glory but in weakness and lowliness to one of the obscure corners of the Roman Empire. His obscure, beggarly life in the great Roman Empire was like the glow of Mercury hidden in the effulgence of the Sun (*Par.* v. 129). Compare the self-abasement of Christ with the glamor of Geryon, whose back, breast, and sides are painted with knots and circlets:

Never did Tartars nor Turks make cloth

> with more colors in groundwork and in pattern,
> nor did Arachne ever put such webs on her loom.
>
> *Inf.* xvii. 16–18

When Geryon appears out of the abyss, Virgil calls Dante's attention to him, saying:

> Behold the beast with the pointed tail
> that can cross mountains and break through walls;
> behold him who pollutes the whole world.
>
> *Inf.* xvii. 1–3

This is an adaptation of the salutation with which John the Baptist pointed out the Son of God to his fellow creatures at the Jordan: *Behold the Lamb of God, behold Him, who takes away the sins of the world* (John 1:29). The sins which Christ takes away are the sins with which Satan pollutes the world. Like Christ, Geryon appears in a dual nature. Christ is the incarnation of mercy, and Satan the incarnation of envy. Geryon is known as a three-headed king in the classical legend. One is rather puzzled to see only one head on Geryon until one comes to see the three heads on Satan at the center of Hell. Geryon's one head is in the imitation of Christ who divests Himself of the majesty of the Holy Trinity in order to come singly to the earth.

Geryon is the beast that St. John saw fighting against the Lamb of God in one of his visions:

. . . soon it (the beast) must arise from the abyss, . . . The sight of this beast . . . will strike awe into every dweller on earth . . . And the ten horns (of the beast) are ten kings . . . All of them have a single policy; they surrender to the beast the power and the dominion which is theirs. And they will fight against the Lamb, but the Lamb will have the mastery of

them; He is the Lord of all lords, King of all kings . . .
(Apoc. 17:8–14).

The ten valleys of the *Malebolge* are the ten kingdoms of
sinners who have surrendered their power and dominion to
the devil's seduction.

The *Ecce Agnus Dei* has a liturgical significance which
brings out the implied meaning of Virgil's *ecco la fiera*. In
the Mass, the celebrant says the *Ecce Agnus Dei* while he
is holding out the host and showing it to the communicants
who are kneeling down at the altar rail to receive the holy
communion. Virgil's *ecco la fiera* should have been said
while Satan was holding out the forbidden fruit to Eve
who was about to swallow it. The fruit of the beast breaks
up the communion between man and God, and the flesh
and blood of the Lamb bring the fallen man back to communion with God. Satan has secured his ten kingdoms of
sin through his own ten sins. In luring away the first man
from the Garden of Eden, he committed all the ten sins
of envy in the *Malebolge*. He seduced and pandered Eve
(*bolgia* 1), through his flattery (*bolgia* 2). He stole the
first man and woman who belonged to God (*bolgia* 3) and
tried to divine the eternal plan of God (*bolgia* 4). His
simony was barratry (*bolgia* 5) and thievery (*bolgia* 7).
His counsel to Eve was a counsel of hypocrisy (*bolgia* 6)
and of evil (*bolgia* 8). He sowed discord between man and
God (*bolgia* 9) and executed his crime in a falsified form
(*bolgia* 10).

The fierce devil reigning over his ten kingdoms of sin is
overthrown by the Lamb. Beatrice says that the earth
shuddered and heaven opened at the triumph of the Paschal
Lamb (*Par.* vii. 46–48). The heaven was opened for the
sinful man. The ten Heavens are the marriage feast which
the Lamb has prepared for the souls who have been en-

chained and enslaved through Satan's ten sins of envy.
Dante sees the trace of the triumph of the Lamb even in
the *Malebolge*. In the sixth *bolgia* he is told by one of the
black angels that the entire Hell felt the impact of a shat-
tering earthquake at the Crucifixion. Dante sees the bridge
over the sixth *bolgia* broken at the earthquake (*Inf.* xxi.
112). While Satan has built up the ten dominions of sin
with his own sins, Christ has prepared the ten Heavens with
His own virtues. Every man lives on the cross road of
Christ's invitation of mercy and Satan's invitation of envy.
The episode of Guido illustrates the decision which the
mortal soul has to make between these two invitations (*Inf.*
xxvii. 64–120). The invitation of mercy can be accepted
only in mercy and the invitation of envy only in envy.
This is the lesson Guido learned.

That Satan aims at disunion and discord is reflected in
the way the devils cooperate in the *Malebolge*. In the fifth
bolgia, the devils fight against one another like mad vultures
(*Inf.* xxii. 133–151). In contrast to this discord and disunion, Christ works in union with the other Two Persons of
the Trinity. Long before Christ becomes incarnate, the bird
of God establishes and rears the Roman Empire whose mature justice and peace sets the proper stage on which the
debt of punishment is to be paid for original sin (*Par.* vi. 4).
The bird of God is the Eagle, the symbol of the Holy
Spirit. The Holy Spirit not only prepared for the Coming
of the Son through the long tradition of prophecy of the
Jews, but also appointed and perfected the tribune of justice
among the Gentiles for judgment on the Son of Man.
Through this judgment, the debt of punishment sinful man
owes to the Father is paid, and the lost man is restored to
the Father.

Satan not only disrupts the families he envies, but
works with his cohorts in discord and disunion to imple-

ment his envy. Christ not only reunites the broken families on which He takes compassion, but works with the other Two Persons in union and harmony to implement His mercy. The work of justification and salvation which Christ works in union with the Spirit for the Father is praised in the prayer for His fidelity:

O Lord, Jesus Christ, Son of the living God, who by the will of the Father, with the cooperation of the Holy Spirit, hast by Thy death given life to the world, deliver me by Thy most sacred Body and Blood from all my sins and from every evil. Make me always cling to Thy commands, and never permit me to be separated from Thee. Who with the same God the Father and the Holy Spirit livest and reignest, God, world without end, Amen. (*The New Roman Missal:* The Communion.)

The nature of Satan's envy and Christ's mercy is illustrated by the bridle and the whip of the Second Terrace. The examples of virtue and sin are given through voices on the Second Terrace, while the examples are shown by sculpture on the First Terrace. The difference between the visual and the audible examples shows the difference between the active and the passive powers. That is, we are quite active in appreciation of the visual art and passive in that of the musical art. It is this difference of sight and hearing, vision and rhythm, that Nietzsche brings out in his masterly distinction of the Apollonian and the Dionysian traditions in the Greek art in *The Birth of Tragedy*. The activity in seeing and the passivity in hearing have recently evoked a new interest in the field of psychiatric phenomenology: "In seeing I direct myself actively to the visible; I 'cast my eyes' upon something. But in hearing I am a receiver; the tones come at me and compel me."[10] Humility and pride belong to the active intellect, and vision is the proper medium for the depiction of their examples. Mercy and envy are of the passive intellect, and hearing is the proper medium for the expression of their examples.

The examples of envy are the voices of Cain and Aglauros (*Purg.* xiv. 133–139). Cain laments over his cursed fate, "Everyone that findeth me shall slay me." Aglauros cries, "I am Aglauros who was turned to stone." These two examples capture the whole scene of the *Malebolge*. The *Malebolge* is the livid stone to which every envious soul is transformed like Aglauros. The *Malebolge* are the valleys in which every envious soul is scourged like Cain.

The three examples of mercy are given by the unseen spirits who give the penitents the courteous invitations to the feast of love (*Purg.* xiii. 25–36). The first voice says "*Vinum non habent* (*They have no wine*)." These three words are the words of Queen Mary to her Son at the wedding feast of Cana, where Christ performed His first miracle by turning water into wine (John ii. 1–11). These three words indeed show her great virtue of mercy. The tenderest prayer to the Virgin calls her the Mother of mercy (*Salve Regina, Mater misericordiae*.)

Great as her virtue is, her virtue only reflects a far greater virtue: the infinite mercy of her Son. When Mary says, *They have no wine*, Christ answers, *My time has not yet come*. His time for the active works of salvation and for the manifestation of His divinity has not yet come, but Jesus takes pity on the wedding party and turns water into wine. He does not display His miracle; the source of the marvelous wine remains hidden even to the master of the feast. The only motive with which Christ works all miracles is the compassion for the misery of the sinners.

This first miracle of Christ exemplifies His entire visible mission. Water and wine are the symbols of humanity and divinity in the Roman Catholic liturgy. While pouring water into wine at the altar, the celebrant prays:

O God, who hast established the nature of man in wondrous dignity and even more wondrously hast renewed it, grant that through the mystery of this water and wine, we may be made partakers of His Divinity, who has deigned to become partaker of our humanity, Jesus Christ . . . (*The New Roman Missal:* The Offertory.)

The wine of the marriage feast to which Christ invites the sinners is the wine of divinity. Before the sinful soul can join the divine feast of wine, it has to pay the debt of punishment for its sin. But man cannot pay for his sin. The Son of God becomes the Son of Man; He has deigned to become the partaker of humanity so that He can take upon His body of flesh the punishment for Adam's sin. This act of mercy is illustrated by the sacrifice of Pylades who offered his life to take the punishment of his dear friend, Orestes (*Purg.* xiii. 31–33). Orestes' was a death sentence. Adam's sin was a mortal sin, whose consequence is death. Like Pylades, the Son of God offers His own life for the mortal punishment of man's sin.

The name of Orestes suggests a chain of vengeance. Agamemnon was killed by his wife in revenge of Agamemnon's sacrifice of Iphigenia; Orestes had to kill his mother Clytemnestra in revenge of his father's death; and Orestes had to be punished for his matricide. This chain of vengeance and re-vengeance is dictated by justice. This dictate of justice is reflected in Justinian's account of the Crucifixion and the destruction of Palestine (*Par.* vi. 88–93). The Crucifixion was the vengeance on original sin, and the destruction of Palestine was the vengeance on this vengeance. How can Christ offer Himself to the punishment for original sin and put an end to the chain of vengeance and re-vengeance? This is possible only through mercy: "Love them from whom you have suffered evil" (*Purg.* xiii. 36). This is the third example of mercy, and it reflects the infinite mercy of Christ which culminates in His last prayer: *"Father forgive them; they do not know what it is they are doing"* (Luke 23:34).

It is the mercy of the Son that the Angelic Poet sings on the second rung of the angelic ladder of divine love. On the first rung of the angelic ladder, the Angelic Poet praised His humility to the Father. On the second rung, he sings the mercy which the Son has shown in co-operation with the Spirit for the restoration of the lost man to the Father out of His fidelity. Thus, the Angelic Poet concludes the first phase in his adoration of the Holy Trinity through the praise of the Son's two virtues exemplified in His visible mission.

chapteR 6

Lesson on the Rung of Meekness and Wrath

The Third Heaven, the Third Terrace, and the Seventh Circle

WE ARE now stepping on the third rung of the angelic ladder of divine love. This rung is grounded on the active irascible power. Since the irascible is the power proper to the animal soul, our poet extensively employs animal metaphors in the construction of the third and the fourth rungs of the angelic ladder. To facilitate the understanding of those metaphors, let us review the essential features of Aristotelian zoology. The animal is distinguished from the rational creature on the one hand and from the vegetable on the other. In distinction from the rational creature, the animal lacks reason. In distinction from the vegetable, the animal has motive power. Whereas the plant is planted in one place, the animal moves around from place to place. Besides the power of locomotion, the animal has the power of sensation. From the power of sensation, the animal derives its power of forming images; this is the power of imagination. The animal can retain the images; this is the power of memory. Memory is the retained images or phantasms. The central organ of an animal is the heart, which heats the blood and controls the body.

In man, the animal power lies between the intellect and the appetite and can go out of its proper bounds in two ways. The animal power may enslave its master, the rational power, or be enslaved to its subordinate companion, the appetite. In either event, the result is a vice. The animal power is a virtue, when it functions as a faithful servant to the intellect and as a dutiful guardian for the appetite.

The Minotaur of the Seventh Circle is the personification of the active irascible which has become vicious. He is a creature of dual nature in which bestial anger overpowers the intellect. The Minotaur gnaws and bites himself "like one whom anger inwardly consumes" (*Inf*. xii. 13–15). The poison of anger torments the owner of anger before anyone else. Virgil immediately fans the Minotaur's rage by recounting his shameful defeat and death at the hand of the Duke of Athens (*Inf*. xii. 16–21). Provoked and outraged at Virgil's pointed insult, the Minotaur plunges around like a bull at the fatal stroke and becomes a helpless victim of his own rage. Taking advantage of this, Virgil and Dante pass through the entrance to the Seventh Circle.

Through this incident, Dante conveys two ideas. First, the animal power is powerless before sound reason. The Minotaur was conquered by the Duke of Athens, the symbol of reason, and now is easily handled by Virgil's reason. Second, Dante demonstrates Aristotle's definition of anger: "Anger may be defined as an impulse, accompanied by pain, to a conspicuous revenge for a conspicuous slight or insult directed without justification towards what concerns oneself or towards what concerns one's friends."[1] The rage of the Minotaur is provoked by insult.

The behavior of the Centaurs illustrates another point of observation which Aristotle makes on anger: "Anger seems to listen to argument to some extent, but to mishear it, as do hasty servants who run out before they have heard the whole of what one says, and then muddle the order, or as dogs bark if there is but a knock at the door before looking to see if it is a friend."[2]

The three Centaurs behave like rash dogs on seeing Virgil and Dante (*Inf.* xii. 58–66). They rush out and one is about to draw his bow without finding out whom he is going to shoot. Virgil laments, "unhappily thy will was always thus rash" (*Inf.* xii. 66). In explaining the identities of the Centaurs, Virgil does not leave out Chiron's function as a teacher of anger: the great Chiron nursed Achilles whom Aristotle was fond to consider as the acme of ire (*Inf.* xii. 71).

The definition of anger as the impulse to revenge for insult is its formal definition. Aristotle also gives its material definition: "Anger is the boiling of the blood around the heart, the animal's central organ."[3] This material definition is well used in the construction of the First Ring of the Seventh Circle. The violent against their neighbors are being cooked in the boiling blood of Phlegethon (*Inf.* xii. 101–102). In contrast, the violent against themselves are transformed into trees and shrubs in a wasteland (*Inf.* xiii. 4–6). The sinners of the First Ring wreaked their anger on their neighbors and those of the Second Ring on themselves. Because the former made the blood of their neighbors boil with their own boiling blood, they lived as it were in a hot blood bath. The latter were like the trees and shrubs which cannot find outlet for their boiling blood of anger except by tearing and breaking off their branches.

When Dante moves into the suicide wood, he hears wailings and moanings from all around and says:

> I *believe* (*credo*) he (Virgil) *believed* that I *believed*
> that so many voices came from people
> hidden from us among the trees; (Italics mine)
> > *Inf.* xiii. 25–27

With this involuted tercet, the poet characterizes the nature of the internalized anger which leads to suicide. Those who take their own lives cannot externalize their anger and vent it on other people, but internalize it into their choking bosoms. They cannot verify the cause of their anger through an open argument; their angry thought always revolves around within the tight knot of anger. Their angry thought is seldom substantiated through objective evidence. To characterize this type of thinking, Dante uses the word belief (*credo*). Belief is faith, that is, "the argument of things which are not seen" (*Par.* xxiv. 65). One does not or need not believe the things which one can see with one's own eyes, but only the things whose objective evidence is beyond one's knowledge. The angry thought degrades itself to a groundless imagination which coils and tangles upon itself, without being able to branch out into the open air like the knotted and snarled branches of the suicide wood.

The well-known episode of the Seventh Circle is the story of Pietro delle Vigne (*Inf.* xiii. 55–75). Pietro was the confidant of Frederick II. Frederick not only confided all his secrets but also entrusted all his power to Pietro. The power and trust Pietro wielded inflamed the envy of others, who finally succeeded in turning Frederick against Pietro and bringing about Pietro's downfall. Pietro says that he inflicted the unjust act of self-destruction upon his just self in order to escape scorn and disdain. Even though he made a cruel end of his life because of envious calumny, he concludes his sad story with a vehement claim that he has never broken faith with his lord.

This episode has been considered as one of the sentimental stories of the *Divina Commedia*. That is, though Dante places Pietro in the Second Ring of the Seventh Circle in a faithful compliance with the ethical doctrines of his Church, he cannot hide his warm sympathetic sentiment for Pietro's firm fidelity to his cruel lord. Is Dante such a sentimental poet as not to be able to resolve the conflict of the dictate of his faith and the demand of his animal sentiment?

Notice the implied comparison between Pietro's oath of fidelity and that of Peter the Apostle. Pietro claims to have had both keys of Frederick's heart (*Inf.* xiii. 58). Peter, the Apostle of the Apostles, received the greatest trust from the greatest Lord: *Thou art Peter, and it is upon this rock that I will build My Church; and the gates of hell shall not prevail against it; and I will give to thee the keys of the kingdom of heaven* (Matt. 16:18). Peter's is the mightiest trust given to a mortal soul.

In spite of this trust, what becomes of Peter's loyalty at the crucial moment? Christ knew the frailty of man and foretold the Apostle's breach of faith just before His Crucifixion. He said, *"Tonight you will all lose courage over Me."* Peter could not believe and protested, *"Though all else should lose courage over Thee, I will never lose mine"* (Matt. 26:31–34). Jesus knew how easy it is to take the oath of fidelity and how hard it is to keep it, and calmly predicted, *"Believe Me, this night, before the cock crows, thou shalt thrice disown Me"* (Matt. 26:34–35). Peter had the courage to contradict his heavenly Lord, *"I will never disown Thee, even if I must lay down my life with Thee"* (Matt. 26:35).

Before the cock crew thrice, Peter learned which fidelity was easier to keep: fidelity to his own life or fidelity to his Lord. He was not given only one chance, but three. Perhaps only after this test of fidelity, Peter may have realized Christ's knowledge of human frailty lying beneath His command: *Love thy neighbor as thyself.* If one loves one's neighbor as much as oneself, one reaches the highest peak of ethical perfection. The Greeks had a maxim of knowledge: the self is the measure of human knowledge. The self is also the measure of human love.

With this maxim of love, we can easily estimate the worth of Pietro's claim for his fidelity to his lord. Could he have kept faith with his lord at a crucial moment, while he could not be faithful to his own life? We need not deny the merit of Pietro's frenzied devotion to his lord any more than we have to deny the merit of Peter's zealous loyalty to his Lord, whatever merit their zeal and frenzy may have. We can still detect the undercurrent of animalistic anger beneath the surface of Pietro's frenzy of loyalty. We can almost hear him say: "You, stupid Frederick, have discarded my priceless loyalty like a worn-out slipper in trust of the calumny and flattery of worthless creatures, and, for this unpardonable wrong and inexcusable slight, let me take revenge on you with the fire of my eternally burning fidelity to you." Anger is the impulse of vengeance for the undeserved slight.

Pietro's vehement claim of his fidelity is the expression of his mixed feeling, the mixture of the impulse for vengeance and the sense of fidelity to his lord. Where do we see the evidence for his mixed feeling? It is in his vehement oath. A violent oath is always a sign of uncertainty of the swearer, which comes from his muddled feeling and his stained conscience. When a husband begins to swear his love and faith to his wife, she may as well take it as a timely warning and symptom of his uneasy conscience.

How do the people who have to live with themselves in anger get along with others? Here again, the self is the measure. Those who cannot keep peace within the kingdoms of their own hearts cannot keep it with others. For this reason, anger against the self is graver than anger against others and the suicides are placed in Hell lower than the tyrants and murderers. Anger in the self always provokes anger in others, and this is expressed in a single tercet:

> *Inflamed* all minds against me,
>   and the *inflamed* so *inflame*d Augustus
>   that my joyous honors changed into dismal sorrow
>   (Italics mine)
>   *Inf*. xiii. 67–69

It is Pietro who sets the flame of envy among his neighbors whose flame of rage inflames Augustus whose flame of ire finally kindles the flame of wrath to consume Pietro's whole animal body.

We can now see who is sentimental, our poet or his reader. The reader is always the measure of his reading: one reads what one desires to read and sees what one deserves to see. The Greeks had a marvelous inkling: the like understands the like. The sentimental reader can read only sentiment. I do not want to deny all sentiment in Dante's handling of Pietro's episode. Dante is a poet of rich sentiment and passionate emotion, but his sentiment and emotion are fully crystallized through his powerful intellect. His sentiment is not a vague haze of feeling, but a translucent crystal. It can dazzle you and baffle you and fool you, but it does reveal itself to a patient eye.

The anger against the self and others has tangible objects, but the anger against God, Nature, and Art has no tangible object for its expression. Having no tangible object, the anger becomes a pervasive torment. This pervasive torment is represented by the flakes of fire showering on the burning desert in the Third Ring of the Seventh Circle, where the sinners are buffeted from all directions (*Inf*. xiv. 13–42).

Unlike most of the shades running about to ease the torment of fire-flakes and burning sand, Capaneus lies on the ground and pretends not to care about the fiery sands and flakes (*Inf*. xiv. 46–72). He proudly slights Jove's power. Though Jove may muster all the might of his kingdom and shower all the thunderbolts of his forge on Capaneus, Capaneus says Jove cannot reap the joy of vengeance (*Inf*. xiv. 52–60). Capaneus ridicules and slights Jove, because anger is the impulse of revenge for insult. But the impulse is a painful one; Virgil says, "No torture, except thy own raving,/ would be pain proportioned to thy fury" (*Inf*. xiv. 65–66). This is the marvel of divine justice; sin is the most fitting punishment for sin.

Among the sinners against Nature, Dante meets his dear old teacher, Brunetto Latini (*Inf*. xv. 22). Brunetto Latini tries to explain the cause of the misfortune of Florence and Dante (*Inf*. xv. 61–78). He believes that the present evil and corruption of the Florentines are the results of Nature's bungling. The Florentines are the hybrid products of the good Romans and the beasts of Fiesole. Nature had a poor fortune in this mixture of different bloods, and the bestial blood of Fiesole has overpowered the sacred blood of the Romans. Not only is the evil of Florence due to the poor workmanship of Nature and her fortune, but Dante's misfortune and exil are also the heartless tricks of merciless fortune. Beneath this seemingly scholarly, objective explanation of evils, Brunetto Latini's tumultuous anger against Nature and her fortune runs like an undercurrent. This is the subtle expression of the anger of the intellectuals who feel that they have been slighted by Nature. His whole discourse amounts to an angry reply to Nature, "Look at yourself and your products and see what a poor artisan you are!"

When Brunetto concludes his angry accounts of Nature's working by warning his pupil to be prepared for even severer dealings from Fortune in the future than what he has already received, Dante tactfully shows his distrust of Brunetto's angry view of Nature:

> What you say about my life I write down
>   and keep to be explained with another text
>   by a lady who will be able to do so if I meet her.
>   *Inf.* xv. 88–90

On the Third Terrace, Dante meets Marco of Lombardy who picks up Brunetto's topic right at the point where Brunetto left it (*Purg.* xvi. 64–129). In response to Dante's question about the cause of evil in the world, Marco sighs as though he had heard the entire discourse between Dante and Brunetto and says that it is the opinion of the blind to attribute all evil to necessity. At this point, it becomes clear that Brunetto's view reflects the state of his soul which is blinded by wrath. Marco's argument is very simple in its outline. Though the initial impulses of man come from the heavens, these initial impulses do not determine man's final decisions and actions. Human actions are subject to the mind which knows right from wrong and which is not subject to stellar influences. The will that is under the control of this unchained mind is free will. Good and evil stem from this free will.

The will which is the subject of Marco's discourse is the executive will whose nature and place we briefly examined in the second chapter of this book. The executive will is the will of prudence. St. Thomas says that prudence is the joint operation of the intellect and the sensitive power.[4] Prudence is the right reason about things to be done. Reason as such considers only universal principles, but the things to be done involve particular desires. In Dante's triadic scheme, the irascible power applies the universal principles of the intellect to the execution of the particular appetites of the concupiscible. This division of power is clearly reminiscent of Plato's theory of state. The intellect plays the role of the philosopher king who formulates laws for the state, and the irascible performs the function of the warrior guardian who applies the general laws and counsel of the philosopher to the government of the productive class.

The division of power and labour between the intellect and the irascible is reflected in the two centers of man. The mind of man is the center of his intellect, and his heart is the center of the animal power. Not to confound these two centers and to keep them in a fine co-operation is the wisdom of prudence. This is the theoretical framework which underlies Marco's discourse on the relation of the secular and the ecclesiastical power. Marco says that evil does not come from corrupt nature but from corrupt leadership. Rome used to keep two separate leaderships: one of the world and the other of God (*Purg.* xvi. 107). But one has quenched the other; the sword has been joined to the crook. The papal authority has swallowed up the political power of the empire. The relation of the Pope and the Emperor is analogous to that of the mind and the heart. Christendom has now to limp on one leg instead of walking securely on two legs. Since the executive power of the Emperor has been liquidated, the laws and precepts of the papacy cannot be implemented and have to remain a bundle of impotent barren principles.

Having lost the heart, the central organ of the body, the Empire has been withering away and falling to pieces. The disruption of the animal body and the corruption of its limbs are inevitable consequences of the loss of the heart. In the Third Heaven, Dante meets Carlo Martello who Dante dearly hoped would become the heart of the Roman Empire and rejuvenate its withering limbs (*Par.* viii. 31). As Carlo describes the four immense territories, Provence, Apulia, Hungary, and Sicily, which he would have inherited but for his early death, the four realms sprawl across the entire Christendom like the four amputated limbs of a dinosaur (*Par.* viii. 58–75). Carlo claims that he would have alleviated a great deal of evil if he had lived longer (*Par.* viii. 51).

Carlo's explanation of the evil in the world completes Marco's discourse. Carlo elaborates the law of heredity which was broached by Brunetto Latini and touched on by Marco of Lombardy (*Par.* viii. 130–135). He explains that the generation of human beings does not follow the laws of heredity. That is why a bad son like Esau is born from a good father like Jacob and a Romulus can be born of a base father. To understand this point, we have to be acquainted with the Catholic doctrine of Creationism. Whereas the production of an animal soul is a process of nature, the human soul is brought into being through God's own creative act.[5] A horse always breeds a horse, but a wise man does not necessarily beget a wise man.

Carlo says that the law of heredity is overruled in the production of human beings in order to ensure the diverse talents required for the maintenance of a society (*Par.* viii. 122–123). As far as Nature functions as the breeding ground of the human souls, he assures Dante, she never fails (*Par.* viii. 114). It is the poor human prudence that disrupts the faithful service of Nature:

> And if the world below thought
> of the foundation nature makes,
> by following it, people would be better off;
>
> But you direct into religion
> one born to bind on a sword,
> and make a king of a born writer of sermons;
>
> Thus it happens that your tracks leave the right road.
> *Par.* viii. 142–148

The doctrine of world government, which has been developed in the Seventh Circle, on the Third Heaven, and on Venus turns out to be an exegesis of St. Paul's doctrine of the Mystical Body of Christ and the gifts of the Holy Spirit:

Now there are varieties of gifts, but the same Spirit; there are varieties of ministers, but the same Lord; and there are varieties of workings but the same God, who works all things in all. Now the manifestation of the Spirit is given to everyone for profit. To one through the Spirit is given the utterance of wisdom; and to another the utterance of knowledge . . . to another interpretation of tongues. But all these things are the work of one and the same Spirit, who allots to everyone according as He will.

For as the body is one and has many members, and all the members of the body, many as they are, form one body, so also is it with Christ.

For in one Spirit we were all baptized into one body . . . and we were all given to drink one Spirit. For the body is not one member, but many . . .

If the whole body were an eye, where would be the hearing? If the whole body were hearing, where would be the smelling? But as it is, God has set the members, each of them, in the body as he willed. Now if they were all one member, where would the body be? . . . And the eye cannot say to the hand, "I do not need thy help"; nor again the head to the feet, "I have no need of you." Nay, much rather, those that seem the more feeble members of the body are more necessary; . . . God has so tempered the body together in due proportion as to give more abundant honor where it was lacking; that there may be no disunion in the body, but that the members may have care for one another. And if one member suffers anything, all the members suffer with it, or if one member glories, all the members rejoice with it (I Cor. 12:4–26).

In his poetic exegesis of St. Paul's doctrine, Dante views

the relation of the Pope and Emperor as analogous to the relation of the Son and the Spirit in the Mystical Body of Christ. The Father has entrusted the government of the world to the visible mission of His Son and the invisible mission of His Spirit. The whole world constitutes the Mystical Body of Christ. The Son is the Head, and the Spirit is the Heart of the Mystical Body. In the government of the world, the Pope is the representative of the Son and the Emperor that of the Spirit. The Son instituted His Church in His visible mission. In the preceding chapter, we saw that the Holy Spirit established and nurtured the Roman Empire in His invisible mission.

It is the role of the Pope to lay down universal laws and it is the function of the Emperor to apply them to particular circumstances. This relation of the legislator and the executor between the Pope and the Emperor reflects the relation of the Son and the Holy Spirit in their co-operation. On the second rung of the angelic ladder, we saw that the Holy Spirit prepared all the particulars for the universal act of the Son for the propitiation of the whole world. It is the same relation of the universal and the particular between the Son and the Spirit which Christ has in mind, when He answers, just before His Ascension, His disciples' question, *"Lord, wilt thou at this time restore the kingdom to Israel?": It is not for you to know the time or dates which the Father has fixed by his own authority; but you shall receive power when the Holy Spirit comes upon you* . . . (Acts 1:7–8).

The power of implementation and execution is of the Holy Spirit. On the other hand, the eternal plan of creation and salvation is of the Son. It is through the Word (the Son) that the Father creates the whole world. It is to the wisdom of the Spirit that the Father entrusts the providence and government of the world. Dante regards the wisdom

203

of prudence and execution as the attribute of the Holy Spirit. The Pope and the Emperor should work in union and harmony for the one body of Christ as do the Son and the Spirit. Since the Pope has swallowed up the power and function of the Emperor, there is no hand to execute laws although there are laws (*Purg.* 16:97). *If the whole body were an eye, where would be the hearing?* Since all the powers of Christendom have been monopolized by the Pope, there is no room for the executive power of the Emperor. *And the eye cannot say to the hand, "I do not need thy help."* But the head (the Pope) has eaten up the heart (the Emperor).

What has become of the Papacy which has usurped the power of the Emperor? It has forgotten its original role. It has become like the intellect which has arrogated the animal power and abandoned its original function. What must become of the man in whom such a misfortune takes place? He becomes a mean, ignoble creature who has lost all the virtues of animal courage and whose intellect is degraded to a despicable slave to concupiscence. Where do we find such a despicable creature? It is in the lowest segment of the Seventh Circle, that is, the usurers (*Inf.* xvii. 43–75). The violent against Art do not retain the animal spirit; they do not even move from their seats. They are brushing off the flakes of fire:

> Not otherwise are dogs busy in summer,
> > now with their muzzles and now with their paws,
> when bitten by gadflies or gnats or fleas.
> > > *Inf.* xvii. 49–51

Dante closely looks into their visages, but they have lost all their individualities. The only things Dante can discern are the pictures of animals on the money pouches hanging from their necks. They have all become like the pictures of animals; they retain only the semblance of animals. You can easily see the depth of degradation which the animal spirit has undergone in the transition from Phlegethon to the sand bar of the usurers, if you compare the animal pictures hanging from the usurers' necks with the beard on Chiron's jaw which he combs with the notch of his arrow (*Inf.* xii. 78). This is the same depravation Carlo laments in his brother, Robert, who has usurped Carlo's son's throne, completely forgotten the spirit of knighthood, and become a greedy hoarder (*Par.* viii. 83–84). Robert's degradation is exactly of the same nature as the corruption of the Vatican, which has abandoned "the cemetery/of the soldiery that followed Peter" and given itself up to an adultery with worldly cupidity (*Par.* ix. 139–142). The corruption of Florence falls into the same category, that is, its desertion of the spirit of Mars for the scum of florins (*Inf.* xiii. 143).

Dante treats domesticated animality with great contempt. His visit to the usurers comes as a trivial interlude between two moments of excitement and horror, i.e., the dramatic emergence of Geryon out of the abyss and the frightful ride on his back down to the abyss. Virgil treats Dante's visit to the usurers as a mere harmless excursion for using up a few extra minutes of time (*Inf.* xvii. 37–42). The category of the violent against Art is a border-line case between the Seventh and the Eighth Circle; their animal anger has become a quasi-guile. That is why Dante sees them after the emergence of Geryon.

In order to show his contempt for the violent against Art, Dante deprives them of two main features of animals, motive force and animal courage. Motion is one of the chief characteristics of animality. For the first time in the descent of Hell, Dante in the Seventh Circle adopts a local guide (*Inf.* xii. 93–100). He crosses Phlegethon on the back of Nessus. For the first time in the ascent of the *Purgatorio*, he employs a penitent as a local guide on the Third Terrace (*Purg.* xvi. 45, 141). Marco walks with Dante the entire course of purgation on that Terrace. For the first time in Heaven, Dante sees a distinctive, circular form of cosmic dance on the Third Heaven (*Par.* viii. 26). Even in the suicide wood, harpies and hounds attack the sinners. But locomotion becomes completely absent with the violent against Art.

The second characteristic of animality is the fierce animal spirit. The animal spirit is evident in the Minotaur, the Centaurs, and the sinners who curse, snarl, and wail. On the Third Terrace, Dante feels the animal temper in his legs, which stagger and reel (*Purg.* xv. 121). The blessed of Venus rush down like a thunderbolt with a resounding Hosanna to meet our pilgrim (*Par.* viii. 22–30). The angel of the Third Terrace does not bother to wait for Dante's request, but gives his benediction before being asked (*Purg.* xvii. 55–63). Notice the breathless haste in Dante's confrontation with the blessed on Venus. Beatrice has no time to say a single word by way of introduction, and Dante's question is abrupt and brisk: "Tell me who you are (the Italian is even shorter: *Di' chi siete?*)" (*Par.* viii. 44; cf. ix. 19). When we follow Dante to the violent against Art, we are struck by the complete absence of the breathless rush and quick temper in those sinners who are squatting like lazy dogs beaten down by the summer heat.

To lose and degrade the lively animal spirit is far more dreadful and disgusting than to be overpowered by it and enslaved to it. How can the force and function of the animal heart be preserved and perfected? The answer is given on the Third Terrace. The penitents begin all their prayers with *Agnus Dei* (*Purg.* xvi. 19). *Agnus Dei* is the animal which Marco keeps in the back of his mind when he talks of the shepherd who chews the cud but has not divided hoofs (*Purg.* xvi. 98). Like every mortal soul, Christ was born with an animal body and an animal heart. But He was full of grace and of truth, because He was anointed with the Holy Spirit (John 1:14; Acts 10:38). Christ not only gives the Holy Spirit as God, but also receives it as man.[6] Isaiah prophesied: *"And there shall come forth a rod out of the root of Jesse: and a flower shall rise out of his root. And the spirit of the Lord shall rest upon him"* (Isa. 11:1–2).

The sanctification of the body of Christ by the grace of the Holy Spirit prefigures the co-operation of the Son and the Spirit for the government of the Mystical Body of Christ. As the animal spirit gives the body strength and courage in order to sustain the workings of the mind, the Holy Spirit fills the Mystical Body with grace and power to sustain the works of the Son. The blessed souls in Venus represent the function of the Spirit in the Mystical Body of Christ. Carlo Martello as the representative of the Spirit was to implement the laws and precepts of the Pope, the vicar of Christ. Rahab rendered her courageous service to Joshua in conquering the Holy Land. Joshua is a pre-figure of Jesus; the Holy Land is the symbol of the Mystical Body; Rahab is the pre-figure of the power and courage the Holy Spirit diffuses into the Mystical Body for the victory of the Head of the Body.

The sanctification of the body of Christ by the Holy Spirit also sets the pattern for every faithful soul. Though Christ was born in weak flesh, He was full of courage and patience. He fearlessly drove the thieves out of the temple and meekly suffered death on the cross. As Christ becomes full of grace and wisdom by receiving the Holy Spirit, so does every baptized soul become powerful and graceful by being sanctified in the Spirit. This is illustrated by the life of Peter the Apostle which is submerged under the episode of Pietro delle Vigne. Peter the Apostle was neither the only one to take the oath nor the only one to disown his

Lord. *Peter said to him, I will never disown thee, though I must lay down my life with thee. And all the rest of his disciples said the like* (Matt. 26:35). But when the moment of test came, *all his disciples abandoned him, and fled* (Matt. 26:56). Peter had a far greater animal spirit than any other apostle, and yet was proved too weak to take upon himself the way of the cross with his Lord.

It was through the grace of the Holy Spirit that the weak Peter became the wise vicar of the Church. On receiving the Holy Spirit, Peter witnessed the realization of Joel's prophecy:

I will pour forth of my Spirit upon all flesh; and your sons and your daughters shall prophesy, and your young men shall see visions, and your old men shall dream dreams. And moreover . . . will I pour forth of my Spirit . . . And I will show wonders in the heavens above and signs on the earth beneath, blood and fire and vapor of smoke. The sun shall be turned into darkness . . . And it shall come to pass that whoever calls upon the name of the Lord shall be saved (Acts 2:17–21).

This prophesied miracle took place not only before Peter's eyes but before Dante's on the Third Terrace. Dante sees visions in rapture (*Purg.* xvii. 13–18). Dante says that his visions are the gift of divine illumination. He wants to say that the visions are the effects of the outpouring grace of the Holy Spirit. By receiving the Holy Spirit, the sinful animal body is being sanctified, and the blood and fire of the animal anger are being purified. Thus the human animal becomes the divine animal like *Agnus Dei*, the supreme animal of God.

The transformation of the human animal into the divine animal is further illustrated by the purgation in the smoke. The purpose of the dark smoke is to close the carnal eyes and open the spiritual eyes. It is through the spiritual eyes that Dante sees the visions while his carnal eyes are unconscious. The spiritual eyes are the eyes of the intellect. Aristotle remarks that reason in the soul is like sight to the eye.[7] Walking through the smoke, Dante leans on Virgil's shoulder (*Purg*. xvi. 9). That is, Dante's animal body walks under the guidance of the eyes of reason.

When Marco and Dante meet, Marco says that the smoke does not allow their seeing each other but "hearing shall keep us in touch in its stead" (*Purg*. xvi. 36). Dante replies, "thy words shall be our escort" (*Purg*. xvi. 45). The Word is the proper name of Christ, the Mind of the Mystical Body. The Body must be guided by and follow the Word. The important feature of purgation is not only the opening of the eyes of the mind, but its concurrent motion, i.e. the movement of the animal spirit in obedience to the vision of the intellect. The penitents do not merely close their carnal eyes and sit down on the ground, but walk the whole length of the course of purgation. The walking with closed eyes represents the exercise of the animal power in concordance with the vision of the intellect.

Our poet illustrates the harmonious relation of the mind and the heart through the metaphor of the epicycle. On reaching Venus, Dante calls our attention to its epicycle (*Par*. viii. 3). What is an epicycle? The epicycle is a circle which revolves in its own orbit while the center of its revolution follows the main circular motion of a planet along its equator. The closer the epicyclical motion is conformed to the main circular motion, the nobler it is (*See Conv*. ii. 4). The relation of the main circle and the epicycle is analogous to the relation of the two centers of motion in man, the mind and the heart. Though the mind and the heart have two separate spheres of motion, it can be said in analogy, the closer the motion of the heart is conformed to the motion of the mind, the nobler it is.

Notice the contrast between the Minotaur's raging motion at the recollection of his ignomious death and Dante's staggering walk during his rapture on the Third Terrace. Both of them are seeing unreal phantasies. Dante can walk half a league, but the Minotaur cannot budge a single step forward from his place. The Minotaur's animal rage overpowers and paralyzes his mental power. It is as though the epicyclical motion of his heart had engulfed the main circular motion of his mind. It is just the other way around with Dante. Try to trace in your mind the lines of the moving feet along the path, and you will see that the motion of the feet resembles the epicyclical motion as the feet go up and down and draw half circles along the path. The epicyclical motion of Dante's heart conforms to the main circular motion of his mind, though his legs stagger and reel. To call our attention to this point, Dante puts a heavy stress on his "measured steps" (*Purg.* xvii. 10).

On Venus, the metaphor of epicycle is more prominent. Each of the blessed appears to be a flame within a flame and a voice within a voice (*Par.* viii. 16–17). Dante meets three spirits in a row, Cunizza, Folco, and Rahab who succeeded in placing the epicyclical orbit of animal passion in perfect conformity to the main orbit of intellect (*Par.* ix). Compare these three blessed souls with the three Florentine intellectuals who form a wheel and keep revolving during their talk with Dante in Hell (*Inf.* xvi. 19–90). The ring of the three intellectuals which is revolving within the Seventh Circle represents the main orbit of the intellect that has been overpowered by the epicyclical orbit of the animal heart. In the Seventh Circle, the main cycle and epicycle have changed their positions. The same disaster has taken place in Lombardy which has been completely denuded of worth and courtesy and whose three virtuous surviving elders long to be removed from the corrupt land by the hand of God (*Purg.* xvi. 115–123). The three virtuous elders are caught in the same helpless position as that of the three intellectuals of the Seventh Circle.

With the blessed whose epicyclical motion of the heart is perfectly conformed to the main circular motion of the mind, the power of memory is also under an orderly control. Memory is an animal power. Cunizza, Folco, and Rahab say in unison that they are no longer tormented by the memory of their past bestial passion and deeds (*Par.* ix. 34, 103, 115). In contrast with this peaceful recollection of their sinful past, the three Florentines of the wrestling ring still grieve over their past like any other sinners of the Seventh Circle (*Inf.* xvi. 45). The notable example of the uncontrollable grief over the past is the Minotaur. Even at a slight mention of his defeat and death, he becomes outraged. The tormenting grief over the past is a vicious animal passion as much as the anger of the present; it is the anger for the self which failed to measure up to its own expectation.

For the orderly subjection of the heart to the mind, it is necessary to overcome wild remorse as much as to subdue present anger. Wild remorse is the sign that one has not yet outgrown the remorseful past. The peaceful recollection of past failure is the proof that the wounds of past anger have been healed. The animal passion may burn itself not only for the past but for the future. The animal soul not only retains images of the past, but forms images for the future. Brunetto Latini's disquieting talk about Dante's rough future provokes in Dante an angry image of the future Fortune holds in store (*Inf.* xv. 55–78).

Dante claims to be prepared for cruel Fortune; he is prepared to face her in ire, "Let Fortune turn her wheel as pleases her,/and the boor his mattock" (*Inf.* xv. 95–96). On Venus, Dante learns how not only remorse for the past but fear of the future are controlled. Carlo concludes his discourse, saying "Hold thy peace, and let the years revolve" (*Par.* ix. 4). The blessed can hold their peace in spite of their knowledge of the future evil waiting for their descendants and kindred, because they can gaze on the divine Mind and Art which govern the world (*Par.* viii. 97–106; ix, 106–108). The government of the world is Providence, that is, the Art of the Holy Spirit which implements the Word of God in the Mystical Body of Christ.

It is through the sanctification of the Holy Spirit that the animal passion, which can easily erupt into a paralyzing rage for the past, the present, and the future, can be perfected into the power of execution and the wisdom of prudence and so revolve in an epicycle faithful to the main circle of the mind. The three examples of wrath on the Third Terrace show the three ways the animal passion can bestialize the rational animal (*Purg.* xvii. 19–39). Procne represents the evil wrath against God and Nature, Haman against neighbors, and Amata against the self. These three examples reflect the three Rings of the Seventh Circle. The third example illustrates how violent anger defeats the aim of the mind. Amata killed herself because of the fear of losing her daughter Lavinia to Aeneas. Lavinia weeps, saying to her dead mother, "Slaying yourself in order not to lose Lavinia,/so lost me" (*Purg.* xvii. 37–38).

"*Beati pacifici* who are without evil wrath"; peace is a gift of the orderly animal passion (*Purg.* xvii. 69). The three examples of meekness illustrate how the animal power is perfected into a peaceful servant of the mind (*Purg.* xv. 88–114). The first example is the scene where the Virgin Mother finds the Child Jesus in the temple after a long search. Every year, the parents of Jesus used to go up to Jerusalem for the paschal feast (Luke 2:41–52). When Jesus was twelve years old, they took Him to the feast. After the paschal feast, they left the city for home and noticed after a whole day's journey that their Son was not in their company. After a long search and inquiry, they found Jesus still in the temple and busily engaged in a debate with the doctors. In spite of anguish and trouble in the search for the Child Jesus who stayed behind without the permission of the parents, the tender Mother did not lose her temper.

The virtue of the Holy Vessel always reflects a far greater virtue. Though Mary's temper is well controlled, you can still detect the trace of anxiety and annoyance in her words: "My son, why hast thou treated us so?" (*Purg.* xv. 90). You can see perfect peace and confidence in the Son's response to the Mother's rebuke: *"Could you not tell that I must needs be in the place which belongs to my Father?"* (Luke 2:49). Any ordinary child of His age would feel a greater anxiety for being abandoned than the parents' anguish for having lost him. But Christ shows no annoyance and tenderly chides His Mother for her anxiety.

"Could you not tell that I must needs be in the place which belongs to my Father?" What does He mean? *These words he spoke to them were beyond their understanding* (Luke 2:50). He remained in the temple. The temple is the tabernacle and the symbol of the Mystical Body of Christ. The sanctification of Christ's animal body by the Holy Spirit is the prefigure of the sanctification of the Mystical Body and the exemplar for the sanctification of the animal body of the baptized. The Child Jesus in the temple was the first manifestation of the grace of the Holy Spirit in His body: *"And the child grew and became strong. He was full of wisdom and the grace of God was upon him"* (Luke 2:40).

What is the effect of the grace of the Holy Spirit on the body of Christ? This is illustrated by the second example of meekness. Pisistratus' wife was outraged by a man who tried to embrace her daughter and begs her husband, the king of Athens, to take vengeance on him. She provokes her husband saying,

> "If thou art truly the lord of the city
>   whose naming caused such strife amongst the gods
>   and from which all knowledge shines forth,"
>   *Purg.* xv. 97–99

The strife was the strife between Minerva and Neptune.[8] Both wanted to have Athens named after them. In the contest, Neptune struck the earth with his powerful trident and produced a horse and Athene produced an olive-tree. The victory was given to Athene, and Athens was named after her. Neptune and his horse are symbols of animal power; Athene symbolizes reason, which has subdued animal power.

The reply of the king of Athens to his raging wife is worthy of the lordship over the city of wisdom, "from which all knowledge shines forth." He graciously says, "What shall we do to those which wish us harm/if we condemn those who love us?" (*Purg.* xv. 104–105). The king of Athens thus subdues the queen's animal passion by reason. Woman is the symbol of carnality and animality in man. Through the grace of the Holy Spirit, the animal heart and power of Christ become perfectly subdued to His mind.

The third example of meekness is the scene of St. Stephen's martyrdom. The Martyr Stephen was one of the lowliest disciples. He was one of the seven deacons appointed to do the lowliest work in the Church, i.e., to take care of the widows who complained of being neglected by the busy Apostles (Acts 6:1–5). But Stephen was *"full of faith and of the Holy Spirit."* The stoning of the first martyr began with his debate with the Jews. The learned Jews were no match for the wisdom of the lowly creature:

Now Stephen, full of grace and power, was working great wonders and signs . . . And they were unable to withstand the wisdom and the Spirit who spoke. Then they bribed men to say that they had heard him speaking blasphemous words against Moses and against God . . . They seized him and brought him to the Sanhedrin . . . (Acts 6:8–12).

Stephen lost no courage before the Sanhedrin and its false witnesses and gave an eloquent lecture in which he explained the divine mission of Christ in a long historical perspective to the "stiff-necked" creatures (Acts 7:1–53). His persecutors could not stand him any more:

They were cut to the heart and gnashed their teeth at him. But he, full of the Holy Spirit, looked up to heaven and saw the glory of God, and Jesus standing at the right hand of God; and he said, "Behold, I see . . ." But they cried out with a loud voice and stopped their ears and rushed upon him . . . And while they were stoning Stephen he prayed and said, "Lord Jesus, receive my spirit." And falling on his knees, he cried out with a loud voice, saying, "Lord, do not lay this sin against them" (Acts 7:54–60).

St. Stephen's martyrdom illustrates the final manifestation of the power of the Holy Spirit in the body of the Son, whose first manifestation was given in the temple of Jerusalem. The Holy Spirit strengthens and sustains the body of the Son throughout His visible mission, in His Mother's womb and in her bosom, in the temple and on the street, in the city and out in the wilderness, until the Lamb of God returns to Jerusalem to become a holocaust for the paschal feast. It is the animal passion of the mob that crucifies the animal body of the Son. When Pilate said that he could not find any guilt in the Lamb of God, the bestial mob demanded: *"His blood be upon us, and upon our children"* (Matt. 27:25). The Lamb of God meekly subjected

Himself to the animal passion of the mob, and rebuked the one who tried to draw his sword for His defense (Matt. 26:53).

Aristotle teaches his rhetoric students that the sting of insult is the most effective weapon in provoking anger. Even the sting of insult has no effect on Christ nailed on the cross: *The people stood by watching; and the rulers joined them in pouring scorn on him; "He saved others," they said; "if he is the Christ, God's chosen, let him save himself." The soldiers too mocked him, when they came and offered him vinegar, by saying, "if thou art the king of the Jews, save thyself"* (Luke 23:35–38). In His agony, He only prayed for His persecutors until He said, *"Father, into thy hands, I commend my spirit"* (Luke 24:46).

St. Thomas says that the Passion of Christ was the greatest sorrow and pain ever inflicted on a human body.[9] *O all ye that pass by the way, attend, and see if there be any sorrow like unto mine* (Lam. 1:12). To suffer the outrage of animal passion in meekness takes a far greater courage than to fight back in valor. It was the animal heart waxed and nurtured in the grace of the Holy Spirit that sustained the Son of God on the way of the cross. The animal heart of *Agnus Dei* was pierced with a spear as the last act of human bestiality to be inflicted on the body of the Son (John 19:34). This is the Sacred Heart which was filled by the Holy Spirit, the Love of God. This is the heart which throbbed and revolved in a perfect conformity to the head of the body. When this heart was pierced, its outpouring love thrilled the entire universe and left a permanent trace at the entrance to the Minotaur's kingdom (*Inf.* xii 34–45). *But Jesus again cried out with a loud voice, and gave up his spirit. And behold, the curtain of the temple was torn in two from top to bottom; and the earth quaked, and the rocks were rent. . . .* (Matt. 27:50–51).

The sanctification of Christ by the Holy Spirit is the

exemplar for all the faithful. This is the second meaning of Stephen's martyrdom. Lowly and weak as he was born, he became full of grace and power and worked great wonders and signs. He saw the visions which the learned could not see. He tried to persuade with reason the bigoted Jews who were stopping their ears. His animal spirit culminated in his meek subjection to the stoning mobs. One can gain the wisdom and meekness to mount on the way of the cross only by receiving the Holy Spirit, as Christ showed by His own example.

It is the meekness of the Holy Spirit that the Angelic Poet sings on the third rung of the angelic ladder of divine love. It is the Holy Spirit Who sanctifies and fortifies the body of the baptized and the body of the Church, the Empire, as He sanctified and fortified the body of the Son. Wisdom from the Holy Spirit opens lowly eyes to the visions of heaven; power from Him strengthens the weak flesh to bear the crown of thorns on this earth.

chapter 7

Lesson on the Rung of Fortitude and Sloth

The Fourth Heaven, the Fourth Terrace, and the Fifth and the Sixth Circles

WE ARE now approaching the fourth rung of the angelic ladder of divine love. This rung is grounded on the passive irascible. While the active irascible is the role of animal power in its relation to the intellect, the passive irascible is its role in its relation to the concupiscible. In the last chapter, we examined how the animal power operates in obedience to the intellect or in defiance of it. In this chapter, we will see how the animal power functions in protecting and guiding the concupiscible. The main task of the irascible as the guardian of the concupiscible is to overcome the obstacles and difficulties in the pursuit of the good. The concupiscible needs no help from the irascible, as long as there is no evil force working against its satisfaction.

Confronted with obstacles and difficulties, the irascible may give up all hope and sink into despair, or renew its vigor and overcome the difficulties. The former is the vice of sloth, and the latter is the virtue of fortitude. The consequence of the battle of the irascible is the satisfaction or the frustration of the concupiscible. The former will be the joy of the irascible; the latter its sorrow. Voice is the medium for the expression of joy and sorrow; the animal weeps and sings with its voice. Voice will be a new element in the metaphor of animal which our poet continues to employ in the construction of the fourth rung of his angelic ladder.

Despair can fall into two classes: the despair of the earthly good and the despair of the heavenly good. The former is represented by the Fifth Circle, and the latter by the Sixth Circle. The sinners who despaired of the earthly good are sinking and moaning in the muddy, stagnant marsh of Styx (*Inf.* vii. 103–130). The filthy water of the Stygian swamp flows down from the three Circles of the concupiscible (*Inf.* vii. 101–102). The stagnant water represents the desires of the concupiscible which have been detached and withdrawn from their objects in despair. A slothful man who shrinks back in despair from the objects of his desire rots in his stagnant power of appetition and shuts himself up in resentment.

In the terminology of the Freudian school, Dante's sloth will be explained as the withdrawal of the libidinal cathexis. What is libido but the concupiscible? Libido is the erotic component of the soul; the concupiscible is the source of love. The source of libidinal energy lies in the deepest level of the psyche, the unconscious. The origin of the concupiscible is in the lowest level of the soul, the vegetative level, which is essentially unconscious. What is the result of the complete withdrawal of libido from its objects? The result is the interesting phenomenon of autism. The ego completely loses its interest in its environment and shuts itself up in its tight shell. Eugene Minkowski called such a psychical status a stagnation of life impetus. Once the libido or the concupiscible stops flowing in the stream of life and shuts itself up, it has to stagnate and decay. From this stagnation arise the unbearable fumes of stench over the Stygian marsh (*Inf.* ix. 31).

In the Sixth Circle, Dante gives the Epicureans as the sample of the despair of the heavenly good (*Inf*. x. 13–15). The Epicureans denied the immortality of the soul and consequently all the possibilities of the heavenly bliss. The despairers of the heavenly good are roasted in open tombs. The difference between the heavenly and the earthly good is represented by the contrast between fire and water. Fire mounts upward; water falls downward. Despite this difference, the two Circles share the common theme of death. One group is crammed in tombs and the other is drowned in a marsh. To live with no lively interest in the world is like being buried alive.

Anger is the psychological concomitant of despair. The anger of despair is sullen rancor; it does not flare up into positive act. There is no guard in the Fifth or the Sixth Circles as in the Seventh, because there is no need to lock up the sullen in prison. To be sure, they can become violent enough for a few rounds of pinching and biting, but they can be left at large with no great damage (*Inf*. vii. 112–114). It is the lack of motive force that distinguishes the passive anger of despair from the active anger of vengeance. Whereas the bloody stream of Phlegethon flows like a torrent, the Stygian marsh stagnates. The flakes of fire in the Seventh Circle are blown in the air, but the fire of the Sixth Circle burns in the tombs.

The cause of positive anger is positive harm received from others, particularly a positive insult or slight. Passive anger arises from the negative cause that the object of one's desire has not been granted. Passive anger is a resentment against the world for its unfairness in the distribution of its fortune. Phlegyas is a good example of the resentment of the sullen. Dante presents his anger as a resentment against deceit (*Inf*. viii. 22–24). When one withdraws one's desire which was once extended into the world like a fresh green shoot of hope, one feels as though the cruel world had lured out his innocent desire only to tantalize, mock, and cheat it.

Resentment becomes indignation when it is expressed in the language of justice and fairness.[1] Filippo Argenti is indignant at the special privilege bestowed on Dante: "Who art thou, that comest before thy time?" (*Inf.* viii. 33). The indignation of the fallen angels at the gate of the Lower Hell rests on the same ground of unfairness: "Who is this rash one, paying not death's fee,/that dares to penetrate into this realm?" (*Inf.* viii. 84–85). Cavalcante's tearful complaint amounts to: "If you, Dante, have gained this privilege of walking through the kingdom of death as a reward for your genius, why is my son, whose genius is equally great, not coming with you?" (*Inf.* x. 58–60).

Our poet himself experiences all the symptoms of despair and resentment. When he reaches the Stygian shore, every star is falling (*Inf.* vii. 98). So fall Dante's courage and vigor. At the threshold of the City of Dis, he becomes such a powerless victim of despair and fear that he loses all his confidence in Virgil's power and begs Virgil to give up the trip. Dante becomes timid and petty. At Argenti's assault, he helplessly lacks courage to fight back in defense. It is Virgil who pushes Argenti back into the swamp (*Inf.* viii. 31–42). If Dante had any sense of manly courage, he would be too ashamed of his cowardice during Argenti's assault even to lift up his face before Virgil. But he is oblivious of his cowardice and proud of praying for the vengeance he could not inflict on Argenti with his own hands (*Inf.* viii. 52–54). The excessive impulse for vengeance is a sign of a frustrated coward who cannot be his own instrument of vengeance. Dante further couches his venom of vengeance in the language of justice. The semblance of justice is the only ointment to alleviate the wounds of humiliation and frustration in a coward.

Positive anger, like the anger of Achilles, can become

the motive force for altruistic act and heroic deed, but passive anger which is essentially rooted in frustrated self-interests allows no room for concern and care for other people. Bottled up in his own frustration, the sullen man loses all sense of communion with his neighbors. The exchange of scorn and insult between Dante and Farinata is briefly interrupted by the emergence of Cavalcante (*Inf*. x. 52–75). After Cavalcante's disappearance, Farinata resumes his quarrel with Dante as though nothing had happened during the interval and shows no concern at all for his tombmate's grief (*Inf*. x. 76–96). It is this sense of discommunion among the sullen that Dante wants to convey through the consistent resistance he meets in his entry to the Fifth Circle. The sullen cannot and do not want to share their grief and agony with others. Try to tell one of them that you understand the agony in his choked heart and that you have even experienced that sort of agony, and you will be scornfully answered: "How dare you presume to enter the kingdom of my agony. You may have seen a great deal of sorrow but not anything like mine. Mine is the thorn buried in the deepest chamber of my heart which no one can see or touch." The sullen man wants to treasure his petty anger in a petty pride.

What is the effect of despair and resentment on the intellect? The intellect bogs down in the mire of rancor. We can see the shortsightedness of the intellect benumbed by rancor in the series of rash judgments and conjectures which Dante himself makes and leads others to make. The series of rash judgments begins with Phlegyas' mistake about the purpose of Dante's trip (*Inf*. viii. 18–24). Virgil has his share of rash judgment in underestimating the obduracy of the fallen angels (*Inf*. viii. 86–117). From the discouraged, broken words of Virgil, Dante draws a conclusion far worse than what Virgil intends to express (*Inf*. ix. 7–15). The series of rash judgment culminates in the pitiful scene where

Cavalcante infers the death of his son from the past tense of a single verb and tumbles back to the bottom of his tomb without bothering to check the validity of his conjecture (*Inf.* x. 67–69).

This is the nature of the intellect which draws a heretical conclusion about the possibility of the heavenly bliss and thereby justifies the despair of it. This is a vicious circle. Despair benumbs the intellect, and the intellect makes a rash judgment to justify the despair. It is this rash intellect which St. Thomas has in mind, when he gives, on the Sun, a long discourse on the danger of rash judgment (*Par.* xiii. 112–142). The intellect which is paralyzed by despair is like the eye whose field of vision is blocked by the thick, foul vapor of Styx (*Inf.* viii. 12).

All the joys and sorrows of the sullen are distilled into their hymn of mire:

> Fixed in the slime they say: "Sullen we were
> in the sweet air cheered by the brightening sun
> because of sulky vapors (*accidioso fummo*) in our
>   hearts;
>
> Now here in this black mire, we curse our luck.
> *Inf.* vii. 121–124

They cannot sing out this hymn of despair in intelligible words, but have to gurgle it in their throats (*Inf.* vii. 125). St. Thomas says that anger destroys and confuses the power of speech, the most intelligible organ for expression.[2] It is because of *accidioso fummo* that the sullen soul has to wallow in the mire of unintelligibility.

By joining the two words *accidioso* and *fummo*, Dante wants to point out the inherent relation between sloth and rancor. Sloth is often taken to mean only laziness or languor, and its inherent relation with despair and rancor is often overlooked. On the Fourth Terrace, Dante again points out the inherent relation between sorrow and sloth. The penitents run and shout in tears of sorrow (*Purg.* xviii. 99). Besides hearing the tearful cries of the penitents, Dante feels the impact of sloth and torpor on his own body. All powers pass away from Dante's legs the moment he steps on the Fourth Terrace (*Purg.* xvii. 73–75). St. Thomas says that the contemplation of divine truth and future happiness is the best remedy for sorrow and sloth.[3] Dante urges his guide to continue his discourse (*Purg.* xvii. 84). Virgil's discourse gives a synoptic view of the *Purgatorio* and explains the source and nature of love. Like the survey of the plan of the *Inferno,* the synoptic view of the structure of the *Purgatorio* is meant to describe the course of pilgrimage and thereby help restore the vigor of the pilgrim who has become weary at the midway of his journey (*Inf.* xi; *Purg.* xvii. 112–139). To know the prospect and retrospect of the course of the journey is a great help to a tired traveller.

Virgil's discourse on human love describes the process in which the human soul falls in love with its object (*Purg.* xviii. 16–33). Mind is awakened to activity by the objects of pleasure. Confronted with an object of desire, the mind forms an image of the object and unfolds it within itself. This image attracts the mind to the object, and this attraction is love. Thus enamoured with the object, the mind never rests until it is united with the object. The demonstration of this discourse is given in Dante's dream of the Siren (*Purg.* xix. 7–24). The Siren appears as a hideous woman with stuttering voice, squint eyes, crooked feet, maimed hands, and sallow hue. But Dante's long gaze works a dramatic change in her appearance. She begins to glow with the color of love and even sing sweet songs until Dante feels captivated by her charm. During the long gaze, Dante has formed the ideal image of his love and shrouded the Siren with his image. Thus he falls in love with the hideous woman.

The dream of the Siren illustrates the function of the irascible power in the awakening of human love. Love is the first of the concupiscible passions.[4] And yet love is not possible without the power of the intellect.[5] But the power of human intellect knows no particular. Love is the joint product of the intellect and the concupiscible. Love is the longing for a particular object, but it has a universal force. It is the imagination of the irascible that performs the crucial function of bringing together the intellect and the concupiscible. The imagination of the animal power provides the medium in which the intellect is awakened to the object of the concupiscible and transforms the object of mere desire into an object of love. Human love always begins with the love of the sensible and grows into the love of the insensible. The ideal image projected to the object of love does not show sensibly the object but only points to the object of love which has transcended the sensible level. St. Bernard says that the principal reason for the Incarnation is to win the love of those who know how to love only carnally.[6]

In the dream of the Siren, Dante's love is re-kindled and his sloth is overcome. Since sloth is the withdrawal of the libidinal cathexis from the objects of desire, its cure requires the expansion of the shrinking libido back to the external world and its re-investment in the objects of desire. The initial, hideous appearance of the Siren reflects the slothful response of Dante's languishing and shrinking eros, and the glow and charm of the Siren shows the vigorous response of his palpitating and expanding libido.

The troublesome feature of the renewal of Dante's appetite is that his libido is creeping back to the earthly good instead of leaping up toward the heavenly bliss. The danger of falling back to the good of flesh and dust is forestalled by the timely intervention of a heavenly lady (*Purg.* xix. 25–27). Dante can detach himself from the bewitching Siren only after seeing her hideous belly and becoming disgusted with its stench. It is still his profit to have renewed his appetite. He climbs up to the next Terrace:

> As a falcon which gazes at its feet,
>> then turns at a call and extends its head
>> through desire for the food that allures it.
>
> *Purg.* xix. 64–66

The dream of the Siren is the effect of Virgil's discourse as well as its demonstration. Dante knows where lies the food of his longing. Virgil has admonished him to spurn the earth with his heels and "turn your eyes to the lure placed/ by the Eternal King in the revolving spheres" (*Purg.* xix. 62–63).

The phenomenon elucidated by the dream of the Siren is the reversal of what takes place in the vision of the Furies (*Inf.* ix. 37–63). The Furies are the women of terror and fright, while the Siren is the woman of enticement and bewitchment. The Siren sings, and the Furies weep. The former glows in love's hue and the latter threaten with the Gorgon's head. Gazing at the Siren warms up Dante's cold limbs, but the vision of Medusa would have turned him into a stone. The Furies represent the shrinking and freezing of libido in despair, and the Siren the renewal and expansion of the shrunken appetite.

The tears of the Furies and the song of the Siren spell out, in a hidden way, the requisite steps for directing the appetite away from the earthly good and toward the heavenly good, if the Furies' tears are taken as the alienation of love from the insensate earthly care and the Siren's song for the lure of the glorious heavenly bliss. On the Sun, two garlands of sparkling lights open Dante's eyes to the truth that poverty is a requisite step in the pursuit of the heavenly bliss. The two circles of the blessed are those who became beggars on the earth to follow Christ's first counsel: "*If thou wilt be perfect, go sell all thou hast, and give to the poor, and follow me*" (Matt. 19:21). St. Thomas and St. Bonaventura, the two chief spokesmen on the Sun, were mendicant monks. While on the earth, St. Thomas preached that Christ was a mendicant and that voluntary poverty is the first foundation for the perfection of charity.[7] The mendicant monks withdrew all their love from the perishable good not in despair, but in hope for the immortal glory.

Both the souls of the Fifth and the Sixth Circles and the souls of the two rings on the Sun have withdrawn their libido from the earthly good, but they differ in the disposal of the withdrawn appetite. The difference is spelled out by the dark vapors over the Styx and the brilliant illumination on the Sun, the bodies wallowing in the mire and the bodies dancing on the Sun, the gurgling in the slime and the singing on the Sun. These differences are the reflection of the contrast between the shrinking and depressive force of despair and the expanding and elating force of hope. The two garlands of lights are even "sweeter in voice than shining in appearance" (*Par.* x. 66).

Dante compares the festivity on the Sun to the Bacchanalian frenzy (*Par.* xiii. 25–27). He saw the foreshadow of this frenzy on the Fourth Terrace (*Purg.* xviii. 93). The song of the theologians surpasses the music of the Muses and the Siren (*Par.* xii. 8). To keep the love of God unsullied from the dust and mire of despair and to sustain it in the Bacchanalian frenzy of hope is the virtue of fortitude. The virtue of fortitude is not only embodied in the two circles of theologians but exemplified by the lives of the two great beggarly saints, St. Francis and St. Dominic. The two saints were two princes specially appointed by Providence to succor the Holy Church, which had reached the nadir of despair and was wallowing in the mire of despondency (*Par.* xi. 28–36).

St. Thomas, the distinguished son of the Dominican order, gives the eulogy of the saint of Assisi. He says that to call the birthplace of St. Francis *Assisi* (I have risen) is to understate the virtue of the saint and that it should be called the *Orient*, the rising Sun (*Par.* xi. 52–54). Even at the early stage of this new sun, the whole earth which was depressed like the Stygian marsh began to feel his rays of heat and love:

> He was not yet far from rising
>   when the earth began to feel
>   some comfort from his great virtue.
>
> *Par.* xi. 55–57

While he was still a youth, he renounced his father and his fortune to be espoused to Lady Poverty,

> She, deprived of her first husband (Christ),
>   for eleven hundred years and more, until he came,
>   remained obscure and despised and without a proposal.
>
> *Par.* xi. 64–66

Though poverty is usually a cause of sloth and languor, St. Francis' marriage with Lady Poverty enflamed his love and zeal and started a stampede of young men to the Lady:

> So that the venerable Bernard
>   first bared his feet, and ran after such peace,
>   and while running seemed to himself too slow.
>
> O unknown riches! O fruitful good!
>   Egidius bared his feet, Sylvester his,
>   following the groom, so pleasing was the bride!
>
> *Par.* xi. 79–84

To wean away all the desires from the earthly attraction is to be wed to Lady Poverty. Through this marriage, the soul can devote its entire being to the love of God. Such an impeccable devotion is the *holy will* (*Par.* xi. 97). The holy will of St. Francis was so pure and unsullied that it still remains one of the central topics in the ethical discourses of our world which knows little and heeds little about the Dark Ages.

St. Bonaventura, the eminent son of the Franciscan order, answers to St. Thomas' eulogy of St. Francis with the eulogy of St. Dominic. He says that St. Dominic was the great partner of St. Francis in the great mission. While St. Francis was wed to Lady Poverty, St. Dominic was wed to the Lady of Faith. He re-equipped and rejuvenated Christ's laggard, timid army of faith. In his battle against the rank host of heretics, he was cruel to his enemies and tender to his friends (*Par.* xii. 88–102). As his godmother had foreseen in her dream, St. Dominic turned out to be a fierce dog with a blazing torch in his mouth (*Par.* xii. 64). As St. Francis gave everything to God, so St. Dominic belonged to God (Dominic means "of God").

St. Francis and St. Dominic accomplished magnanimous works at the most depressive era in the entire history of the Church, while most of their fellow Christians were "gurgling in their throats" to no purpose (*Inf.* vii. 125). Magnanimity and magnificence are the important components of fortitude.[8] Magnificence and magnanimity mean the undertaking of some great and honorable tasks and to do so requires a broad, noble mind, great courage, and boundless hope. It also requires great expenditures. Having forsaken all their wealth, St. Francis and St. Dominic had no resources for great expenditures except their souls. The two beggarly monks accomplished with bare hands the great task which was too big even for battalions of cardinals and bishops.

Compare the two monks with the most arrogant soul in the Sixth Circle, whom Dante designates as "magnanimous" (*Inf.* x. 73). Keenly conscious of his nobility and magnanimity, Farinata wants to know Dante's ancestry before doing anything else with him and does not hide his contempt in his inquiry (*Inf.* x. 42). St. Francis did not derive his nobility and magnanimity from his ancestors. He came in fact from a humble tradesman and stood above all the spurious claims and marks of nobility:

> Nor did baseness of heart weigh down his brow
> for being the son of Pietro Bernardone,
> nor for appearing so marvelously despised.
> *Par.* xi. 88–90

Farinata is too petty to have any concern even for the grief of his tombmate, Cavalcante, for all his claim and pretense of being a magnanimous soul. While the two poor monks had hearts and minds broad enough to take upon their shoulders the care of the entire Christendom, Farinata does not have a heart large enough to encompass one single tomb. In describing the inmates of his tomb, Farinata says,

> "With more than a thousand lie I here;
> here within is the second Frederick
> and the Cardinal; and of the rest I speak not."
> *Inf.* x. 118–120

If Dante were to ask why Farinata would not speak of the rest, what reason would he give? We can fairly well guess; he would answer, "How do you expect me to know and remember all these countless souls, worthless except for a few famous ones like the cardinal and the emperor?"

The final contrast between the heavenly and the hellish magnanimity comes in the difference between the celestial and the infernal eulogy. St. Francis is praised by a distinguished son of the Dominican order, and St. Dominic by an eminent son of the Franciscan order. The Angelic Doctor concludes the praise of the Seraphic Father by denouncing the decadence of his own order, and the Seraphic Doctor concludes the praise of the Cherubic Father by exposing the corruption of his own order. The two rival orders are not only happy to praise each other's merit but eager to denounce their own demerit. To see the merit of others with adoring eyes and to expose one's own demerit with a merciless hand is a mark of a magnanimous mind. Compare these eulogies with the words of scorn and insult exchanged between Dante and Farinata (*Inf*. x. 46–99). They irritate and debase each other by the childish boasts of their own sides and the petty ridicules of each other's side. Their quarrel only reflects the paltry minds of the combatants.

What is it that brings about the difference between a magnanimous soul and a paltry soul? What is it that makes a great soul great and a puny soul puny? The magnitude and stature of a soul is determined by its hope. A soul which sets its highest hope on the trifles of the earth and wallows in its mire cannot but be paltry and petty. A soul which sets all its hope on the great glory of heaven and vibrates in the angelic vigor cannot but be magnificent. While the paltry soul is blinded by the Stygian vapor, the magnificent soul glows like the Sun. This is the wisdom of Solomon of the *Sole*, the greatest wisdom ever possessed by a human being except Christ and Adam (*Par*. xiii. 46–111).

The Angelic Doctor explains the origin and nature of Solomon's wisdom. When Solomon was asked by God what he wanted to receive from Him, Solomon wished to have "*a wise and understanding heart*" (Wisdom 7:7; *Par*. xiii. 93). St. Thomas says that Solomon's wisdom is not any of the intellectual virtues which are employed in philosophy, science, and mathematics, but regal prudence. His wisdom is prudential wisdom. What is prudential wisdom? It is practical wisdom. While theoretical wisdom deals only with theories, practical wisdom is concerned with the practical problem of choice. Choice involves the counsel of the intellect and the desires of the concupiscible. The wisdom of Solomon's understanding heart lies in its marvelous capacity of mediating the intellect and the concupiscible.

In the last chapter, we saw how Dante employs the epicycle of Venus in his illustration of the prudence of the heart in its obedience to the intellect. We shall now see how he uses the dual spiral motion of the Sun to elucidate the wisdom of the heart in mediating the desires of the concupiscible and the counsel of the intellect (*Par.* x. 7–33). The Sun spins along at the cross section of the two spiral motions (*Par.* x. 14, 32). By combining the two spiral motions, the Sun can fulfill the task of being the minister of Nature. Without the marvelous dual motion, Dante says, every potency on the earth would be dead. The Sun as the union of the two spiral motions represents the Holy Spirit. The Holy Spirit proceeds from the Father and the Son.[9] The Spirit is the combined breath (*spira*) from the Father and the Son; the Spirit is the union of the spirations of the Father and the Son:

> Gazing upon His Son with the Love (Spirit)
>   which both (Father and Son) eternally breathe
>   (*spira*) forth,
>   the primal and ineffable worth
>
> Made everything that revolves through mind
>   or through space and with such order
>   that whoever looks on it cannot fail to see His effect.
>
> *Par.* x. 1–6

The Power of the Father is the source of the creative force, and the Wisdom of the Son is the fountain of the exemplars of created things. It is the function of the Holy Spirit to bring together the Power and the Wisdom in the government of the world. This is Providence. What is Providence but God's prudence? Divine providence is administered in the temporal world by the Holy Spirit.[10] This is the answer to Virgil's puzzle. In explaining the nature of love on the Fourth Terrace, Virgil admits that the original source and cause of the human impulses is the puzzle which he can never hope to explain and which he would like to leave to Beatrice (*Purg.* xviii. 57, 73). The Holy Spirit is the Gift of gifts; all the motive forces of creatures come through the mediative function of the Spirit. This is what the Angelic Poet means in saying that every potency on earth would be dead except for the Sun's dual spiral motion.

The function of the irascible in mediating the intellect and the concupiscible resembles the dual spiral motion of the Spirit. The intellect provides the universal principles and resembles the Word of God, the Son, and the concupiscible is the source of the appetitive force and resembles the Power of the Father. The important difference between the Power of the Father and the appetite of the concupiscible is that the former is the source of all values (*lo primo et ineffabile valore*) from which all good emanates and the latter is the origin of the powers which seek the good for satisfaction (*Par.* x. 3). In the Aristotelian tradition, the intellect and the appetite are the two principles of motion, the universal and the particular. The irascible combines these two principles of motion into concrete acts, as the Spirit combines the two spiral motions to give life to the world. The Holy Spirit is the Lord and Giver of life, who proceedeth from the Father and the Son:

Et in Spiritum Sanctum, Dominum, et vivificantem, qui ex Patre Filioque procedit (The Nicene Creed).

As every potency on earth would be dead without the Sun's mediational function, so every potency of the soul would be dead without the mediational function of the irascible. The death which comes from the failure of the irascible in its mediational function is represented by the Fifth and the Sixth Circles. We have noticed that death is the common feature of the two groups of sinners in the two Circles: one group is buried in the mire and the other in the fiery tombs. The Fifth Circle is in the Upper Hell, and the Sixth Circle in the Lower Hell; the former is in the region of the concupiscible and the latter in the region of the intellect. The separation of these two Circles by the impenetratable fortification means the total failure of the irascible in its function of mediation. Instead of providing the crucial function of uniting the two principles of motion, the irascible is divided against itself and has lost all its motive force. The sinners sink in the tomb or in the mire.

The mediational function of the Holy Spirit is further illustrated by the miraculous succor of the Church which the Spirit effected through St. Francis and St. Dominic. St. Francis is the Seraphic Father, the exemplification of the concupiscible. St. Dominic is "a splendor of Cherubic light," the exemplification of the intellect. These two princes are the "two wheels" with which the Spirit performed the miracle. The two circles of the theologians represent the two types of theology, the Franciscan and the Dominican, the theology of love and the theology of intellect. Their union is represented by the third circle which appears and encircles the two circles of theologians just before Dante leaves the Sun. Dante hails the third circle in a single line: "Oh true sparkling of the Holy Breath (*santo spiro*)" (*Par.* xiv. 76).

We can now see the nature of the Bacchanalian frenzy which fills the festivity and singing on the Sun (*Par.* xiii. 25–27). The frenzy is from the Holy Spirit. *Be not drunk with wine . . . but be filled with the Spirit* (Eph. 5:18). The penitents who run on in two groups on the Fourth Terrace are already anticipating and imitating the two spiral motions on the Sun. They are already infused with the Bacchanalian frenzy of the Spirit (*Purg.* xviii. 93).

The wisdom of Solomon is the wisdom which comes from the Holy Spirit and which reflects His Providential wisdom. The height of prudential wisdom is the wisdom of theology. Theology is not a theoretical science, but a practical one.[11] Theology deals with the end of man, and the ends of man are matters of prudence. The wisdom of theology is the highest prudential wisdom, because theology treats the highest end of man. The Angelic Doctor says that theology is "the wisdom above all human wisdom; not merely in any order, but absolutely."[12] St. Thomas on the Sun exemplifies the best specimen of prudential wisdom in his discourse. Cautioning against the rash judgment of the muddled intellect, he opens his discourse with clear distinction of terms and their senses and carefully qualifies his conclusions to avoid all possible misunderstandings (*Par.* xiii. 109–142).

At the opening of his *Summa*, St. Thomas defines theology as the elucidation and articulation of the revealed truth which is accepted in faith.[13] By infusing the theologians with the Bacchanalian-like zeal of the Holy Spirit, the Angelic Poet expresses his view that theology is a gift of the Spirit. Christ promised this gift before His Ascension: *Many things yet I have to say to you; you cannot hear them now. But when he, the Spirit of truth, has come, he will teach you all truth* (John 16:12–13). The first manifestation of this promised appearance was given shortly after His Ascension:

*They were all filled with the Holy Spirit, and they began to
speak with divers tongues, according as the Holy Spirit gave
them to speak . . . And all were amazed and perplexed, saying to one another, "What does this mean?" But others said in
mockery, "They are full of new wine." But Peter . . . lifted
up his voice . . . "Men of Juda . . . let this be known to you
. . . These men are not drunk, as you suppose" (Acts 2:4–
15).*

By placing Solomon among the theologians, Dante shows
the link between the Judaic tradition of prophecy and the
Christian tradition of theology. Both prophecy and theology are the gifts of the Holy Spirit and their purpose is
to elucidate the nature of the ineffable good. This is the
way Solomon understood the origin and purpose of his
wisdom:

*Wherefore I wished, and understanding was given me: and I
called upon God, and the spirit of wisdom came upon me
. . . she is the breath of the power of God and a certain
emanation of the glory of the almighty God . . . she is the
brightness of eternal light, and the unspotted mirror of God's
majesty, and the image of his goodness (Wis. 7:7–26).*

The mirror of images which reflects God's majesty and
goodness is theology. The nature of the triune God does
not yield itself to direct perception and apprehension. "The
soul never thinks without image."[14] In thinking of God
whose nature is essentially supersensible, man has to rely
on his sensible images. These images are metaphors and
analogies. Solomon made an imaginative use of the power
of imagery in his Canticle of Canticles. His wisdom was
the unspotted mirror of sensible image for the reflection of
the supersensible truth; he deserves to be placed on the
Sun, the highest sensible image of the divine light.

Indispensable as they are, the images can never fully

represent the nature of God. Imagery is a dangerous medium; it not only reveals but also obscures. Fully aware of the difficulty of using imagery for the illustration of the things whose order of existence surpasses the sensible level, St. Thomas instructs us to see not only the historical or literal sense of images but their spiritual sense.[15] What is the spiritual sense? It comprises the allegorical sense, the moral sense, and the anagogical sense (cf. Dante's dedicatory epistle to Can Grande). Our poet wants his readers to understand his Angelic Epic as a theological poem:

> O ye, who have sane intellects,
>   consider well the doctrine here concealed
>   under the veil of my strange verses.
>
> *Inf.* ix. 61–63

Our Angelic Poet also wishes to tell us that "the veil" is the veil of imagery. He repeats the word *imagini* three times while he is describing the splendor of the theologians on the Sun (*Par.* xiii. 1, 7, 10). He further instructs us that what is veiled under his imagery is that which transcends our mortal sense:

> For it as far transcends our sense
>   as the movement of Chiana is transcended
>   by the motion of that heaven
>   which surpasses all the rest.
>
> *Par.* xiii. 22–24

The image in a theological song also performs exactly the same function as the image in the dream of the Siren. As the image lures out and attaches carnal love to the Siren, so the image entices and elevates spiritual love to God. The difference between the song of the Siren and the Song of Songs is the difference between the flesh and the spirit. The heavenly lady rips open the Siren's belly; the belly is the source of the concupiscible. Our poet witnesses this at a prophetic hour (*Purg.* xix. 4). That is, he will see how the belly of the concupiscible is ripped open and purged on the three top Terraces. The singing of the theologians is also prophetic. What is prophecy but the vision of the future?[16] The theologians sing of the Trinity (*Par.* xiv. 28–33). Our poet will see the Trinity as the object of appetition on the three top Planets.

What is going to become of the body when its sensitive power is wholly absorbed into the spiritual good? What is going to become of "the wise and understanding heart" of Solomon in the kingdom of spirit? This is the topic on which Solomon gives his wise counsel to Dante (*Par.* xiv. 43–60). On the Day of Resurrection, when the blessed recover their bodies, their bodies will be spiritual in proportion to their spiritual bliss. Dante does not forget the bodies of the damned. The heretics will also recover their bodies, and their bodies will be buried in the eternally burning tombs where their souls are already buried (*Inf.* x. 10–12). We can say that their bodies will be carnal in proportion to their carnal bliss.

The virtue and the sin of the passive irascible which we have seen in Heaven and Hell are crystallized in the whip and bridle of the Fourth Terrace. The two examples of sloth are the Israelites who lost courage and hope in their strenuous return to the Holy Land and the Trojans who despaired of Aeneas' mission and failed to reach Latium (*Purg.* xviii. 133–138). The former is the despair of the divinely appointed goal, and the latter the despair of the humanly appointed goal. The former reflects the Sixth Circle; the latter the Fifth Circle.

The two examples of fortitude are Mary's haste and Caesar's haste (*Purg.* xviii. 100–105). As soon as the Eternal Virgin received the Angelic Annunciation of the Miraculous Conception, she rose up in haste and ran to Elizabeth, the mother-to-be of John the Baptist (Luke 1:39). The fortitude of the Virgin Mother lies in her vigor and eagerness to meet her cousin whose son is to prepare the way of repentance for her own Son. From the moment of the Miraculous Conception to the moment of the Resurrection, the Holy Mother was always the first to look after and stand by her Son.

The virtue of the Holy Vessel reflects a far greater virtue of the Holy Spirit: *No sooner had Elizabeth heard Mary's greetings, than the child leaped in her womb; and Elizabeth herself was filled with the Holy Spirit* (Luke 1:41). The Holy Spirit sanctifies Elizabeth's womb immediately after the sanctification of Mary's womb. The haste and vigor of the Holy Spirit is further illustrated by the haste and vigor of Caesar. The Emperor is the image of the Holy Spirit on the earth, and Caesar was the first Emperor of the Roman Empire. Caesar wastes no time in rushing to Spain after his attack on Marseilles in his conquest of Lerida.

Like Caesar, the Holy Spirit always is active in accomplishing His invisible mission: from the sanctification of Mary's womb to that of Elizabeth's womb, from the sanctification of Jews to that of Gentiles. Before the Advent of the Son, the Holy Spirit prepared not only the temple of Jerusalem in which Christ was to be sacrificed, but the justice of Rome under which He was to be judged. After the Ascension of Christ, the Holy Spirit is poured out not only over the Jews but over the Gentiles. The activity of the Holy Spirit is fully reflected in the frenzy of the Apostles who bestow the grace of the Spirit on the Jews and the Gentiles in Jerusalem and Rome, in Juda and Asia Minor, as is recorded in the Acts, the Gospel of the Holy Spirit. *Be not slothful in zeal; be fervent in spirit, serving the Lord, rejoicing in hope* (Rom. 12:11–12).

The fortitude of the Spirit is reflected in the strenuous command which the Spirit of the Lord gave to Paul, the

Vessel of the Holy Spirit: "Be steadfast; for just as thou hast borne witness to me in Jerusalem, bear witness in Rome also" (Acts 23:11). The whole world is held together as one world by the Holy Spirit, as the Father and the Son are brought together into the Holy Trinity through the mediation by the Spirit of the two spiral motions. For this mission of cosmic mediation, the Spirit constantly works back and forth between the Jews and the Gentiles, between heaven and earth, and between the Father watching from heaven and the Son walking on the earth.

It is the fortitude of the Holy Spirit that our Angelic Poet sings on the fourth rung of the angelic ladder of divine love. While the meekness of the Spirit is exemplified by the Sacred Heart of Jesus in its obedience to the mind of the Son, the fortitude of the Spirit is reflected in His union of the two spirations from the Father and the Son for the quickening and governing of the whole world. The former is elucidated by the epicycle of Venus, and the latter by the dual spiral motion of the Sun. Thus the Angelic Poet concludes the second phase in his adoration of the Holy Trinity through the praise of the two virtues of the Holy Spirit as exemplified in His invisible mission.

chapteR 8

Lesson on the Rung of Liberality and Avarice

The Fifth Heaven, the Fifth Terrace and the Fourth Circle

T HE fifth rung of the angelic ladder of divine love is built upon the active concupiscible. Because the concupiscible arises out of the vegetative level of the soul, the metaphor of the plant will begin to function extensively. The active concupiscible is the power that aims at growth and expansion of the individual. The growth and expansion of the concupiscible also covers the generation of posterity, because the bearing and rearing of the offspring are the expansion and extension of the individual. Thus, the problem of birth and death and the relation of father and son will constitute the central themes which the Angelic Poet sings on the fifth rung of his angelic ladder.

When the growth and expansion of the individual are sought in the external treasures of the earth, the active concupiscible becomes the sin of avarice or prodigality. In the Fourth Circle, the avaricious and the prodigal are engaged in the busy task of pushing heavy weights with their chests (*Inf.* vii. 25–27). *Wherever your treasure is, there will your heart be also* (Matt. 6:21). The avaricious and the prodigal prostitute their hearts in treasures of dust and become unrecognizable and sordid like the dust (*Inf.* vii. 52–54).

Virgil says that weary souls will not have a moment of repose for all the gold beneath the moon (*Inf.* vii. 64–66). Whether they gain or lose, they will consume themselves, howling and rolling for all eternity in a whirlpool of hoarding and spending. St. Bernard says that to seek the consummation of desires in the earthly good is the fruitless labor of eternal self-consumption.[1] It is with the curse of self-consumption that Virgil greets Plutus, ". . . consume thyself internally with thy greedy rage" (*Inf.* vii. 9). Dante shows his contempt by talking to no one and recognizing no one as he does among the violent against Art.

On the Fifth Terrace, our poet meets Hugh Capet and Adrian V, as representative of covetous secular power and of covetous ecclesiastical power. Pope Adrian recounts his avaricious life (*Purg.* xix. 97–117). His heart was so consumed by avarice that he never knew any rest. Avaricious throughout his life, he finally achieved the papal mantle. During the short period of about a month in which he wore the mantle, Adrian V learned "how heavy the great mantle weighs on him who keeps it above the mire" (*Purg.* xix. 103–104). Through this bitter crowning experience of his avaricious career, he came to realize the vanity of avaricious ambition and reached the moment of his late conversion.

Huge Capet identifies himself as "the root of the evil tree/which overshadows the entire Christendom" (*Purg.* xx. 43–44). He then narrates the avaricious history of the Capetian dynasty (*Purg.* xx. 52–96). He was born a son of a butcher in Paris, and his avaricious hands grasped the royal rein of the realm. This seed of avarice grew into the horrible tree of the Capetian dynasty. Every new fruit on this tree far surpassed all previous ones in the sin of avarice so that the former seemed to "atone" for the sins of the latter.

The avaricious tree of the Capetian dynasty is going to be the tree on which the second Crucifixion will be enacted (*Purg.* xx. 68–90).

The Pope who will be crucified by Hugh Capet's descendant is Boniface VIII, a descendant of Adrian V on the tree of the avaricious Papacy. Just as the two armies of the Fourth Circle come to a violent clash and curse each other, so the avaricious dynasty and the avaricious Papacy will keep up their conflict and struggle until their greedy drive re-enacts the Crucifixion. This is the crucifixion of the king of cupidity upon the tree of cupidity. The tree of cupidity comes into contrast with the tree on Mars, the luminous white cross (*Par.* xiv. 97–102). There the cross shines like the Milky Way, and the warriors of the cross are freely gliding within the framework of the cross:

> From horn to horn, from summit unto base,
>   were moving lights that sparkled mightily
>   in meeting one another and in passing.
>
> So, on earth, particles long and short,
>   straight and aslant, fast and slow,
>   changing aspect, are seen moving
>
> Through a ray of sunlight which often streaks the shade.
> *Par.* xiv. 109–115

The warriors of the cross are martyrs and crusaders. These warriors embody the virtues which are as complementary or as contrary as the sins of the avaricious and the prodigal in the Fourth Circle. The avaricious consume themselves in making their fortune and the prodigal in wasting it. To crusade is to sacrifice oneself against the foes of Christ; to be martyred is to offer the same sacrifice by being attacked by His foes. Both the Fourth Circle and Mars are permeated by the militant spirit of aggression. Without the aggressive spirit, one cannot achieve growth and expansion.

243

Beneath these points of apparent similarity, the Fourth Circle and Mars present a few points of striking difference. The warriors of the cross are not divided from each other like the two files of the warriors of fortune, but freely mingle with each other. The two beams of the cross meet at one point, whereas the two files of the warriors of wealth clash with each other at two points. The sinners blame and curse each other in their encounter, but the blessed sparkle and flash in their meeting and passing. The howling and yelling of the greedy whirlpool comes in contrast with the martial hymn on the cross of Mars:

> And as viol and harp, tuned in harmony
> with many strings, make only a sweet tinkling sound
> to one unfamiliar with the music
>
> So from the lights I saw in the cross
> a melody sounded which carried me away
> without my understanding the hymn.
>
> *Par.* xiv. 118–123

The glories and riches in which the warriors of the cross are clothed transcend all the glories and riches of the dust. Dante calls Cacciaguida "a living topaz, adorning with your gem this precious jewel (Mars)" (*Par.* xv. 85–86). Their glory is the glory of God. On reaching Mars, our poet exclaims, "O Elios! who dost so glorify them!" (*Par.* xiv. 96). Our Lord on the cross cried out, *"Eli, Eli . . ."* (Matt. 27:46). The Son of God was crucified in weakness and lowliness but raised in power and glory by His Father: *What is sown corruptible, rises incorruptible; what is sown unhonored, rises in glory; what is sown in weakness, is raised in power* (1 Cor. 15:42–43).

The cross of Mars shows how the warriors of faith are raised in power and glory from their lowly and weak death on the cross like Christ. Mars burns like a red fire (*Par.* xiv. 87). Christ flashes forth from the cross like a lightning, and every warrior is like a blazing torch (*Par.* xiv. 104). Cacciaguida darts down like a meteor to receive his great-great-grandson (*Par.* xv. 19–24). When Cacciaguida names eight warriors for Dante, each of them flashes forth like a lightning flash and wheels with joy like a top whipped by a lash (*Par.* xviii. 34–51).

To put on the cross of Elios is to divest oneself of the glories and wealth of the earth for the glory and riches of Eli. Cacciaguida calls his death the dismantling of the deceitful world, "the love of which corrupts so many souls" (*Par.* xv. 147). The mantle is the extension of the individual and as such is the symbol of all the riches which the active concupiscible seeks. While the heavenly glory is the mantle of God, the earthly wealth is the mantle of Satan. It is with the mantle of dust that Satan has seduced man. As one has to be crucified on the cross of Eli for the mantle of Eli, so one has to be crucified on the cross of Satan for the mantle of Satan. As Christ called out for Eli on the cross, Plutus calls out for Satan before he falls, "Pape Satan! pape Satan, aleppe!" (*Inf.* vii. 1). The meaning of Plutus' cry is unintelligible; the meaning of Christ's cry was unintelligible to His hearers. The cross of Eli is the cross of power and glory, but the cross of Satan is the cross of impotence and ignominy. Plutus disgracefully falls to the ground:

> As sails swelled by the wind
> > fall entangled when the mast breaks,
> > so the cruel monster fell to the ground.
> > > > *Inf.* vii. 13–15

The power of avarice which is rooted in gold and silver is one of the easiest to break down for all its appearance of militant spirit. We can see this among the many warriors of fortune who are the easy preys to nervous breakdown in today's world. The idol of wealth is the most ungodly of all the idols Satan provides:

Fear we never the gods that ungod themselves so plainly! Wood and silver and gold, that watch the world as a scarecrow over a herb-garden; wood and silver and gold, patient of the birds that perch on them as bush of white-thorn, or corpse left to lie in a dark alley! From the purple robes that rot on them, you may learn they are no gods; they, too, shall be eaten away when their time comes, and be disgrace to the country-side (Baruch 6:68–71).

Virgil handles Plutus like a scare-crow and leaves him behind like a corpse in a dark alley.

The cross of Satan is the cross of injustice, and the cross of Eli is the cross of justice. St. Thomas says that justice means the right relation of the creature to the Creator.[2] By swallowing the fruit Satan offered, man lost his right relation with his Creator. This is the disruption of the original order and justice. The disorder of man's appetite is a consequence of the loss of the original justice.[3] The cross of Eli restores man to the Creator and consequently brings about order in his appetite. The disorder and conflict among the sinners of the Fourth Circle reflect the disorder and conflict of the active concupiscible in a man who has become a son of Satan through the power of avarice and prodigality, and the order and harmony of Mars reflect the order and harmony of the active concupiscible in a man who has been adopted as a son of Eli through the power of the cross.

To be adopted as a son of Eli, one has to be born anew: *What is born by natural birth is a thing of nature, what is born by spiritual birth is a thing of spirit. Do not be surprised, then, at my telling thee, you must be born anew"* (John 3:6–7).

246

Statius arises as a re-born soul. The re-birth of Statius is marked by two events which recall the Advent and the Resurrection of Christ. The entire mountain of the *Purgatorio* shakes as in an earthquake and all the penitents sing in a resounding chorus: *"Gloria in excelsis Deo"* (*Purg.* xx. 136). This is the angelic hymn the shepherds heard on mountainsides at the birth of Christ. This violent event takes Dante and his guide by surprise and holds them in suspense. A little later, Statius appears to them as Christ appeared after His Resurrection to two of His disciples on their way to Emmaus (*Purg.* xxi. 7–15). Statius informs our pilgrims that the earthquake marked his rising from the dust of the Fourth Terrace after the completion of his penance.

The Advent and the Resurrection are the two terminal points of one lesson Christ wished to teach the sinful souls, i.e. how to die in flesh and be born in spirit. A sinful soul can be born anew as an adopted son of God only through the power of Christ on the cross and only in imitation of His re-birth.

Do you not know that all we who have been baptized into Christ Jesus have been baptized into his death? For we were buried with him by means of Baptism into death, in order that, just as Christ has arisen from the dead through the glory of the Father, so we may also walk in newness of life. For if we have been united with him in the likeness of his death, we shall be so in the likeness of his resurrection also (Rom. 6:3–5).

The penitents are lying in the dust, i.e., they are waiting in their burial ground for the day they can rise like Statius through the glory of the Father.

Our poet develops the theme of rebirth very gradually and steadily. When he meets Pope Adrian, he notices only the groaning and weeping and says that the penance of the Fifth Terrace is the bitterest on the entire *Purgatorio* (*Purg.*

xix. 71–75, 117). Adrian V explains that the penitents have
to keep their faces turned away from heaven and to the
dusty ground because they turned away their desires from
heaven for the treasures of the dust (*Purg.* xix. 97–98).
This is the exile of the sinful soul to the earth. *So the Lord
God drove him out from the Garden of delight, to cultivate
the ground from which he came* (Gen. 3:23). The penitents
are groaning and moaning in their exile for adoption as the
sons of the Father; they say, "*Adhaesit pavimento anima
mea* (My soul cleaveth unto the dust)" (*Purg.* xix. 73).

*Comfort this earthly exile; do not refuse me the knowledge of
thy will. Crushed lies my spirit, longing ever for thy just
awards . . .*
    My soul cleaveth to the dust, *restore life to me, as thou
promised. Deign, now, to show me thy will, thou who hast
listened when I opened my heart to thee. Direct me in the path
thou biddest me to follow, and all my musing shall be of thy
wonderful deeds. Despair wrings tears from me: let thy promise
raise me up once more* (Psalm 118[119]: 19–28).

When our poet meets Hugh Capet, he sees the nature of
penance in a clearer light. He recognizes Hugh Capet's pain
as labour pain:

> And by chance I heard someone ahead of us
>   invoke "Sweet Mary" in his tears
>   as a woman does in childbirth.

> And he continued, "Thou wast so poor!
>   as can be seen by that hostelry
>   where thou didst lay down thy holy burden."
>   *Purg.* xx. 19–24

Invoking the miracle of the birth of the Son, Hugh Capet
is labouring for the birth of his own soul as an adopted son
of God. As Christ was born in the exile of dust, the peni-

tents are being born in the exile of dust. When Christ foretold His disciples of His impending death, they became very
sorrowful. To cheer up His sorrowful disciples, Christ
explained His death as labour pain:

*Amen, amen, I say to you, that you shall weep and lament,
but the world shall rejoice; and you shall be sorrowful, but
your sorrow shall be turned into joy. A woman about to give
birth has sorrow, because her hour has come. But when she has
brought forth the child, she no longer remembers the anguish
for joy that a man is born into the world* (John 16:20–21).

The bitterest pain of the whole *Purgatorio* is forgotten in
the joy that shakes the whole mount. This is the joy of
re-birth. Because the penance is labour pain, the weepings
are called the pains of maturation (*Purg.* xix. 91–92). The
penitents distill through their eyes, drop by drop, the evil
of their old greed (*Purg.* xx. 7–9). In spite of the severe
pain of penance, the penitents are unwilling to interrupt
their weeping. Adrian is very anxious to get rid of Dante's
interruption:

> "Now go your way; I'd have you stay no more:
>   your lingering disturbs my weeping
>   whereby I mature that of which you spoke."
>   *Purg.* xix. 139–141

It is quite understandable and excusable for one in the
middle of labour pain to desire no interruption and dis-
turbance.

Statius explains the process of re-birth (*Purg.* xxi. 58–66).
The penitents have to stay prostrated on the ground as long
as their desires cleave to the dust. There can be conflict
between the will and the desire. The will may aspire to
heaven, but the desire may still cling to the dust. The divine
justice allows perfect freedom to the human will and desire

whether it burns for heaven or clings to earth. When the desire is perfectly cleansed and freed from the bondage of the dust, the soul can rise up from the dust and start on the holy way:

> It (the *Purgatorio*) trembles here when a soul
>   feels cleansed so that it may go up,
>   and such a shout accompanies it.

> Will alone gives proof of the purity
>   which takes the soul by surprise, and helps it
>   when it is free to change its cloister.
>
> *Purg.* xxi. 58–63

The relation of the desire to will is quite analogous to the relation of the baby in the womb to its mother. The baby does not come out of the womb at any moment the mother wishes, but takes its own time. The desire has to mature and be delivered in its own schedule. The only thing the penitents can do is to wait in tears and groans like women in labour pain. Through this metaphor, Dante conveys the old truth that the desire is the hardest thing for the will to control and that it takes a great deal of time and patience to discipline the desire and appropriate it as a part of the true self.

Before meeting Statius, Dante grieves over the severe penance imposed on this Terrace (*Purg.* xxi. 6). His grief almost amounts to indignation, and his grief and indignation recall the sorrow and indignation of the Apostles over the death and burial of Christ. At the earthquake Dante's anxiety and indignation turn into tension and suspense as the Apostles' sorrow and indignaiton changed to tension and suspense on the early Easter morning:

> Never did ignorance so strive
>   in me, making me so eager
>   to know, if my memory does not err,

As I then seemed to have, while pondering;
>   but in our haste I was not bold enough to ask,
>   nor could I discover anything by myself.

Thus I went on, timid and pensive.
>   *Purg.* xx. 145–151

When Statius appears, he greets Virgil and Dante with the benediction of peace which Christ gave His disciples appearing after the Resurrection: "God give you peace" (*Purg.* xxi. 13 and Luke 24:36). *Gloria in excelsis Deo, et in terra pax hominibus bonae voluntatis.* Peace is the gift which Christ brings to the earth at His Advent and leaves on the earth after His Ascension. But this gift is bestowed only on the man of good will. Peace is the harmony of appetite which is possible only to the justified will, whose desires are wholly attuned to God.[4] The desires of the concupiscible which have been attuned to God are like the holy strings of Mars (*Par.* xv. 1–3). On the other hand, the desires which have been alienated from God have to war against one another as in the whirlpool of the Fourth Circle. While the chains of covetous desires shackle down the soul to the dust, the chains of holy desires bind the soul with the love of God.

>   So enamoured was I with the hymn
>   that until then nothing had ever bound me
>   with such sweet ties.
>   *Par.* xiv. 127–129

To be born as a son of God is to burn up all the chains of the earthly desires and to be bound with the chain of holy love. To burn up all the ties of the dust is the sacrifice of holocaust. This is martyrdom. On reaching Mars, our pilgrim first offers with all his heart his silent prayer of *olocausto* (*Par.* xiv. 89). While the warriors of the cross are burning their hearts in the fire of holocaust on Mars, the children of cupidity burn their hearts in the mockery of Fortune (*Inf.* vii. 27, 62).

Holocaust presents the paradox of life and death: one is born into the spiritual world only through death in the carnal world. At the earthquake which signals the birth of a new life, Dante feels the shock and dread of death:

> When I felt the mountain shake like a thing falling,
>   so that a chill gripped me,
>   as it does someone going to his death.
>
> *Purg.* xx. 127–129

Christ demonstrated this paradox of life and death with His Crucifixion and Resurrection, and told his disciples: *If anyone wishes to come after me, let him deny himself, and take up his cross and follow me. For he who would save his life will lose it; but he who loses his life for my sake and for the Gospel's sake will save it* (Mark 8:34–35).

To die on the cross is to divest the soul of the old sinful self and clothe it with the new holy self. The old sinful self is the mortal self. Death comes into the self through its sin. The mortal soul can conquer death only by burning up the old sinful self, desires cleaving to the dust, in holocaust. It is through the holocaust of the sinful desires that the re-born soul arises from the chain of dust and conquers the sting of death. This is the theme of the martial hymn on Mars: "Arise and conquer" (*Par.* xiv. 125).

The birth of a soul is a highly individual matter. This is one of the few things which cannot be achieved in a collective measure. The travails on the Fifth Terrace are highly individualized:

Now one speaks loudly, another low,
    according as an impulse spurs him
    with a greater or a lesser force.

Purg. xx. 118–120

The individuality of labour pain is preserved in the distinctly individualized splendors and motions on Mars (*Par.* xiv. 112–114). The children of cupidity retain no individual traits. When the individual is identified through his property, he becomes indiscernible.

The sense of horror and disgust which comes from the total loss of individuality among the children of cupidity is heightened by Dante's hint that these souls are also undergoing the labour pain in their own ghastly way. At Virgil's rebuke, Plutus falls flat on the ground and takes the same posture as that of the penitents in travail. In his rebuke, Virgil refers to the "proud adultery" (*Inf.* vii. 7–12). Plutus seems to prostrate himself to give birth to his adulterous child. In describing the pains of the covetous sinners, Dante carefully picks the words suggestive of labour pain: *nuove travaglie* (fresh travail) (*Inf.* vii. 20). The *nuove travaglie* stings Dante's heart as the travail of the penitents does (*Inf.* vii. 36; *Purg.* xxi. 6). The covetous soul is an adulterous child. Every soul is a seed sown by God, but a covetous soul prostitutes itself and is born as a bastard of Satan. Because a covetous soul is an adulterous child of Satan, I would like to propose that Plutus's cry *"Pape Satan, pape Satan . . ."* is quite likely to mean *"Padre Satan, padre Satan"* (*Inf.* vii. 1).

The theme of adultery is fully developed in Cacciaguida's history of Florence (*Par.* xv. 97–132; xvi. 46–154). In Cacciaguida's days, Florence was securely protected within the "ancient circle," and her citizens lived in a sober and chaste peace. In their chaste life, the Florentines embodied the virtues of the two patrons of their city, Mars and John the Baptist. Their fair and reposeful life was disrupted by the influx of the vulgar outsiders into the city. The entire population of Florence was contaminated by the greedy newcomers. The mingling of the persons was the source of the city's ailments, just as surplus food is the cause of harm to the body.

As the city grew beyond its original boundaries, her iniquities also grew and multiplied. The city folk became ferocious slaves of luxury and wealth. The old martial courage degenerated into bestial force for internecine fights. John the Baptist was debased to the image on a florin. The adulteration and corruption of Florence culminated in the outbreak of the bitter feud between the Guelfs and the Ghibellines. The outbreak of this feud came with an act of adultery: Buondelmonte's desertion of his bride on the eve of his nuptials (*Par.* xvi. 136–141).

The adulterous history of Florence recaptures the initial adultery of the human race. The life of Adam and Eve was sober and chaste until Satan intruded into the Garden of Eden and captivated them with the chain of cupidity. The covetous feud of the Guelfs and the Ghibellines in Cacciaguida's description becomes almost of the same nature and form as the feud between Hugh Capet's descendants and Adrian's successors and the strife in the Fourth Circle. As the long feud between the Capetian dynasty and Adrian's papacy makes its final atonement by re-enacting the Crucifixion, so the long strife between the Guelfs and the Ghibellines culminates in their holocaust at the mutilated statue of Mars (*Par.* xvi. 145–147).

As the two covetous armies of the Fourth Circle keep clashing with each other and howling against each other at "the two points of the Circle," the two Florentine armies of cupidity repeat an endless conflict and clash between Mars and the Baptist: the two points marking the ancient circle of the city (*Inf.* vii. 44; *Par.* xv. 97; xvi. 47). While the tonsured heads are found among the parties of covetous feud in the Fourth Circle, the clergy on the earth has become an adulterous step-mother to her children and one of the most degenerate groups in the feud of the Guelfs and the Ghibellines (*Inf.* vii. 38; *Par.* xvi. 58–60). These children of adultery have completely forgotten and deserted the Holy Land which is theirs by right (*Par.* xv. 142–144). The Holy Land is the symbol of the kingdom of heaven. It is adultery to desert what is one's own and to be enslaved to what does not belong to one.

Whether one is reborn as an adopted son of the Father or as a greedy bastard of Satan, one dissolves the natural tie and enters a new order. When Dante kneels down before Pope Adrian, Adrian reminds him of Christ's teaching on the order of the heavenly kingdom: "they neither marry, nor are given in marriage" (*Purg.* xix. 137). Adrian tells Dante to "straighten your legs, get up, brother!" (*Purg.* xix. 133). Adrian is no longer the holy father to Dante but only a brother. The earthly relations and the natural ties have been dissolved and superseded. The mistake and correction between Adrian and Dante are repeated between Virgil and Statius. Statius who has revered Virgil as his poetic father stoops down to embrace Virgil's feet, and Virgil calls Statius "brother" in his humble refusal of Statius' filial reverence (*Purg.* xxi. 97, 131).

The children of the adulterous greed forget and dissolve their natural ties too. The descendants of Hugh Capet sell their daughters and haggle over their price (*Purg.* xx. 80). Hugh Capet laments:

> O avarice, what more can you do
>   since you have so drawn my race to yourself
>   that it has no care of its own flesh.
>   *Purg.* xx. 82–84

If the natural ties of blood and family are dissolved in the kingdom of spirits, how should we account for the special joy and delight in Dante's meeting with his great-great-grandfather Cacciaguida? Is our poet contradicting his own view of natural nobility, becoming a helpless victim of his petty pride, and leaving an indelible blemish on his Angelic Epic? No, he cannot; he wishes to convey a far more significant thing than a petty pride of ancestry. In order to avoid that misunderstanding on the part of his readers, our poet gives a special warning. This special warning is Beatrice's smile whose intention our poet points out by his allusion to the warning cough "at the first trespass writ of Guinevere" (*Par.* xvi. 15). Beatrice's warning against trespass is not given to Dante who is already in the kingdom of absolute truth, but to us who are still in the realm of error.

Cacciaguida's special joy on receiving Dante represents the joy of the heavenly Father on welcoming His prodigal son returning from his exile of greed. We should recall the parable of the return of a prodigal son (Luke 15:11–24). A younger son runs away from his father's home and wastes his fortune in riotous living. He cannot get work even as a swineherd. Remembering how many servants there are in his father's house, he resolves to return to his father and ask to be employed as a mere servant:

And he arose, and went on his way to his father. But, while he was still a long way off, his father saw him and took pity on him; running up, he threw his arms around his neck and kissed him. . . . The father gave order to his servants . . . Bring out the best robe . . . Then bring out the calf . . . let us eat, and make merry; for my son here was dead, and has come to life again; was lost, and is found (Luke 15:20–24).

Like the father of the parable, Cacciaguida has long waited for the coming of Dante and rushes down to meet him (*Par.* xv. 20, 49–51). As the father of the parable forgets all the cares and chores of the day in his joy of welcoming his once lost son, the heavenly Father imposes silence on the sweet lyre and stills the sacred strings (*Par.* xv. 4–6). Dante's joy is so great that he feels he has touched the limit of "my grace and my paradise" (*Par.* xv. 36). To see the heavenly Father is the limit of grace and the apex of bliss. The Father does not send Himself as He does His Son and His Spirit on a mission to the earth, but waits in His mansion for the return of the adopted sons. Cacciaguida's joy is the joy of the heavenly Father for the son who has come back to life from death (*Par.* xv. 58–60).

It is through his sin that man alienates himself from the bounty of divine grace, suffers spiritual death, and becomes a prodigal son wandering in the wilderness of evil. His return from death to life is to become a member of the Mystical Body of Christ, and this is possible by eating the flesh of the Son of Man and by drinking His blood. *Hic est enim calix sanguinis mei, novi et aeterni testamenti: mysterium fidei, qui pro vobis et pro multis effundetur in remissionem peccatorum.* (For this is the chalice of my blood of the new and eternal covenant: the mystery of faith, which shall be shed for you and for many unto the forgiveness of sins—*The New Roman Missal*, the Consecration.) This is the solemn statement which the Son of God pronounced while giving the blood of divine life to His disciples and asking them to drink it and which is recited at the consecration of the chalice of wine for the re-enactment of the holy sacrifice during the Mass. It is to this solemn pronouncement that Cacciaguida's greeting of joy on welcoming Dante makes a veiled reference:

> "O sanguis meus, *o superinfusa*
> *gratia Dei, sicut tibi, cui*
> *bis unquam coeli ianua reclusa?*"

("O blood of mine, O grace of God
poured over thee! to whom was Heaven's gate
ever twice thrown open as to thee?")

Par. xv. 28–30

The prodigal son of the parable resolves for himself to return to the mansion of his father, but no sinner can of his own will alone repent his sin and resolve to mount up to the mansion of the heavenly Father because his sin is mortal. The sinner can come back from death to life through the mystery of faith which is possible only through the outpouring of grace and can mount up to the mansion of the Father through the mystery of rebirth as a member of the Mystical Body of His Son. This is possible only by drinking from the chalice of His blood. *O sanguis meus* is the joyous greeting of the heavenly Father to Dante on the miraculous occasion of his rebirth and return from the world of sin and death through the mystery of His own blood.

To avoid any misunderstanding of this symbolic representation, Dante always calls his great great-grandfather "my father (*padre mio*)" and never "my grandfather" or "my great-great-grandfather" (*Par.* xvi. 16; xvii. 106). Cacciaguida in turn addresses himself to Dante as my "son (*figlio*)" (*Par.* xvii. 94). Our poet further stresses the father-son relation between himself and Cacciaguida by comparing their meeting to the meeting of Aeneas and his father in the Elysian Fields (*Par.* xv. 25–27). When Dante inquires about Cacciaguida's ancestry, he prefaces his inquiry with his derision of the "puny blood-nobility" on earth. The blood-nobility is nothing more than one of the many objects of the earthly greed (*Par.* xvi. 7–9). Cacciaguida shows the same derision of the noble blood ties, by saying nothing of the details of his ancestry (*Par.* xvi. 43–45). In answering Dante's inquiry, Cacciaguida does not only keep in silence his ancestral background but recounts his birth in the language and context of the heavenly family:

> Mary, besought with deep cries, yielded me,
> and in your ancient Baptistry at once
> a Christian I became and Cacciaguida.
> *Par.* xv. 133–135

Cacciaguida identifies Mars as the fifth branch of the tree "which has its life from the top" (*Par.* xviii. 29). The ten Heavens constitute one immense family tree, and its root is the Father in heaven. It is in the context of this heavenly family tree that we should understand the imagery of a tree used in the discourse between Dante and Cacciaguida such as *Oh leaf of mine* (*Par.* xv. 88), *I was your root* (*Par.* xv. 89), *Dear root of mine* (*Par.* xvii. 13), Why does Dante take this oblique way to represent the joy of the heavenly Father at the return of his lost son? He gives us the reason:

> Nor did he hide his meaning from choice
> but from necessity, for his thought
> rose above the range of mortals.
> *Par.* xv. 40–42

This is the same reason why Christ gave His lessons in parables to mortals.

It is from Cacciaguida that Dante hears the long awaited prophecy about his future (*Par.* xvii. 46–142). Cacciaguida predicts a destiny of bitter exile lying before Dante. The last advice Dante seeks from his "Father" is on the dilemma about his epic. If he reveals all his visions in their nakedness, he will earn the ire of the whole world. If he hides any of his visions, he will be branded as a timid warrior of Truth for all eternity. Cacciaguida gives Dante martyr-like encouragement:

259

Nonetheless, set aside all falsehood,
make your entire vision manifest,
and let there be scratching where the itching is.
Par. xvii. 127–129

Dante is destined and commanded to be a prophet in exile for the entire Christendom, which has become a kingdom of adultery. His destiny reminds us of another great prophet of exile, Ezechiel:

I was sharing the lot of exiles by the river of Chobar, when heaven opened, and I saw a vision of God . . . Rise up, son of man, . . . I am sending thee on an errand to the men of Israel, this heathen brood that has rebelled and forsaken me . . . Never fear them, son of man, never let rebuke of theirs dishearten thee (Ezech. 1:1; 2:1–6).

The scene of adultery our prophet in exile witnesses is not very different from what Ezechiel saw:

Silver and gold of mine, thy adornment and my gift, should they be turned into gods of male form, at thy harlot's whim? . . . to these gods thou wouldst bring sons and daughters of thine and mine, consecrating them to death. Could not thy wanton desires rest content, without immolating my own sons as victims to such as these? (Ezech. 16:17–21).

As Cacciaguida bids Dante to reveal his entire vision, so the Lord commanded Ezechiel, *And now, son of man, do thou confront Jerusalem with the record of her misdoings* (Ezech. 16:1–2). The Lord commanded Ezechiel to eat the scroll of the bitter prophetic words:

Son of man, he told me, eat thou must what eat thou canst; here is the scroll for thy eating. After that, go and give my message to the sons of Israel. Thereupon I opened my mouth,

*and he gave me the scroll to eat, promising me safe digestion
and a full belly with the gift; and indeed, it was sweet as
honey when I ate it* (Ezech. 3:1–3).

Dante also relishes the bitter scroll of prophecy which he
gulps down from the hand of his Father:

> Now that blessed soul was rejoicing
>   in its thought alone, and I was tasting mine,
>   tempering the bitter with the sweet.
>
> *Par.* xviii. 1–3

Why does Dante receive the prophecy of his role as a
prophet in exile on Mars? He has to face his prophetic
mission in the spirit of the warrior of the cross. What is the
spirit of the warrior of the cross? It is to bear the witness
of holocaust to Truth.[5] It is one thing to have the vision
of truth and another to manifest it. Dante not only sees
the warriors of the cross on Mars, but also learns their
courage of manifestation and expression. Time and again,
he is encouraged and commanded to manifest his inward
desires and to express his hidden will (*Par.* xv. 67–69, xvii.
1–12). This is the training to launch the prophet on the
hard way of manifesting his whole vision to the whole
world.

The seven examples of avarice on the Fifth Terrace are
the examples of the sins which St. Thomas calls the seven
daughters of avarice (*Purg.* xx. 103–117). These seven
daughters all belong to the greedy army howling and rolling
for the treasures of the dust. They have all become the
adulterous children of Satan. Avarice is the way to prostitute the soul made in the image of God to adultery with the
devil so that it becomes unrecognizable.

The three examples of liberality show the liberality of
the Father in the adoption of the sinful souls as His sons

261

(*Purg.* xx. 20–33). The first example is the poor circumstances under which the Holy Mother gave birth to her Son. The Holy Mother's poverty at the birth of the Son reflects the will of the Father. The Father wishes His Son to be a child of poverty so that the Son can inherit the riches of the Father. Every soul has to be a child of poverty on earth to inherit riches in heaven. A soul whose desires are satiated by the treasures of the dust has no room left to appreciate the treasure of heaven.

When a soul lives in poverty, it is always subject to the temptation of greed. The second example of liberality shows how a poor soul can overcome the temptation of greed and preserve its virtues. Fabricius "did desire to possess virtue with poverty,/rather than great riches with iniquity" (*Purg.* xx. 26–27). To seek iniquitous riches is to court the favor of Satan. The Son of God was born and lived in poverty but resolutely rejected the temptation of the earthly glories and riches even after fasting forty days and forty nights in the desert:

Once more, the devil took him to the top of an exceedingly high mountain, from which he showed him all the kingdoms of the world and the glory of them, and said, "I will give thee all these if thou wilt fall down and worship me." Then Jesus said to him, "Away with thee, Satan; it is written, Thou shalt worship the Lord thy God, and serve none but Him" (Matt. 4: 8–10).

The Father does not wish to strangle His adopted sons in poverty. He provides His children liberally with all the necessaries out of His bounty. The liberal provision of the Father is explained by the liberal example of St. Nicholas, who secretly provided three maidens with large sums of money which not only rescued them from dire straits of poverty but enabled them to marry with dowries. The

adoption of a sinful soul as a son of God is a marriage.
The Father provides not only for the daily need of His
sons but also for the costly preparation for their nuptials in
heaven. The liberality of the Father is understood by His
Son better than anyone else:

*Look at the birds of the air: they do not sow, or reap, or gather
into barns; yet your heavenly Father feeds them. Are you not
of much more value than they? . . . See how the lilies of
the field grow; they neither toil nor spin, yet I say to you
that not even Solomon in all his glory was arrayed like one of
these. But if God so clothes the grass of the field, which
flourishes today but tomorrow is thrown into the oven, how
much more you, O you of little faith! Do not fret then, saying,
"what shall we eat, what shall we drink . . . ?" for your Father
knows that you need all these things. But seek first the kingdom of God and his justice, and all these things shall be given
you besides* (Matt. 6:26–33).

To seek the kingdom of God and its justice is to be born
and adopted as the son of the heavenly Father. It is for the
preparation for this heavenly goal that the Father provides
the mortal souls with the inexhaustible riches of the earth.
To mistake the riches of the dust for the final end in themselves and cling to them is to prostitute one's soul in adultery
with Satan.

It is the liberality of the Father that the Angelic Poet
sings on the fifth rung of the angelic ladder of divine love.
The heavenly Father has opened the gate of His mansion
to the sinful souls in the earthly exile with the blood of His
only-begotten Son. He has shown the way for the exiled
soul to return to Him. He raises in power and glory every
soul who takes up the cross and dies in the world of sin and
flesh in the imitation of His Son.

chapter 9

Lesson on the Rung of Temperance and Gluttony

The Sixth Heaven, the Sixth Terrace, and the Third Circle

THE sixth rung of the angelic ladder of divine love is built upon the passive concupiscible, which aims at the nourishment and preservation of the individual, while its active power strives for the growth and maturation of the individual. The virtue of the passive concupiscible is temperance, and its vice is intemperance and gluttony.

The gluttons in the Third Circle are submerged under eternal rains. Rain is the symbol of life and food for plants. The rain for the gluttons is not the rain of refreshment and comfort but of exhaustion and torment:

> I am in the third circle of the rain,
> > eternal, accursed, cold, and heavy:
> > its measure and kind never change.
>
> Large hailstones, dirty water, and snow
> > pour down through the dark air;
> > the ground that receives them stinks.
>
> > > > > *Inf.* vi. 7–11

When the appetite becomes a compulsion, food and drink

become the unbearable instruments of torture. When the gluttons try to refrain from food, they suffer from their gnawing compulsion to eat. When they give way to their compulsion and gorge themselves, they suffer in remorse and self-contempt. This perpetual torment and dilemma of gluttons is presented in a single tercet:

> The rain makes them howl like dogs;
>> they use one side to shelter the other;
>> often they turn and twist, the impious wretches.
>>> *Inf.* vi. 19–21

In spite of all the eating and howling, the gluttons have lost all their vigor and languish in lethargy. They are lying on the ground, and Ciacco says, "I languish in the rain" (*Inf.* vi. 37, 54). The gluttons rot like weeds in the mud. They have become blind. The eyes constitute one of the distinctive features of animals and the guiding organs for their locomotion. Ciacco falls to the ground like a soulless body:

> He twisted his straight eyes asquint,
>> looked at me a little, then bent his head,
>> and fell to the level of the other blind ones.
>>> *Inf.* vi. 91–93

St. Thomas says that gluttony is more disgraceful than any other vice.[1] The punishment of the Third Circle is more disgusting than any other punishment (*Inf.* vi. 48). The digust and horror of gluttony are personified in Cerberus:

> Cerberus, the fierce and the cruel beast,
>> barks doglike with three throats
>> over those submerged there.

His eyes are red, his beard greasy and black,
   his belly large, his paws armed with claws;
   grasping the spirits, he flays and tears them.

Inf. vi. 13–18

In spite of their fierce appearance, the gluttons are most easily subdued. When Cerberus trembles with his gluttonous compulsion, Virgil calms him down with a handful of earth:

As a barking dog, longing for food,
   grows quiet after he has seized it,
   since he thinks only of eating,

So did those filthy heads of the demon Cerberus.

Inf. vi. 28–31

St. Thomas calls gluttony a childish sin.[2] The combination of disgust and weakness makes the gluttons extremely sensitive about their appearance like children. Fully knowing the glutton's childish sensitivity, Dante takes special care not to hurt Ciacco's feeling. Ciacco asks whether Dante can or cannot recognize him (*Inf.* vi. 40–42). Ciacco is so disfigured that Dante cannot recognize him, but Dante tactfully attributes his failure of recognition to Ciacco's internal anguish rather than to his external transformation (*Inf.* vi. 43–45). In his tactful reply, Dante is not telling a lie but the truth; the external disfigurement is the expression of the internal compulsion.

The penitents of the Sixth Terrace abstain from all food and drink in their absolute fast. They are disfigured through their abstinence as much as the gluttons. Dante cannot recognize Forese Donati until he hears his old friend's voice (*Purg.* xxiii. 43–45). The penitents are so emaciated that their bodies seem to be composed of only bones and skins. Though they look twice dead, they do not languish like gluttons. St. Thomas says that the dullness of sense is an effect of gluttony and its keenness an effect of abstinence.[3] The penitents are nimble and agile. They move so fast that Dante cannot keep pace with them.

The purpose of purgation is to intensify the appetite for the heavenly food (*Purg.* xxiv. 106–111). Since their vice was a childish one, the penitents behave like children in their penance (*Purg.* xxiv. 108). They are looking up to the tree of the heavenly food with the eagerness and wholesomeness of child-like appetite. Before they can be allowed to drink from the fountain of the heavenly nourishment, they must cleanse their appetite of the dust and sanctify it. They strive to intensify their holy appetite as much as they can. There is no limit to the reception of the heavenly food except the limit of appetite. For the purification and intensification of their desires, the penitents expose themselves to the temptation of the tree:

> The fragrance which comes from the fruit
>   and from the spray on the verdure
>   gives a craving to eat and drink.
>
> *Purg.* xxiii. 67–69

They wait in tears and prayers for the day when their craving will be satisfied. Dante compares them to a throng of pilgrims (*Purg.* xxiii. 10–24). They have to walk in thirst and pray in tears until they reach the Holy Land. Their agony reminds us of the long period of tearful waiting which the Psalmist has left in his song: *O God, my whole soul longs for thee, as a deer for running water; my whole soul thirsts for God, the living God; shall I never again make pilgrimage into God's presence? Morning and evening, my diet still of tears!* (Psalm 41[42]:1–4).

Whereas the gluttons are full of stench, the tree on the

Sixth Terrace bears wholesome and sweet fruit (*Purg.* xxii. 130). The tree tapers downward. The trees of the earth taper upward because they are drawing nourishment from the ground. The tree which tapers downward draws its nourishment from heaven above. Aristotle says that the root of a plant plays the same function as the head of an animal does, i.e., a plant receives its nourishment from the root and an animal from the mouth of its head.[4] He further says that a tree can be said to be standing on its head and upside down. Plato calls man a plant not of the earth but of the firmament.[5] The tree which tapers downward represents the state of the soul which is nourished by the heavenly food, i.e., a plant of the firmament.

The clear water which sprinkles the leaves of the tree is the heavenly nourishment (*Purg.* xxii. 137–138). The clear water falls down from rock to rock and resembles the water God gave the Israelites in the scorching desert.

But the people, thirsting for lack of water, grew loud in their complaints against Moses: "Didst thou bring us away from Egypt, they said, only to let us die here, with our children and our cattle, of thirst?" . . . So the Lord bade Moses march out at the head of the people . . . he was to carry in his hand the staff which he had used to smite the river. "I will meet thee," he said, "at the rock of Horeb; thou hast but to smite that rock, and water will flow out of it . . ." (Exodus 17: 3–6).

Forese Donati explains the power and source of the water from the rock: "From the eternal counsel/a power descends to the water, and through it to the tree . . ." (*Purg.* xxiii. 61–62). The fragrance of the tree and the spray awaken such an unbearable torment that Donati compares his agony to the one in which Christ on the cross cried out, "*Eli, Eli, why hast thou forsaken me?*" (Purg. xxiii. 71–74):

268

My God, my God, why hast thou forsaken me? Loudly I call, but my prayer cannot reach thee. Thou dost not answer, my God, when I cry out to thee day and night. Thou dost not heed. Thou art there nonetheless, dwelling in the holy place . . .

I am spent as spilt water, all my bones out of joint, my heart turned to molten wax within me, parched is my throat, like clay in the baking, and my tongue sticks fast in my mouth . . . Only life is left me; save that. . . .

Then I will proclaim thy renown to my brethren where thy people gather, I will join in singing thy praise . . . (Psalm 21[22]).

This psalm gives almost a literal description of the "sweet wormwood of torments" (*Purg.* xxiii. 86). On the third rung of the angelic ladder, we have seen that the grace and strength of the Holy Spirit sustained the Son throughout the agony and torment He suffered in His body. It is the power from the eternal counsel (of the Spirit) in the clear water that not only gives the penitents the torment but enables them to bear it (*Purg.* xxiii. 61–62). The agony of Christ and that of the penitents are only to prepare the praise of the Father, i.e., to show how the power of the Father raises the souls from the agony on the cross to the heavenly feast. The penitents sing in tears: *Labia mea Domine* (O Lord open thou my lips; and my mouth shall show forth thy praise) (*Purg.* xxiii. 11). They are waiting and praying "to proclaim thy renown." The praise of the Lord is the only sacrifice His creatures can offer:

Listen my people . . . listen, Israel, to the protestation I make thee; I the God thou ownest as God. I do not find fault with thee over thy sacrifices; why all day long thy burnt offerings smoke before me . . . I own already every wild beast in the forest . . . Wouldst thou have me eat bull's flesh, and drink the blood of goats? The sacrifice thou must offer to

God is a sacrifice of praise, so wilt thou perform vows to the most High. So, when thou criest to me in time of trouble, I will deliver thee; then thou shalt honor me as thou wilt (Psalm 49[50]: 7–15).

The Eagle on Jupiter is the bird that sings the praise of the Lord:

> So I saw that emblem which was woven
>   of the praises of divine grace become such
>   with songs as only those who rejoice up there can
>   know.
>
> Par. xix. 37–39

Our poet gradually prepares his reader for the bird of God on Jupiter. When he comes to the first tree of the Sixth Terrace, he intently looks for birds through the green leaves of the tree (*Purg.* xxiii. 1–3). He compares the throng of penitents to a flock of birds:

> As the birds that winter along the Nile
>   sometimes form flocks in the sky and then
>   go in file to fly with greater speed,
>
> So all the people who were present there,
>   turning their faces, hastened their steps,
>   and leanness and desire made them fleet.
>
> Purg. xxiv. 64–69

At Dante's arrival on Jupiter, the countless birds which compose the Eagle spell out letter by letter: *Diligite iustitiam qui iudicatis terram* (Love justice, ye that be judges of the earth) (*Par.* xviii. 91–93). The birds remain for a while in the formation of the last letter M. The M transforms itself into the Eagle by adding the head and neck on its top (*Par.* xviii. 94–108). The M constitutes the body of the Eagle and requires only a head and a neck to become the complete Eagle. On the Sixth Terrace, Dante sees the germ of the celestial Eagle in the face of every penitent:

> Their eye pits looked like rings without gems;
>   whoever reads OMO (*homo*) in the face of man
>   would easily have recognized the M.
>
> *Purg.* xxiii. 31–33

The celestial Eagle is the perfected form of the *Homo Dei*. The perverted form of the *Homo Dei* is Cerberus. With his three throats, Cerberus is the M planted upside down. The shapes and postures of the three forms of the M indicate the three different modes of nutrition the *Homo Dei* draws. The two eyes and one mouth are the three organs through which the *Homo Dei* absorbs nourishment. The eyes represent the organs for spiritual food, and the mouth the organ for material food. All these three organs for the absorption of food in a glutton have been degraded and defiled in the food of dirt and mud. Cerberus has three throats and three mouths. While his two eyes have become dull, his gullets become ravenous. Cerberus blindly gulps down a handful of dirt, and the gluttons are blind (*Jnf.* vi. 25–30, 93).

The blessed birds of the Eagle feed on spiritual food with their eyes. Their sight is "one of the rays of the Mind/ with which everything is replete" (*Par.* xix. 53–54). The bird uses its throat and mouth for the praise of the Lord:

> I seemed to hear the murmuring of a stream
>   cascading clear down from rock to rock,
>   showing the abundance of its high source;
>
> And as at the neck of a lute
>   the sound takes its form, and as the wind
>   at the vent of a pipe fills with sound,

So, without suspense of long delaying,
 that murmur of the eagle swelled and rose
 up through the neck as if it were hollow.

There it became voice and issued forth
 out of the beak in the form of words,
 such as my heart that inscribed them awaited.
Par. xx. 19–30

The stream which cascades down from rock to rock flows out from the source whose water the woman of Samaria asked for to quench her thirst. The Eagle shows its perfect satisfaction of thirst after singing out with the celestial water as the medium:

As a lark soaring in the air
 first sings and then is silent, content
 with the last sweetness which satisfies it,

So the image appeared to me satisfied
 under the imprint of the Eternal Pleasure.
Par. xx. 73–77

Because the birds drink the celestial water from God and sing it out to praise His glory, they are the media for the reflection of God's bounty and glory:

Each spirit looked like a small ruby
 in which a ray of sunlight burned
 and in my eyes was reflected.
Par. xix. 4–6

The water which the Eagle drinks is the same water which falls from a high rock on the Sixth Terrace and sprinkles the leaves of the tree (*Purg.* xxii. 137–138). The penitents cannot drink from the cascading water, because they are not yet prepared to do so. The M of the penitent has yet to develop its head and neck. A bird cannot drink without using its head and neck. The birds of Jupiter are the birds which our pilgrim looks for among the green leaves of the tree (*Purg.* xxiii. 1–3). Plato said that man is a plant not of the earth but of the firmament. Our poet says that the plant of the firmament is the celestial bird on Jupiter. While our pilgrim looks for birds in the leaves of the tree on the Sixth Terrace, he sees flowers of the tree among the birds of Jupiter (*Par.* xix. 22–24).

Cerberus is also a tree; he is a tree of three trunks firmly rooted in the ground. Though Cerberus takes nourishment from the dirt like a tree he does not enjoy the peace of vegetative existence. He lives in the turmoil of thirst and hunger which can never be quenched. He perpetually clamors with his hungry cries:

> So did those filthy heads of the demon Cerberus,
> who thunders over the shades,
> making them wish they were deaf.
>
> *Inf.* vi. 31–33

This is the song which the gluttons sing in praise of the Lord.

The stream from which the birds of Jupiter drink is the spring of grace (*Par.* xx. 119). This grace is sanctifying grace and is different from prevenient grace. While the soul is moved toward God through prevenient grace, it is accepted into the Body of Christ and nourished in it through sanctifying grace. In the last chapter, we saw how a sinful soul is born as an adopted son of God. We now see how the adopted sons of God are nourished in the spring of the Holy Spirit. The spring of grace is the spring of the Holy Spirit: *We too, all of us, have been baptized into a single body by the power of a single Spirit, Jews and*

Greeks, slaves and freemen alike; we have been given drink at a single source, the one Spirit (1 Cor. 12:13).

The joyous song of the Eagle reflects the unity of the members of the divine body, all of whom drink from the same fountain:

> As a single heat makes itself felt
>   from many coals, so, from many loves
>   a single sound issued from that image.
>
> *Par.* xix. 19–21

The unity of the Eagle represents the harmony of desires among the members of the divine body. When the Eagle speaks, its "I" and "mine" signify "we" and "our" (*Par.* xix. 10–12). This is the essence of justice. The laws are not enacted and enforced for private profit, but for the common good of the whole community.[6] Justice is the concord of private appetites and their subjection to the common good. Injustice is the discord of private appetites which seek gratification at the expense of the public good. Thus defined in terms of the concord and discord of private appetites, justice is an attribute of temperance, and injustice an attribute of intemperance.[7]

While all the birds of Jupiter constitute one body, the gluttons have no bond of community. The contrast between the Third Circle and Jupiter shows the intimate relation between individuality and the community. Individuality can never be attained and developed outside the bond of community. No individual is recognized and named in the Third Circle except Ciacco. Even Ciacco, the only glutton with whom Dante exchanges a few words, is too disfigured to retain any trace of individuality. "Ciacco" is not his proper name, but his gluttonous nickname (*Inf.* vi. 52). Ciacco introduces himself with his nickname and does not bother to mention his real name. The penitents are very happy to be called by their names in spite of their disfigurement (*Purg.* xxiv. 26). The birds on Jupiter have developed individualities of high degrees; each of them has a distinct role to play and a unique place to occupy in the divine body. Individuals with no bond of communion are no longer individuals. Individuals become individuals only by becoming members of a proper community.

Once the community loses the bond of justice, the community becomes a sack of warring appetites. The howling Cerberus is such a sack of warring appetites. Florence has also become such a sack (*Inf.* vi. 63–75). The Church has become a temple of warring appetites where the money changers sell and buy the bread of the Father (*Par.* xviii. 121–136). On the Sixth Terrace, new concord replaces the old discord. A spark of new friendship is kindled between Dante and Forese Donati who exchanged scurrilous sonnets during their sojourn on the earth (*Purg.* xxiii. 46–48). The spirit of concord shines through in Donati's account of the mutual care among members of his family. Through his wife Nella's flood of tears, Donati hastened and expedited his course of purgation (*Purg.* xxiii. 87). Donati is happy in praising the virtue and glory of his sister Piccarda (*Purg.* xxiv. 13–15). Every member of the family is concerned with the welfare of other members. This is the spirit of justice. The bond of care extends from the living to the dead, and from the repentant to the blessed. It is in this spirit of mutual care and concern that Bonagiunta foretells Dante of the kind reception he will have from an unknown lady of Lucca in the course of his exile (*Purg.* xxiv. 43–48). The spirit of justice is the spirit of the good Samaritan.

Our pilgrim also develops a great sense of concern for the well-being of others. This is the concern which Dante holds for virtuous heathens. In spite of all their virtues and merits, the heathens have to be eternally damned simply because they are not given grace. Is it not a great injustice to give the pagans no chance at all for their salvation? This concern is the great, long fasting which our pilgrim would like to be relieved of on Jupiter (*Par.* xix. 25–78). This is the hunger for justice. Dante dare not point out what seems to be a grave injustice on the part of God. He is fully aware of the Apostle Paul's admonition: *Nay, but who art thou, O man, that bandy words with God?* (Rom. 9:20). The Eagle reads and propounds the question which is gnawing into Dante's trembling heart.

The Eagle answers Dante's question by explaining justice, creation, and election. The origin and measure of justice is the divine will; the will and desire of God is living justice (*Par.* xix. 68, 86). Justice on the part of the creatures is the effect of the primal justice, that is, the reflection and imitation of the primal justice (*Par.* xviii. 116–117). St. Thomas says that the natural law is the reflection of the divine law and that human law is derived from natural law.[8] Creatures are just only insofar as their desires and wills are in harmony with the divine will (*Par.* xix. 88). It is presumption by creatures to pass judgment on the will of God using the human standard, the presumption of measuring the measure of all with the measured (*Par.* xix. 79–81). To see through the foundation of divine justice is beyond the capacity of the created intellect. The created intellect which tries to understand the ultimate mystery of the divine will is like the feeble eye which tries to fathom the bottom of the ocean from its surface (*Par.* xix. 55–60).

It is not for creatures to pass judgment on the Creator, but for the Creator to pronounce judgment on His creatures. The Eagle pronounces its thunderous judgment on the perverted rulers of Christendom (*Par.* xix. 103–148). The Father in heaven is the Ruler of all rulers: *See, where he stands, the Ruler of all, among the rulers assembled, comes forward to pronounce judgment on the rulers them-*

*selves! Will you never cease perverting justice, espousing
the cause of the wicked? (Psalm* 81[82]: 1–2).

The divine will wills the greatest and the highest good
(*Par.* xix. 85–87). The entire creation is the expression of
the infinite good (*Par.* xix. 40–45). God wishes to share
His good with His creatures. Every creature is a receptacle
for the good emanating from God, and no creature is large
enough to absorb all the good in God (*Par.* xix. 45). Whatever a creature receives from God is a free gift; no one is
entitled to what one receives. The rule of human justice
is to render each one his own due, and this rule cannot be
applied to the distribution of divine gifts.[9]

Grace is the highest gift of God. Through grace a mortal
creature attains life everlasting in the kingdom of God
(Rom. 6:22). Divine grace so far surpasses the level of
desert and merit that no creature merits the gift of grace
through its virtues.[10] No mortal can by his nature even
desire the glory and bliss of heaven, because heavenly glory
far surpasses the level of human desire (*Par.* xix. 13–15).
The will of God is the only principle through which the
gift of grace is distributed.[11] Even the blessed who see God
face to face do not yet know all the elect (*Par.* xx. 133–
135). It is far beyond the comprehension of all creatures
how the grace of the Holy Spirit works through the souls
of mortals: *The wind* (the breath of the Holy Spirit)
*breathes where it will, and thou canst hear the sound of it,
but knowest nothing of the way it came or the way it goes*
(John 3:8).

Because of the unfathomable mystery in which grace
works, St. Thomas admits the possibility of invisible
sanctification.[21] He believes that baptism is absolutely necessary for salvation (*Par.* xix. 103–105). While baptism is
a visible manifestation of a visible desire, St. Thomas
ponders, may grace work invisibly through the innermost

heart of man? Our poet sees an unbelievable instance of the invisible sanctification in Ripheus. Who would believe that the Trojan, Ripheus, is saved? (*Par.* xx. 67–69). The power of grace worked internally and invisibly in the soul of Ripheus:

> The other (Ripheus), through grace
>> which is distilled from so deep a spring
>> that no creature ever saw to the bottom,
>
> Put all his love below on uprightness;
>> wherefore, from grace to grace,
>> God opened his eyes to our future redemption.
>> *Par.* xx. 118–123

Another testimony to the mystery of grace is the Emperor Trajan. His soul was rescued from Hell after his death, and he was given a second chance to believe what he did not believe in his first life. This special privilege was given in response to the pious prayers of Gregory. Trajan believed in his second life and was saved (*Par.* xx. 106–117). The special gifts and privileges given Trajan and Ripheus were special exceptions to the justice of the divine court. St. Thomas says that clemency is a part of temperance.[13] God tempered His justice with mercy:

> The kingdom of the heavens suffers violence
>> only from warm love and living hope
>> which vanquish the divine will.
>
> Not as men overcome each other,
>> but because it wishes to be overcome
>> and, vanquished, it conquers with its own kindness.
>> *Par.* xx. 94–99

The heavenly justice is not tempered only for Ripheus

and Trajan. The election and salvation of every mortal soul is violence to the justice of the heavenly court, because the sinful soul does not merit life everlasting in the mansion of God but deserves only death in the kingdom of sin. The opening of the kingdom of heaven for sinful souls is itself the violation of divine justice. *Ever since John the Baptist's time, the kingdom of heaven has suffered violence* (Matt. 11:12). The salvation of Ripheus and Trajan is not the only miracle which divine grace works in its inscrutable way, but the redemption of every sinful soul is an unfathomable mystery.

In spite of the inscrutable way in which divine grace works, the predestination of all the souls is determined for all eternity. Predestination is a feature of the eternal justice which leaves nothing to blind chance (*Par.* xx. 52–54). The sons of eternal bliss and the sons of eternal perdition are determined even before their birth. This is God's election on which we can be instructed by St. Paul:

It is not that the word of God has failed. For they are not all Israelites who are sprung from Israel; nor because they are the descendants of Abraham, are they all his children . . . That is to say, they are not sons of God who are the children of the flesh, but it is the children of promise who are reckoned as posterity . . . before the children had yet been born, or had done aught of good or evil, in order that the selective purpose of God might stand, depending not on deeds, but on him who calls, it was said to her: "The elder shall serve the younger"; as it is written, "Jacob I have loved, but Esau I have hated" (Rom. 9:6–13).

The election of blessed souls and the reprobation of perverted souls is determined by the will of God before the foundation of the world.[14] Every gift from above and every station assigned to a mortal soul are the free gifts from God. God distributes these free gifts as He wills and not as His creatures deserve, because no creature deserves anything in its own right. Even the deeds and virtues of the creature arise from the gifts the creature receives from God and do not constitute an independent ground for merit and desert. It is ultimately the will of God that gives the initial promise to every soul and settles its final destiny. Reprobation as well as election is a part of Providence.[15] The selective purpose of God stands not on the deeds of those who are called but on Him who calls. Does this mean a whimsical injustice on the part of God? *By no means! . . . the effect comes, then, from God's mercy, not from man's will . . . Pharaoh, too, is told in scripture, "This is the very reason why I have made thee what thou art, so as to give proof in thee, of my power, and to let my name be known all over the earth* (Rom. 9:11–17).

"*To give proof of my power*" and to "*let my name be known,*" that is, the manifestation of God's power and name is the ultimate purpose of all creation and emanation, whether God saves or damns. This is why the Eagle presents each of the six souls making up the Eagle's eye with the proclamation *ora conosce* (now he knows) (*Par.* xx. 40, 46, 52, 58, 64, 70). For a proper understanding of this point, we should be acquainted with the Angelic Doctor's doctrine of emanation.[16] Creation is the outpouring of the infinite goodness of God. It is through this outpouring that God manifests His boundless bounty. The plurality and inequality of the grades of being are essential to perfect manifestation of the divine Good. One angel and one animal can reflect more perfectly the divine Good than one angel and one angel. St. Thomas concludes: "Hence, there would not be a perfect likeness of God in the universe if all things were of one grade of being. For this reason, then, is there distinction among created things: that, by being many, they may receive God's likeness more perfectly than by being one."[17]

The entire chain of being can be divided into different grades of being. It can be, for example, divided into the incorruptible and the corruptible good.[18] The former reflects the nature of God better than the latter, but the two together manifest the divine good better than either one of them alone. It is in the light of the principle of emanation and reflection of the divine Good that we should understand the predestined difference between the two sons of Isaac. The two grades of man, the virtuous and the depraved, reflect the infinite divine good better than any one of the two grades alone. It is also in the spirit of divine reflection that Dante divides Heaven into heavens and Hell into hells.

The redeemed and the damned alike are created for the manifestation of God's power and the praise of His name. Of all the levels of manifestation of the divine nature, the intuitive vision of God is the highest. The principle of multiplicity and inequality operates also in the vision and knowledge of God. The many and diverse forms of the beatific vision manifest the divine good more perfectly than one uniform grade and pattern would. The six souls who make up the Eagle's eye have come to know different aspects of the divine will and justice through their redemption. This is true not only of the six distinguished souls, but of all the redeemed. The salvation of every soul is a unique mystery and comes to reveal a unique aspect of the unfathomable divine will. If the Eagle were to present individually all the souls on Jupiter, it would manifest each of them to the world with the proclamation *ora conosce* (now he knows).

All creatures exist for the praise of the Lord, but only the blessed praise the Lord willingly and knowingly. All the blessed praise the Lord, but only the birds of Jupiter sing the honor and power of the Lord. The fountain of their song is the spring of the Holy Spirit. The pupil of the Eagle is none other than King David, "the singer of the Holy Spirit" (*Par.* xx. 37–39). His Book of Psalms is a stream of songs He sang with the inspiration of the Holy Spirit. Our poet understands his Angelic Epic as a song of praise which flows out of the holy spring of the Spirit like King David's Psalms.

On the Sixth Terrace, Bonagiunta is anxious to find out the secret of Dante's *dolce stil nuovo*, the new rhymes beginning "Ladies who have intelligence in love . . ." (*Purg.* xxiv. 49–51). "Ladies who have intelligence in love" is the first ode Dante composed after a resolve which marked a significant development in his long career of singing. In the first part of *La Vita Nuova*, our poet raves with the torment and agony of his heart which is feeling the first shaft of Love. Even in this early stage, our poet is quite sure of the divine origin of love which begins to claim lordship over his passionate heart; but his tender young heart is too tormented to sing of anything but its own torment.

When the initial shock of love's shaft is gone, our poet begins to think of more than "myself." "Having said enough concerning myself," he resolves to sing of "another matter" (*La Vita Nuova*, xvii). He resolves to praise the lady of his love. "The Ladies who have intelligence in love" is the first ode our poet sings after this significant resolve:

> Ladies that have intelligence in love,
>> Of mine own lady I would speak with you;
>> Not that I hope to count her praises through,
>> . . . .
>
> *La Vita Nuova*, xix (The Rossetti Translation)

Dante strives to sing the praise of His Love, but he comes to realize that he has yet to grow far more mature to be able to sing it properly. Thus he closes the adolescent stage of his singing to wait for the "time as I could discourse more worthily concerning her" (*La Vita Nuova*, xliii). *La Divina Commedia* is the love song which the Angelic Poet sings as a full-fledged bird of the Holy Spirit. How far has our angelic bird grown from *La Vita Nuova* to *La Divina Commedia?* Our poet describes himself as a full-fledged bird to Bonagiunta:

> "I am one who,
> when Love inspires, takes note
> and as he dictates within, I write."
> *Purg.* xxiv. 52–54

How was the bird as a youngling?

> Woe's me! by dint of all these sighs that come
>   Forth of my heart, its endless grief to prove,
>   Mine eyes are conquer'd, so that even to move
>   Their lids for greeting is grown troublesome.
>
> They wept so long that now they are grief's home
>   And count their tears all laughter far above:
>   They wept till they are circled now by Love
>   With a red circle in sign of martyrdom.
>
> These musings, and the sighs they bring from me,
>   Are grown at last so constant and so sore
>   That Love swoons in my spirit with faint breath;
>
> Hearing in these sad sounds continually
>   The most sweet name that my dear lady bore,
>   With many grievous words touching her death.
>   *La Vita Nuova*, xl (Rossetti Translation)

The distance our Angelic Poet has travelled from *La Vita Nuova* to *La Divina Commedia* is the distance from raving to writing, that is, from the thought that raves in

283

the tormented heart to the thought that writes itself down with an instinctive hand. The former is the song of agony and the latter the song of joy. The former is praise in struggle and the latter is praise in instinct. The distance between these two epochs in Dante's career of singing is illustrated by the contrast between the birds of the Sixth Terrace and the birds of the Sixth Heaven. While the penitent birds struggle with their instinct, the blessed bird of the Eagle rejoices in the perfect mastery of its instinct:

> He who paints there has no one to guide him,
> but guides himself: from him we recognize
> that instinctive power which designs a nest.
>
> *Par.* xviii. 109–111

Our poet illustrates the distance between the singing of the penitent bird and that of the blessed bird or between the song of agony and the song of joy with the difference between the psalmist in the struggle with his agony and the psalmist in the mastery of his instinct. The penitents sing *Labia mea Domine*:

Sprinkle me with hyssop, and I shall be cleansed; wash me, and I shall become whiter than snow. Make me to hear joy and gladness, let the bones thou hast crushed rejoice . . . Create a pure heart for me, O God, and renew in me a steadfast spirit. Cast me not away from thy face, and take not thy holy spirit from me . . . O Lord, thou wilt open my lips, and my mouth shall declare thy praise (Psalm 50[51]9–17).

The difference between the penitent bird and the blessed bird is the distance between raving and writing. While the praise of the former is raving in the contrite heart and waiting for the opening of the lips, the praise of the latter spells itself out letter by letter. The birds of Jupiter write out *Diligite iustitiam qui iudicatis terram* (*Par.* xviii.

91–93). While the crawling and raving in torment is the singing of the psalmist in agony, the soaring and writing in delight is the singing of the psalmist in joy: *Joyful the thoughts that well up from my heart, the king's honor for my theme; my tongue flows readily as the pen of a swift writer. Thine is more than mortal beauty, thy lips overflow with gracious utterance* (Psalm 44[45]:1–3).

The difference between *La Vita Nuova* and *La Divina Commedia*, between the crawling baby bird and the soaring full-fledged bird and between the raving psalmist and the writing psalmist is the difference between prevenient grace and sanctifying grace, the difference between raving and writing.

Our Angelic Poet is quite conscious of the spring of the Holy Spirit as the source of his inspiration and makes a special invocation on Jupiter for the first time since his invocation at the beginning of his ascent of the *Paradiso:*

> O divine Pegasea, thou
> > who givest glory and long life to genius
> > and thence, through thee, to cities and kingdoms,
>
> Illumine me with thyself that I may set forth
> > their figures as I have conceived them;
> > let thy power appear in these brief verses!
> > > *Par.* xviii. 82–87

The kingdom of heaven is a kingdom of justice where all desires vibrate in harmony with the divine will. The kingdom of justice is the imperial family where the Father in Heaven is the Father of all sons and the familial empire where the Father in Heaven is the Ruler of all rulers. In the last chapter, we saw how the Father of all sons adopts sinful souls as the members of the divine family through the blood of His only begotten Son. In this chapter, we have seen how the Ruler of all rulers nourishes His adopted

285

sons as the members of the divine empire through the fountain of His own Spirit.

Cacciaguida on the Cross of Mars represents the tenderness and joyfulness of the Father in welcoming the return of His prodigal son from exile. The voice of the Eagle on Jupiter represents the majesty and dignity of the Emperor in governing the princes of His Empire as members of one body. While Cacciaguida calls his great-great-grandson "my son," the Eagle intends to mean "we" and "our" with the words "I" and "mine" (*Par.* xix. 10–12). "We" and "our" are the proper forms of the royal address. When the Ruler of all rulers said, "I am that I am"; He meant, "We are that we are."

The sinful soul which has been alienated from God is justified when its active concupiscible is attuned to the will of the Father through its adoption as a son of the Father and when its passive concupiscible is nourished in harmony with the will of the Emperor through its sanctification as a prince of His empire. The adoption through the blood of the Son and the sanctification in the stream of the Spirit are the two phases of one enterprise: the justification of the estranged creature. The former is active and external, and the latter is passive and internal. To take up the cross and follow the Son is active, and to receive grace and to be nourished in the stream of the Spirit is passive. The cross of the Son is visible and the breath of the Spirit is invisible. The latter works in the heart, and the former is carried on the back. These differences between the justification of the active concupiscible and that of the passive concupiscible are distilled into the contrast between the string music of the Cross on Mars and the vocal music of the Eagle on Jupiter.

Both the string music of the Cross and the vocal music of the Eagle are the expression of one joy, the joy of justification, and both sing the bliss of one beatitude: "Blessed are they who hunger and thirst for justice, for they shall be satisfied" (*Purg.* xxii. 6; xxiv. 151). The hunger is satisfied in the justice of adoption, and the thirst is quenched in the justice of sanctification. It is with the virtue of liberality that the Father of all fathers adopts sinners as His sons through the visible mission of His Son. It is with the virtue of temperance that the Emperor of all emperors nourishes adopted sons as the princes of His Empire through the invisible mission of His Spirit.

The desires of the passive concupiscible which have not been justified are the sins of intemperance and gluttony. The two examples of intemperance represent two types of the perverted appetite which you can find in the Third Circle (*Purg.* xxiv. 121–126). In the Third Circle, Dante names two creatures, Cerberus and Ciacco. Cerberus represents those who have never been called to drink from the spring of the Holy Spirit, and Ciacco represents those who have been called but not elected into the divine body. Cerberus knows of no better drink than the wine of mud for his thirst, and his perversion is represented by the first example of intemperance, the Centaurs who were gorged and heated with wine and abandoned themselves to blind revelry (*Purg.* xxiv. 121–123).

Ciacco's perversion resembles the second example of intemperance, the fate of the soldiers who were eliminated from Gideon's army:

Gideon . . . led his army to the Spring of Harad . . . "This is a great army thou hast with thee," the Lord told Gideon. "I must not grant victory over Madian to an army like this, or the Israelites would boast that they had no need of me; that their own strength had brought them deliverance. Make it known . . . that any man who shrinks back or is afraid is free to go home." So twenty-two thousand of his men . . . went back home, and left him with only ten thousand. But the Lord said to Gideon, "Thy army is still too great. Take them down to the waterside, and I will test them there . . ." And when they reached the water, the Lord's command to Gideon was, "Separate those who lap the water like dogs, and those who go down on their knees to drink . . ." (Judges 7:1–5).

The Lord commanded Gideon to send home all those who went down on their knees to drink. Out of many thousand, only three hundred men survived this final test and were given the victory over Madian. *Many are called, but few are chosen* (Matt. 22:14). Only those who do not *kneel down* to drink from the spring of the earth are chosen to drink from the stream of the Holy Spirit. If all the called were elected, they would boast that "their strength had brought them deliverance."

The three examples of temperance show how the Father elevates to the fountain of His Spirit those who do not kneel down to the spring of the dirt (*Purg.* xxii. 140–154). The first example is Mary's concern for the marriage feast at Cana. She thought more of the feast than of her mouth and asked her Son to provide wine when the feast ran out of wine. The mouth is the symbol of the passive concupiscible, and Mary uses her mouth more for the satisfaction of others' desire than her own. This is temperance. Through Mary's virtue and pleading, the feast at Cana was provided with wine.

The Virgin Mother's virtue reflects a far greater virtue; the temperance of the Father in sending His Son to the earth and pouring out the stream of grace on the mortal souls. Wine is the symbol of grace; the grace of the Holy Spirit is the wine for the heavenly feast. Since Adam forfeited grace through his sin, revelry on earth was like a feast that ran out of wine. To bring the wine of grace to the feast of man, the Father sends His Son to the earth. Grace comes with Christ. As the Virgin Mother asked her Son to give wine for the wedding feast of Cana, so the Father in heaven asked His Son to give wine for the feast of the earth.

The second example of temperance explains how the mortal soul should prepare for the drink from the fountain of the Holy Spirit. The second example is that of the ancient Roman women who were content with plain water for their drink and Daniel who despised food and gained wisdom. The Roman Empire is the manifestation of the Holy Spirit in Dante's view, and the Roman women prepared their race for this special gift of the Spirit through their temperate diet. Daniel also prepared himself with his lean diet for the grace of the Lord (Dan. 1:8–9). One who kneels down to the food and drink of the earth as the ultimate source of pleasure and satiates his hunger and thirst cannot drink from the fountain of the Spirit. Those who wish to drink the wine of heaven should despise the meat and wine of the earth.

The third example is the delight of the golden age and John the Baptist in their austere diet. The golden age is the age of innocence and grace. Innocence and grace of the golden age were lost through gluttonous appetite for the food and drink of the dirt. Christ comes to restore the gluttonous man to the grace of the golden age, and John the Baptist prepares for His coming in the austere diet of the golden age: *and he* (John) *ate locusts and wild honey. And thus he preached, One is to come after me . . . Jesus came . . . and was baptized by John in the Jordan. And even as he came up out of the water he saw the heavens opened and the Spirit, like a dove, coming down and resting upon him* (Mark 1:6–10). Thus mankind is restored to the original justice of the golden age, and the wine of the Holy Spirit comes back to the feast of man.

It is the temperance of the Father that our Angelic Poet sings on the sixth rung of the angelic ladder of divine love. The Father tempers His justice to give the wine of heaven to mortal souls. To drink from His wine, the mortal soul has to bring its desires into unity with the divine will. The unity of all desires in the will of God is justice and peace. *The kingdom of God does not consist in food and drink, but in justice and peace and joy in the Holy Spirit* (Rom. 14:17). The bond of the Holy Spirit is the peace of heaven, and the stream of His grace is the wine of the blessed.

chapter 10

Lesson on the Rung of Spiritual and Carnal Love

The Seventh Heaven, the Seventh Terrace, and the Second Circle

W E HAVE reached the seventh rung of the angelic ladder of divine love. This rung is built on the power of love. What is love? St. Thomas defines love as the power of union.[1] The soul becomes one with what it loves. To become one with another self is to go out of oneself and to dwell in the other self.[2] To be carried out of oneself and to abide in another self is the *ecstasy* of love. Love longs for union and ecstasy. The love of God is spiritual love, because God is pure spirit. Spiritual love brings the soul to ecstatic union with God. *God is love, and he who abides in love abides in God, and God in him* (1 John 4:16). The love of flesh is carnal love. It is carnal love that brings two bodies of flesh into a carnal union.

The Second Circle is the kingdom of lust. St. Thomas says that lust is blind, rash, thoughtless, and inconstant.[3] Our poet of love crystallizes all the attributes of carnal love:

> Now I begin to hear the notes of sorrow,
> now I have come to where
> loud cries beat upon my ears.

The Fragile Leaves of the Sibyl

I have reached a place mute of all light
   which roars like a sea in a tempest
   when beaten by warring winds.

The infernal storm which never rests
   leads the spirits in its sweep;
   whirling and beating, it torments them.

Inf. v. 25–33

The power of lust has no power to maintain its own integrity and purity. One moment an infatuated lover may swear his love for all eternity, and the next moment his "eternal" love may crumble to an eternally irretrievable ruin. All the illustrious heroes and heroines of lust in the Second Circle had to break the fidelity and integrity of their carnal love: Dido had to break faith with the ashes of Sichaeus for Aeneas; Helen of Troy had to desert Menelaus' bed for Paris; Achilles had to side with the Trojans for the hand of Polyxena; finally Empress Semiramis had to legalize her tempestuous lust in imperial decrees (*Inf.* v. 52–69). The irrevocable ruin of carnal integrity is the most dreadful source of remorse and lamentation for the heroes and heroines of lust:

When they arrive before the ruin,
   there the shrieks, the moaning, and the lamentation;
   there they blaspheme the divine power.

Inf. v. 34–36

They will soon forget their shrieks and moanings, get on a new tide of lust, and swear their new love in the name of God whom they have just blasphemed in their lamentation over the ruin of the old tempest of their lust. Thus they will make another round of lust and come back to the same ruin:

And, as starlings are borne by their wings
    in the cold season, in a broad and dense flock,
    so that blast carries the evil spirits.

Here, there, up, and down, it blows them;
    no hope ever comforts them
    of rest or even of less pain,

And as cranes go chanting their lays,
    making a long line of themselves in the air,
    so I saw coming, uttering laments,

Shades borne by that strife of winds.
                          Inf. v. 40–49

The lovers are responsive to the call of love. When our poet invites Paolo and Francesca in the name of love, they respond quickly and gently. Spontaneity is the singular feature of love:

As doves summoned by their desire,
    with wings raised and firm, sail through the air,
    borne to their sweet nest by their will alone.
                          Inf. v. 82–84

Thus the two lovers come to Dante. They have become one body in the ecstatic union of their bodily love. Francesca repeats *pace* (peace) twice in her greeting to Dante (*Inf.* v. 92, 99). Peace is that which the carnal lovers long for more than anything else in the tumult of carnal ecstasy. Francesca explains the nature and destiny of carnal love:

Love, which flames quickly in gentle hearts
    was kindled in this soul (Paolo) by the fair body
    taken from me; the manner still offends me.

293

> Love, which absolves no one beloved from loving
> caught me so strongly with his charm
> that, as you see, even now it leaves me not.   ˙
>
> Love led us to one death together.
> Caina waits for him who quenched our lives.
>
> *Inf.* v. 100–107

These three tercets portray the birth, growth, and death of carnal love. The first of the three tercets describes the birth of love. St. Thomas says that the bodily sight is the beginning of carnal love.[4] Paolo's love was kindled by Francesca's fair body. Love is born in a gentle heart. Malicious, cold, calculating people seldom become the victims of carnal passion.

The second tercet shows the usual response to love; it is very hard and seems to be even cruel to reject love. Love demands to be justified and revered as the duty which allows no exemption. Thus love gains the mastery over its victims only to lead them to the common destiny. The common destiny of carnal love is death. Carnal love consummates itself only through its self-consumption. Francesca cannot bring the third tercet of her love story to its consummation. Her love story comes to an abrupt, destructive end at the end of the first line of the last tercet, and her sweet love changes into a bitter ire of vengeance in the second line.

Notice the difference in tempo of the three tercets, each of which begins with "love." "Love" in lines 100 and 103 is separated from its verb by a qualifying clause which runs the whole length of the line. "Love" in line 106 is immediately followed by its verb. The difference in tempo of the three tercets reflects the difference of the three stages of love: birth, growth, and death. In the first and the second tercets, "love" moves back and forth between the two lovers. In the last tercet, "love" grips them together and casts them into one death.

The love of flesh cannot escape its doom without being transmuted into the love of spirit. It is through the fire of the top Terrace that carnal love is transmuted into spiritual love. The purgatorial fire is fanned by the blasts which blow upward, that is, by the blasts of flesh bent toward heaven (*Purg.* xxv. 113). The penitents are burning themselves in the fire, singing *Summa Deus clementiae* (*Purg.* xxv. 121).

> Father of mercies infinite,
>   Ruling all things that be,
> Who, shrouded in the depth and height,
>   Art One and art Three;
>
> Accept our chants, accept our tears,
>   A mingled stream we pour;
> Such stream the laden bosom cheers,
>   To taste Thy sweetness more.
>
> Purge thou with fire the o'ercharged mind,
>   Its sores and wounds profound
> And with the watcher's girdle bind
>
>   .   .   .   .
>
> *The Roman Breviary*, Saturday at Matins

The penitents sing and weep like cranes in flight as the carnal lovers do (*Purg.* xxvi. 43–48). The singing and weeping of the former is a "mingled stream," whereas the singing and weeping of the latter is "unmingled." As the Angelic Doctor quite well understood, men are more ashamed of venereal acts than of any other acts and the sin of lust is the most shameful sin.[5] In Francesca's account of her sinful act, you cannot detect a tinge of her shame but only a pitiful adoration of her sinful love (*Inf.* v. 127–138).

For the penitents, the torture of their shame is as unbearable as the torment of the fire (*Purg.* xxvi. 81). The weeping and singing of the carnal lovers is also unmingled because their recollection of the past happy love gives them nothing but pain. Francesca says, "There is no greater pain/ than to recall a happy time in wretchedness" (*Inf.* v. 121–122). The penitents recall the sad past but look forward to the happy future. Arnaut Daniel tells Dante:

> I am Arnaut, and now I go singing and weeping.
>   Sadly I regret my past folly
>   and rejoicing see ahead the joy I hope for.
>   *Purg.* xxvi. 142–144

The mingled stream of sorrow and joy, regret and hope, flesh and spirit, has to become a pure stream for the ecstatic union of the soul with its Creator. How can carnal love with "its sores and wounds profound" be transformed into pure spiritual love? What is the nature of this miraculous transformation? Our poet views this miraculous transformation as a process of assimilation. He presents his doctrine of assimilation in his account of the genesis of the human soul. When the First Mover breathes the spiritual soul into the sensitive soul nurtured in the womb of Mother Nature, the spiritual soul transforms and assimilates the sensitive soul into itself. This process of assimilation is like the "heat of the sun which becomes wine/ when joined to the juice taken from the vine" (*Purg.* xxv. 77–78).

We can infer from this metaphor of assimilation that spiritual love transforms and assimilates carnal love into itself just as the spiritual soul transforms the sensitive soul. This view echoes St. Paul's teaching that the natural is for the preparation of the spiritual and that the spiritual is for the consummation of the carnal:

Mankind begins with the Adam which became, as Scripture tells us, a living soul; it is fulfilled in the Adam who has become a life-giving spirit. It was not the principle of spiritual life that came first; natural life came first, then spiritual life; the man who came first came from earth, fashioned of dust, the man who came afterwards came from heaven, and his fashion is heavenly (1 Cor. 15:45–47).

It is spiritual love that performs the function of leaven in the purgatorial fire. It is again spiritual love that pulls Dante's body into the fire. When he is told that he has to be burned in the fire, he shudders with horror (*Purg.* xxvii. 15). The love of spirit is frightful to the body of flesh. Moses was frightened when he was told to face God. At the germinal stage of his love, our poet saw "the figure of a lord of terrible aspect" who held in his hand Dante's flaming heart and fed it to the lady of his love (*La Vita Nuova*, iii).

In his attempt to persuade Dante to step into the fire, Virgil appeals to the authority of his reason and counsel and reminds him of all the great perils through which Virgil guided him. Virgil says *"ricordati, ricordati* (remember, remember) . . ."* (*Purg.* xxvii. 22). Virgil then appeals to Dante's sense of animal courage and says *"pon giù, pon giù* (put aside, put aside all fear)" (*Purg.* xxvii. 31). And yet Dante stands back from the fire like a firm rock. Virgil's final appeal is to Beatrice: "Now see, my son,/ this wall is between you and Beatrice" (*Purg.* xxvi. 36). At her name, the stony Dante softens and revives like Pyramus at the sound of Thisbe's name (*Purg.* xxvii. 37–40). Virgil's first appeal is to the counsel of the intellect, his second appeal to the courage of the irascible, and his final appeal to the love of the concupiscible. Just as Francesca and Paolo respond effortlessly to Dante's call of love, so Dante rushes into the fire of love at Virgil's appeal to Beatrice, the love of God. Love is conquered only by love. It is Dante's love of God that pulls his body into the fire and transforms its wounded carnal love into a pure spiritual love.

Within the fire, Virgil constantly talks of Beatrice. The fire does not singe a single hair (*Purg.* xxvii. 27). While the blast of lust brings the carnal lovers to the inevitable ruin, the purgatorial fire preserves and consummates carnal love. It is through the power of spiritual love that the penitents regain their chastity. What is chastity but the purity and integrity of love? Virgil calls the fire "the womb of these flames"; the fire is the womb where carnal love is reborn as spiritual love. The fire is the fire of the Father who is "shrouded in the depth and height" and who purges the penitent's love of "its sores and wounds profound." In the fire, Dante hears the voice of the Son calling His beloved to the mansion of His Father: "*Venite, benedicti patris mei*" (*Purg.* xxvii. 58). The fire of the Lord does not burn up but purifies His beloved: *And the Lord appeared to him in a flame of fire out of the midst of a bush; and he saw that the bush was on fire and was not burnt* (Exod. 3:2).

Our poet conceives the birth of his *dolce stil nuovo* out of the troubadour poetry as the transformation of carnal love into spiritual love. When he meets Guido Guinizelli in the fire, Dante calls him his father, the father of the "sweet and gracious rhymes of love" (*Purg.* xxvi. 97–99). The troubadour poetry sings of carnal love, and the sweet, new style of spiritual love. The latter arises out of the former. This is the way Solomon's Canticle of Canticles came to birth and life.

The impact of carnal love song is portrayed in Francesca's love story:

> One day, for our delight, we were reading
> of Lancelot, how love constrained him;
> alone we were and without any suspicion.

Several times that reading urged our eyes to meet,
  and changed the color of our faces;
  but one moment alone overcame us.

When we read how the longed-for smile
  was kissed by such a lover,
  he, who shall never be separated from me,

Kissed my mouth all trembling.
  A Galeotti was the book and he that wrote it;
  that day we READ in it NO FURTHER.
                                        Inf. v. 127–138

This account of the powerful impact of the reading of
the love story should be read with the knowledge of the
dramatic conversion of St. Augustine on reading St. Paul,
the Vessel of the Holy Spirit. At the critical stage of his
struggle against lust, the great saint of lust was led by a
child's refrain *Tolle lege! Tolle lege!* to the Epistle to the
Romans in which the Apostle of love propounds the birth
of spiritual love out of carnal love:

I was . . . weeping . . . when, lo, I heard the voice . . .
chanting and repeating, "Take up and read; take up and read."
Immediately my countenance changed . . . I rose up, interpreting it no other way than as a command to me from Heaven
. . . So quickly I returned to the place where . . . I put down
the volume of the apostles . . . I grasped, opened, and in
silence read that paragraph on which my eyes first fell—"*Not
in rioting and drunkenness, not in chambering and wantonness,
not in strife and envying; but put ye on the Lord Jesus Christ,
and make not provision for the flesh, to fulfill the lusts thereof.*"
NO FURTHER would I READ, nor did I need . . .[6]

Carnal love begins with delight and ends in tears; spiritual
love buds in weeping and blossoms in joy. The end of
carnal love is eternal death, and that of spiritual love is life

everlasting. Spiritual love can be born out of carnal love as the second Adam can come out of the first Adam. The emergence of the second Adam out of the first Adam is the rebirth of *amor* as *caritas*, and this is the miracle that took place in Augustine as the effect of reading Paul.

Our poet joins, in the fire of purgation, Guido and Arnaut, the two great fore-runners of the sweet new style. The sweet new style which has emerged from the troubadour tradition has to be purged in the fire of the Lord for the holy mission of singing the love of the Lord. Dante's love of Beatrice buds in the customary form of sensuous delight as firmly established by the tradition of troubadour poetry; his love takes its root in his animal heart at the bodily sight of her sensuous beauty (*La Vita Nuova* ii). Dante's long career of singing is the strenuous, sustained effort of spiritualizing the love in his animal heart. It is this love in his animal heart that our poet burns in the fire. He plunges into the fire for Beatrice and burns himself for Beatrice. The purgatorial fire perfects his spiritual idealization of the Beatrice who came in flesh and gives the final touch to his preparation for meeting the Beatrice who is to come in spirit. The fire of purgation performs for the *dolce stil nuovo* the same function which the fire of a burning coal performed for the foul lips of Isaias:

I saw the Lord sitting upon a throne high and elevated: and his train filled the temple . . . And they cried . . ." Holy, Holy, Holy, the Lord God of hosts, and the earth is full of his glory . . ." And I said, "Woe is me, because I must needs keep silence; because I am a man of unclean lips, and I dwell in the midst of a people that hath unclean lips, and I have seen with my eyes the Lord of hosts." And one of the seraphim flew to me: and in his hand was a live coal . . . And he touched my mouth, and said: "Behold this hath touched thy lips . . ." And I heard the voice of the Lord, saying: "Whom shall I send,

and who shall go for us?" And I said: "Lo, here am I. Send me"
(Isa. 6:1–8).

Our poet saw the Lord of the most high in the vision of
Beatrice:

> Then lifting up mine eyes, as the tears came,
>   I saw the angels, like a rain of manna,
>   In a long flight flying back heavenward;
>   Having a little cloud in front of them,
>   After the which they went and said, 'Hosanna!'
>   And if they had said more, you should have heard.
>   Then Love spoke thus: "Now all shall be made clear:
>   Come and behold our lady where she lies."

.   .   .   .

La Vita Nuova, xxiii (Rossetti Translation)

Our poet is seized by a dreadful sense of humility at this
vision of Beatrice's departure from the world of flesh. He
prays for the hand of death. With Beatrice's departure,
Dante begins to die to be born again and meet her in the
world of spiritual love. This long process of rebirth is perfected in "the womb of these flames." After being burned
and cleansed in the flames, our poet becomes pure and
sacred enough to proclaim his holy vision.

In the Seventh Heaven, Dante sees spiritual love in its
highest intensity and purity. Beatrice cannot smile; her
smile would burn the mortal Dante into ashes (*Par.* xxi.
4–6). For the same reason, the sweet symphony of the
Paradiso has to be suspended on Saturn to save Dante's
mortal body (*Par.* xxi. 58–60). The entire Heaven of Saturn
is adorned with nothing but simplicity and austerity like the
famed ruler of the golden age (*Par.* xxi. 25–27). Love requires no adornment other than its own sublimity. Jacob's
Ladder rises from this Heaven and soars beyond the range

of Dante's sight (Par. xxi. 28–30). On this Ladder, a great throng of splendors are flying up and down in perfect freedom. Jacob's Ladder is the symbol of the burning love for God. Abraham is the father of faith, and Isaac is the son of hope. Isaac is the hope given as a reward for Abraham's faith. Jacob is the love which arises out of Abraham's faith and Isaac's hope, and his ladder is the ladder of divine love at whose top Jacob sees the Lord. The seven Planets are the steps leading up to this ladder of divine love (*Par.* xxi. 7). As St. Augustine says, all the virtues are for the perfection of the love of God.[7]

Our pilgrim talks with Peter Damian and St. Benedict on Jacob's Ladder. Dante is quite anxious to find out why Peter Damian and no other is assigned by love to the office of receiving him on Jacob's Ladder (*Par.* xxi. 73–79). Our poet's inquiry touches on the root and cause of love. Peter Damian says that he cannot answer Dante's question and that even a seraph cannot see the mysterious ground of divine love (*Par.* xxi. 88–96). The cause and fountain of divine love is buried in the deepest abyss of the Supreme Essence and is far beyond the finite range of the created vision.

Divine love is the causeless cause of all things. It can explain many things, but nothing can explain it. To explain a thing is to show its cause. Divine love can be shown as the cause of all things, but nothing can be shown as the cause of divine love. Even the Incarnation of the only-begotten Son can be explained as the effect of God's love. *God so loved the world that he gave his only-begotten Son* (John 3:16). Even the Apostle of Love cannot give the cause for God's love of the world. Divine Love is *causa sui*. Even carnal love demands to be honored as *causa sui*. When Francesca says that love absolves no one beloved from loving, she adores love as the supreme command beyond all causes and reasons. She is quite right; love, carnal and spiritual, transcends the level of reason. Our poet himself experiences the supra-rational power of love at the purgatorial fire. The power of love enables him to penetrate the barrier which neither reason nor courage can.

After severely admonishing Dante against the futile attempt to fathom the mysterious ground of love, St. Peter Damian describes his austere ascetic life on earth (*Par.* xxi. 106–117). Compare the description of his hermitage:

> Between the two shores of Italy
> not far from your native land, crags rise
> so high that thunder sounds much lower down.
> *Par.* xxi. 106–108

with the description of Francesca's native city:

> The city where I was born
> lies on the shore where the Po descends
> with all its tributaries to find peace.
> *Inf.* v. 97–99

The spiritual love of Peter Damien rises above all the disturbances of the earth and soars toward heaven, and the carnal love of Francesca collects all the filthy streams into itself and flows down to the ocean of perpetual turbulence.* The former is exalting, and the latter is debasing.

Peter Damian's ascetic life was as pure and as simple as the crags on which he lived. With little food and care for his body, he chiefly lived on the spiritual food of contemplation (*Par.* xxi. 115–117). He says that Peter and Paul

---

* The description of Peter Damian's hermitage is a depiction of the *Purgatorio*, and the description of Francesca's native city is a depiction of the *Inferno*.

came "lean and unshod" but the modern shepherds have become fat beasts:

> Now the modern shepherds want someone
>   to prop them on this side and that, so portly are they,
>   and one to lead and one behind to hold their trains.
>
> They cover their palfreys with their mantles,
>   so that two beasts go under one cloak.
>   O Patience, that endures so much!
>
> *Par.* xxi. 130–135

Our poet here further develops his doctrine of the spiritualization of carnality. The ascetic life is the necessary means for converting the love of flesh into the love of spirit. The shepherds are entrusted with the holy mission of leading their flocks to the chaste love of God, but they have degraded themselves into beasts.

At Peter Damian's denunciation of bestial shepherds, all the blessed flock around St. Peter and shout such a thunderous cry that Dante becomes pale and breathless. This thunderous cry shows Dante the intensity of the chaste love which smolders like a volcano under snow. At the thunder of love, Dante is vanquished with stupor (*Par.* xxi. 142; xxii. 1). Before the purgatorial fire, he feels "like one who is laid in the grave" (*Purg.* xxvii. 15). On hearing Francesca's love story, he swoons and falls like a dead body (*Inf.* v. 142).

All these three scenes of stupor and shudder portray the climax of love, rapture and ecstasy. The self loses itself in its selfless union with the beloved. St. Bernard calls such an ecstatic love the fourth degree of love:

When shall the mind experience affection like this, so that, inebriated with divine love, forgetful of self, and become to its own self *like a broken vessel*, it may utterly pass over into

God, become one spirit with Him, and say: *My flesh and my heart hath fainted away . . .*[8]

Dante passes away under the impact of carnal love, but does not lose his consciousness under the impact of the purgatorial fire and the thunderous cry on Saturn. The Second Circle is the perfection of carnal ecstasy, but the Seventh Terrace and the Seventh Heaven are only the previews of spiritual ecstasy.

The most brilliant light on Jacob's Ladder is St. Benedict. He compared his Holy Rule for his monks to Jacob's Ladder.[9] His twelve rules are the twelve steps of this Ladder. By climbing these twelve steps of humility, one comes to the love of God. He says that the two sides of the ladder are the soul and the body. This metaphor is the first concrete elucidation of St. Paul's doctrine of the spiritualization of carnal love. St. Benedict on Jacob's Ladder readily acknowledges the grave difficulty of transmuting the frail flesh of mortals into spiritual love (*Par.* xxii. 85). St. Benedict says that the transformation of the frail flesh into pure spirit is a far more wondrous miracle than the miracle of turning back the flow of the Jordan or of opening of the Red Sea (*Par.* xxii. 94–96). As St. Paul says, the birth of the spiritual man out of the natural man is the miracle which has become possible through the power of the Incarnate Word.

St. Benedict stands as the witness and symbol of the permanent victory of the spirit over the flesh in Christendom. He embodied and exemplified his Holy Rule through a brilliant monastic career which he opened in a cave. He brought the light of Christ to the barbaric invaders who had almost extinguished the flame of the Western civilization and sowed the seed which was to blossom as the flower of the Christian civilization among the crude pagans. The Benedictine Monastery on Cassino is the symbol of the conversion of the flesh to the spirit:

> The summit of the mountain on whose slope
> Cassino lies was once frequented
> by deceived and ill-disposed people,
>
> And I am the one who first took there
> the name of Him who brought to earth
> the truth that exalts us.
>
> And so much grace shone upon me
> that I redeemed the surrounding villages
> from the impious cult which seduced the world.
>
> *Par.* xxii. 37–45

St. Benedict's account of his career is at once modest and presumptuous. He is modest in claiming to have redeemed only a few surrounding villages whereas his fabulous work transformed the entire Western world. Modesty, tenderness, and patience permeate his entire discourse. Our poet presents St. Benedict as the personification of love as explained by St. Paul: *Love is patient, is kind; love does not envy, is not pretentious, is not puffed-up, is not ambitious, is not self-seeking, is not provoked; thinks no evil, does not rejoice over the wickedness, but rejoices with the truth; bears with all things, believes all things, hopes all things, endures all things* (I Cor. 13:4–7).

St. Benedict's account of his own career is also presumptuous. He claims, "I redeemed (*retrassi*)* the surrounding villages/ from the impious cult that seduced the world" (*Par.* xxii. 44–45). Power of redemption lies only with God. No mortal creature can claim to have redeemed even a single soul; even the highest angel can function only as an instrument in the divine mission of redemption. When St. Francis and St. Dominic are praised for their great works on the Sun, they are hailed as the two wheels of

---

* *Retrassi* does not literally mean *redeemed* but *reclaimed*; *reclaim* has the figurative meaning of *redeem* because redeeming lost souls means to reclaim the perverted souls.

Providence, i.e., only a pair of powerful instruments of the Holy Spirit in His mission of redemption. Furthermore, Benedict's claim of redemption is not of a local but cosmic dimension. He claims to have redeemed the villages from the impious cult that "seduced the world." His claim is not only presumptuous but blasphemous and impious, if taken at face value.

Why does the saint of chaste and tender love seem to revel in impiety and blasphemy? The saint does not receive Dante as a mere saint of love but as the Father for all the sons of saintly love. St. Benedict stands with St. Peter Damian on Jacob's Ladder as the symbol of the Father in union with His Son through His Spirit. St. Benedict is the founding father of the Benedictine order, and St. Peter Damian is a distinguished son of that order. Jacob's Ladder is the symbol of love, and love is the proper name of the Holy Spirit. The Father loves His Son through His Spirit. St. Benedict gave his sons the Holy Rule which he compared to Jacob's Ladder. When St. Benedict says that he is the one who first took the name of the Son to deceived people, he means to say that he stands for the Father who sent His Son to the sinful world (*Par.* xxii. 40–42).

Dante's overt wish to see St. Benedict unveiled is his veiled wish to see the Father in His Essence (*Par.* xxii. 60). Beatrice's allusion to Semele reflects the longing to see the Divine Essence (*Par.* xxi. 4–6). Semele longed to see the undisguised godhead of Jupiter. Filial love is chaste love; nothing can be so chaste. Filial love wells up in Dante already on the Seventh Terrace. He adores Guido as *father* of his sweet new style (*Purg.* xxvi. 94–99). But Guido calls him "brother" and makes it clear that he is not the proper object of Dante's filial worship (*Purg.* xxvi. 115). Guido's only request is for Dante to say a *Pater Noster* for him (*Purg.* xxvi. 130). By this request, Guido wishes to point out "our Father" to whom both Guido and Dante should give filial devotion. It is through this bond of filial love that the penitents can embrace one another with a fraternal kiss (*Purg.* xxvi. 32). Filial love is the foundation for fraternal love, because the bond of brother and brother stems from the bond of father and son.

Filial and fraternal love finally bring about the harmony and unity of the family. St. Benedict standing with his son on the Ladder, and his son receiving his brother, Dante, for his father, and Dante wishing to see his father's face, represent the joy and peace of the family living and breathing in chaste love. While chaste love is the tie that holds together the family, lust is the poison that corrodes the family. Helen of Troy disrupted the families of Menelaus and of Paris and further brought the two families into a lethal war. Cleopatra poisoned her Egyptian family. Paolo and Francesca overturned the familial order in their wanton sexual excursus.

The seventh rung of the angelic ladder is the seat of judgment, because it is the rung of love. Everyone is judged for his love. Minos of the Second Circle passes judgment on the sinners:

> There Minos stands, horrible and snarling,
>   examining the offenses, judging,
>   and sending down as he girds himself—
>
> I mean that when an ill-born soul
>   comes before him, it confesses wholly,
>   and that discerner of sin,
>
> Seeing what place in Hell belongs to it,
>   encircles himself with his tail as many times
>   as the degrees he wants it to descend.
>
> *Inf.* v. 4–12

Minos passes his judgment with his tail, because all sinners are judged for carnal love. The end of carnal love is the body, and the end of the body is the tail. Purgation is spiritualization; damnation is carnalization. All penitents are judged for spiritual love; all sinners for carnal love (cf. Ch. 3). Since the end of carnal love is the body, the end of which is the tail, the proper measuring stick for the extent of carnal love is the tail of Minos. (This symbolic significance may be particularly noted in the remarks found in *Inf.* v. 4, 20).

Penitents are tested for their works on the seven Terraces: *The work of each will be made manifest, for the day of the Lord will declare it, since the day is to be revealed in fire. The fire will assay the quality of everyone's work; if his work abides which he has built thereon, he will receive reward; if his work burns, he will lose his reward* (I Cor. 3:13–15). Dante's works on seven Terraces pass the test of fire, and qualify him to receive the reward of the seven beatitudes pronounced on the seven Terraces. This reward is Beatrice, in whom all promises of the seven beatitudes come to be one.

In the fire, Dante hears the voice singing *Venite benedicti patris mei* (*Purg.* xxvii. 58). This is the voice which the blessed will hear from the Son of Man on the Day of Last Judgment: *Then the king will say to those on his right hand, "Come, blessed of my Father, take possession of the kingdom prepared for you from the foundation of the world"* (Matt. 25:34). The voice singing *Venite benedicti patris mei* gives Dante a preview of the general judgment. St. Thomas says that every man has to pass through two judgments.[10] As an individual, one has to receive judgment right after death. As a member of the race, one has to be judged at the Last Judgment. The former is a particular and the latter a general judgment. The former is a private manifestation of divine will; the latter its public manifestation. The former is rendered individually, and the latter collectively.

Our pilgrim is given a full preview of the general judgment on Saturn. The austerity and solemnity of Saturn which is devoid of music and smiles prefigure the solemn and awesome atmosphere in which the Son of Man will come for the Judgment: *The sun will be darkened and the moon will not give her light . . . and they will see the Son of Man coming upon the clouds of heaven with great power and majesty. And he will send forth his angels with a trumpet and a great sound, and they will gather his elect from the four winds, from one end of heaven to the other* (Matt. 24:29–31).

The great throng on Jacob's Ladder represents the host of angels who will accompany the Son of Man at the Judgment. Jacob saw a throng of angels descending and ascending his ladder. Peter Damian's denunciation of the shepherds and the thunderous cry of the host of the blessed prefigure the Son's pronouncement of His Judgment. St. Benedict who gathers all the blessed and sends them upward like a whirlwind represents the Father who will receive with His tender hands all the souls who pass the Son's stern Judgment. Peter Damian judges on the ladder of love, and St. Benedict gathers the blessed through the ladder. The Son will judge with the Spirit, and the Father will receive the blessed through the Spirit. The Spirit is the Love of God. The Judgment on the love of creatures will be the Judgment on the Love of God.

Love is the power of union. Spiritual love is the power for the union with God, and carnal love is the power for the union with the animal. The two examples of lust on the Seventh Terrace are "Sodom and Gomorrah" and "Pasiphaë enters the cow that the young bull may haste to her lust (*Purg.* xxvi. 40–42). The first example is recited by those who could not keep their lust within the limits set by human institutions, and the second example is recited by those who could not keep their lust within the limits set by nature. Though the penitents are divided into two files, the carnal sinners of the Second Circle are not divided into two groups. The carnal lovers of the Second Circle have become real beasts through their perfect carnal love. Semiramis and Helena, Cleopatra and Dido, mingle with one another in perfect ease.*

The three examples of chastity show how the Father in heaven loves the chastity of His creatures (*Purg.* xxv. 128–135). The first example is *Virum non cognosco* (I know not a man), the response of the chaste Virgin to the Annunciation. The chaste love of the Virgin reflects the chaste love of the Father. St. Ambrose calls God the King of virgins and the Lover of chastity in one of his prayers. The Father's chaste love is the love which He bears for the Son through His Spirit. It is the chaste love of the Father that is exemplified in the Miraculous Conception. The Son is conceived in the chaste womb of the Virgin by the Holy Spirit. It is with the same chaste love that the Father loves all His sons. *God so loved the world that he gave his only-begotten Son* (John 3:16).

The Father accepts into the bower of His love only chaste creatures. This is explained by the second example of chastity. As Diana expels out of her wood those who have been contaminated by the poison of Venus, the Father keeps out of His kingdom all creatures defiled by bestial lust. Heaven is all holy and too chaste to allow any room for wantonness.

The stern, austere, and chaste love of the Father should

* We have so far maintained that the examples of sin on each Terrace reflect the design of the corresponding Circle in Hell, but have to admit that the Seventh Terrace is an exception to this general rule. The conspicuous feature of this exception is the presence of sodomites, who call upon the names of Sodom and Gomorrah in their penance. In the *Inferno*, it is not the Circle of lust but the Circle of wrath to which sodomites are condemned.

not be mistaken for sterile frigidity. God rejoices in His creatures as a bridegroom does in his bride. The Virgin Mother is not the only bride of the Father, but every chaste creature is His bride. The union of the Father and His adopted sons in spiritual love is like the union of husband and wife in chaste love. This joyous feature of God's love is explained by the third example of chastity.

It is the love of the Father that the Angelic Poet sings on the seventh rung of his angelic ladder of divine love. The Father loves His children as He loves His only begotten Son; He fills the world with His chaste love. Every sinful soul who is adopted through the blood of the Son and who is sanctified by the grace of the Holy Spirit is united with the Father in the bond of His love. It is through love that every soul becomes perfect and abides in God. *And to crown all this, love; that is the bond which makes us perfect* (Col. 3:14). On the fifth, the sixth, and the seventh rungs, our poet has praised the three virtues of the Father: His liberality for the adoption of the sinners as His sons, His temperance for their sanctification and His love for them as His chaste brides. Thus our poet concludes the final phase in his adoration of the Holy Trinity through the praise of the three virtues of the Father. On the seventh rung of the angelic ladder, the Angelic Poet has given us his final benediction: *Blessed are the pure in heart, for they shall see God* (*Purg.* xxvii. 8). With purity of heart, we will see the Holy Trinity face to face on the remaining three rungs of the angelic ladder.

chapter **11**

Retrospect and Prospect on Jacob's Ladder

H AVING mounted Jacob's Ladder, Beatrice tells Dante to "look down and see what a great universe/ I have already put beneath your feet" (*Par.* xxii. 127–129). Our pilgrim sees the seven Planets revolving below him and smiles at the paltry appearance of our earth:

> I turned my eyes down through all the seven spheres,
>   and I saw this globe of ours such
>   that I smiled at its sorry semblance.
> Par. xxii. 133–135

The vast distance which our poet has traversed shows the height of virtue that he has attained through his imitation of the Holy Trinity. To climb the first seven rungs of the angelic ladder is to learn the seven virtues which have been exemplified by the Three Persons of the Trinity. The imitation of the Trinity means the wonderful working of the Three Persons in making the soul god-like:

I cannot fail to notice the wonderful working of the Holy Trinity, and to see how, although the Three Persons are all one

313

in the unity of the God-head, each performs a separate task in co-operation with the others. For in the first stage of our journey we see the working of the Son; and in the second, the action of the Holy Spirit; while the third stage is in the care of God the Father.[1]

The seven steps we have mounted can be called the seven steps of imitation, and the seven steps are divided into three phases of imitation. In the first phase which is composed of the first and the second rungs, we learned the works and virtues of the Son in His visible mission. In the second phase which is composed of the third and the fourth rungs, we saw the gifts and virtues of the Holy Spirit in His invisible mission. In the final stage which is composed of the fifth, the sixth and the seventh rungs, we learned of the care and love of the Father who receives into His imperial family and His familial empire His sons adopted through the blood of His Son and sanctified through the grace of His Spirit.

Our poet characterizes the three phases of holy imitation by matter, motion, and form. The dominant characteristic of the first phase is matter: the pearly substance of the Moon and the fishpool-like watery substance of Mercury. The salient feature of the second phase is motion: the epicyclical motion of Venus and the dual spiral motion of the Sun. The prominent aspect of the third phase is form: the Cross on Mars, the Eagle on Jupiter, and the Ladder on Saturn.

These main characteristics of the three phases illustrate three doctrines: (i) concretion, (ii) creation, (iii) salvation. Every concrete entity is a union of form and matter. This is Aristotle's definition of substance. The substantial union of form and matter is brought about by the power of motion. The three phases of matter, motion, and form illustrate the three principles of concretion in their co-operation.

314

The process of creation is the formation and generation of creatures out of the formless matter: *In the beginning God created heaven and earth. And the earth was void and empty, and the darkness was upon the face of the deep. And the spirit of God moved over the waters* (Gen. 1:1–2). The Spirit of the Lord moves over the formless matter, and *informed* creatures come out of the formless matter as a consequence of the motion of the Spirit. The process is the sequence of matter, motion, and form.

The process of salvation is the same as the process of creation. Christ is the foundation of salvation (1 Cor. 3:11). The souls that are baptized on this foundation are entrusted to the care of the Holy Spirit. The Spirit governs and guides the baptized souls to their proper end.[2] The proper end is the Father who has sent His Son and His Spirit for the mission of salvation. The foundation is indicated by the matter of the first phase, and the government by the motion of the second phase. The end is indicated by the form of the third phase. The distinctive form is the end of every teleological motion.

Concretion, creation, and salvation are the three concurrent and continuous phases of one enterprise. Both creation and salvation are the processes of concretion. Creation is the beginning of salvation, and salvation is the end of creation.

Let us shift our eyes from retrospect to prospect. Before telling Dante to look down and see the seven Planets he has traversed, Beatrice says to him, "You are so close now to the ultimate bliss" (*Par.* xxii. 124). He is about to see the Three Persons on the highest three rungs of the angelic ladder. On the first seven rungs of the angelic ladder, he encountered the Three Persons only in their symbolic appearances. From now on, our Angelic Poet will rip open his veil of symbolic presentation and reveal the Three Persons in intuitive manifestation.

315

The manifest presentation of the Three Persons will follow the same order as their symbolic presentation. On the eighth rung of the angelic ladder, we shall see the Son in His visible mission from the Father. On the ninth rung, we shall see the Holy Spirit in His invisible mission from the Father. On the highest rung, we shall see the Father in union with His Son and His Spirit. In these three manifest visions of the Trinity, we shall also see the functions of the Three Persons:

You see that those whom the Son first humbled by precept and example, and over whom the Spirit then shed love, have finally been received in glory by the Father. The Son makes disciples, the Paraclete consoles friends, the Father exalts his children. But because not only the Son but also the Father and the Holy Spirit are truly called Truth, it follows that one and the same Truth, without violating the distinction of persons, performs these three things on the three steps. On the first it (the Son) instructs, as a teacher; on the second it (the Spirit) consoles as a friend or brother; on the third it (the Father) draws close, as a father his children.[3]

On the eighth rung of the angelic ladder, we will see how our pilgrim is instructed and humiliated. On the ninth rung, we will see how he is consoled and strengthened. On the highest rung, we will finally see how he is glorified in his ultimate beatific vision. These three final steps are the steps of faith, hope, and charity. Faith, hope, and charity are the three phases of one growth; faith is the beginning of charity and charity the end of faith. We have now to see how the seven steps we have traversed are related to these three final steps.

Both the first seven steps and the final three steps are steps of virtues. Virtues can be classified into two groups: orientational and operational. Orientational virtues only orient the soul to its end and do not give it the actual power to achieve the end. Operational virtues give the soul the power of operation in achieving the end. The theological virtues only direct the soul to the supernatural end, and the infused virtues give the power of operation for that end.[4] The former are orientational virtues, and the latter operational virtues.

The relation of orientational and operational virtues is the relation of form and matter. As the form becomes substantial by having the matter for its content, orientational virtues become substantiated by having operational virtues for their contents. The three theological virtues are substantiated by the seven virtues developed on the Seven Terraces. The seven virtues on the seven Terraces can be divided into two groups. The four virtues on the Lower *Purgatorio* proper are natural virtues, and the three virtues on the Upper *Purgatorio* proper are infused virtues. Humility, mercy, meekness, and fortitude are possible to a natural man. The three virtues on the Upper *Purgatorio* proper are: the power to be born as a son of the Father through the blood of His son; the power to be sanctified in the grace of His Spirit; and the power to be spiritualized in the fire of His love. These three powers are not possible for natural man; these virtues are powers infused by God. This grave difference between the natural virtues and the infused virtues is marked by the emergence of Statius. Virgil can guide Dante through the four natural virtues, but has to rely on a Christian to guide him through the three infused virtues.

The three infused virtues are the operational virtues of faith, hope, and charity. On the Fifth Terrace, a soul is reborn as an adopted son; this is the effect of faith as the power of operation. On the Sixth Terrace, the penitents are waiting for the day when they will be allowed to drink from the stream of grace; this is the working of hope as an operational power. *But if we hope for what we do not*

317

see, we wait for it in patience (Rom. 8:25). On the Seventh Terrace, love is perfected; this is the substantiation of charity as the power of operation.

The three highest Planets also represent the three virtues of faith, hope, and charity as operational virtues. The Cross on Mars is the symbol of faith established by the Son and substantiated in the Father. Faith comes with the visible mission of the Son, and its end is the return of the faithful to the Father. *He who believes in me, believes not in me but in him who sent me* (John 12:44). The Eagle on Jupiter is the symbol of hope infused by the Holy Spirit and substantiated in the Father. Hope comes through the invisible mission of the Spirit, and its end is to endure for the hope of seeing the Father. *We wait for it in patience. But . . . the Spirit comes to the aid of our weakness* (Rom. 8:26). The Ladder is the symbol of love perfected for the vision of the Father. Dante is anxious to see his Father's face unveiled on Saturn.

The three functions of the Three Persons should not be confused with the three divine attributes. The three attributes are the Power of the Father, the Wisdom of the Son, and the Love of the Holy Spirit. Faith is established by the Wisdom of the Son; hope is sustained by the Love of the Spirit; charity is consummated by the Power of the Father. Dante perhaps wants to point out these three functions of the Three Persons when he presents the three upper Planets in the form of a triune relation (*Par.* xxii. 145).

While the three upper Planets represent the three operational virtues of faith, hope, and charity, the four lower Planets represent the four natural virtues. On the Sun, St. Thomas says that Adam was "the full animal perfection" at his creation. Adam's bliss was the bliss of a perfect natural man. He did not have the theological virtues in his innocent stage. His virtues were the four natural virtues represented by the lower four Planets. His natural perfection is explained on the Sun, because the Sun represents the highest of the four natural virtues.

The seven virtues displayed by the seven Planets are also represented by the seven ladies who accompany Beatrice on her coming to the Terrestrial Paradise. The seven ladies are the three theological virtues dancing along on the right wheel of the chariot and the four natural virtues dancing along the left wheel (*Purg.* xxix. 121–132). They sing, "Here we are nymphs and in heaven are stars" (*Purg.* xxxi. 106). They are the seven virtues represented by the seven Planets in heaven. The three ladies of theological virtues correspond to the top three Planets, and the four ladies of natural virtues to the lower four Planets. The four ladies are led by one of them who has three eyes in her head (*Purg.* xxix. 132). This lady is the symbol for the highest of the four natural virtues which is represented by the Sun. We have seen the crucial function the Sun plays in mediating the higher three and the lower three Planets. We have also seen the three Circles on the Sun.

The seven virtues are further represented by the seven stars Dante sees on the *Ante-Purgatorio*. He first sees the four bright stars "never yet seen save by the first people" at the foot of the *Purgatorio* (*Purg.* i. 24). He sees the four stars of natural virtues at the original site of the Garden of Eden. The four stars represent the four natural virtues which adorned Adam at his natural perfection. Cato is now shining under the rays of the four stars. In the third chapter of this book, we saw that Adam would be standing like Cato if he had not fallen. Cato under the rays of the four stars is the memory of Adam at his natural perfection.

Before his fall, Adam had virtues of the will but had no virtues of the appetite. In Chapter 3, we saw that the intellect and the irascible constitute the two features of the will, the absolute will and the executive will, and that the concupiscible is the source of the appetite. St. Thomas distinguishes two elements, the formal and the material, in original sin.[5] Original sin is formally the rebellion of the will against the Creator and materially the submission of the appetite to mutable good. St. Augustine says that concupiscence is the guilt of original sin.[6] That is, the appetite becomes inordinate and disorderly when the will attempts to seek ultimate bliss in the natural order. Aristotle makes a similar observation on the incontinent appetite.[7] The lower animals are never incontinent, but only the higher animals which have the faculty of universal judgment. Aristotle says that incontinence is the effect of the misapplied universal judgment on appetite. For example, an incontinent man reasons, "Everything sweet ought to be tasted; this is sweet; therefore, I must eat this." Thus, he comes to eat everything sweet.

The will is the faculty of universal judgment. The appetite becomes incontinent and inordinate when the will turns away from the principle of spiritual life and clings to natural good as the source of the ultimate bliss. Before the fall, the appetite was orderly but not virtuous. Virtues are the habits which man acquires through habituation or infusion.[8] The appetite before the fall was orderly not through habituation or infusion, but by nature. What is in man by nature is not virtue.[9] Adam's appetite was not virtuous before his fall but became vicious through his fall. Before his fall, Adam was adorned with the four natural virtues of the intellect and the irascible as indicated by the rays of the four stars on Cato. After his fall, Adam became the slave of the seven capital sins as shown by the seven Circles of the *Inferno* proper. In Dante's view, the three vicious powers of the concupiscible constitute the fertile ground for the infusion of operational virtues for the achievement of the supernatural end. Furthermore, the four natural virtues can be converted to the ancillary powers for infused virtues. The transformation of the vicious powers of the concupiscible into infused virtues is performed on the three upper Terraces, and the conversion of the four natural virtues to ancillary virtues for infused virtues is performed on the four lower Terraces. The converted natural virtues come under the generic name of infused virtue, because their conversion is performed not in the order of nature but in the order of grace. Thus all the seven powers of the soul become operational virtues for spiritual life as indicated by the seven ladies who function as the handmaids of Beatrice, the love of God.

Dante sees three stars at the top of the *Ante-Purgatorio* proper (*Purg.* viii. 85–93). The three stars represent the theological virtues. They were not seen by the first parents in the stage of their innocence; Adam and Eve knew of no supernatural end before their fall. The contrast between the seven stars on the *Ante-Purgatorio* and the seven ladies on the top of the *Purgatorio* shows the difference between the seven virtues as orientational powers and the seven virtues as operational powers. The seven ladies are the handmaids to Beatrice. On the top of the *Purgatorio*, the seven virtues are the powers of operation. While the seven virtues operate like handmaids on the top of the *Purgatorio*, they are only orientational virtues on the *Ante-Purgatorio*. The seven virtues illuminate for the soul the end which is as remote from the soul as the stars in the sky. The virtues have yet to be substantiated to become powers of operation.

To be sure, the four stars of the natural virtues are powers of operation for Cato and were so for Adam before his fall. The four stars are operational virtues for the natural end, but are not so for the supernatural end. How do the four natural virtues become powers of operation for the supernatural end? Our poet here again solves the problem by the principle of appropriation. On the eighth rung of the angelic ladder faith, substantiated on the fifth rung, will appropriate the two virtues of the intellect developed on the first and the second rungs. Faith involves the consent of the intellect for the acceptance of the revealed truth. The virtues of the intellect are properly appropriated into faith as auxiliary powers.

On the ninth rung of the angelic ladder hope, substantiated on the sixth rung, will appropriate the two virtues of the irascible developed on the third and the fourth rungs. St. Thomas says that hope is the first of the irascible passions. The virtues of the irascible are properly appropriated into hope as ancillary powers. On the highest rung of the angelic ladder, love perfected on the seventh rung will bring together all the powers that have been consolidated and appropriated on the eighth and the ninth rungs, and thereby appropriate all the powers developed and substantiated on the first six rungs.

The construction of the highest three rungs is perhaps the most intricate feature of the entire Angelic Epic. Let me try to explain it in greater detail. The power of the fifth rung will be the principal power for the construction of the eighth rung, and the powers of the first and the second rungs its ancillary powers. The main purpose of the Procession of the Revelation on the top of the *Purgatorio* is the baptism of Dante in the water of Lethe, that is, his rebirth as an adopted son of God. For the fulfillment of this purpose, the power of rebirth and travail developed on the Fifth Terrace will function as the principal power. In this process of baptism and rebirth, Dante will be humiliated. He will survive this humiliation with the humility gained on the First Terrace. The angels will implore Beatrice to show him mercy. *Blessed are the merciful, for they shall receive mercy*. Dante receives the intercession of mercy for the mercy gained on the Second Terrace.

In the Starry Heaven, Dante will see the Garden of the Rose. The chief figure of this Garden is Christ whom Dante saw flashing forth on Mars. The soil of the Garden reflects the material substances of the Moon and Mercury, which represent the two virtues of the Son. In the construction of the Garden on the Starry Heaven, the Sixth Heaven provides the principal feature and the First and the Second Heavens the ancillary features.

In the construction of the ninth rung, the virtue of the sixth rung will be the principal power and the powers of the third and the fourth rungs the ancillary powers. After the Ascension of the Griffin, Beatrice sits down on the root of the tree of the forbidden fruit and shows Dante the seven catastrophes falling on the Chariot. This is the Tribulation of the Tabernacle. The Tabernacle of the Holy Spirit has to suffer the violence of evil and wait in patience for the final bliss. The main purpose of the Tribulation is the sanctification of the Tabernacle. The power developed on the Sixth Terrace is the principal power in the sanctification of the Tabernacle. The Tabernacle is tested and tried under the tree whose offshoots we saw on the Sixth Terrace. The virtues of meekness and fortitude developed on the Third and the Fourth Terraces function as the ancillary powers in surviving the seven catastrophes on the Tabernacle. Throughout the seven catastrophes Dante patiently waits and hopes in meekness and fortitude.

In the construction of the *Primum Mobile*, the Sixth Heaven provides the main feature and the Third and the Fourth Heavens the ancillary features. The center of the nine angelic rings is the Holy Spirit. We saw the Eagle, the symbol of the Spirit, on the Sixth Heaven. The nine angelic orders revolve in the form of nine concentric circles. The circular motion is the characteristic feature of the Third and the Fourth Heavens which represent the two virtues of the Holy Spirit. The grand motion of the nine angelic orders on the *Primum Mobile* is the consummation of the epicyclical motion of Venus and the spiral motions of the Sun, just as the august Garden of the Starry Heaven is the consummation of the pearly substance of the Moon and the watery substance of Mercury.

In the construction of the highest rung, the power developed on the seventh rung is the principal power and the powers consolidated and appropriated on the eighth and the ninth rungs are ancillary powers. Jacob's Ladder leads to the Empyrean. The spiritual love perfected in the Seventh Heaven is consummated in the highest Heaven. Our pilgrim was received by the founder of the Benedictine order and one of its distinguished sons on Saturn. In the Empyrean, he will be received by the most prominent member of the Benedictine order, the venerable St. Bernard. In his Angelic Epic, our poet shows his warmest reverence for the Benedictines. He firmly believes that the Benedictine order as nurtured in the grace of the Holy Rule is the orthodox heir to the elegant Pauline tradition which struggles for the transformation of the defiled flesh into the spiritual blossom. He further believes that his Angelic Epic is the poetification of St. Paul's legacy as lived and developed by the Benedictines under the Holy Rule.

In the Mystical Rose of the Empyrean, the confirmed angels of the *Primum Mobile* and the redeemed souls of the Starry Heaven come together in the heavenly feast. The Son of the Starry Heaven and the Holy Spirit of the *Primum Mobile* come into the triune union with the Father on the Empyrean. The visions of the Eighth and the Ninth Heavens are united in the vision of the Tenth Heaven. The eighth and the ninth rungs provide the ancillary powers in the construction of the highest rung, and the seventh rung provides the principal power. The power perfected on the seventh rung brings together all the power of the first six rungs in the ultimate beatific vision, by appropriating the powers and visions of the eighth and the ninth rungs.

The construction of the highest three rungs rests on the

principle of cumulative representation whose example we saw in the construction of the lowest Circle of Hell. *Giudecca* is the cumulative representation of the three Rings of the lowest Circle. The eighth rung will be the cumulative representation of the fifth, the first, and the second rungs; the ninth rung will be that of the sixth, the third, and the fourth rungs. The tenth rung will cumulatively represent the seventh, the eighth, and the ninth rungs. The tenth rung is a cumulative representation of the second degree, because it brings into its cumulative representation the eighth and the ninth rungs which are cumulative representations of the first degree.

The cumulative representation in Hell is not limited to the Ninth Circle. The *Inferno* is the inverted reflection of the *Paradiso*. When we view the *Inferno* in isolation, we can see the principle of cumulative representation governing the entire structure of the *Inferno*. We have seen that the three Rings of the *Inferno* are cumulatively represented in the three persons of Lucifer and that the three persons of Satan imitate the three divine attributes. *Caina* is the inverted imitation of Love, *Antenora* is that of Wisdom, and *Tolomea* is that of Power. *Caina* is the cumulative representation of the Circles of the concupiscible, because *love* is the first of the concupiscible powers. *Antenora* is the cumulative representation of the Circles of the irascible, because *wisdom* of prudence is the distinctive feature of the irascible. *Tolomea* is the cumulative representation of the Circles of the intellect, because the intellect is the highest *power* of the soul.

The cumulative representation of Hell is exactly opposite to that of Heaven. While the cumulating Heaven is higher than the cumulated Heavens, the cumulating Circle is lower than the cumulated Circles. What does it signify? The effect of accumulation in Hell is dispersion. The purpose of real accumulation is to appropriate and preserve what is accumulated. For this reason, the cumulating medium should be bigger than the cumulated. For example, the Starry Heaven is far greater than the Heavens of Mars, Venus, and the Sun; the former appropriates, preserves, and magnifies all the things it gathers from the latter. The first Ring of the Ninth Circle appears to be cumulative of the three Circles of the concupiscible, but the former is far smaller than the latter. Consequently, the former cannot bring together the substantial contents of the latter and appropriate and preserve them. The effect of the apparent cumulative representation in Hell is dispersion. Everything in Hell is an inverted imitation of Heaven.

The effect of the cumulative representation is attrition and dispersion in Hell, and appropriation and accumulation in Heaven. This is the difference between the real and the inverted cumulative representation. Because of this difference, you feel the emptiness of Hell at the end of the descent of the *Inferno*, and the fullness of Heaven at the end of the ascent of the *Paradiso*. The Empyrean is the fullest sphere of being and the bottom of Hell is the emptiest place of being not only on the poem's doctrinal ground but in its actual emotional impact on the readers. I do not wish to mislead you to assume that the principles of cumulative representation of Heaven and Hell work independently. Sin and evil have no power of independent existence. Heaven encloses Hell; divine good encompasses Satanical evil. It is only within the total framework of cumulative representation of the entire cosmos that the *Inferno* reveals its structure and function.

Let us examine a few more principles of representation which our poet uses extensively in the construction of his Angelic Epic. The few principles which need to be examined at this point are intuitive representation, reflective representation, concurrent representation and co-referent representation.

326

For the explanation of intuitive representation, let us take the episode of Count Ugolino. Our poet presents that episode as the inverted version of the Last Supper. He provides all the essential details which are necessary to make that episode a crystallized inversion of the Last Supper. Where the essential details are lacking, he creates them. He says everything essential and necessary except the things which are too obvious.

In presenting the episode, our poet does not discursively explain the meaning of the episode but leaves it for the intuitive understanding of the readers. He does not say that the episode of Count Ugolino is the inverted imitation of the Last Supper; that to live in pride is like locking up oneself in prison; that Count Ugolino fed on the flesh of his sons whereas the Son of Man fed His children with His flesh and blood; or that one can participate in the communion of divine food only in humility. He leaves the meanings of the episode to the intuitive understanding of his readers. Whenever a poem has to go into a discursive explanation of its theme, it has usually failed to be a poem. A virtuous man is a virtuous man, not because he talks of virtues, but because he embodies them. A poem is a poem, not because it speaks of a poetic theme, but because it incarnates the theme.

Readers of the *Divina Commedia* are often perplexed at Dante's extensive, inexhaustible allusion to classical legends and contemporary events, to profane legacies and sacred traditions, to philosophy and theology, etc. You will be surprised to know how carefully and elaborately he provides all the essential details in every scene of his epic. To be sure, the long span of time between Dante and us has made many things obvious in his days obscure and unintelligible to us. In spite of this great barrier, you can understand the meaning of almost every major scene in the *Divina Commedia* within the *Commedia*, i.e., without consulting external commentaries on the allusions the poet makes. But you can do this only if you can grasp the inter-relation of the essential details of the scene and if you can place the scene in its proper thematic context of the entire epic. In explaining the meaning of the many episodes such as those of Ugolino, Ulysses, Pietro, Francesca, Romeo, I have seldom felt the need to go beyond the essential details given in the *Commedia* except for the obvious things which the poet has left for our intuitive comprehension.

Let me warn you against two types of commentaries which can distract your eyes from seeing the intuitive essence of the Angelic Epic—the misleading and the irrelevant commentaries. As an example of the misleading, let us take commentaries on the third circle of light on the Sun. You will find a great number of commentaries on the nature of the theology represented by this third circle and on its relation to the other circles. These commentaries can mislead you to look for what is not there and distract you from seeing what the poet shows you. Our poet identifies the nature of the third circle by hailing it: "Oh true sparkling of the Holy Breath" (Par. xiv. 76). *Santo spiro* is the Holy Spirit, and the function of the third circle is to show that the two circles of theologians are inspired by the Spirit.

As an example of irrelevant commentaries, let me give you the usual comments on Romeo's career on Mercury. Many commentators will tell you how the poor and cruel lot of Romeo reflects Dante's own career of poverty and exile. This is an irrelevant commentary. It is irrelevant to the understanding of the *Commedia* as a poem to know how well the *Commedia* portrays Dante's personal life or whether he wrote it in an ivory tower or on the thorny road of exile. The *Commedia* is not meant to be a diary but a poem; it is not meant to be a portrayal of private experience but the incarnation of public truth. I have no objection to knowing the personal life of a poet as such. I warn you against the irrelevant commentary simply because it distracts you from seeing the Romeo episode as an intuitive representation of the mercy of Christ in inviting the sinful souls as the brides of the heavenly nuptials.

Now the reflective representation. Let us take the relation of the *Paradiso* and the *Inferno*. The *Inferno* is the inversion of the *Paradiso*. The former is like the image of the *Paradiso* reflected in a mirror. The image in a mirror presents the original in its inverted form. If you look at your image in a looking glass, the image of your right eye appears as the left eye of your image in the mirror.* Satan is the inverted image of the Holy Trinity. Ulysses' episode is the inversion of Romeo's episode. The wrestling ring of the three Florentine intellectuals is the inversion of the epicyclical motion of Venus. The petty quarrel between Farinata and Dante is the inversion of the eulogies on St. Francis and St. Dominic on the Sun.

You can never understand the *Inferno* until you come to see the original whose inversion is the *Inferno*. To take the *Inferno* at its face value is like taking the sum of a wrong calculation at its face value. You can never understand a wrong calculation until you figure out its error and find out its right sum. All the great episodes in Hell have been taken as nothing more than comical relief for the over-burdened readers or as the frivolous products of Dante's capricious imagination simply because the *Inferno* has been taken not as an inverted image but as an original. Only when you see the *Inferno* as an inverted image, can you see that the great episodes in Hell propound the major themes of the epic.

While you have to see the *Inferno* as the reflection of the *Paradiso* to understand it, you also have to see the *Paradiso*

* It was as when a man stands on his head, resting it on the earth, and holds his feet aloft by thrusting them against something: in such a case right and left both of the man and of the spectators appear reversed to the other party (The *Timaeus* 43E).

as the original of the *Inferno* to understand it. The understanding of error is as indispensable to the understanding of
truth as the comprehension of truth is indispensable to the
comprehension of error. Thus it is necessary to see Dante's
three worlds in mutual reflection. It is through the reflective representation that the three worlds reflect one another
and illuminate one another.

Let us begin with Dante's dedicatory epistle to Can
Grande in which he explains the different meanings of
his epic. In his discussion of the different meanings of
symbol, Dante does not distinguish two different media for
the diversification of the meanings of a symbol. These two
media are the levels of meaning and the references of
meaning. The liberation of Israel may have moral and
historical significance. These two meanings are differentiated by the two levels of meaning: the moral level and
the historical level. The moral meaning of the liberation
of Israel may refer to the individual soul or the whole race.
The historical meaning of Israel cannot refer to the individual soul, but only to Israel.

The moral meaning is a symbolic meaning, and the historical meaning is the literal meaning. The former can refer
to more than one object, and the latter only to one object,
the subject of fact and history. The unique feature of a symbol is that it can have not only many levels of meaning but
also many referents for its sense even on the same level.
When a symbol has more than one referent, I propose to
call it a co-referent symbol or a co-referent representation.
For example, when Dante stands before Beatrice, he stands
as the symbol simultaneously referring to the individual and
the race. His judgment before Beatrice may have different
levels of meaning, historical, moral, allegorical, and anagogical. On each of these levels except the historical and the
literal, Dante stands as the symbol simultaneously referring

330

to the individual, the Christian, the Church, and the whole race.

Of all the possible referents for the symbols in the *Commedia*, our poet keeps the two referents, the individual and the community, in their inseparable relation and in the prominent foreground. For this purpose, he opens his *Commedia* with the conspicuous conjunction of the singular and the plural pronouns:

> In the middle of the journey of *our* life (*nostra vita*)
> *I* came to *myself* (*mi ritrovai*) in a dark wood,
> where the straight way was lost.
>
> *Inf*. i. 1–3

Dante undertakes his epic journey as the *I* of the individual and as the *We* of the race.

One symbol may signify more than one event on the same level and to the same referent. I propose to call such a symbol a concurrent symbol or a concurrent representation, because it represents concurrently more than one event. For example, the Beatricean Procession represents two events: the First and the Second Comings of Christ. The coming of Beatrice recalls the First Coming of Christ in weakness and humility and anticipates His Second Coming in majesty and glory. These two events can be represented by one symbol, because the Second Coming is the fulfillment of the First Coming and the First Coming is the preparation for the Second Coming. The two Comings of Christ are the two terminal ends of one great event, that is, His visible mission. Thus the two events can be represented by one symbol. The symbol is a concurrent symbol because it looks concurrently backward to a past event and forward to a future event.

We have examined five principles of representation: intuitive, reflective, co-referent, concurrent, and cumulative representation. This examination of Dante's principles of representation is far from systematic and exhaustive, but will be of some help for the intuitive understanding of the three ecstatic visions our poet will unfold on the highest three rungs of his angelic ladder of divine love.

chapter **12**

Vision on the Rung of Faith and Revelation

The Fixed Stars, the Coming of Beatrice, the Upper Ante-Purgatorio, and the Limbo

Our Angelic Poet is about to show us the only-begotten Son in the visible mission from the Father: to render visible the invisible truth. The Word of God becomes flesh and dwells among us for the Revelation. The vision of the Son in flesh will be the concrescence of what we have seen on the first, the second, and the fifth rungs of the angelic ladder.

The First Circle of the *Inferno* is the eternal abode for those who lived in natural virtue but died in the stain of original sin. In this valley of sinless sin, Dante hears no lament but only sighs "which made the eternal air tremble" (*Inf.* iv. 27). The sighs come from "the sadness without torment" (*Inf.* iv. 28). Virgil explains that no one has been saved out of the Limbo except the patriarchs and prophets whom Christ rescued when He came down to the Limbo crowned with "the sign of victory" (*Inf.* iv. 52–63). Salvation comes only through faith.

Among the sinless pagans, Dante meets three groups of distinguished shades. These three groups soar above the rest through their eminent virtues and talents, which are the highest achievements that mortal creatures can attain in the order of nature. The first of these three groups are the four ancient poets (*Inf*. iv. 85–90), who have come out to receive Dante and Virgil and lead them into the Noble Castle. Inside the Castle, Dante first sees a group of virtuous statesmen (*Inf*. iv. 121–129). Seated higher than the statesmen are men of wisdom and science presided over by Aristotle (*Inf*. iv. 130–151).

The Noble Castle is encircled by seven walls and a fair rivulet, which protect the meadow of fresh verdure from the surrounding "trembling air" (*Inf*. iv. 106–111). The "trembling air" is the air of evil, the dominion of the devil; the seven walls stand for the protection against the seven capital vices with which Satan infects the lower atmosphere. The meadow of fresh verdure represents the height of natural perfection and bliss in the world of sin and under the light of natural reason. The eminent pagans show no positive sign of joy but live in the somber air of dignity:

> There we saw people dignified and grave,
> of great authority in their semblance;
> they spoke seldom, and with soft voices.
>
> *Inf*. iv. 112–114

Why does Dante pick the three groups of eminent pagans? Aristotle distinguishes three levels of life: the contemplative, the active, and the productive. The productive life is to make things; the active life is to do things; the contemplative life is to know things. Knowledge itself can be divided into three levels. Theoretical science is for contemplation, practical science for action, and productive science for production. The production and distribution of the necessaries come under the government of active life, and the active life prepares for contemplation, the highest bliss of man.

334

The order and co-operation of these three levels of life are essential for the well-being of the state and the soul. In the state, the three levels are represented by three classes of people: men of wisdom, the governing class, and the productive class. In the individual, the three levels of life are represented by the three levels of the soul. The principle of the virtuous life is the same for the individual and the community. It is because of this close affinity between the life of the individual and that of the community that Socrates in the *Republic* wants to take the state as the "large writ" example of the soul.

The three groups of eminent pagans in the Noble Castle represent the three levels of life in perfection. Aristotle and his men of wisdom stand for contemplation, the kings and rulers for action, and Homer and his poets for production. The Noble Castle is the co-referent representation of the natural bliss of the individual and the community, where the three levels of life are in the perfect stage of union and function.[1]

On the Upper *Ante-Purgatorio*, Dante meets two groups of penitents and one poet. The first group consists of those who repented at the last hour of their violent death, and in the second group are the rulers and princes in the Flowery Valley. Between these two groups, Dante runs into Sordello. The Upper *Ante-Purgatorio* resembles the Limbo in a few respects. The pagan nobilities are sitting in the Noble Castle, and the Christian nobilities in the Flowery Valley. Dante meets a thick throng of plain pagans on the outskirts of the Noble Castle, and a heavy crowd of plain Christians a little below the Flowery Valley. He names no one in the former group and recognizes no one in the latter group (*Purg.* v. 58–59). Virgil and Dante are led into the Noble Castle by the four ancient poets, and into the Flowery Valley by the Mantuan poet.

There are also a few points of striking difference between

335

the Limbo and the Upper *Ante-Purgatorio*. The pagans lived in virtue, but the Christians lived in sin. Whereas the crowd of virtuous heathens stands cold and aloof from Dante, the thick throng of sinful Christmas flocks around him, shoving him and pulling him in order to secure prayers from their relatives and friends (*Purg.* vi. 1–12). The pagan nobilities are protected by the seven walls of the Noble Castle, but the Christian nobilities of the Flowery Valley have no power of self-protection. The Noble Castle can keep its meadow of fresh verdure undefiled by the "trembling air" of the devil's lower atmosphere, but the Flowery Valley has no walls to prevent the intrusion of the serpent into its meadow. The negligent Christian princes are protected by the angels from the bosom of Mary (*Purg.* viii. 25–37).

The Noble Castle is illuminated by the light of natural reason, and the Flowery Valley by the Sun in the day time and by the three stars at night. Whereas the light of natural reason conquers a little hemisphere, the three stars illuminate the whole pole (*Inf.* iv. 69; *Purg.* viii. 90). The men of contemplation are seated a little above the men of action in the Noble Castle, but there is no man of contemplation sitting with the Christian rulers in the Flowery Valley. The Christian princes forgot that action is only the necessary preparation for contemplation, which for Christians is the contemplation of divine truth. Action in this world is the preparation for contemplation in the other world. The Christian princes took the active life for the ultimate end and neglected their supernatural end. The three torches are now pointing out the end of contemplation which the princes have neglected through their preoccupation with the earthly activities.

As the beauty of the Noble Castle represents the natural good that pagans achieved through their virtuous activities, so the splendor of the Flowery Valley represents the earthly glory which Christians achieved through their sinful activities:

> Gold and fine silver, crimson and white lead,
>   indigo, bright and clear,
>   fresh emerald, at the moment it is split,
>
> Would be surpassed in color by the grass
>   and by the flowers within the hollow
>   as the lesser is by the greater.
>
> *Purg.* vii. 73–78

Because the beauty and glory of the Christian princes are the fruits of sinful activities, the serpent wants to crawl into the Valley and claim it as its due. You can find no trace of joy in the Noble Castle or in the Flowery Valley. The pagan nobles sit in the air of majesty and dignity, but the Christian princes beg for the mercy of the Mother of mercy like little children. The Christians sing the *Salve Regina:*

Hail, holy queen, mother of mercy, our life, our sweetness, and our hope! To thee do we cry, poor banished children of Eve, to thee do we send up our sighs, mourning and weeping in this valley of tears. Turn then, most gracious advocate, thine eyes of mercy towards us; and after this our exile show unto us the blessed fruit of thy womb, Jesus. O clement, O loving, O sweet Virgin Mary!

The Flowery Valley is a valley of tears. The princes of the Valley now realize that they mistook the exile in Eve's sin for their permanent home and their ultimate end. They now realize that weeping and mourning are the only fruits of all their sinful labours and that they neglected the only fruit of bliss, the fruit of Mary's womb.

The difference between Limbo and the Upper *Ante-*

337

Purgatorio is twofold. The Christians are in the world of grace, and the pagans are in the world of nature. The Christians lived in sin, and the pagans lived in virtue. What were the sins of the Christians? Their sins were pride, envy, and avarice, the sins that we saw on the first, the second, and the fifth rungs.

Envy was the sin of the violently slain. They chant the *Miserere*, a prayer of mercy (*Purg.* v. 24). The penitents on the Second Terrace are chanting the Litany of the Saints, also a prayer of mercy (*Purg.* xiii. 50). The first two speakers of the violently slain are Cassero and Buonconte da Montefeltro (*Purg.* v. 64–132). The former was a Guelf and the latter a Ghibelline leader. One Guelf and one Ghibelline on the Second Terrace present the feud between their two parties as the culmination of envy corroding all Christendom, and talk of the Arno Valley and Romagna as the symbols of the degenerate, envious race (*Purg.* xiv. 1 ff.). The Arno and Romagna figure prominently in the stories of Cassero and Buonconte (*Purg.* v. 69, 94, 96, 125). La Pia of Sienna, the city of envy, reminds us of Sapia of Sienna (*Purg.* v. 133; xiii. 109).

The violently slain resemble not only the sinners of the Second Terrace but also the sinners of the *Malebolge*. They roam about like the sinners of the *Malebolge*. Envious malice keeps people roaming about and working evil for other people. The devils lay their snares of envy and roam through the world seeking the ruin of the souls (The Prayer to St. Michael). The violently slain are not yet ready to put the curb on their envy and sit down like the penitents of the Second Terrace.

The devil's envious snares and roaming are illustrated by the episodes of Buonconte da Montefeltro on the *Ante-Purgatorio* and his father Guido da Montefeltro (*Purg.* v. 85–129; *Inf.* xxvii. 62–129). After many years of fraudulent life, Guido tried to convert to the way of truth and became a monk. In spite of this resolve, he continued to walk the way of malice right up to the moment of his death. On his death, there came to claim his soul St. Francis, the founder of his monastic order, and a black cherub. The black cherub won Guido's soul, because Guido died in the snare of the devil.

Guido's son was bitterly engaged in a battle of envy right up to the hour of his death. He was mortally wounded in the battle and died during his escape. Just before losing consciousness and life, he called on Mary. His soul was also claimed by an angel from Heaven and a devil from Hell. The angel won and the devil lost.

The fate of the soul after death depends solely on the state of the soul at the moment of its death. If the soul dies in the snare of the devil, it will stay in it for eternity. If the soul dies in repentance and grace, it will reach the kingdom of heaven. Because of this decisive significance of the last hour, the *Ave Maria* ends with the plea for the last hour: "Holy Mary, Mother of God, pray for us sinners, now and at the hour of our death." Buonconte fortunately remembered his *Ave Maria* well and saw its efficacy.

The devil was so enraged with the loss of Buonconte's soul that he decided to wreak his anger on his body. He raised a storm and washed down the body into the Arno. The devil is the prince who has power over the lower atmosphere. Buonconte's soul escaped the devil's snare, though his body was caught in the devil's storm. Cassero's is another case in which the devil's snare failed. While he was running away from his assassins, he ran into the marshes and got entangled in the mire and reeds (*Purg.* v. 67–84). He says that he would have escaped from his assassins if he had run toward La Mira. The mire was the snare the devil prepared for Cassero. The devil caught his body but not his soul. It is only through malice and envy that a soul comes into communion with the devils. The devil's snare of envy does not prevail unless the victim is already caught in his own snare of envy.

The relation of the Flowery Valley and the Ninth Circle is first indicated by Nino in the Valley, whose grandfather Count Ugolino is in the bottom of Hell (*Purg.* viii. 53–81; *Inf.* xxxiii. 1–75). While Count Ugolino feasted on the flesh of his children, Judge Nino is waiting for his daughter's prayer. The Ninth Circle is the imperial court of Satan, and the ten valleys of the *Malebolge* are the ten kingdoms of envious snares surrounding Satan's inner court. The relation of the Flowery Valley to the unshriven is analogous to the relation of Satan's inner court to the *Malebolge*. While the violently slain were roaming about for their malicious works, the princes of the Flowery Valley sought their bliss in the kingly glory of the earth. To forget the Father in heaven and seek the ultimate bliss in the kingly glory of the earth is pride.

It is the power of repentance that saved the negligent princes from Satan's inner court and the unshriven from the ten kingdoms of the *Malebolge*. While the unshriven are roaming about like the sinners in the *Malebolge*, the negligent princes sit tight like the princes of pride in Satan's inner court. The Flowery Valley is Mary's bosom; Sordello calls it a "bosom (*grembo*)" (*Purg.* vii. 68). The negligent princes are like babies nestling in their mother's bosom. The sinners of pride on the First Terrace are reciting the *Pater Noster* and walking toward their Father. The negligent princes are sitting in their Mother's bosom and calling for her mercy. (*Salve Regina, Mater Misericordiae*). Though they have been saved through their faith, their faith is still in the infant stage.

What is the nature of faith in its infant stage? It is insubstantial. The powers of the soul have not yet become the powers of operation for faith; they are still in sin. The soul whose powers are in sin is a shrine of the devil; the devil can come into it and abide in it. The *Ante-Purgatorio* is within the range of the devil's atmosphere. As soon as the rays of the sun are withdrawn, the devil can crawl back into the soul whose faith is still in its infant stage and whose sinful powers are still alive. Just before the sunset, the penitents recite *Te lucis ante:*

> Let dreams depart and phantoms fly,
>> The offspring of the night
> Keep us like shrines, beneath Thyne eye,
>> Pure in our foes' despite.
>> (*The New Roman Missal*, p. 1791)

Evil dreams and phantoms are the works of the devil.[2] At sunset, two angels come down from Mary's bosom with two flaming swords (*Purg.* viii. 25–27, 37–39). The anticipated serpent soon appears, but is easily repelled by the angels' blunted swords.

The two holy angels stay on in the Flowery Valley, standing on its banks and keeping the negligent princes under their watchful eyes. This event dramatizes the concluding prayer of the compline hymn:

> Visit, we beseech Thee, O Lord, this habitation,
>> and drive far from it all snares of the enemy.
> Let Thy holy angels dwell herein to keep us in peace:
>> and may Thy blessing be upon us always.
>> (*The New Roman Missal*, p. 1792).

The repulse of the serpent reenacts the victory of the second Eve promised by God. *She is to crush thy head, while thou dost lie in ambush at her heels* (Gen. 3:15). This is the promise God made to the first Eve on her expulsion from the Garden of Eden for having eaten the bitter fruit under the enticement of the serpent. On the stealthy approach of the serpent to the Flowery Valley,

341

our poet refers to the serpent, calling it "perchance such as gave to Eve the bitter food" (*Purg.* viii. 99). By this allusion, he wishes us to understand that the swift repulse of the snake by the angels from Mary's bosom is the fulfillment of the promised vengeance. The repulse of the serpent further indicates the helplessness of the sinner under the devil's domination. The princes of the Flowery Valley are totally powerless to block the serpent's invasion. They are saved only by the angels from Mary's bosom.

Nino's pathetic dependence on his daughter's prayer reflects Adam's dependence on Mary for salvation. Nino is bitter about his wife's re-marriage to the viper of the Milanese and expects no help from his unfaithful wife. He is anxious to have his daughter's prayer because she is innocent and her prayer has efficacy. Adam's wife was poisoned by the viper of the *Malebolge* and was of no help for his salvation. He had to wait for the fruit of the womb of his daughter Mary who was conceived without the stain of the viper's poison. Nino is the co-referent symbol of both the race and the individual, anxiously waiting in the vale of tears for the holy prayer of the Eternal Virgin.

What was Sordello's sin? His sin was of the active concupiscible. He tries to embrace Virgil's feet as Statius does. Statius' sin was also of the active concupiscible. Both of them were poets. The active concupiscible is the power of production, and poetry is the productive art *par excellence*. Production as an act differs in its consequence from action and contemplation. Doing and knowing as acts terminate in the doer and the knower, but making as an act goes outside of the maker and terminates in the thing that is made. The production of works of art is the extension of the artist; a poem is a baby produced by the poet. The power of producing poems, the power of making fortunes, and the power of giving a new birth to the soul all belong to the active power of the concupiscible.

It is by poets that Virgil and Dante are led into the Noble Castle, the Flowery Valley, and the Terrestrial Paradise. Production is not an act of virtue, whereas action and contemplation are acts of virtue. Action is the act of moral virtues, and contemplation is the act of intellectual virtue. Production is a mere art and an instrument to prepare for and lead to the acts of the moral and intellectual virtues. This is the reason why poets lead Virgil and Dante to the Noble Castle, the Flowery Valley, and the Terrestial Paradise. The Noble Castle represents the action and contemplation of the natural man, the Flowery Valley those of the infant Christian, and the Terrestrial Paradise those of the mature Christian.

The function of the poet-guides is related to the function of the active concupiscible as the power of birth. The four ancient poets help Dante to be born as a virtuous pagan; they accept him as a member of their elite circle. Sordello helps Dante to be born as an infant Christian in the Flowery Valley; Dante spends the night in the Flowery Valley as an infant Christian in Mary's bosom. Statius helps him to be born as a mature Christian; Statius helps Dante cross Lethe and regain Beatrice.

Sordello stoops down to embrace Virgil's feet (*Purg.* vii. 10–15). Virgil stands on a far higher level than Sordello, insofar as their natural virtues and talent are concerned. Virgil's bones were buried by Octavian, but he cannot rise to the glory of the Heavenly Empire (*Purg.* vii. 6). Virgil cannot do what Sordello can do with the power of faith:

> "I am Virgil, and for no other fault
>   did I lose Heaven except not having faith."
>
> *Purg.* vii. 7–8

Virgil cannot be born as an infant Christian, whereas Sordello can.

Statius also stoops down to embrace Virgil's feet. Virgil

does allow Sordello to embrace his feet but does not allow Statius to do the same (*Purg.* xxi. 130–132). This shows the difference between Sordello and Statius as Christians. Statius has perfected the power to be born as an adopted son of God, but Sordello's power for rebirth remains still in sin. Statius can lead Dante to the top of the *Purgatorio*, but Sordello only to the Flowery Valley. The Terrestrial Paradise soars high above the lower atmosphere, but the Flowery Valley is within the range of the foul vapors.

As we have seen on the fifth rung of the angelic ladder, the sin of the active concupiscible is the adultery of the soul, i.e., to mistake the exile for the permanent habitat, to desert what is one's own by right and birth and to be wed to what is alien and improper. Sordello embodied all these features of adultery in his career. He was a poet of exile by choice. He forsook not only his native Mantua but even his native language. He did not write in his native tongue but in Provencal.

Sordello now appreciates his native Mantua. He drops his haughty mien and gladly embraces Virgil on the mere discovery that Virgil is a Mantuan shade. This moving scene between the two Mantuan shades touches off Dante's bitterest lamentation over the widowed state of Italy (*Purg.* vi. 76–151). Italy has been made a poor, sickly widow by the Emperor's desertion and neglect of what is his own by right. Dante's lamentation makes the Flowery Valley a co-referent symbol of desertion and neglect of one's due and proper end. The Flowery Valley is a vale of tears which has to mourn and weep for the self-imposed exile and desertion of its rulers. As the negligent princes neglected the care of their souls, so they failed to take a proper care of their cities and states. They allowed the serpent to creep into their souls and their kingdoms (*Purg.* vii. 94).

The Terrestrial Paradise is the co-referent symbol of the individual soul and the community against which the serpent's power does not prevail. Virgil gives Dante his final counsel:

> Expect no further word or sign from me;
>   free, upright, and whole is your will;
>   it would be wrong not to do as it pleases.
>
> Therefore, over yourself, I crown and mitre you.
>   *Purg.* xxvii. 139–142

Our poet has gained the lordship over his soul by returning pure and whole to the original nest of the human race. The Terrestrial Paradise is man's original nest, and the Flowery Valley is his nest of exile. The latter is the vale of tears, but the former the garden of delight. Dante meets Matelda dancing and singing the psalm *Delectasti* (*Purg.* xxviii. 80). This psalm sings the joy in the works of the hands of the Lord (Ps. 92). In the long course of his pilgrimage, Dante meets the expression of impeccable joy for the first time.

On reaching the original nest of the human race, Dante feels refreshed and revived like a pilgrim returning home (*Purg.* xxvii. 111). When he arrived in the Flowery Valley, he felt the keen homesickness of a pilgrim (*Purg.* viii. 1–6). In his descent to the Limbo, he trembled in fear and dread. He overcame fear and dread by the time he reached the Flowery Valley, but was struggling against the tiredness and loneliness of his exiled soul. The lordship over his soul means the wholesome delight he enjoys in the Garden of Delight. This delight is the natural bliss Adam and Eve exchanged for the tears and toils under the dominion of the serpent. The natural bliss is not Dante's final end; he will not long retain the lordship over his soul. A power far mightier than Virgil will soon claim the lordship over Dante's free soul.

Beatrice is going to come to take over Dante from Virgil. Dante has to cross Lethe to regain Beatrice. He walked across the rivulet around the Noble Castle as if on solid ground (*Inf.* iv. 109). Lethe is only about three paces in its breadth, but he will have a little difficulty in crossing it (*Purg.* xxviii. 70–75). Let me first recall the outline of the Beatricean Procession as it unfolds itself. The seven golden candlesticks appear and move toward Dante under the resounding chant of the *Hosanna*, and the seven bands of light stretch behind the seven candlesticks like a rainbow. Behind the candlesticks come the twenty-four elders who are dressed in white and move in two lines. Then come the four beasts, each with six wings and crowned with olives. The four creatures enclose the triumphal chariot drawn by the Griffin. The Griffin is a composite animal: a lion with an eagle's head. His two wings stretch high above the range of the mortal's sight. Seven ladies come dancing along the two wheels of the Chariot. The Chariot is followed by two old men walking abreast, four men of humble appearance, and a solitary old man moving in a trance. These seven are crowned with garlands of roses and other vermilion flowers.

The whole Procession comes to halt before Dante with a thunderclap. The twenty-four elders turn about toward the Chariot, and one of them cries thrice, "*Veni, sponsa, de Libano* (Come with me from Lebanon, my spouse)." A host of angels appear above the Chariot, sing *Benedictus qui venit* (Blessed art thou who come), and scatter flowers while singing *Manibus O date lilia plenis* (O give lilies with full hands). Under this shower of flowers, Beatrice emerges:

> Thus, within a shower of blossoms,
> thrown by angelic hands, which rose
> and fell on and around the chariot,
>
> Underneath a white veil, crowned with olive,
> a lady appeared to me, under a green mantle,
> dressed in the color of living flame.
>
> *Purg.* xxx. 28–33

Dante trembles in anguish and tension at the re-awakening of his ancient love. Overpowered by the tension, he turns around for Virgil's comfort only to find:

> But Virgil had left me without his company,
> Virgil, my beloved Father, Virgil,
> to whom I gave myself up for my salvation;
>
> *Purg.* xxx. 49–51

Beatrice calls Dante by his name and tells him to wait for the real occasion to shed his tears. The veil drops from her head, and she appears "queenlike in bearing yet stern." She begins to chastise and humiliate Dante, her faithful one (Dante is the contraction of Durante), for his unfaithful past. He lowers his eyes and cannot bear seeing even his image in the water of Lethe. The angels intercede with the plea which Dante is too confounded to speak out for himself:

(In te, Domine, speravi) *In thee, O Lord, do I put my trust, let me never be confounded; in thy faithful care deliver me. Bow down thy ear to me, make haste to rescue me . . . Into thy hands I commend my spirit: thou wilt deliver me, O Lord, thou faithful God . . . I will triumph and exult in thy mercy, for thou hast regarded my misery, thou hast helped my soul in distress. Thou hast not given me over into the power of the foe, but thou hast set my feet in a spacious place* (Psalm 30 [31]:1–9).

This psalm gives expression to Dante's profound gratitude to the Lord who has faithfully delivered His unfaithful son from "the power of the foe" and set him on the top of the *Purgatorio*. Beatrice briefly recounts her faithful effort to save the unfaithful Dante. Dante is not an ordinary creature, but was born and reared with the "bounty of graces divine." Beatrice specially sustained him with her visible counte-

347

nance and guided him with her youthful eyes in his younger days. When she was raised from flesh to spirit, she became less precious to him. He forsook her and delivered himself up to idols. All her efforts proved to be of no avail in saving the wayward Dante, and she had to visit the portal of the dead to bring him to the place where he is standing now.

Dante cries out like the shooting of an over-strained cross-bow and admits Beatrice's accusation in tears. She tells him to lift up his beard and look at her. At this "last venom of her argument," he loses all his power of resistance, lifts up his chin, and breaks down. When he regains his consciousness, he finds himself drawn across Lethe by Matelda and hears *Asperges me.* The four ladies take him before the breast of the Griffin, on which Beatrice's eyes are fixed. He sees the two natures of the Griffin reflected in Beatrice's eyes. This is the unveiling of her first beauty, which he sees while in the care of the four ladies. Her second beauty is her mouth, which is unveiled through the intercession of the three ladies:

> O splendor of the living, eternal light!
>   Who has become so pale in the shade of Parnassus,
>   or drunk so deeply at its fountain,
>
> That he would not seem to have a clouded mind
>   in trying to describe you as you appeared
>   when you revealed yourself in the open air,
>
> Uncovered save for the harmonious spheres?
>   *Purg.* xxxi. 139–145

Then the Procession turns around and moves toward the tree which has been molested by Adam and Eve. The whole company hails the Griffin for not injuring the tree with its beak, and the Griffin responds, "Thus is preserved the seed of all justice." The Griffin ties the pole of the Chariot to the

348

foot of the "widowed trunk," and the withered tree bur-
geons forth in a fresh new color. Dante falls asleep. On
waking up, he sees the Griffin mounting to Heaven with its
company and Beatrice sitting at the foot of the tree with
the seven ladies forming a ring around her.

This is a rough outline of the Procession of the Revelation.* Let us now examine the Procession as the concurrent
representation of the First and the Second Coming of Christ
and then as the co-referent representation of His Coming
to the individual and to the race. We shall first view the
Procession as the First Coming of Christ. Christ came in the
fullness of time (Gal. 4:4). He came under the justice and
peace of the mature Roman Empire, and this is represented
by the order and peace of the Terrestrial Paradise. John the
Baptist preached repentance at the Jordan to prepare the
way of the Lord; a solitary lady sings on the bank of Lethe
of the deserted Garden (Luke 3:3–4; *Purg.* xxviii. 40–42).
When John saw Christ coming towards him, he said,
"Behold, this is the Lamb of God . . . I have come to
make him known to Israel" (John 1:29–30). On the appearance of the Procession, Matelda calls Dante's attention,
saying, "My brother, behold and hearken" (*Purg.* xxix. 15).
Dante is the symbol of the elect race.

The divine truth unfolds itself under the illumination of
the seven gifts of the Holy Spirit, which are represented by
the seven candlesticks. Under the illumination of the candle
lights, Dante sees for the first time his image reflected on

* For the detailed and profound meanings of particular symbols in the
explanation of the Beatrician Procession, I will rely on two admirable
authorities: J. S. Carroll, *Prisoners of Hope* (London: Hodder and
Stoughton, 1906); C. S. Singleton, *Dante Studies* 2 (Cambridge: Harvard University Press, 1958). I will not try to specify which of the two
authorities I rely on for the origin and meaning of each symbol, mainly
because I rely on both authorities in many cases. I am especially indebted
to Professor Singleton for the idea that the Beatrician Procession is the
concurrent representation of the First and Second Coming of Christ.

the water of Lethe (*Purg.* xxix. 64–66). The recognition of the self as made in the image of God becomes possible with the divine illumination. The twenty-four elders represent the twenty-four books of the Old Testament. They are followed by the four beasts, the four Gospels of the New Testament. The four Gospels are followed by the seven Epistles. The four beasts surround the Chariot; the Church is established on the four Gospels.

The Griffin draws the Chariot; Christ is the head of the Church (Eph. 1:22). The Incarnation is the marriage of Christ to His Church. The Procession sings *Veni, sponsa, de Libano*, the call for the divine spouse, and the angels scatter lilies for the bride. At the appearance of Beatrice, Virgil vanishes. So divine wisdom supervenes over natural wisdom. Beatrice's chastisement and humiliation represent Christ's chastisement and humiliation of Israel for her unfaithfulness. As Dante was not an ordinary man but a special creature born and reared in the bounty of grace, so Israel was not an ordinary people but the elect race, God's chosen one. The visions and dreams which Beatrice has shown have been of no avail in rescuing the wayward Dante from his perversion; the dreams of the patriarchs and the visions of the prophets were of no use in saving Israel from her idolatry.

Dante's immersion in Lethe represents the baptism of Christ in Jordan, which instituted the sacrament of baptism. Baptism is the remission of all sins. The water of Lethe washes away all the memory of sin. To forgive is to forget. *I will not remember any more all his sins* (Ezech. 18:22). The unveiling of Beatrice's eyes and mouth represents the two special gifts Christ gave His disciples. He showed them His divinity and gave them the Last Supper. The unveiling of Beatrice's eyes stands for the manifestation of Christ's divinity to His disciples, and the unveiling of her mouth represents the Last Supper. The vision of Christ's divinity is the joy of the eye, and the participation in the Last Supper is the joy of the mouth. Christ showed His divinity in works and gave the Last Supper in rest from works. Beatrice's eyes are unveiled while Dante is in the care of the four ladies of natural virtues, and her mouth is unveiled when the three ladies of supernatural virtues take over Dante from the four ladies. The relation of the natural virtues and the supernatural virtues is that of work and rest.

The return of the Chariot to the tree of the forbidden fruit symbolizes the Crucifixion. By the Crucifixion, Christ pays the debt of punishment for original sin and restores original justice. The revival of the tree stands for the restoration of original justice. The tree embodies God's first decree to man and is the symbol of law and justice. The stricken tree is the Old Law, and the revived tree is the New Law. The New Law fulfills the Old Law. Dante's awakening from his slumber represents the Resurrection and his vision of the ascending Griffin, the Ascension. Dante compares his awakening to the scene of the Transfiguration; the Transfiguration was ordained to give the chosen Apostles a preview of the Resurrection.

The Procession also anticipates the Second Coming of Christ. The Procession is the procession of glory and majesty. Christ came in weakness and lowliness in His First Coming, but will come in majesty and glory in His Second Coming. The formation of the Procession is largely drawn from the apocalyptic vision in which John saw Christ in His Second Coming:

Round it were twenty-four seats, and on these sat twenty-four elders, clothed in white garments . . . Lightnings came from the throne, and mutterings, and thunders, and before it burned seven lamps, . . . round the throne itself, were four living creatures . . . they cried unceasingly, "Holy, Holy, Holy is the Lord God . . ." the twenty-four elders fell down in wor-ship . . . crying out, Thou, our Lord God, claimest as thy due glory and honor and power (Apoc. 4:4–11).

A host of angels arise over the Chariot and sing just before the emergence of Beatrice, as the blessed will rise from their graves at the last trumpet call, singing *Alleluia* (*Purg.* xxx. 13–18). The singing of the angels anticipates the singing with which the resurrected will greet the Son of Man on His Second Coming. Dante bows down before Beatrice as the redeemed will prostrate themselves before the Judge. Beatrice's judgment on Dante prefigures Christ's Judgment on all the redeemed. Dante stands before Beatrice as the symbol of all the faithful and elect who will stand before the Judge for His stern Judgment.

In the construction of the Procession, our poet draws from Ezechiel as well as from John (*Purg.* xxix. 92–105; Ezech. 1:4–14). Ezechiel's vision was of the First Coming and John's of the Second Coming. The combined use of these two visions indicates that the Procession is the concurrent representation of the First and the Second Coming. The Procession recalls the First Coming, which is the beginning of the Second Coming, and anticipates the Second Coming, which is the fulfillment of the First Coming.

Christ comes not only to the race as a whole but into the heart of each of His elect. It was through Beatrice that Christ came into Dante's heart. He was told this in one of his early love-dreams: "(My son), it is my will that thou compose certain things in rhyme, in which thou shalt set forth how strong a mastership I have obtained over thee through her (Beatrice) and how thou wast hers even from thy childhood" (*La Vita Nuova,* xii).

In another vision, he saw Beatrice following Joan and coming toward him. He explains the significance of this vision: ". . . her name, Joan, is taken from that John who went before the True Light, saying, "I am the voice of one crying in the wilderness: Prepare ye the way of the Lord" (*La Vita Nuova*, xxiv).* As Joan prepared the way of Beatrice, the True Light, in her first coming, so Matelda prepares the way for Beatrice's coming on the Terrestrial Paradise. Joan was called the Spring by many; Matelda is the maiden of the eternal spring of the Garden of Delight.

When Christ comes into the heart of the faithful, He abides in it as His tabernacle. *You are the temple of the living God* (2 Cor. 6:16). The Chariot is the co-referent symbol of the universal Church of the race and the individual temple of God in the heart of each Christian. Beatrice's emergence on the Chariot recalls her emergence in Dante's heart as the tabernacle of the Lord. His vision of the Griffin's dual nature in the reflection of Beatrice's eyes recalls that Dante came to see the nature of the Son of Man through Beatrice's flesh.

The Procession not only recalls Beatrice's first coming but also anticipates her second coming. Beatrice will come for the second time, when Dante divests himself of his life on earth and climbs to the top of *Purgatorio* in sheer spirit. She came in weakness and lowliness in her first coming, but will come in majesty and glory in her second coming. Her first and second comings are teleologically related like the First and the Second Coming of Christ. Her second coming will be the fulfillment of her first coming. On Beatrice's appearance on the Chariot, Dante feels the re-awakening of the great power of his childhood love and every drop of his blood trembles as it did at her first coming (*Purg.* xxx. 34–48). Beatrice's second coming will bring to fruition the flame of love which she kindled in young Dante's heart at her first coming.

The Procession is the concurrent representation of the

---

* This is another point which I owe to Professor Singleton.

First and the Second Coming of Christ and of Beatrice's first and second coming. It is a co-referent representation of the visible manifestation of the divine truth to the individual and the race or of the visitation of Christ to the public tabernacle and the private tabernacle.

Let us now see how the cumulative representation functions in the Procession. The main purpose of Dante's ordeal is to be reborn in faith. The power of rebirth was developed on the Fifth Terrace. At the venom of Beatrice's accusation, Dante breaks down and loses consciousness. We can imagine him falling down on the ground and taking the same posture as that of the penitents in labour pain on the Fifth Terrace. He regains his consciousness in the water of Lethe. He is reborn in this baptismal rite; baptism is the sacrament for rebirth. He stands as a reborn soul before Beatrice on the other side of Lethe.

Before going through this travail of rebirth, he is subject to a bitter humiliation. He can live through the ordeal of humiliation with the virtue of humility gained on the First Terrace. Though he has been unfaithful, he is allowed to be reborn through the mercy of the Lord. Dante begs for mercy through the intercession of the angels (*In te, Domine, speravi*). *Blessed are the merciful, because they will receive mercy*. One has to be merciful to receive the mercy of the Lord. Dante receives God's mercy through his mercy developed on the Second Terrace. The effect of divine mercy is to open the mortal's eyes to the divine good. On the Second Terrace, the penitents are waiting for God's mercy to open their eyes like the two blind men at Jericho. Dante's eyes are opened to the divine good through mercy; Beatrice's eyes and mouth are unveiled for Dante.

The theme of rebirth culminates at the simultaneous vanishing of Virgil and emergence of Beatrice. At this critical moment, the angels scatter flowers and sing:

354

All proclaimed, *"Benedictus qui venis"*
and scattering flowers above and around,
"Manibus, O date, lilia plenis!"

> *Purg.* xxx. 19–21

The first of the two chants is a nuptial song, and the second a dirge of Virgil's own composition.[3] The combination of the nuptial song and the dirge marks the birth of divine wisdom and the death of natural wisdom. Dante feels both the dread of death and the tremor of birth. Divine truth supervenes over the human truth; spiritual man is born out of natural man. The Procession is the concrescence of the virtues developed on the First, the Second, and the Fifth Terraces; that is, it brings the virtues into a joint fruition.

The final end of the Incarnation is not to regain Eve's lost Garden for man, but to create Mary's Rose Garden. Eve is the thorn and Mary is the rose. The thorn came out of Adam, and Christ is the fruit of the Rose. In the Flowery Valley, we heard the *Salve Regina:* "after this our exile show unto us the blessed fruit of thy womb Jesus." Dante comes to see the blessed fruit of the Rose in Mary's Rose Garden on the Starry Heaven. Dante arrives on the Heaven of the Fixed Stars in the atmosphere of the dawn, and Beatrice is like a mother bird anxious to fetch food for her baby, who

> Anticipates the dawn on the open branch,
> and with ardent affection waits for the sun,
> looking intently for the day to break.
>
> *Par.* xxiii. 7–9

The dawn is the Eternal Virgin out of whom emerges the Sun, the Son of Man. The heaven grows brighter and brighter, and Beatrice points out "the hosts of Christ's triumph" (*Par.* xxiii. 20). There instantly emerges the Sun

355

under whose rays the Garden of Rose shines and grows
(*Par.* xxiii. 28–33). Dante cannot endure the brilliant light
of the Sun, and Beatrice explains that there is no power to
withstand the might of the Sun:

> It is the wisdom and the power
> > that opened the pathway between heaven and earth
> > for which there has been such long desire.
> >
> > *Par.* xxiii. 37–39

The Sun is "the Wisdom and the Power." Wisdom is the
attribute of the Son, and Power is that of the Father. The
effulgence of the Sun stands for the triumph of the Son in
His visible mission from the Father.

The torch of the Angel Gabriel wheels around the Rose,
singing and praising the Eternal Virgin as he did at the
Annunciation (*Par.* xxiii. 94–108). Christ and Mary ascend
to the higher heaven, leaving behind the lilies of the Garden.
This recalls the Ascension of Christ and the Assumption of
the Queen of Heaven. The host of the redeemed break out
in *Regina coeli:*

> O Queen of heaven, rejoice, Alleluia,
> For He Whom thou wast meet to bear, Alleluia,
> Hath risen, as He said, Alleluia.
> Pray for us to God, Alleluia.
> Rejoice and be glad, O Virgin Mary, Alleluia.
> For the Lord hath risen indeed, Alleluia.

This antiphon is known as the Proclamation of the
Resurrection to the Queen of Heaven and used to be sung
during the octave of Easter, that is, the week following
Easter Sunday. It is the proclamation of the triumph foretold at the Annunciation and of the vengeance promised at
the expulsion of Eve from Eden (Luke 1:33; Gen. 3:15).
The *Regina Coeli* proclaims the final fruition of the blessed

fruit which was sown in Mary's womb at the Annunciation. This blessed fruit in glory and power is the food with
which Beatrice is anxious to feed her baby bird.

The three Apostles examine Dante on his understanding
of faith, hope, and charity after the Ascension of Christ.
The three Apostles represent the Apostolic Church which
Christ has left on the earth to continue His visible mission.
Dante stands before the Apostles as the co-referent symbol
of all the faithful and the individual Christian to be instructed and guided by the Apostolic Church. The Apostles
embody the virtues on which they examine Dante. St. Peter
exemplified faith through his own life. So did St. James
with hope and St. John with charity. This is the way the
Apostolic Church should discharge her mission, that is,
through the eloquence of personal examples.

Adam's discourse on the nature of Eden and its loss is
intended primarily to dramatize his fate, which began with
the loss of Eden. After losing Eden, he was exiled to the
vale of tears. What was his lot there? Judge Nino in the
Flowery Valley is the answer to this question. Adam had
to wait for the fruit of Mary as Judge Nino is waiting for
the prayer of his daughter in the valley of tears. After
his death, Virgil told Dante, Adam had to wait for the
coming of Christ in the Limbo. He has now gained Mary's
Rose Garden many thousand years after losing Eve's
Garden.

The Rose Garden has arisen from the garden of sin. Sin
came into the earth through Adam's sin; the innocent earth
became the sinful ground. Because of sin, the Son of God
came down to the earth. Christ would not have come but
for sin.[4] The Son of God has sown the seed of heavenly
bliss in the garden of sin. He explained His mission with the
parable of the sower, "He who sows the good seed is the
Son of Man. The field is the world; the good seed, the
sons of the kingdom" (Matt. 13:37–38). The soil of earth

357

which has been polluted by Satan's sin becomes the fertile soil for the Rose Garden. We have seen how Christ has transformed through His Incarnation the ice of Cocytus into the pearly substance of the Moon and the livid stone of the *Malebolge* into the watery substance of Mercury. The regenerated substances of the Moon and Mercury constitute the soil of the Rose Garden on the Starry Heaven.

The tree which grows on the soil of the Rose Garden is the Cross of Mars. The Heaven of Mars shows how the sinful souls in exile can be grafted to the tree of Eli: *Abide in me, and I in you. As the branch cannot bear fruit of itself unless it remain on the vine, so neither can you unless you abide in me. I am the vine, you are the branches* (John 15:4–5). The lilies of the Rose Garden on the Starry Heaven are the souls which have been grafted to the tree of Eli as its branches and nurtured in the soil of sin. The Moon and Mercury show the soil of the Rose Garden; Mars shows the tree of the Rose Garden. The former show how the soil of sin is converted into the soil of virtue, and the latter shows how a soul can be grafted from the tree of Satan to the tree of Eli. The Starry Heaven is the concrescence of the powers displayed on the Moon, Mercury, and Mars, i.e., their blissful fruition.

To be born as one of the lilies of the Rose Garden is the final end of the mourning and weeping in the vale of tears:

> Here they live and rejoice in the treasure
>   which they earned with tears in the exile of Babylon,
>   where they spurned its gold.
>
> *Par.* xxiii. 133–135

The vision of the Rose Garden is the fulfillment of the dear wishes of those who sing the *Salve Regina* in the Flowery Valley.

The mission of the Apostolic Church is to cultivate the

Garden which the Son of God has established on the earth and to wean away the exiled souls from their adultery with Satan. The Church has been degraded and abused for the gratification of the avaricious appetite. St. Peter cannot restrain his indignation over the one who "usurps my place, my place, my place" and "has made of my burial-ground a sewer of blood and filth" (*Par.* xxvii. 22–26). The Bride of Christ who has been nurtured by the blood of the Apostles for the care of God's tillage on earth is being used by the disciples of Lucifer for the ruin of the baptized (*Par.* xxvii. 22–56).

Dante takes another look at the THRESHING FLOOR on his way up to the *Primum Mobile* (*Par.* xxvii. 79–87). The threshing floor which now appears on the visible side of the earth is the Mediterranean area, known as Christendom. This is the special area selected by Christ for the sowing ground of the Rose Garden. It is with the baptism of faith that the seeds are sown in this ground. It is with the test of faith that the fruits of the seeds will be winnowed. This was foretold by John the Baptist: *He will baptize you with the Holy Spirit and fire. His winnowing fan is in his hand, and he will thoroughly clean out his* THRESHING FLOOR *and will gather his wheat into barns; but the chaff he will burn up with the unquenchable fire* (Matt. 3:11–12).

It is the blessed fruit of Mary's womb that our Angelic Poet sees on the eighth rung of the angelic ladder of divine love. The blessed fruit is the Wisdom of the Son shining in the Power of the Father. The Son is the foundation of all salvation; He is the Sun of the *Fixed Stars.*

chapter 13

Vision on the Rung of Hope and Sanctification

The Primum Mobile, the Tribulation of the Chariot, the Middle Ante-Purgatorio, and the Vestibule to the Inferno

Our Angelic Poet is now going to show us the Holy Spirit in His invisible mission. His invisible mission is to strengthen and sanctify the faithful in their journey from their exile on the earth to the mansion of the Father. The seed that is sown by the blood of the Son is nurtured by the grace of the Holy Spirit. The vision of the Spirit will be the concrescence of what we have seen on the third, the fourth, and the sixth rungs of the angelic ladder.

In the Vestibule to the *Inferno*, an immense throng of shades run around like herds of nomadic beasts:

> Strange tongues, horrible outcries,
>   words of pain, tones of anger,
>   voices loud and hoarse, and the sounds of blows
>
> Made a tumult which is whirling always
>   through that air, forever dark,
>   as sand eddies in a whirlwind.

Inf. iii. 25–30

The Vestibule bears a striking resemblance to the three

Circles of the irascible. A tone of anger pervades the former as it does the latter. The vocal utterance of the trimmers is totally unintelligible whereas the verbal expressions of anger are intelligible in the Fifth, the Sixth, and the Seventh Circles. Dante cannot point out the ground and the object of the trimmers' anger, though he can perceive their anger through the tone of their cries. This is the way we come to notice the anger of brute animals.

The Vestibule is the natural perfection of animal nature, while Limbo is the natural perfection of human nature. The trimmers are indistinguishable from nomadic beasts. Virgil says that they share their lot of indiscrimination and indistinction with "that caitiff choir of the angels who were neither rebellious nor faithful to God" (*Inf.* iii. 37–39). Decisive choice of good and evil is the unique human privilege, and the trimmers never exercised this human privilege. They lived like animals without bothering to take a stand on the problem of good and evil. They are without blame and without praise (*Inf.* iii. 36). Blame and praise are given for virtues and sins, which are the consequences of choice. Animals have neither virtue nor sin, because they have no will of choice. The Vestibule is devoid of sin like Limbo, but it is devoid of virtue, too.

If they were neither for nor against God and lived neither in virtue nor in sin, how did they live? They lived only for themselves (*Inf.* iii. 39). Animals have the instinctive bond of herds but no communal bond of mutual interest. We have seen the total disintegration of communal bonds in the Third Circle where gluttons languish in the mire. The appetite of the gluttons is vicious, but that of the trimmers is not. The appetite of an animal seldom becomes vicious. Acts of virtue and vice are the acts of universal judgments. Because they are the acts of the universal judgment, they constitute the communal bond between the individual and his community. The individual reflects and embodies the public interest of his community in his acts of virtues and sins.

The royal will embodies the entire public interests of the kingdom. Not every man can become a king, but every man can become an individual through the identification of his self with his world. The private individual and the public community grow through their mutual interaction. The private individual can be the mirror for the reflection of the interests of the public community, and the public community can be the domain for the execution of the interests of the private individual. In this mutual interaction, the individual becomes more than a self and the community becomes more than a herd.

Acts, virtuous or sinful, are the attempts at the mutual identification of the individual and the community. In this mutual interaction, the acts of virtue bring about concord between the individual and his community, and the acts of vice bring about discord between the private individual and his public world. Nonetheless, the acts of vice reflect the individual's interest in his world; no vice is possible without the individual's interest in his world. For example, the vices of slander and envy are possible only if the sinner has some interest in the people he slanders and envies. In the examination of the seven virtues of the Holy Trinity, we have seen that the holy virtues are rooted in the communal bonds of the Three Persons. For example, the humility of the Son lies in His submission to the will of the Father, and the meekness of the Holy Spirit is manifested through the Body of the Son. Furthermore, all divine virtues culminate in the Love through which the estranged man is brought back into communion with the Father as the only-begotten Son is brought into union with the Father through the Holy Spirit, the Love of God. The Holy Trinity is the model of all communities, and the communal bond of the Three Persons is the ultimate source of all virtues. Sins are the sinful imitations of the holy bond of the Three Persons. Neither virtues nor sins are possible for the man who has dissolved all his communal bonds and lost all his interests in his world.

The trimmers lived only for themselves and in a total dis-identification with their public world. Many of those who seem to live blamelessly are the despicable creatures who do not have even some vicious interests in their world. They always follow the blind herd (*Inf.* iii. 52–54). Their mode of existence is that of fashion and vogue. They follow one fashion after another as the winds of fashion blow. Their only torment and fear is to fail to get on the ever-changing tides of fashion and to be left behind as a straggler. This torment and this fear are the wasps and the hornets of their lives:

> These wretches, who had never really lived,
>   were naked and stung constantly
>   by hornets and wasps that were there.
>   *Inf.* iii. 64–66

They are despised both by God and by His enemies (*Inf.* iii. 63). They are so despicable that Virgil tells Dante not to spend his precious time looking on them. Their number is greater than the number of the sinners in any other region of the *Inferno*. The Vestibule is the outermost Circle of the *Inferno*. Astonished at their number, Dante exclaims, "I should never have believed/ death had undone so many" (*Inf.* iii. 56–57). To be a real sinner is to be in the elite.

On the Middle *Ante-Purgatorio*, Dante meets two groups of shades who lived in sin but sustained their hope of salvation. The first of the two groups roam about like shepherdless sheep just below the steep cliff, and the second group are squatting just above the cliff. The first group are the excommunicate, and the second group are the indolent. The former's was the sin of the active irascible, and the latter's the sin of the passive irascible.

The excommunicate rebelled and fought against the Church in their anger (*Purg.* iii. 136). Manfred lived in contumacy of the Holy Church until he was mortally stabbed in one of the battles against the forces of the Pope (*Purg.* iii. 118–145). At the moment of his death, he gave himself up to God and was pardoned in spite of his horrible transgressions. His body was disinterred by the order of the Pope and deposited on the banks of the Verde (Hope) "with tapers quenched." The papal curse could not condemn Manfred's eternal soul, "so long as hope bears a leaf that is green" (*Purg.* iii. 135).

The excommunicate lived in bestial anger, but did not lose their hope of salvation. Their hope is an infant hope, because it has not been substantiated by the virtue of the irascible. They anticipate the purgation on the Third Terrace where the model for purgation is *Agnus Dei* (*Purg.* xvi. 19). The excommunicate have calmed down their anger and behave like a flock of sheep (*Purg.* iii. 79–85). The sheep of the excommunicate have yet to pass the stage of the herd instinct. They feel, think, and move like a herd of sheep. But the *Agnus Dei* is not an animal of mere herd instinct, but an individual of the highest order. The penance of the Third Terrace is to walk individually through dark smoke. The lambs of the Third Terrace have the wisdom of knowing what they are doing and where they are going. The excommunicate became shepherdless sheep by rebelling against the shepherd in anger.

The steep cliff is very hard to climb and resembles the steep slope which leads from the Circles of the passive irascible to the Circles of the active irascible. On reaching the top of the cliff, Dante gets exhausted and sits down as he does on reaching the Fourth Terrace. A group of indolent souls are lounging in the shade (*Purg.* iv. 103–105). One of them is sinking his head between his knees and reminds us of the slothful souls sinking in the marsh of Styx (*Purg.* iv. 106–108). This is an old friend of Dante, Belaqua. Before discovering his identity, Dante jokes with Virgil about his laziness. Belaqua shows his sullen humor in his retort to Dante, "Now you go up, who are valiant" (*Purg.* iv. 114).

Virgil shows Dante the relationship of the Sun's path to the two hemispheres (*Purg.* iv. 61–75). This explanation anticipates Dante's discovery of the dual spiral motion of the Sun on the Fourth Heaven (*Par.* x. 7–21). As the Sun brings into union the two principles of spiration, so the passive irascible has to mediate and unite the virtues of the intellect and the virtues of the concupiscible. The indolent neglected this crucial duty of their passive irascible. The virtue of hope is the virtue of the passive concupiscible. The hope of the indolent is an infant hope, because it has not been substantiated by the mediation of the passive irascible.

The infant hope of the passive concupiscible is represented by the steep cliff. The cliff is so steep that Dante says:

> One can walk at Sanleo and get down to Noli;
>   one can mount Bismantova to its summit
>   with feet alone; but here a man must fly,
>
> I mean with the swift wings and with the plumes
>   of great desire. . . .
>
> *Purg.* iv. 25–29

The purpose of purgation on the Sixth Terrace is to grow wings and plumes of desires to become the heavenly birds (Cf. "bird imagery" of the Sixth Terrace). Hope becomes a mature hope, when it welds together the three powers of the passive concupiscible, the active, and the passive iras-

cible. The separation of the excommunicate and the indolent by the steep cliff represents the inchoate state of hope
which has yet to be substantiated through the concrescence
of the three operational powers for hope.

Dante experiences the force of mature hope in his ordeal
of witnessing the seven catastrophes falling on the Chariot.
After the ascension of the Griffin, Beatrice remains as the
guardian of the Chariot. The seven ladies form a ring with
the seven lights of the Holy Spirit (*Purg.* xxxii. 98). The
universal Church is entrusted to the government of the
Holy Spirit.[1] Beatrice tells Dante that he will be a forester
for a while with her before becoming a citizen of that
Rome of which Christ is a Roman (*Purg.* xxxii. 100–102).
She tells him to watch the Chariot. The Chariot goes
through seven catastrophes (*Purg.* xxxii. 109–160). At the
end of the catastrophes, the seven ladies sing out a psalm of
tribulation:

(Deus, venerunt gentes) *O God, the heathen have invaded
thine inheritance, they have defiled thy holy temple, they have
reduced Jerusalem to ruins . . . We are become a reproach to
our neighbors, a laughing-stock and mockery to them . . .
How long, O Lord? Wilt thou be angry forever? . . . Help
us, O God of our salvation, for the glory of thy name . . .
Let the avenging of thy servant's blood, which has been shed,
be made known among the heathen before our eyes. Let the
groaning of the captives come unto thee; according to the
might of thine arm set free those who are doomed to death . . .*
(Psalm 78 [79]:1–11).

While listening to this lamentation and imploration,
Beatrice changes her countenance as Mary did at the scene
of the Crucifixion and then replies by reciting Christ's
words to His disciples before His departure from the earth:
*A little while, and you shall see me no longer: and again, and
a little while, ye shall see me, because I go to the Father*

(*Purg.* xxxiii. 7–12). Beatrice arises and walks toward the fountain of Eunoë and Lethe, with the seven ladies marching ahead of her. On the way, she tells Dante to be free of all fear, and promises him divine vengeance on those who have defiled God's tabernacle (*Purg.* xxxiii. 31, 43).

The seven catastrophes represent the seven major crises which the Universal Church of Rome has had to go through since its establishment. The Chariot is the co-referent symbol of the individual tabernacle and the universal tabernacle. Every baptized soul has to go through a series of tribulations and catastrophes; it has to be invaded and defiled. The seven virtues developed on the Seven Terraces cannot provide an adequate protection to the tabernacle against the heathens. No mortal soul can preserve its tabernacle in sanctity with its own power. We cannot sustain the hope of salvation without the sanctifying grace of the Holy Spirit just as we cannot gain faith in salvation without the aid of the Incarnate Word.

Dante only watches and listens throughout the seven catastrophes. The two virtues developed on the Third and the Fourth come to his aid. The impetuous Dante shows no trace of anger in witnessing the seven catastrophes; neither does he lose courage and despair. Dante endures, in meekness and fortitude, the tribulation on the tabernacle.

The lamentation of the seven ladies at the dreadful fate of the Chariot recalls the moaning and weeping on the Sixth Terrace. The mortal soul can do nothing in attaining the heavenly bliss except to wait in moaning and weeping. It is through the agony of waiting and weeping that the sinful soul comes to learn the power of grace. On the Sixth Terrace, we learned that God allowed only a few of Gideon's army to march to the victory in order to demonstrate His power: *And the Lord said to Gideon: "The people that are with thee are many, and Madian shall not be delivered into their hands. Lest Israel should glory*

against me, and say: 'I was delivered by my own strength' "
(Judges 7:2).

Fully knowing the source and purpose of salvation, the seven ladies implore, "Help us, O God of salvation, for the glory of thy name" (*Deus, venerunt gentes*). How long does the fragile tabernacle have to be defiled by the hands of the heathen and wait in agony for sanctifying grace? "How long, O Lord? Wilt thou be angry forever?" Beatrice consoles, "A little while, and you shall see me again." This is the consolation of the Holy Spirit Who "strengthens and comforts us as His friends and brothers."[2]

On the Heaven of the *Primum Mobile*, Dante sees the nine angelic orders. At the opening of her discourse on the Ninth Heaven, Beatrice speaks of the inevitable degeneration of an innocent baby into a sinful man (*Par.* xxvii. 121–138). This is the lesson which Dante learned in witnessing the desecration of the Chariot on the top of the *Purgatorio*. In contrast with the human tabernacles of the Holy Spirit, the confirmed angels are the wondrous tabernacles which have never been defiled (*Par.* xxviii. 53). Thus it is proper that the dispensation of grace be entrusted to the angelic orders. It is through the ministration of the angels that the weak human tabernacle can be rescued from its inevitable course of degeneration and nurtured in the stream of grace.

The angelic hierarchies appear in nine concentric circles around a point of an infinitely small magnitude and of an immeasurably intense light (*Par.* xxviii. 16–35). It is not one of the angels but Beatrice who explains the angelic orders. She is an angel; our Angelic Poet once called her "this youngest of the angels" (*La Vita Nuova*, ii). The highest order is the smallest circle and nearest to the center, and the lowest order is the widest and farthest from the center. The nearer the circles are to the center, the faster they move. The speed of each angelic order reflects its knowledge and love of God. The center of the nine an-

gelic orders is the Holy Spirit in His invisible mission from
the Father:

> The order of the universe, which holds its center
>   motionless and moves all the rest around,
>   begins here as from its starting point,
>
> And this heaven has no other *where*
>   but the divine mind where is kindled
>   the Love that turns it and the Power it rains down.
>
> Light and Love enclose it in one circle
> Par. xxvii. 106–112

Love is the attribute of the Holy Spirit and Power that
of the Father. The Holy Spirit is the Love that transmits
the Power of the Father for the quickening and governing
of the whole world. What is the Power of the Father? It is
the Power of Light which is the source of all existence and
life. On the Sun, we learned that every potency would be
dead without the governing function of the Spirit. The
Spirit governs the entire universe with the Power of the
Father.

The Spirit is the Providence of the universe. In the Third
Heaven, Dante learned that imperial power comes from
Providence (*Par.* viii. 97 ff.). On the Sun, he also learned
that Providence appointed St. Francis and St. Dominic as
the two princes for the succor of the Church. He further
learned that the Holy Spirit inspires the prophets and the
theologians for the elucidation of man's supernatural end.
Beatrice assails the preachers who neglect the Gospel in
their preaching and feed their sheep with the winds of jest
and trifles (*Par.* xxix. 94–126). The Gospels were written
under the special inspiration of the Holy Spirit and are
the highest gifts of the Gift.

The motion of the nine concentric rings of the angels

around the Holy Spirit is the proper manifestation of the invisible mission of the Holy Spirit, because the Spirit moves and quickens the entire creation. We saw the preview of the motion of the nine angelic orders in the epycyclical motion of Venus and the dual spiral motion of the Sun. The Holy Spirit is the spiration of the Father and the Son. The Spirit also spirals out all His gifts to the entire creation.

The angelic orders are the angelic choirs constantly singing the praise of the Lord (*Par.* xxviii. 94). We have seen the Eagle of the Holy Spirit singing the praise of the Lord on Jupiter. What is the nature of the angelic hymn of praise? The solemn hymn of the angelic choirs is their majestic ministerial function as represented by the splendid motion of the nine concentric circles. The angels are the ministers of the Holy Spirit entrusted with the mission of governing the whole universe. The nine concentric rings of the angels constitute the cosmic communal bonds which hold together the entire creation in order and splendor. This is the angelic hymn in praise of the Lord. The caitiff choir of angels in the Vestibule have no communal bonds; they live only for themselves. The angels shown in the *Primum Mobile* live for the whole world and move in the cosmic communal bonds.

As the Eagle explains the course of creation and salvation, so too does Beatrice (*Par.* xxix. 40 ff.). The important point, implicit in the Eagle's account and explicit in Beatrice's, is that even the angels have been exalted only through the grace of the Spirit (*Par.* xxix. 61–66). The bliss of seeing the divine essence far surpasses the nature and power of all creatures, human and angelic, corruptible and incorruptible.

Throughout Beatrice's discourse in the *Primum Mobile*, Dante seldom talks. His silence reflects the nature of hope. To be in hope is to wait in patience. This he does not only during the vision of the angelic orders but during that of Jupiter. He does not speak out his burning question on the fate of the virtuous heathens but waits for the Eagle to read it (*Par.* xix. 22–33). There is a striking difference between the two waitings of Dante on Jupiter and in the *Primum Mobile*. On Jupiter, he cannot hide his anguish and tension. On the *Primum Mobile*, he fully displays his serenity and confidence. He does not get excited and angered even at Beatrice's mention of the evils on the earth. For the first time in his ascent of the *Paradiso*, our Angelic Poet reposes in angelic serenity. Dante sees the ground of his hope in the vision of the Holy Spirit and His angelic ministers, and virtues separately displayed on Venus, the Sun, and Jupiter mellow in their reposeful concrescence in the *Primum Mobile*.

The nine angelic orders fade away one by one like stars at sunrise, leaving the light of the Holy Spirit to shine alone (*Par.* xxx. 6–14). The ministration of the angels becomes no longer necessary for the soul fully prepared for the beatific vision: *Thou shalt no more have the sun for thy light by day, neither shall the brightness of the moon enlighten thee: but the Lord shall be unto thee for an everlasting light, and thy God for thy glory* (Isa. 9:19). In the highest Heaven, our pilgrim will be illuminated by the direct rays of God and no longer by His reflected rays. The function of the reflected rays of the angelic ministers is to nurture, guide, and bring the soul where it can be exalted by the immediate divine illumination.

Not only the angelic Church but also the human Church comes to the end of its ministration when the soul is fully sanctified in hope. While Beatrice and Dante are walking over to the source of Lethe and Eunoë, leaving the molested Chariot behind, she tells him, "Know that the Chariot the monster broke was and is not" (*Purg.* xxxiii. 34–35). Dante has been fully sanctified and requires no further ministration of the Chariot.

It is the spiral motion of the Holy Spirit that our Angelic Poet sees on the ninth rung of the angelic ladder of divine love. The spiral motion is the Love of the Spirit revolving in the Light of the Father and governing with His Power. The grace which flows out through His spiral motion nurtures and sanctifies the seeds of the faithful sown by the sower of the Divine Word. The Spirit is the Motion of all motion; He is the center of the *Primum Mobile*.

chapter 14

Vision on the Rung of Charity and Beatification

The Empyrean, the Rivers, and the Mount of Delight

WE ARE at last about to stand on the apex of the angelic ladder of divine love. Our Angelic Poet will show us all the angels and all the redeemed together in one feast of one love in which they will participate on the Day of Judgment when they finish their works as ministers of the visible mission of the Son and of the invisible mission of the Spirit. He will also show us the Son and the Spirit not in missions from the Father but in union with the Father. He will further show us the face of the Father unveiled as Benedict promised on the Heaven of Love. The ultimate vision on the Empyrean will be the final concrescence of all the visions on the nine rungs of the angelic ladder and the final consummation of all the powers of the soul.

The virtue of charity is the spark of life. Not to have God as the final end is to be spiritually dead. The dead souls are the evil harvest from the tree of Adam and assemble on the shore of Acheron:

> As in autumn the leaves fall
> one after the other, until the branch
> sees all its spoils upon the ground,

> So the evil seed of Adam
> fell to that shore . . .
>
> *Inf.* iii. 112–116

Charon pronounces his dreadful intention, "I come to take you to the other shore/ into eternal darkness, into fire, and into ice" (*Inf.* iii. 85–87). The naked souls "change color and gnash their teeth" (*Inf.* iii. 101). They will gnash their teeth once more on the Day of Judgment:

But the harvest is the end of the world, and the reapers are the angels. Therefore, just as the weeds are gathered up and burnt with fire . . . The Son of Man will send forth his angels, and they will gather . . . and cast them into the furnace of fire, where there will be the weeping and the gnashing of teeth (Matt. 13: 39–42).

The dark land trembles violently, and Dante loses his consciousness in the crimson light flashing out of a sudden blast (*Inf.* iii. 130–136). This is the concurrent representation of the individual death of the soul and its final extinction on the Day of Judgment.

The penitents arrive at the foot of the *Purgatorio*, singing the psalm *In exitu Israel de Aegypto*:

When Israel went out of Egypt, the house of Jacob from a barbarous people, Juda was made his sanctuary, Israel his kingdom. The sea saw and fled, the Jordan turned backwards . . . Our God is in heaven; he has done all things whatsoever he would. Their idols are silver and gold, the work of the hands of men. They have mouths, and speak not; they have eyes and see not . . . Like unto them shall be they that make them, everyone that trusts in them . . . The Lord remembers us and will bless us . . . Heaven is the heaven of the Lord, but the earth he has given to the children of men. The dead do not praise the Lord, nor anyone that goes down to the grave. But we bless the Lord both now and forever (Psalm 113[114]).

374

This is the psalm that remembers the miracle of the Exodus. It used to be sung as the dead were carried to the church. The death of the faithful is his liberation from the slavery of sin, and his liberation is as miraculous as the Exodus. Casella informs Dante that the blessed souls assemble on the shore of the Tiber where they are "garnered" into the angel's vessel (*Purg.* ii. 100–103). They are not the tares to be burned, but the wheat to be garnered. The mouth of Tiber is the port of Rome; the penitents are the wheat raised in the vineyard of the Church. The mouth of Tiber is the port of liberation. The Exodus of the soul from bondage is a miracle which annuls the laws of nature and which transcends human power; this is reflected in the supernatural method which the celestial pilot employs in carrying the blessed over the ocean (*Purg.* ii. 31–33).

The miracle of the Exodus is possible only for those who trust in God. The idolaters remain with their idols in the kingdom of death. The idols are "the works of the hands of men." The guards of Hell are the idols, and the idolaters become like them. The Lord has given over the earth to the idolaters. The faithful will secure the Holy Land and be made the tabernacle of the Lord. The Israelites spent forty years before crossing the Red Sea and forty years in the desert between the Red Sea and the Jordan. The first forty years were meant for the liberation of Israel from the idolatrous empire and the second forty years for the purification of Israel from the stain of slavery.

Like Israel, every soul has to go through the period of liberation and the period of sanctification before entering the Holy Land. This was exemplified by the Son of Man. He spent forty days in the wilderness at the beginning of His mission to overcome Satan's temptation and forty days after arising out of the grave before His Ascension (Matt. 4:2; Acts i. 3). Our pilgrim spends three nights in the kingdom of sin and three days in the desert of purgation.

He comes out of the Infernal Empire to the base of the *Purgatorio*, as Israel came out of the Egyptian Empire by crossing the Red Sea. When he has emerged out of the grave of sin, he finds himself in the atmosphere as refreshing as at the dawn of the first Easter:

> A sweet color of oriental sapphire
>   which was forming in the clear sky,
>   pure from zenith to the horizon,
>
> Restored delight to my eyes
>   as soon as I came out of the dead air
>   that afflicted both my eyes and lungs.
>
> *Purg.* i. 13–18

The death of flesh for the life of spirit is represented by Cato who died for the sake of his liberty (*Purg.* i. 70–75). Cato further stands for the love of the Father. He had almost a paternal love for his second wife Marcia. When she wanted to be married to Hortensius, he magnanimously granted her wish. Marcia wished to come back to Cato on the death of Hortensius, and he joyfully accepted her return. Marcia's desertion and return represent the soul's rebellion against God and its return to Him. Like Marcia, the human soul is the second bride to God, the angel being the first bride. The divine bridegroom would not keep the bride against her will when she wants to go away but joyfully receives her back when she wants to return.

Cato is now separated from Marcia by the distance between the *Inferno* and the *Purgatorio*. The immense chasm which separates Marcia from Cato characterizes the state of charity of the penitents arriving at the bottom of the *Purgatorio*. We have seen how the Upper and the Middle *Ante-Purgatorio* represent infant faith and infant hope. The penitent's love of God is as remote from its destination as Marcia is from Cato. The chasm which separates the penitents from God is as hard to traverse as the chasm which separates Marcia from Cato. The chasm can be bridged only by the power of grace and not by human power. This is meant when Cato says that he cannot show the way for Dante and Virgil but they will be guided by the rays of the Sun in their ascent (*Purg.* i. 107).

The light of the Sun guides Dante; the pillars of fire guided Israel in the desert. Moses, who led his people across the Red Sea and to the Jordan, was not allowed to enter the Holy Land. Virgil who guides Dante through the *Inferno* and to the top of the *Purgatorio* is not allowed to cross Lethe. It was Joshua, one of Moses' lieutenants, who led Israel across the Jordan into the promised land. It is Statius, one of Virgil's assistant guides, who crosses the stream of Lethe with Dante. With her amorous valor Rahab helped Israel's entry into the Holy Land from the other side of the Jordan (*Par.* ix. 115 ff.). Dante finds Matelda with her eyes "shining under the eyelids of Venus" on the other side of Lethe (*Purg.* xxviii. 65). She pulls him from the front through the water of Lethe. It is again Matelda who leads Dante to the joint fountainhead of Lethe and Eunoë and explains the mysterious way the two rivers function (*Purg.* xxxiii. 118 ff.). It was from Rahab that Israel gained the secret knowledge of the land of milk and honey and the city of Jericho (Joshua 2).

After crossing the Jordan, Israel is prepared to become the sanctuary of God in the Holy Land. After drinking from Lethe and Eunoë, our pilgrim becomes fit to be the tabernacle of God in heaven:

> I came back from the most holy waters,
>   born again, like young plants,
>   renewed by their new foliage,

Pure and prepared to mount to the stars.

Purg. xxxiii. 142–145

One of the conspicuous discrepancies between the biblical Eden and Dante's Eden is the number, the names, and the nature of the rivers. *Genesis* counts four rivers in the Garden of Eden, but Dante shows only two in his Terrestrial Paradise. Dante's two rivers do not bear any of the names of the four rivers of the *Genesis* but the names of the two rivers of Hades. Hades was known to have two rivers, the river of forgetfulness and the river of good memory.* Though we don't find four rivers in Dante's Terrestrial Paradise, we do find four rivers in his Hell. The two rivers of the Terrestrial Paradise coincide in name with the two rivers in Hades, and the four rivers of the *Inferno* coincide in number with the four rivers of Eden. What does Dante want to show by these coincidences? He wishes to show the nature of his *Inferno* and of his Terrestrial Paradise and their relation to the Garden of Eden.

The four rivers stand for the powers and virtues. *A spring rose out of the earth, watering all the surface of the earth* (Gen. 2:6). The spring is the source of life; its water gives life to the earth. In the early Christian tradition, the four rivers of Eden were specially identified with the virtues of the soul.**

. . . the first of these rivers is prudence which means the very contemplation of truth . . . and that (second) river . . . is

---

* Lethe means the oblivion of Evil, Eunoë the remembrance of Good. In the Greek mysteries, it was believed that two rivers flow through Hades—the river of oblivion and the river of memory. *See* W. W. Vernon, *Readings on the Purgatorio of Dante*, Vol. II, pp. 460–461 (London: Methuen & Co., 1907); J. S. Carroll, *Prisoners of Hope*, p. 384 (London: Hodder & Stoughton, 1906).

** It is again Professor Singleton's admirable work that has called my attention to the significance of the Neoplatonic interpretation of the rivers in the other world.

very hot and burning, signifies fortitude, prompt and swift in the heat of action. And the third, the Tigris . . . signifies temperance . . . Of the fourth river, it is not said what it flows against or what land it compasses, for justice pertains to all parts of the soul because it is the very order and equity of the soul, by which the three others are bound in harmony.[1]

These four powers of the soul in their degenerate state are represented by the four rivers in Dante's Hell (*Inf.* xiv. 94–120; *Purg.* xxviii. 139–144). Cocytus represents the degenerate intellect whose function is "the very contemplation of truth." Phlegethon represents the degenerate irascible; fortitude is one of the virtues of the irascible. The second river is "very hot and burning." So is Phlegethon. The marsh of Styx collects its water from the three Circles of the concupiscible (*Inf.* vii. 100–102). Temperance is the generic virtue of the concupiscible, and Styx represents the degenerate concupiscible. St. Augustine says, "Of the fourth river, it is not said what it flows against or what land it compasses, for justice pertains to all parts of the soul . . ." Of the four rivers in the *Inferno*, Acheron alone neither represents any power of the soul nor accommodates any group of sinners.

St. Augustine says that justice pertains to all parts of the soul "because it is the very order and equity of the soul, by which the three others are bound in harmony." Justice is the harmony of the three powers of the soul, and injustice is their disharmony. Acheron represents the injustice by which the three powers of the sinful soul are bound in disharmony.

Justice not only lies in the internal relation of the soul but also in its external relation to its Creator. On the first seven rungs of the angelic ladder, we learned that a just soul restores the internal order of its three powers by imitating the Three Persons of the Holy Trinity and that an unjust

379

soul loses its internal order through its inverted imitation of the Three Persons. Everything in the world derives its being from the Creator; the Creator is the only *causa sui*. Every soul exists and grows as an image of God, i.e., through its imitation of the Trinity. The problem which confronts the fate of every soul is not *what* it is to imitate, but *how* it is to imitate the model of all imitation. The intellect becomes virtuous through a just imitation of the Son, the irascible through a just imitation of the Spirit, and the concupiscible through a just imitation of the Father. The three powers become sinful through the inverted imitation of the Three Persons.

The internal justice of the soul is inseparably interlocked with its external justice. It is through justice that the soul gains its internal order and gives itself back to its Creator. It is through injustice that the soul loses its internal order and is lost from its Creator. It is the inseparable relation of the soul's internal and external justice that lurks behind the first two of the three tercets written above the gate of the *Inferno*:

> Through me is the way into the city of sorrow;
> through me the way into the pain eternal;
> through me the way among the people lost.

> Justice moved my High Maker;
> Divine Power made me,
> Wisdom Supreme, and Primal Love.

Inf. iii. 1–6

The soul that goes through this gate is an inverted image of the Three Persons; it derives its inverted image from the Trinity as its High Maker. Through inverted imitation, the soul is alienated from God and lost to Him. The internal conflict and disorder of the soul which stems from the inverted imitation is the pain eternal. The city of sorrow is the co-referent symbol of the sinful soul and the sinful community.

While the four rivers of the *Inferno* show the origin of the degenerate powers and the effect of their degeneration, the two rivers of the Terrestrial Paradise show the origin of the regenerate powers and the effect of their regeneration. Lethe and Eunoë bear the names of the rivers in Hades; the degenerate powers of Hell are the origin of the regenerate powers in the Terrestrial Paradise. The two rivers of the Terrestrial Paradise differ from the four rivers of Eden both in number and name because the regeneration of the degenerate powers is not simply the restoration of the four virtues of innocence which have been lost through original sin.

The regaining of lost innocence is not the regaining of Eden, but the gaining of the Terrestrial Paradise. What is the difference between the regaining of Eden and the gaining of the Terrestrial Paradise? This difference is the difference between Cato adorned with the rays of the four holy stars and Beatrice surrounded by the ring of the seven ladies. Adam in Eden was the natural man in perfection, but Dante in the Terrestrial Paradise is the spiritual man in perfection. The four rivers of the *Inferno* represent the degeneration of the natural man, and the two rivers of the *Purgatorio* represent the regeneration of the degenerate natural man into the spiritual man. The four rivers flow down from the Garden of Eden, "the faithful cradle of Rhea's son" (Mount Ida), and the two rivers have a legendary original in Hell. The Jordan flowed backward for Israel's entry into the Holy Land; Lethe and Eunoë flow upward figuratively speaking for Dante's flight into the Holy Heaven.

The two rivers and the four rivers demonstrate the power that woman holds over the fate of man. The four rivers flow down from Eden to Hell through the power of Eve, and the two rivers flow up from Hades to the Ter-

restrial Paradise through the power of Mary. The first
Adam falls through the first Eve, and the second Adam
arises from the second Eve. The four rivers show the genesis
of the seven sins which man gains through the first Eve, and
the two rivers show that of the seven virtues which man
gains through the second Eve. Lethe washes off the traces
of the seven sins which man inherits as a son of the first
Eve, and Eunoë preserves the works of the seven virtues
which man gains as a son of the second Eve. Man gains the
seven virtues by climbing the seven Terraces, i.e., by imitating the seven virtues of the second Eve with her gracious
aid. The water of Lethe and Eunoë does not take effect until
one drinks from both (*Purg.* xxviii. 130–132). The only
way to purge sins is to purify the sinful powers and to
transform them into virtuous powers, because both sin and
virtue reside in the same power. The purgation of sins and
the cultivation of virtues, the extinction of the traces of sin
and the preservation of the works of virtue, are the two
features of one task.

Man rises and falls through woman; he would be standing like Cato at the original site of Eden but for his en-
tanglement with the woman of his flesh. At the outset of
his pilgrimage, Dante tries to climb up the mount of delight
and soon becomes a helpless victim of three beasts. The
three beasts stand for the three powers of the soul which
have been degenerated and carnalized through Eve whom
Adam called his flesh and bone. Dante conquers these three
beasts of sin and converts them into the seven ladies of
virtue by wading through the *Inferno* and by climbing up
the *Purgatorio*.

How does Dante, the helpless victim of the three beasts,
become their conqueror and further transform the carnal
beasts into the spiritual ladies? He does it with the power of
the ladies. When Dante is frightened at the enormousness of

the task he has readily undertaken at Virgil's advice, Virgil consoles him by explaining that he will be assisted by the three heavenly ladies throughout his journey (*Inf.* ii. 10–117). It is through the omnipresent power of the ladies that Dante descends to the bottom of Hell and ascends to the top of Heaven. Beatrice comes down to Limbo to send Virgil to Dante. He is protected in the Flowery Valley from the serpent by the angels from Mary's bosom. Lucia carries him to the gate of the *Purgatorio* proper. On every Terrace, Dante imitates the virtues of the Trinity through Mary's reflection. He is saved from the bewitchment of the Siren by a heavenly lady. Matelda receives him on the Terrestrial Paradise. With Beatrice, he sails through the ten Heavens. Dante is elevated to the ultimate bliss through the intercession of the Queen of Heaven.

The Queen of Heaven is the lady of all ladies. She tells Lucia to look after Dante, and Lucia sends Beatrice to aid him. The Queen of Heaven is the prime mover of Dante's journey and its final destination. It is through her virtue that the four rivers of the *Inferno* flow up to the Terrestrial Paradise and become the two rivers, while the four rivers of Eden have become the four rivers of Hell through Eve's sin. The second Eve is impossible without the first Eve; Mary's virtue is impossible without Eve's sin. Mary is the end of Eve, and Eve the beginning of Mary.

The fall of the first Adam and the rise of the second Adam are inseparably related as the two phases of one eternal plan of salvation, just as the sin of Eve and the virtue of Mary are. The *Inferno* is an essential feature of the eternal design of the Creator:

> Before me nothing was created,
> > but the eternal, and eternal I endure:
> > abandon all hope, ye that enter here.
>
> *Inf.* iii. 7–9

Dante falls through Eve and rises through Mary. He rises to the highest Heaven. The highest Heaven is the heaven of pure light. The pure light is the Light of the Father. Dante is going to see the face of the Father unveiled, and his love will be consummated in rapturous joy:

> Light intellectual, full of love,
>> Love of the true good, replete with joy,
>> Joy that transcends every sweetness.
>
> *Par.* xxx. 40–42

Dante is suddenly swathed and blinded in an outburst of effulgence (*Par.* xxx. 49–51). This is the light that is to elevate Dante's sight for the vision of the divine essence. The vision of the divine essence far surpasses the proper power of any creature and requires God's special illumination. Dante soon feels himself "mount my proper self" (*Par.* xxx. 57). He comes to be more than a human self to see the divine essence; he becomes God-like for the vision of God. At the beginning of his pilgrimage, Dante wakes out of a terrible slumber and comes to himself (*Inf.* i. 1–12). He does not remember how he got lost in the dark wood. Every soul is born in the revelry of the sin of Adam and cannot recall how it got lost in the orgy of sin. The Angelic Epic is the account of the soul's adventure of becoming God-like from the moment of coming back to itself from the revelry of sin to the moment of going out of itself in the ecstasy of divine love.

With his deiform vision, Dante sees the river of light flowing between two banks covered with marvelous spring flowers (*Par.* xxx. 61–69). The living sparks of angels issue from the river of light, settle on the blossoms, and then plunge back to the marvelous swirl of the river. Beatrice explains to Dante that the marvelous scenery of the river is a shadowy preview of what he is going to see anon (*Par.*

xxx. 76–78). On drinking from the river of light, he sees
the oblong river change into a circular ground of festivity,
and the flowers and the sparks transform themselves into
the two courts of heaven for the great feast of divine love
(*Par.* xxx. 82–96). The two courts of heaven, the confirmed
angels and the redeemed souls, now appear in all the glory
they will have on the Day of Judgment (*Par.* xxx. 45).

What is signified by the mysterious change of the oblong
scenery of the river into the circular scenery of festivity?
The scenery of the river of light is the concrescence of the
Seventh, the Eighth, and the Ninth Heaven. The living
sparks on the river of light are the confirmed angels which
we saw in the Heaven of the *Primum Mobile,* and the
blossoms on the banks of the river are the flowers of the
Rose Garden which we saw in the Heaven of the Fixed
Stars. The river of light is the stream of love which we saw
in the form of a ladder rising from the Heaven of Saturn.
The two courts of heaven are brought together in the stream
of one love. On the Heaven of Saturn, Dante was given a
preview of this scene:

> I saw also descend upon the steps
>   so many splenders that I thought every light
>   in the heaven had been poured down on it.
>
> And, as by natural custom, the daws
>   set out at the beginning of the day
>   to warm their chilled feathers;
>
> Then some go away without returning,
>   others fly back to where they started,
>   and still others make wheeling sojourn;
>
> Thus a similar movement appeared
>   to occur in that sparkling
>   as soon as it reached a certain step.
>
> > *Par.* xxi. 31–42

The River of Light is the cumulative representation of Saturn, the Fixed Stars, and the *Primum Mobile* and thus brings into the concrescence of one love all the virtues developed in the long course of Dante's journey.* The transformation of the oblong river scene into the circular feast scene marks the final moment of fruition. The teleological movement is the linear movement toward the circular end; that is, the movement can be represented by the straight line which extends to the end, and the end by the circle which brings together all the segments of the straight line to one eternal bloom and preserves them in their concrescent totality. On Saturn, we noted that Jacob's Ladder is the co-referent symbol of the human love and the divine love. Man's love of God is infused by the Holy Spirit, God's love of man.[2] Man's love of God returns to its primal source in the stream of love, the river of light in the Empyrean. The transformation of the oblong river scene into the circular feast scene is the co-referent symbol of the concrescence of human love and divine love.

The end is the end of the whole. The beginning must then be the beginning of the whole. The Day of Judgment will show the eternal plan as it has happened, and the Day of Creation has shown the eternal plan as it will happen. The Heaven of Pure Light gives the retrospect of Dante's

---

* The River of Light should be understood in connection with the rivers of the *Inferno* and of the *Purgatorio*. Light is the symbol of the spiritual order. The four rivers of Hell flow down from the Garden of Eden, and the River of Light flows out of the Heaven of Light. The four rivers of Eden stand for the powers of natural life, and the River of Light for the powers of spiritual life. The natural powers of the soul which have degenerated through the loss of innocence are regenerated and become the spiritual powers for the bliss in the spiritual order. The powers whose regeneration is perfected in the water of Lethe and Eunoë mount to the Heaven of Light in the form of Jacob's Ladder and constitute the River of Light. The apex of Jacob's Ladder is the River of Light. In the highest Heaven, Jacob's Ladder changes its vertical form into the horizontal form of the river because the Empyrean affords no further height for the Ladder to mount.

whole adventure, and the Dark Wood gives the prospect of his whole journey. The Dark Wood is the preview of the *Inferno;* the Mount of Delight is that of the *Purgatorio;* the Rising Sun is that of the *Paradiso.*

He gets lost with a heavy slumber in the Dark Wood; he falls into the kingdom of eternal darkness in a stupor on the shore of Acheron. He remembers neither how he got lost in the Dark Wood, nor how he crossed Acheron. When Dante reaches the foot of the Delightful Mountain, there the valley ends (*Inf.* i. 13). When he reaches the foot of the *Purgatorio,* there the valleys of the *Inferno* end. He recovers the true way along "the desert strand" at the foot of the Delightful Mountain; he finds, after a little search, the way of purgation at the foot of the *Purgatorio* (*Inf.* i. 29). Dante compares the transition from the Dark Wood to the foot of the Delightful Mountain to an escape from the dangerous sea to the safe shore (*Inf.* i. 22–24). The transition from the *Inferno* to the *Purgatorio* is the escape from the ocean to the shore. The Mountain of Delight is illumined by the rays of the Sun, and so is the *Purgatorio* (*Inf.* i. 17).

He conquers the three beasts of the Mountain with the aid of the three ladies in heaven. He not only climbs to the top of the Mountain but flies up to the Sun. The Sun is the preview of the *Paradiso.* Our poet concludes the last canto of his last canticle: "the Love that moves the Sun and the other stars." The Sun over the Mount of Delight not only shows the final destination of Dante's adventure but also points to the Love that has brought him back to himself. At the end of his journey, Dante will lose himself in the Love that will move him as one of the stars along with the Sun.

Before leaving the Dark Wood, let us face one dark question: Where is Paul, of whom Dante spoke at his initial recognition of the dreadful gravity of his momentous voyage? He can be found nowhere in Dante's vast cosmos. Why? Because Paul is everywhere. At the outset of the journey, our poet compares his task to Paul's trip to the third heaven for the "confirmation of that faith which is the entrance to the way of salvation" (*Inf.* ii. 28–30). What is Paul's faith? His faith is the faith in the birth of the spiritual man from the death of the natural man. Paul's faith is the central theme for the Angelic Epic, just as the faith of Aeneas is the central theme for the *Aeneid*. Dante does not encounter Paul in his journey for the same reason that Aeneas does not run into Aeneas in his trip. The *Aeneid* sings the faith of Aeneas in the glory of the Roman Empire to emerge out of the ashes of Ilium.*

The Angelic Epic sings the faith of the Chosen Vessel in the glory of the spiritual man to blossom out of the sin of the natural man:

Mankind begins with the Adam who became, as Scripture tells us, a living soul; it is fulfilled in the Adam who has become a life-giving spirit. It was not the principle of spiritual life that came first; natural life came first, then spiritual life; the man who came first came from earth, fashioned of dust, the man who came afterwards came from heaven, and his fashion is heavenly. The nature of that earth-born man is shared by his earthly sons, the nature of the heaven-born man, by his heavenly sons; and it remains for us, who once bore the stamp of earth, to bear the stamp of heaven (I Cor. 15:45–49).

* The ashes of Troy are the cumulative symbol of the mortal consequences of pride:

> I saw Troy in ashes and in ruins.
>   O Ilion! thee how base and vile
>   it showed—the sculpture which there is discerned.
>   *Purg.* xii. 61–63

As the glory of the Roman Empire grows out of the ashes and ruins of Troy, so does the splendor of the City of God evolve out of the woes and sins of the City of Dis.

The splendor of the Mystical Rose is the spiritual glory which has blossomed from the fertile soil of the sin of the natural man. The Mystical Rose of the Empyrean forms a vast amphitheatre on whose thousands of petals are seated the redeemed souls crowned and robed in white. Above this august blossom of the Mystical Rose, the host of angels hovers and sings like a swarm of bees. This is the City of God (*Par.* xxx. 130). Upon this City, the Holy Trinity shines in the form of a single star of a threefold light (*Par.* xxxi. 28). All the members of the City of God are gazing on the Holy Trinity. This is the rapturous communion of all the saints.

When our pilgrim turns around to seek Beatrice's explanation of the Mystical Rose, he is startled at an elderly man standing like "a tender father" in Beatrice's place (*Par.* xxxi. 55–63). Dante exclaims, "Where is she?" The elderly man explains that Beatrice has asked him to take her place in order to bring Dante's love to its final consummation (*Par.* xxxi. 64–66). He guides Dante's eyes to Beatrice now back on her throne on the third highest tier of the Mystical Rose and sitting beside the ancient Rachel. Beatrice looks back to Dante, and he offers his final prayer to her:

> "O lady, in whom my hope hath vigor,
>   and who for my salvation didst endure
>   to leave in Hell thy footprints,
>
> In all the things that I have seen
>   I recognize the grace and the might
>   of thy power and thy excellence.
>
> Thou hast drawn me from slavery to liberty
>   by all those paths, by all those methods
>   which thou hadst the power to employ

Preserve thy munificence in me,
>   so that my soul which thou hast made whole
>   may leave the body, pleasing unto thee."
>   *Par.* xxxi. 79–90

The elderly man with the appearance of a tender father reveals his identity:

>   And the Queen of Heaven for whom I am
>   all burning with love, will grant us every grace,
>   because I am her faithful Bernard.
>   *Par.* xxxi. 100–102

At this unveiling of the identity of St. Bernard, Dante gazes upon the abbot of Clairvaux with the wonder and awe of a pilgrim who looks on the Veronica and says in thought, "My Lord Jesus Christ, true God,/ and was this then the shape of Thy countenance" (*Par.* xxxi. 100–108). St. Bernard was Dante's favorite saint. Our poet took the saint's *Steps of Humility* and his exegesis of the Canticle of Canticles as the model for his epic. Dante held the saint in pious reverence. At the initial appearance of St. Bernard, our poet says that the saint looks like a tender father. We can understand the profound filial affection in which our poet holds his favorite saint. His pious reverence becomes so profound that it has definitely reached the stage where it could be taken for an impious idolatry in the mansion of the Father. However inexpressible the joy of gazing on the face of the saint, how can he dare compare his joy to the joy of seeing the trace of the countenance of "My Lord" and "true God"?

Does our pilgrim wish to defile the most sacred Heaven with his impious idolatry? No, certainly not. St. Bernard stands there not as a saint but as the symbol of the Father of all the saints. Dante's three guides are conceived as the symbols of the Three Persons of the Holy Trinity. Virgil is the symbol of the Son, Beatrice is that of the Holy Spirit, and St. Bernard is that of the Father.

The function of the Son is to show how to die and be buried in sin and how to be reborn in grace. Virgil shows Dante the way into the underground world of sin and takes him down to the bottom of perdition. It is Virgil who wrenches Dante from the bottom of the sinful grave and takes him out to the world of grace. Virgil's function is to show Dante the way of the Crucifixion and the Resurrection. Virgil wishes to make a veiled announcement of his function, when he tells Dante at his initial appearance that he was born *sub Julio* (*Inf.* i. 70). His birth *sub Julio* is meant to help us to conceive his function in the light of the visible mission of the Son, Who *"sub Pontio Pilato passus, et sepultus est. Et resurrexit tertia die, secundum Scripturas"* (The Nicene Creed). Christ rose again on the third day; Virgil emerges with Dante out of Hell on the third day. On seeing Christ after His Resurrection, the disciples "came up and embraced his feet and worshipped him" (Matt. 28:9). On meeting Virgil on the *Purgatorio*, his disciples in poetry try to embrace his feet and worship him.

Virgil leads Dante to the top of the *Purgatorio* and stays with him until the Griffin comes. Virgil vanishes before the emergence of Beatrice. Beatrice is the symbol of the Holy Spirit. The Holy Spirit comes to continue the works of the Son: *"If I do not go, the Advocate will not come to you; but if I go, I will send him to you. And when he has come, he will convict the world of sin, and of justice, and of judgment"* (John 16:7–9). Beatrice convicts Dante of sin, and of justice, and of judgment. After the Ascension of the Griffin, Beatrice remains alone with the Chariot. The seven lights of the Holy Spirit form a ring around her; she is the symbol of the Holy Spirit in charge of guiding the Church. On the Sun, Beatrice is the center around which revolve the two circles of theologians under the inspiration of the Eternal Breath. On the *Primum Mobile*, she is the one who explains the nine orders of the angelic ministers for the invisible mission of the Holy Spirit.

The function of the Holy Spirit is to nurture and bring the baptized soul to the Father. Beatrice brings Dante to St. Bernard. Of the Three Persons, the Father alone is not sent on mission. The Father abides in the peace and joy of contemplation:

> So I was gazing upon the living love
> of him (Bernard) who in this world,
> through contemplation, enjoyed that peace.
>
> *Par.* xxxi. 109–111

Saint Bernard not only looks like a tender father (*tenero padre*) but Dante addresses him as the "Holy Father" (*santo padre*) (*Par.* xxxii. 100).

The mission of the Son is to establish faith. Virgil constantly talks of faith. The mission of the Spirit is to strengthen hope. Beatrice comes crowned with olive and her eyes are emeralds (*Purg.* xxx. 31, 68; xxxi. 116). She vouchsafes for Dante's hope to the Apostle of hope (*Par.* xxv. 49–57). Dante opens his final prayer to Beatrice, "O Lady, in whom my hope hath vigor" (*Par.* xxxi. 79). When Beatrice is relieved of her mission and goes back to her seat, Dante changes his form of address to her from "voi" to "tu." This shift in the forms of address is accompanied by the change in the syllabication of her name. While she is performing the mission of the Holy Spirit, "Beatrice" is syllabicated as in *beatus* and *beati*. When she is addressed by "*tu*," "*e*" and "*a*" of "Beatrice" are contracted into one syllable.

The Father waits in His mansion to embrace His children who are adopted through the blood of His Son and sanctified through the grace of His Spirit. The mansion of the Father is the bower of love where the love of the pilgrim is finally consummated. St. Bernard announces at his appearance that his intention is to bring Dante's love to its final fruition. This is the promise which Father Benedict gave Dante on Saturn when Dante expressed his wish to see his face unveiled (*Par.* xxii. 61–63). The promise of Father Benedict has now been fulfilled, and Dante gazes on the face of St. Bernard with the awe and wonder of seeing the face of the Lord and the true God.

The Three Persons of the Holy Trinity are at once transcendent and immanent. The Three Persons transcend all creation. On the Heaven of Fixed Stars, Dante cannot bear the effulgence of the Son. On the Heaven of the *Primum Mobile*, he is at a loss to describe the infinite chasm between him and the light of the Holy Spirit. In the Empyrean, Dante, the great master of imagery, cannot find any better metaphor than the triune circle of three colors for the presentation of the Father in union with His Son and His Spirit. While the transcendent Trinity is impersonal and aloof, the immanent Trinity personally resides in the heart of man. The three guides represent the Three Persons who personally instruct, comfort and embrace the mortal creature in its valiant struggle to overcome the bondage of the sinful exile, to return to its Creator, and to repose in the feast of the Mystical Rose.

The venerable Bernard explains the Mystical Rose. He first points out the Queen of Heaven. She is sitting at the "eastern" end of the Mystical Rose. Dante compares the Queen's throne to "the oriental region of the horizon" out of which the Sun rises (*Par.* xxxi. 118–128). The Sun has fully risen on the Empyrean. Below the throne of the Queen, there sit in a vertical column Eve, Rachel, Sarah, Rebecca, and Ruth (*Par.* xxxii. 4–12). Directly facing the Queen and at the "western" end of the Mystical Rose, there is seated John the Baptist. Below his seat, Francis, Benedict, and Augustine are sitting in a vertical column (*Par.* xxxii. 31–36).

The line of women below the Queen of Heaven and the line of men below John the Baptist divide the whole Mystical Rose into two equal halves. One of these two sides is for the Old Church and the other for the New Church. The former group lived under the Old Law and the latter under the New Law. What does our poet wish to convey by this elaborate arrangement of the Mystical Rose? The Mystical Rose is the Mystical Body of Christ. Christ was born twice, once in flesh and once in spirit, because He was of dual nature. He was born in flesh from Mary and in spirit from John the Baptist. Mary gave Him His body in Bethlehem. The Spirit of the Lord descended on Him when John baptized Him in the Jordan. The line of women below the Queen's throne shows the line of flesh out of which the body of Christ emerged. The line of men below the throne of the Baptist is the line of spirit whose initial birth John witnessed at the Jordan. The three saints who constitute the line of spirit are Francis, Benedict, and Augustine. We encountered these three saints as the exemplars of spiritual love while we were climbing the first seven rungs of the angelic ladder. On the Sun, St. Thomas characterized St. Francis as burning with seraphic love. On Saturn, we met St. Benedict as the symbol of chaste love. In the Second Circle, we noticed that Francesca's episode shows the birth of St. Augustine's spiritual love out of his lust.

The line of Hebrew women below the Queen of Heaven is the line of chaste flesh, and the line of Christian men below the Baptist is the line of chaste spirit. The faithful of the Old Church have been born into the Mystical Body of Christ through the line of the carnal mothers, and the faithful of the New Church have been born into the Mystical

394

Body through the line of the spiritual sons. The two halves of the Mystical Rose can be traced back to the two sides of Jacob's Ladder. The Mystical Rose evolves out of the River of Light, which in turn arises out of Jacob's Ladder. Spirit and Flesh constitute the two halves of the Mystical Rose; the soul and the body are the two sides of Jacob's Ladder.[3]

The children of the flesh can be called the children of the night, and the children of the spirit can be called the children of the day. The throne of the Queen marks the end of the night because she is seated at the end of the line of carnal mothers, and the throne of the Baptist marks the beginning of the day because he is seated at the top of the line of spiritual sons. Both of them stand on the borderline between the day and the night. St. Mary is flanked by Adam and Peter; she is related to Adam in flesh and to Peter in spirit. John the Baptist is flanked by Anna and Lucia; he is related to Anna in flesh and to Lucia in spirit.

Thus in the *Rosa Mystica*, come together spirit and flesh, Jews and Gentiles, the children of light and the children of darkness; and all alike rejoice in the divine effulgence of the Sun, which has fully risen over the mist of dust and dispelled the darkness of sins. This scene of joy and light is what the Prophet Isaias foresaw in one of his visions:

Arise, be enlightened, O Jerusalem: for thy light is come, and the glory of the Lord is risen upon thee. For, behold, darkness shall cover the earth and a mist the people: but the Lord shall arise upon thee and his glory shall be seen upon thee. And the Gentiles shall walk in thy light, and kings in the brightness of thy rising. Lift up thy eyes round about and see: all these are gathered together, they are come to thee. Thy sons shall come from afar and thy daughters shall rise up at thy side (Isa. 60:1–4).

The Mystical Rose is the Mystical Body of Christ. We

can see its two constituents in the scenery of the river of light out of which the Mystical Rose has evolved. We noted that the stream of light in the river is the co-referent symbol of the divine and the human love. The divine love is the Spirit of the Lord. The Spirit of the Lord is also the source of the human love of God. No mortal soul can have love for God unless it is given by the Love of God. In the stream of light, the love which has been given to the soul from God returns to its original source. The River of Love flows over the Garden of the Rose. The Stream of the Spirit and the Garden of the Flesh come together to constitute the Mystical Rose. The Mystical Rose is the Rose of the Queen of Heaven that is quickened and diffused by the Spirit of the King of Heaven. The Flesh of the Queen provides the bodily frame of the Mystical Body of Christ, and the Spirit of the Lord provides the life-giving breath of the Mystical Body (cf. the three phases of matter, motion, and form of the first seven rungs of the angelic ladder). The Eternal Virgin is the Queen of Heaven because she is the Mother of the Mystical Body.

The Head of the Mystical Body is Christ. Through the three constitutive elements of the Mystical Body, all the blessed stand in a threefold relation to the Father. They become the sons of His divine family through the only-begotten Son, the prince of His divine empire through His governing Spirit, and His divine brides through His Eternal Virgin. We saw these three relations of the blessed to the Father on Mars, Jupiter, and Saturn. The Mystical Body is one holy, catholic Church.

Why does our pilgrim get fully oriented with the Mystical Rose before his vision of the Divine Essence? Why does he spend so much time on the Rose instead of directly confronting the Lord and seeing every thing through the beatific vision of His Essence? Because no mortal soul can see God except as a member of the Mystical Body of Christ.

The beatific vision of God is the communion of the divine food for the saints. All the blessed participate in this holy communion as one body: *The cup of blessing that we bless, is it not the sharing of the blood of Christ? And the bread that we break, is it not the partaking of the body of the Lord? Because the bread is one, we, though many, are one body, all of us who partake of the one bread* (I Cor. 10: 16–17).

St. Thomas, the saint of the Holy Eucharist, preaches that the Holy Eucharist is the universal food for the universal church "because the life it confers is not the life of an individual man, but, from its very nature, the life of the whole world."[4] The principle of the holy communion is the same on earth and in heaven. Our pilgrim has to become a member of the Mystical Body of Christ before he can participate in the holy communion.

The significance of the communal bond in the life of man constitutes one of the essential differences between the Catholic Church and the Protestants. The Catholic Church holds the bond of the fellow creatures as an indispensable condition for establishing the union between the creature and the Creator, but the Protestants in general stress the significance of individual independence even at the expense of the communal bond. Kierkegaard, one of the most eminent Protestant theologians, proclaims that to be a true Christian is to become a solitary individual and stand alone in the face of God. In this individual confrontation with God, Kierkegaard insists, all the communal bonds among the fellow creatures are dissolved and all the ethical relations are superseded and suspended.*

* The Protestants protest against the communal bond of the universal Church before anything else. Martin Luther's protestation *Here I stand* can be taken to proclaim *Here I stand alone outside the communal bond of the Church.* S. Kierkegaard was a member of the Lutheran Church, and his definition of faith as *to stand alone in the face of God* can be regarded as the expansion of Luther's protestation *Here I stand.* For

397

The Fragile Leaves of the Sibyl

Dante's *Divina Commedia* extols a diametrically opposite doctrine. No mortal creature can dare stand alone before God. There are not many places for the solitary individuals to stand in Dante's vast cosmos. The ice-bound Cocytus is almost the only place for solitary individuals. Even the carnal feast of Cocytus is impossible without the bond of pride. Even the defiant rebellion against God is not possible without the power of the communal bond. Satan, the greatest of the highest angelic order, can never stand alone against God but only with the host of black angels. The vestibule to the *Inferno* shows the fate of the individuals who have transcended the communal bond. What is their fate? They ceased to be individuals.

Sin and virtue are possible only for the individual who stands in communion with his fellow creatures. The fall of Adam was possible only through his familial bond with Eve. Without this familial bond, Adam would be a solitary individual and be standing alone in the deserted Eden. The rise of the second Adam was also possible through His carnal bond with the second Eve. Neither the first Adam falls nor the second Adam rises as sheer private individuals but as public individuals of the universal community.

The communal bond is the foundation of existence and the measure of individuality. No soul can maintain its existence without participating in the chain of being. The participation in the chain of being is possible only through communal bonds. As we climbed the angelic ladder, we learned that the communal bond is the measure of individuality. The greater communal bond the soul moves in, the higher individuality it achieves. The trimmers of the Vestibule lived only for themselves and in a total alienation from the communal bond. They have achieved no individ-

Kierkegaard's doctrine of faith, see *Fear and Trembling, the Sickness unto Death, Concluding the Unscientific Postscript*, etc., all published in English translation by the Princeton University Press.

uality at all. The Holy Mother lives for the care of all her children and moves in the universal communal bond. She is the Universal Mother and the greatest individual.

The ethical relations among fellow creatures are the requisite conditions for establishing the just union between the creatures and their Creator: *If therefore thou offerest thy gift at the altar, and there thou rememberest that thy brother hath anything against thee, leave thy offering before the altar, and go first to be reconciled to thy brother; and then come and offer thy gift* (Matt. 5:23–24).

Christ comes in the fullness of time; the Son of Man comes to mankind under the justice and peace of the Roman Empire. The justice and peace of the Roman Empire are nothing other than the fullness of the ethical relation the mortal creatures have to establish among themselves as the requisite condition for the restoration of the right relation between man and God. The Procession of the Revelation cannot be unfolded in the Flowery Valley. The order and peace of the Terrestrial Paradise—the order and peace among the creatures—are the main pillars to sustain the sacred stage on which man can receive the Coming of the Lord and from which man can fly up to the mansion of the Father.

The ethical bonds are the beginnings of the universal bonds that are to be perfected in the Mystical Body of Christ. The Mystical Body of Christ is the familial empire and the imperial family which perfects the ethical relations of the blessed. The Holy Trinity Itself is the exemplar of all communal bonds. The Holy Trinity is the Lord God of Hosts (*Sanctus, Sanctus, Sanctus, Dominus Deus Sabaoth. Pleni sunt cæli et terra gloria tua. Hosanna in excelsis.*) The Three Persons work in the most intimate union with the hosts of ministers in guiding every step of the soul on its way of salvation from the beginning to the end. The Holy Trinity is the God-head of the universal communal

399

bond, and no one can participate in this universal communion without becoming a consecrated member of the Mystical Rose. *We too, all of us, have been baptized into a single body by the power of a single Spirit* (I Cor. 12:13). All the blessed are consecrated in the single body of the only-begotten Son by the single love of the same Spirit for the threefold union with the universal Father.

Having fully oriented the new pilgrim as a full member of the Mystical Rose, St. Bernard tells him to feast his eyes on the beauty of the Queen of Heaven (*Par.* xxxii. 85–93). St. Bernard says that the Eternal Mother bears the closest resemblance to Christ and that her brightness will give Dante's eyes the final preparation for the vision of God. The marvelous vision of the Queen holds Dante in a wondrous suspense. We have seen on the seven Terraces that the Holy Queen with her virtues is the most marvelous medium for the reflection of the divine virtues of the Holy Trinity.

Gabriel is singing, "*Ave Maria, gratia plena*," with his wings spread before the Holy Mother, and his sacred canticle of divine love is answered from every side by the blest Court (*Par.* xxxii. 88–105). The Son of God was conceived in the immaculate womb of the Holy Mother by the Holy Spirit, the Love of God. Every blessed soul in the Mystical Rose is a son of God who has been nurtured in the universal womb of the Eternal Virgin by the Love of God. The winged, spiral motion of Gabriel is the co-referent symbol of the Holy Breath (*sancta spira*) of the Eternal Love which quickens the Son of Man and each adopted son of God with its flame of love in the Mystical Rose of the Holy Mother. Dante has become the newest son of the Queen of Heaven through the Eternal Flame of the Holy Love.

St. Bernard now begins his holy prayer to the Queen of Heaven and asks for her intercession for the consummation of Dante's love. It is through her that God has come to man. It is also through her that man comes to God. In his holy prayer, St. Bernard stands on the burning love he has faithfully borne to the Mother of God. He dedicated to the Holy Mother all the numerous monasteries he established on the earth. The mansion of the Father is the bower of love. For the consummation of love, a prayer of love is dedicated for the intercession of love.

St. Bernard was well known for his eloquence. The Holy Mother is said to have moistened his lips with the milk from her breast in a dream and to have given him his famed eloquence. Whether we believe this legend or not, we can not doubt that his prayer for Dante is a torrent of divine eloquence. His holy prayer falls into three parts: salutation, adoration, and imploration.

The salutation presents the Queen of Heaven as the supreme embodiment of all the mysteries of creation and redemption:

> Virgin Mother, daughter of thy son,
> lowly and exalted far above all creatures,
> the final terminus of the eternal design.
>
> *Par.* xxxiii. 1–3

She is the Eternal Virgin and the Universal Mother, and the mother of the God and His daughter. This mystery exemplifies the universal mystery that the heavenly glory emerges from the hellish sin. If man had not fallen, he would have only the natural bliss. It is because of sin that God has become man. *It is not the healthy who need a physician, but they who are sick. For I have not come to call the just, but the sinners* (Mark 2:17).

It is because of sin that man becomes the partaker of divinity. Satan, the highest angel, has performed a crucial function for the elevation of man to the angelic level. Man holds the lowest grade of all intellectual substances. Woman is the lower form of man. The Eternal Virgin was one of the lowliest women. She has now become "the final terminus of the eternal design" because the final end of the eternal plan is to bring the Mystical Rose to its full bloom and because the flesh of the lowliest woman constitutes the bodily frame of the Mystical Body. The lowliest of the lowly has been exalted high above all creatures, while Lucifer the highest of the highest angelic order has been cast down to the lowest point of the cosmos. The Eternal Virgin was the first to see this profound mystery of the divine will and replied to Elizabeth's salutation to her as the Mother of God:

My soul magnifies the Lord; my spirit has found joy in God, who is my Savior, because he has looked graciously upon the lowliness of his handmaid. Behold, from this day forward all generations will count me blessed; because he who is mighty, he whose name is holy, has wrought for me his wonders. He has mercy upon those who fear him, from generation to generation; he has done valiantly with the strength of his arm, driving the proud astray in the conceit of their hearts; he has put down the mighty from their seat, and exalted the lowly; he has filled the hungry with good things, and sent the rich away empty handed. He has protected his servant Israel, keeping his merciful design in remembrance, according to the promise which he made to our forefathers, Abraham and his posterity for evermore (Luke 1:46–55).

The adoration of the Queen sings her supreme virtues which have paved the way for the ascent of her children from the exile on the sinful dust to the Mystical Rose:

> Thou art the one by whom human nature
> was so ennobled that its Maker
> did not disdain to become its creature.

> Within thy womb was rekindled the love

through whose warmth this flower
has blossomed in eternal peace.

Here thou art for us the noonday torch
of charity, and down below, among mortals,
a living fount of hope.

Lady, thou art so great and hast such worth
that whoever has grace and yet does not turn to thee,
would have his longing fly without wings.

Thy kindliness succors not only those
who ask, but many times
freely foreruns the request.

In thee is mercy, in thee pity,
in thee munificence, in thee whatever
in created being is of excellence.

Par. xxxiii. 4–21

The first half of the six tercets praises the Queen for her
great works as the Mother of God, and the second half for
her works as the Mother of all sinful souls. As the Mother
of God, the Queen has become the foundation of faith, the
fountain of hope for the Church Militant, and the nectar
of charity for the Church Triumphant. The first three
tercets sing the Holy Mother as the portal through which
God has come to man.

As the Mother of all human souls, she bestows wings and
plumes on the weary souls struggling on their way to the
court of heaven. When Dante comes back to himself in the
dark wood, he experiences the first effect of grace. He
struggles in vain to climb the Mount of Delight. He there
learns that "whoever has grace and yet does not turn to
thee, would have his longing fly without wings." It is with
the aid of the heavenly ladies, the wings and plumes from
Mary that Dante has waded through the *Inferno,* climbed

up to the top of the *Purgatorio* and flown to the Empyrean.

Mary is so merciful that she does not bother to wait for the request but foresees it. Even before Dante thinks of asking for her aid, the Mother of mercy takes pity on the lost Dante and tells Lucia to go to his aid. Lucia asks Beatrice to look after Dante, and Beatrice comes down to Hell to send Virgil to guide him through the kingdom of sin to the summit of the mountain of grace. The Queen of Heaven embodies all the excellent virtues in such a perfect manner that she is the sole model for the penitents' imitation of the Holy Trinity on the seven Terraces. The second half of the six tercets of adoration praises the Queen as the Mother of all the faithful, through whom man comes to God.

St. Bernard now implores the Queen for the consummation of Dante's long adventure from the bottom of Hell to the top of Heaven:

> Now, this man who from the deepest well
> of the universe even to here
> has seen the spiritual lives, one after another,
>
> Implores thee of thy grace for the power
> with which to uplift his eyes
> still higher toward the final bliss.
>
> And I who never burned for my own vision
> more than I do for his, proffer thee all my prayers
> and may they be not insufficient,
>
> In order that thou scatter for him every cloud
> of mortality with prayers of thine, so that
> the joy supreme may be unfolded to him.
>
> And further do I pray thee, Queen who canst do
> all thou wilt, that thou keepest
> his affection sound after so great a vision.

May thy protection overcome human ferments;
 Behold Beatrice with so many of the blessed
 folding hands for my prayers.
Par. xxxiii. 22–39

Beatrice and all other blessed fold hands and join in
St. Bernard's prayer. This is the communion of the saints.
Greatly pleased by the devout prayer of her faithful Bernard, the Queen of Heaven looks toward Bernard and
Dante (*Par.* xxxiii. 40–45). The most gracious advocate is
now turning her eyes of mercy toward Dante to show him
the blessed fruit of her womb. (*Eia ergo, advocata nostra,
illos tuos misericordes oculos ad nos converte. Et Jesum
benedictum fructum ventris tui, nobis post hoc exsilium
ostende—Salve Regina*, one of the favorite prayers of St.
Bernard.) It was with the kind aid of the Queen that Dante
took the first step toward heaven. It is with her merciful
intercession that he is now to uplift his mortal eyes toward
the final bliss.

With his tender smile, St. Bernard signals Dante to lift
up his eyes. Our pilgrim has already started to gaze boldly
into the rays of the deep light (*Par.* xxxiii. 49–54). In the
fountain of light, he first sees "the scattered leaves of all the
universe, bound by love in one volume" (*Par.* xxxiii. 85–
87). Dante's vision of all reality through the vision of the
divine Mind is not only theologically justifiable,[5] but poeti-
cally substantiated. By the time he uplifts his eyes for the
beatific vision of the Divine Essence, he has presented the
Heaven of Light in such a way as to bring into one grand
concrescence all the things he has seen in the long course
of his pilgrimage. The highest Heaven is not only the
culmination of his journey but its final summation. The
Empyrean reflects the height and the breadth of the entire
cosmos.

405

In the angelic vision of the divine Mind, Dante sees the universal mystery of substance and accidents:

> Substance and accidents and their relation
> as though together fused in such a way
> that what I speak of is one simple flame.
>
> The universal form of this complex
> I believe I saw....
>
> > *Par.* xxxiii. 88–92

He now sees the Three Persons in Their singularity and equality:

> Within the deep and clear subsistence
> of the great light three circles of three colors
> and of one dimension appeared to me,
>
> And one seemed to be reflected from the other
> as Iris by Iris, and the third
> seemed fire breathed equally from both.
>
> > *Par.* xxxiii. 115–120

He now sees the Three Persons in Their unity:

> O Light Eternal, abiding in Thyself alone,
> Thou alone understanding Thyself, and Thou
> understood by Thee, Thou dost love and smile on
> Thyself.
>
> > *Par.* xxxiii. 124–126

He now sees the mystery of the Incarnation. The Circle of the Son transforms itself into the human form and simultaneously retains its original color and form (*Par.* xxxiii. 127–145). While our pilgrim is struggling to understand how the divine circle and the human image can cohere with each other, he comes to see the mystery of the Incarnation in a sudden flash of light. In this final vision, our pilgrim sees not only how God becomes a man but also how man becomes a god. On the apex of the angelic ladder which Dante has climbed through the imitation of the Holy Trinity, he has become God-like. Man has been made partaker of His Divinity, who has deigned to become partaker of our humanity. *Da nobis per hujus aquae et vini mysterium, ejus divinitatis esse consortes, qui humanitatis nostrae fieri dignatus est particeps, Jesus Christus . . .* (*The New Roman Missal,* the Offertory).

It is the Father in His triune union with His Son and His Spirit that our Angelic Poet sees on the apex of the angelic ladder of divine love. For this ultimate vision, our pilgrim is first consecrated into the Mystical Rose in which he comes to stand in a triune relation with the Holy Trinity. He then lifts up his mortal eyes toward the final bliss through the tender mercy of the Queen of Heaven with whose loving-kindness he took the first step on his adventurous journey from the Dark Wood to the Heaven of Light. Thus, in the bosom of the Holy Mother, through whom God has become a man, man comes to be a god.

Notes

Notes to Chapter 1

1 Lecture X, 1818, The Viking Portable *Coleridge*, p. 405–406.
2 *Dante Studies*, I, 30.
3 *The Poetry of Dante*, ch. 3.
4 *Nicomachean Ethics* vii. 4, 1148^a 12.
5 *Ibid.*, vii. 6, 1149^a 30.
6 *Ibid.*, vii. 6, 1149^b 13.
7 *Ibid.*, vii. 6, 1149^b 1.
8 *La Divina Commedia*, the argument for *Canto IX* of the *Inferno*.
9 *S.T. I–II*, q. 84, a. 4.
10 *The Poetry of Dante*, ch. 3.

Notes to Chapter 2

1 *De Anima* ii. 1.
2 *S.T. I*, q. 77, a. 1.
3 *S.T. I*, q. 77, a. 4.
4 *S.T. I*, q. 77, a. 4.
5 *S.T. I*, q. 81, a. 2.
6 *S.T. I–II*, q. 23, aa. 2 and 4.
7 *S.T. I–II*, q. 23, a. 3.
8 *S.T. I*, q. 81, a. 2.
9 *S.T. I–II*, q. 30, a. 2.
10 *S.T. I*, q. 81, a. 2.
11 *Nicomachean Ethics* i. 13; 1102^a 34ff.
12 *S.T. I–II*, q. 46, a. 4; II–II., q. 142, a. 2.
13 *S.T. I*, q. 77, a. 3.
14 *S.T. I–II*, q. 41, a. 1.
15 *S.T. I*, q. 77, a. 3.
16 *De Civitate Dei* xiv. 7, 9.
17 *S.T. I–II*, q. 25, a. 2.
18 *S.T. I*, q. 78, a. 2.
19 *S.T. II–II*, q. 123, a. 1.
20 *S.T. II–II*, q. 35, a. 1.
21 *De Anima* i. 1, 403^a 31.
22 *S.T. I*, q. 63, a. 2; q. 82, a. 5.
23 *S.T. I*, q. 63, a. 2.
24 *Nicomachean Ethics* vii. 6, 1149^b 5.
25 *S.T. I*, q. 63, a. 2.
26 *De Grad. Humil.* i. 2; iv. 14.
27 *S.T. I*, q. 82, a. 3; *De Veritate*, q. 21, a. 3.
28 *S.T. I–II*, q. 63, a. 3.
29 *S.T. I–II*, q. 72, a. 4.
30 *S.T. I–II*, q. 77, a. 5.
31 *S.T. II–II*, q. 162, a. 3.
32 *S.T. I*, q. 63, a. 3.

Notes

[83] *De Grad. Humil.* iv., 15.
[84] *S.T. I–II*, q. 58, aa. 4 and 5.
[85] *S.T. I*, q. 43, a. 4.
[36] *S.T. I*, q. 43, aa. 5 and 7.
[37] *De Grad. Humil.* vii., 21.

[38] *De Grad. Humil.*, iii., 6.
[39] *De. Civ. Dei* xi., 11–13.
[40] *De Civ. Dei* xii. 9.
[41] *S.T. I*, q. 57, a. 2.
[42] *S.T. I*, q. 38, a. 2.

Notes to Chapter 3

[1] *Nicomachean Ethics* i. 7, 1098ᵃ 17; x. 6, 1176ᵃ 32; *S.T. I*, q. 48, a. 1.
[2] *Summa Contra Gent.* ii. 53, 4.
[3] *S.T. I*, q. 67, a. 1.
[4] *S.T. I–II*, q. 72, a. 5.
[5] *S.T. I–II*, q. 37, a. 1.
[6] *Nicom. Ethics* ix. 8, 1168ᵇ 31.
[7] *S.T. I*, q. 77, a. 3.
[8] *S.T. I*, q. 62, a. 2.
[9] *S.T. II–II*, q. 8, a. 4; John 8:12.
[10] *S.T. I–II*, q. 67, a. 1.
[11] *S.T. I–II*, q. 67, a. 1.
[12] *S.T. I*, q. 64, a. 4; q. 114, a.1.
[13] *De Moribus Eccles.* xv.
[14] *S.T. I–II*, q. 63, a. 3.
[15] *S.T. I–II*, q. 63, a. 3.
[16] *S.T. I–II*, q. 63, a. 4.
[17] *Summa Contra Gent.* iv. 83, 12.
[18] *S.T. I–II*, q. 65, a. 4.
[19] *S.T. I*, q. 12, a. 6.
[20] *S.T. I*, q. 26, aa. 1 and 2.
[21] *Summa Contra Gent.* iii. 57.
[22] *S.T. II–II*, q. 24, a. 1.
[23] *Summa Contra Gent.* iii. 58; iv. 91.
[24] *S.T. I*, q. 12, a. 6.
[25] *S.T. I–II*, q. 62, a. 4.
[26] *S.T. I*, q. 26, a. 4.
[27] *S.T. I*, q. 12, a. 5.
[28] *S.T. I–II*, q. 62, a. 1.

[29] *S.T. I–II*, q. 69, a. 2.
[30] *S.T. I*, q. 12, a. 11.
[31] *S.T. I–II*, q. 87, a. 2.
[32] *S.T. I*, q. 48, a. 1.
[33] *S.T. I*, q. 49, a. 1.
[34] *S.T. III*, q. 1, a. 3.
[35] Luke 20:36; *De Civit. Dei* xii. 9; *S.T. I*, q. 108, a. 8.
[36] *Gen. ad lit.* xii. 35.
[37] *Ep. ad Discor.*, xii. 35.
[38] *De Anima* iii. 5; 430ᵃ 24.
[39] *S.T. I–II*, q. 67, a. 1.
[40] *Summa Contra Gent.* iv. 97.
[41] *Summa Contra Gent.* iv. 86, 89.
[42] *Summa Contra Gent.* iv. 85.
[43] *Summa Contra Gent.* iv. 86.
[44] *Summa Contra Gent.* iv. 89.
[45] *S.T. I–II*, q. 30, a. 1, ad 1.
[46] *S.T. III*, Suppl., q. 85, a. 1; *Summa Contra Gent.* iv. 82, 7.
[47] *S.T. III*, q. 45, a. 2.
[48] *De Anima* iii. 9, 432ᵃ 25.
[49] *Nicom. Eth.* i. 13, 1102ᵇ 13.
[50] *S.T. I*, q. 77, a. 4.
[51] *Itin.* iii. 5.
[52] *S.T. I–II*, q. 63, a. 3.
[53] *De Grad. Humil.* ix. 27.
[54] *Sermo in Cant.* ii. ᵒ
[55] *Itin.* i. 3.
[56] *Itin.* i. 5.

Notes to Chapter 4

1 *S.T. I*, q. 63, a. 3.
2 *S.T. I*, q. 63, a. 4.
3 *De Grad. Humil.* ix. 25.
4 *Sermo 37 in Cant.*, 6.
5 *De Diligendo Deo* ii. 4.
6 *De Diligendo Deo* ii. 4.
7 *De Diligendo Deo* xiii. 36.
8 *S.T. I–II*, q. 109, a. 7.

9 *S.T. II–II*, q. 24, a. 3.
10 *De Grad. Humil.*, Preface.
11 *S.T. I*, q. 111, a. 2.
12 *S.T. II–II*, q. 186, a. 6.
13 *De Grad. Humil.* iv, v, vi.
14 *S.T. III*, q. 65, a. 6.
15 *S.T. III*, q. 27, a. 2.

Notes to Chapter 5

1 *S.T. II–II*, q. 36, a. 1; q. 30, a. 2.
2 *Nicom. Eth.* vii. 6, 1149[b] 15.
3 *Nicom. Eth.* vii. 6, 1149[b] 15.
4 *S.T. I*, q. 63, a. 2.
5 *S.T. I*, q. 59, a. 4.
6 *S.T. I–II*, q. 93, a. 3.

7 *S.T. I–II*, q. 96, a. 1.
8 *De Veritate*, q. 28, a. 1.
9 *S.T. I–II*, q. 106, a. 2.
10 Erwin Straus, *The Existence*, ed. by Dr. Rollo May, (New York, 1958), p. 159.

Notes to Chaper 6

1 *Rhet.* ii. 2, 1378[a] 31.
2 *Nicom. Ethics* vii. 6, 1149[a] 25–29
3 *De Anima* i. 1, 403[a] 32
4 *S.T. I–II*, q. 58, a. 5.

5 *Summa Contra Gent.* ii. 86, 87.
6 *De Trin.* xv. 26.
7 *Top.* i. 17; 108[a] 11.
8 Ovid, *Metamorph.* vi. 70–80.
9 *S.T. III*, q. 46, a. 6.

Notes to Chapter 7

1 *Rhet.* ii. 8, 1386[b] 9.
2 *S.T. II–II*, q. 158, a. 7.
3 *S.T. I–II*, q. 38, a. 4.
4 *S.T. I–II*, q. 25, a. 2.
5 *S.T. I*, q. 20, a. 1.
6 *Sermo 20 in Cant.*, 6.
7 *S.T. II–II*, q. 186, a. 3; q. 187, a. 5.
8 *S.T. II–II*, qq. 128 and 129.

9 *S.T. I*, q. 28, a. 4; q. 36, a. 3.
10 *S.T. I*, q. 43, a. 3.
11 *S.T. I*, q. 1, aa. 1 and 2.
12 *S.T. I*, q. 1, a. 6.
13 *S.T. I*, q. 1, a. 1.
14 *De Anima* iii. 7, 431[a] 16.
15 *S.T. I*, q. 1, a. 10.
16 *S.T. II–II*, q. 174, aa. 1, 2, and 3.

Notes

Notes to Chapter 8

1 *De Diligendo Deo* vii, 19.
2 *De Veritate*, q. 28, a. 1.
3 *S.T. I–II*, q. 85, a. 3.

4 *S.T. II–II*, q. 29, a. 3.
5 *S.T. II–II*, q. 124, aa. 4 and 5.

Notes to Chapter 9

1 *S.T. II–II*, q. 142, a. 4.
2 *S.T. II–II*, q. 142, a. 2.
3 *S.T. II–II*, q. 15, a. 2; q. 148, a. 6.
4 *De Anima* ii. 1, 412^b 3.
5 *Tim.* 90A
6 *S.T. I–II*, q. 90, a. 2.
7 *De Mon.* III. xiv. 11.
8 *S.T. I–II*, q. 95, a. 2.
9 *S.T. II–II*, q. 58, a. 11.
10 *S.T. I–II*, q. 112, aa. 1, 2, and 3.

11 *S.T. I–II*, q. 114, aa. 3, 4, and 5.
12 *S.T. III*, q. 68, a. 2.
13 *S.T. II–II*, q. 157, a. 3.
14 *S.T. I*, q. 23, a. 4.
15 *S.T. I*, q. 23, a. 3.
16 *Summa Contra Gent.* II. 45.
17 *Summa Contra Gent.* II. 45, 3.
18 *S.T. I*, q. 48, a. 2.

Notes to Chapter 10

1 *S.T. I–II*, q. 28, a. 1.
2 *S.T. I–II*, q. 28, aa. 2 and 3.
3 *S.T. II–II*, q. 153, a. 5.
4 *S.T. I–II*, q. 27, a. 2.
5 *S.T. II–II*, q. 151, a. 4.
6 *Conf.* viii. 12.

7 *De Moribus Eccles.* xv.
8 *De Diligendo Deo* x. 27.
9 *The Rule for Monks*, vii.
10 *S.T. III, Suppl.*, q. 69, a. 2; q. 88, a. 1.

Notes to Chapter 11

1 *De Grad. Humil.* vii. 20
2 *S.T. I*, q. 43, a. 3.
3 *De Grad. Humil.* vii. 20
4 *S.T. I–II*, q. 63, a. 3.
5 *S.T. I–II*, q. 82, a. 3.

6 *Retract.* i. 15.
7 *Nicom. Eth.* vii. 3, 1146^b 35–1147^b 6.
8 *S.T. I–II*, q. 63, aa. 2 and 3.
9 *S.T. I–II*, q. 63, a. 1.

Notes to Chapter 12

1 *De Monarchia* i. 4.
2 *S.T. II–II*, q. 154, a. 5.
3 *Aeneid* vi. 884

4 *S.T. III*, q. 1, a. 3; *De Monarchia* iii. 4.

Notes

Notes to Chapter 13

1 *S.T. II–II*, q. 1, a. 9; John 26: 12–13.

2 *De Grad. Humil.* vii. 20.

Notes to Chapter 14

1 Augustine, *De Gen. Contra Manich.*, PL 34, 203.

2 *S.T. II–II*, q. 24, a. 2.

3 *The Rule for Monks* vii.

4 *Comment. on St. John's Gospel* vi. 52, Lecture vi.

5 *De Veritate*, q. 2, a. 7.

Bibliography

I. THE ORIGINAL TEXT AND TEXTUAL CRITICISM OF LA
   DIVINA COMMEDIA
   La Divina Commedia di Dante Alighieri, ed. and annot. by
   C. H. Grandgent, rev. ed., D. C. Heath & Co., Boston, 1933
   Readings on the Inferno of Dante, by the Hon. William
   Warren Vernon, in two volumes, Methuen & Co., London,
   1906
   Readings on the Purgatorio of Dante, by the Hon. William
   Warren Vernon, in two volumes, the Macmillan Co.,
   London, 1889
   Readings on the Paradiso of Dante, by the Hon. William
   Warren Vernon, in two volumes, the Macmillan Co.,
   London, 1900

II. THE ENGLISH TRANSLATIONS OF DANTE'S WORKS
   The *Inferno*, the *Purgatorio*, and the *Paradiso* of Dante
   Alighieri, the Temple Classics, in three volumes, J. M.
   Dent & Sons, London, 1958
   The Divine Comedy, trans. and ed. by Thomas G. Bergin,
   Paolo Milano, Laurence Binyon's translation of La Divina
   Crofts Classics, Appleton-Century-Crofts, N.Y., 1955
   The Divine Comedy, trans. by H. R. Huse, Rinehart
   Editions, Rinehart & Co., N.Y., 1959
   The Portable Dante, the Viking Portable Library, ed. by
   Commedia and D. G. Rossetti's translation of La Vita
   Nuova, The Viking Press, N.Y., 1955
   Il Convito, the Banquet of Dante Alighieri, trans. by

415

Bibliography

Elizabeth P. Sayer, George Routledge & Sons, London, 1887

The De Monarchia of Dante Alighieri, ed. and trans. by Aurelia Henry, Houghton, Mifflin & Co., Boston, 1904

III. ANCIENT PHILOSOPHY AND PSYCHOLOGY
The Dialogues of Plato, trans. by B. Jowett, in two volumes, Random House, N.Y., 1937, especially *Phaedo*, the *Republic*, and *Timaeus*
The Basic Works of Aristotle, ed. by Richard McKeon, Random House, N.Y., 1941, especially *De Anima, Metaphysica, Ethica Nichomachea*, and *Politica*.
Saint Thomas Aquinas, the *Commentary on Aristotle's De Anima*, trans. by K. Foster and S. Humphries, Yale Press, New Haven, 1959

IV. MEDIEVAL PHILOSOPHY AND THEOLOGY
The Basic Writings of Saint Augustine, ed. by Whitney J. Oates, in two volumes, Random House, N.Y., 1948 especially the *City of God* and *On the Trinity*
St. Bernard de Clairvaux, *On the Song of Songs*, Sermones in Cantica Canticorum, trans. and ed. by a Religious of C.S.M.V., A. R. Mowbray & Co., London, 1952
Saint Bernard, *the Steps of Humility*, Gradibus Humilitatis, trans. by Geoffrey Webb and Adrian Walker, A. R. Mowbray & Co., London, 1957
The Book of Saint Bernard on the Love of God, De diligendo Deo, ed. and trans. by Edmund G. Gardner, J. M. Dent & Sons, London, 1916
Saint Bonaventura, *the Mind's Road to God*, Itinerarium Mentis ad Deum, trans. by George Boas, the Liberal Arts Press, N.Y., 1953
Saint Thomas Aquinas, *Summa Theologica*, in three volumes, trans. by the Fathers of the English Dominican Province, Benziger Brothers, N.Y., 1947–1948
Saint Thomas Aquinas, *On the Truth of the Catholic Faith*, Summa Contra Gentile, in four volumes, trans. by Anton C. Pegis, James F. Anderson, Vernon J. Bourke,

Charles J. O'Neil, Image Books, Garden City, 1955–1958
Saint Thomas Aquinas, *Truth*, De Vertitate, in three
volumes, trans. by Robert W. Mulligan, James, McGlynn,
Robert W. Schmidt, Henry Regnery Co., Chicago, 1952–
1954
Anton C. Pegis, *St. Thomas and the Problem of the Soul in
the Thirteenth Century*, St. Michael's College, Toronto,
1934

V. THE SCRIPTURE AND LITURGY OF THE CATHOLIC
   CHURCH
   The Holy Bible, New American Catholic Edition, Ben-
   ziger Brothers, N.Y., 1950
   The Holy Bible, trans. by Ronald Knox, Sheed and Ward,
   N.Y., 1950
   Rev. F. X. Lasance and Rev. Francis Augustine Walsh,
   the New Roman Missal, Benziger Brothers, N.Y., 1954
   The Roman Breviary, an English Version, in Four Parts,
   compiled by the Benedictine Nuns of the Abbey of Our
   Lady of Consolation at Stanbrook in Worcestershire,
   Benziger Brothers, N.Y., 1937
   William O'Shea, *the Worship of the Church*, a Companion
   to Liturgical Studies, the Newman Press, Westminster,
   1957

VI. THE COMMENTARIES AND CRITICISM OF LA DIVINA
    COMMEDIA
    J. S. Carroll, *Exiles of Eternity*, *Prisoners of Hope*, and
    In Patria, Hodder and Stoughton, London, 1904–1911
    Charles S. Singleton, Dante Studies 1 (Elements of Struc-
    ture) and 2 (Journey to Beatrice), Harvard University
    Press, Cambridge, 1954 and 1958
    George Santayana, *Three Philosophical Poets*, Lucretius,
    Dante and Goethe, Harvard University Press, Cambridge,
    1910
    Benedetto Croce, the *Poetry of Dante*, trans. by Douglas
    Ainslie, Henry Holt & Co., N.Y., 1922

Index

Index

Index

desire, *see* appetite *and* the concupiscible

despair, 39 f, 74, 218 ff; despair of the earthly good, 40, 67, 219; despair of the heavenly good, 40, 67, 219 f

devil, *see also* Satan, 66 ff, 86, 145, 148, 181, 185, 221 f, 340 f, 398; devil's dominion, 92; devil's envy, 43, 170 f, 182, 186 f; devil's snare, 338 ff

Diana, 311

Dido, 292, 311

discommunion of the sinners, the, 83, 99

Divine Essence, the, 74 f, 99, 302, 307, 370, 384, 396, 405; Divine Nature, 72, 106 f

dolce stil nuovo, the, 282, 298, 300

Dominic, St., 39, 54, 227, 229, 231, 234, 306, 329, 369

Dominican order, the, 228, 231, 234

Donati, Forese, 266, 268, 275

drink, *see* food and drink

eagle, 149 f, 177 f, 186; the Eagle of Jupiter, 37 f, 55, 63, 65, 270 ff, 280, 282, 286, 318, 370

Ecce Agnus Dei, the, 185

ecclesiastical power, the, 200, 242

ecstasy, 291, 304 f, 384

Eden, the Garden of, 86, 113 f, 182, 185, 319, 341, 345, 353, 355, 357, 378, 381

election, the doctrine of, 276 ff

Eli (Elios), 244 ff, 268 f, 358

Elizabeth, 165, 238 f

Elysian Field, the, 3, 258

emanation, the doctrine of, 277, 280 f

Emperor, the, 200, 203 f, 239, 286

Empire, the, 54, 200, 217, 285 f, 314, 396, 399

Empyrean, the, *see* the Heavens of the *Paradiso*

end, 77 ff, 106, 110 f, 125, 235, 315, 317, 386; natural end, 8 f, 49, 78, 95 f, 110, 113, 125, 127, 321; supernatural end, 8 f, 49, 78, 87, 95 f, 125, 127, 235, 317, 321, 336

envy, 13, 42 ff, 51 ff, 56 f, 108, 169 ff, 338

Epicureans, the, 220

epicycle of Venus, the, 209 ff, 232, 240, 323

estrangement from the Creator, the, *see* the alienation from the Creator

Esau, 201

Eucharist, the Holy, 162, 174, 185, 397

Eunoë, 74, 367, 371, 377, 381 f

Eve (the first), 23, 86, 112 ff, 166 f, 182, 185, 321, 341, 345, 348, 355 ff, 382 ff, 393, 398

Eve, the second, 112, 114, 166, 254, 341, 382 f, 398

evil, 9, 60, 110, 190, 199 ff, 212, 218, 326, 361

excommunicate, the, 73, 364 ff

exile, 248 f, 263, 328, 337, 344 f

Exodus, the, 89, 375

Ezechiel, 260 f, 352

Fabricius, 262

faculty of the soul, *see* the power of the soul

faith, the theological virtue of, 8, 21, 47, 68 ff, 87, 95, 105, 194, 235, 302, 316 ff, 333 ff, 403

fall, man's, 86, 112 ff, 126, 181

family, 139 f, 182, 186 f, 256, 259, 285, 308, 314, 396, 398 f

Farinata, 40, 222, 230 f, 329

father, 200, 241, 258, 287, 307 f, 389 f

Father in heaven, the, *see* the Trinity

Fathers of the early Church, the, 47

Faust, the, 23

feast, 183, 189; the heavenly feast of divine love, 74, 99, 106, 159, 189, 269, 288, 324, 373 ff

Fixed Stars, the Heaven of, *see* the Heavens of the *Paradiso*

flesh, *see also* carnality, 45, 49, 72, 111 ff, 163, 182, 189, 207, 237, 297, 304 f, 327, 376, 394 f, 402; the flesh and blood of the Son, 42,

Index